Early Christianity accord
Traditions in Ac

Early Christianity according to the Traditions in Acts

A Commentary

Gerd Lüdemann

Fortress Press   Minneapolis

Translated by John Bowden from the German
Das frühe Christentum nach den Traditionen der Apostelgeschichte.
Ein Kommentar,
published 1987 by Vandenhoeck & Ruprecht, Göttingen,
with further material by the author.

Library of Congress Cataloguing-in-Publication Data

Lüdemann, Gerd
  [Frühe Christentum nach den Traditionen der Apostelgeschichte.
English]
  Early christianity according to the traditions in Acts/Gerd
Luedemann: [translated by John Bowden from the German].
    p.   cm.
  Translation of: Das Frühe Christentum nach den Traditionen der
Apostelgeschichte.
  ISBN 0–8006–2314–2
  1. Bible. N.T. Acts—Commentaries. 2. Bible. N.T. Acts—
History of Biblical events. 3. Bible. N.T. Acts—History of
contemporary events. 4. Church history—Primitive and early church,
c.a. 30–600. I. Title.
BS2625.3.L8313 1984
226'.607—dc20   89–7853

Printed in Great Britain

1–2314

93 92 91 90 89 1 2 3 4 5 6 7 8 9 10

Dedicated to the June Ramsey Sunday School Class,
First Presbyterian Church,
Nashville, Tennessee

Contents

Preface

The basis of the introductory chapter is my inaugural lecture in Göttingen, given on 1 February 1984. The first version of the commentary which follows came into being while I was Visiting Professor at Vanderbilt Divinity School between February and April 1984, and I produced a further draft during a sabbatical semester which I was able to spend there in 1985. The English edition of this book is dedicated to the June Ramsey Sunday School Class in Nashville, Tennessee, members of which heard a popular version of this commentary, discussed it with me, and showed great kindness to all my family. I would like to thank Dean Jack Forstman as a representative of all my colleagues in Nashville who extended such warm hospitality. My thanks also to Dr Jürgen Wehnert, Silke Röthke and the students who helped me: Astrid Berger, Andrea Kaiser, Gebhard Löhr, Vera Lohrmann, Rainer Reuter and Heike Wehnert, along with Dr Friedrich Wilhelm Horn of Göttingen. I am further grateful to Professor Christoph Burchard of Heidelberg for a critique of the whole book, to Professor Ulrich Luz of Bern for his views on the introductory chapter and the approach, and to my publisher, Dr Arndt Ruprecht, for his constant interest in a commentary which came into being out of scholarly necessity and is not part of any series. I have taken note of literature which has appeared since and am grateful to the translator, Dr John Bowden, or his great care and creative empathy with my way of thinking. Finally, words cannot express what I owe to my wife Elke and our four daughters Amrei, Eyke, Marei and Reiga.

Where no other indication is given, the translations are my own.

Göttingen, 29 June 1986/5 March 1989

The Historical Value of the Acts of the Apostles

I

When Adolf (von) Harnack wrote that sentence which was so much discussed in the subsequent period, namely that in criticism of the sources of earliest Christianity we are moving backwards to the tradition (1897, X), what he said applied particularly to Acts, a source which in his view is one of the pillars for our historical knowledge of early Christianity, along with the letters of Paul and Eusebius's *Church History*. Harnack provided support for his thesis between 1906 and 1911 in three brilliant monographs: I. *Lukas der Arzt* (1906), II. *Die Apostelgeschichte* (1908), III. *Neue Untersuchungen zur Apostelgeschichte* (1911). They mark the end of nineteenth-century critical research into Acts (on this see especially McGiffert, *Beg.* II, 363-433; Mattill 1959, 20-206; Kränkl 1972, 16-36; Gasque 1975, 21-106). The latter began with the criticism of Ferdinand Baur. After a hesitant beginning, on the basis of a comparison of the historical information in the letters of Paul with that in Acts, Baur had come to the conclusion that a 'comparison of these two sources... (must) lead to the conclusion that given the vast difference between the accounts on the two sides, historical truth can only be either on the one side or the other' (1845, 5). In the first part of his book on Paul (1845, 15-243; 1866, 19-272), this basic thesis from the introduction is applied to, or justified in the case of, every chapter of Acts. There Baur discusses 'The Life and Activity of the Apostle Paul', following the sequence in Acts. This results in a kind of commentary on Acts with the main purpose of extracting its historical elements. The criteria Baur uses for discovering its historical value are a comparison with the letters of Paul, a history-of-religions comparison, literary criticism and tendency criticism. However, according to Baur, on the narrative level only a few sections of Acts have any positive historical value. This is further diminished because the author of Acts used Paul's letters. On the other hand, Baur argued that the traditions used by Acts are very important. He could therefore write: Acts 'remains... an extremely important source for the history of the apostolic period, but also a source from which a truly historical picture of the persons and circumstances depicted in it can be gained only through strict historical criticism' (1845, 13; 1866, 17). Strict historical criticism made use of the question raised by tendency criticism about the purpose of Acts (for this

1

cf. also Schneckenburger 1841 with Baur's remark: 1845, 5f.; 1866, 8f.). According to Baur, Acts was written in the second century in order to reconcile the warring parties of the Paulinists and the Judaists (1845, 5f.; 1866, 8f.). This perspective of tendency criticism was followed subsequently by Baur's pupils Albert Schwegler (1846, 73ff.) and Eduard Zeller (1845, 318), who equally decisively put in question the value of Acts as a historical source for the things described in it. Furthermore Baur's criticism of Acts was reinforced in a brilliant way in 1870 by Franz Overbeck, who claimed to be a member of the Tübingen school in an allegorical sense (1903, 3), in his new edition of Wette's commentary. Granted, Overbeck did not define the purpose of Acts in the same way as Baur. He argued that its author was almost unaffected by the old party divisions and wrote as a Gentile Christian (cf. also Overbeck, 1872), naively transferring his own circumstances to the earliest apostolic period (cf. the commentary by Schmidt 1910, 32f.). Acts 'is the attempt of a Gentile Christianity itself already strongly influenced by primitive Christian Judaism to come to terms with the past, and especially to argue with its own origin and its first founder Paul' (Overbeck 1870, XXXI). But Overbeck agreed completely with Baur on the inner obligation to investigate early Christianity purely in historical terms (Overbeck 1903, 4). As Zeller (1854, 489-524) had already done before him, he refined the source-critical method beyond Baur (see his comments on the 'We source' [1870, XXVII-LII]), but similarly did not think much of the historical value of Luke's account (for Overbeck's analysis of Acts see also Emmelius, 1975).

Now it would certainly be wrong to get the impression that the criticism of Acts by Baur and Overbeck was generally acknowledged during the nineteenth century. On the contrary, at regular intervals it was the target of scholarly and unscholarly criticisms (see the examples in Lüdemann 1983, 27-31). At the same time it has to be recognized that for decades the Tübingen School's criticism of Acts (and particularly its detailed analysis) remained the natural starting point for criticism from the liberal-critical side (cf. only Pfleiderer 1902; Weizsäcker 1902) until Adolf von Harnack struck his weighty counter-blow at this very point. After stating the opinion quoted at the beginning of this introduction as to the increasing credibility of the tradition of the early church, between 1906 and 1911 Harnack produced a three-volume defence of Luke and rated the historical value of Luke's account incomparably higher than did the Tübingen School and the liberal theologians who followed it (cf. Schürer 1906 and Holtzmann 1908 for criticism of Harnack). In Harnack's view, early Christian tradition (the earliest text is around 185: Irenaeus, *Adversus Haereses* III, 1) is right in saying that Paul's companion Luke was the author of the Gospel and Acts. He introduces himself in the 'we passages', which along with all the other texts in the second part of Acts are valuable, historically accurate eye-witness reports. The account in Acts 1-12 of events at which Luke was not of course present as an eye-witness derive from different sources of varied quality.

The difference between Harnack and the Baur school in their estimation of the historical value of Acts could therefore hardly be greater, and we may describe the Tübingen School's and Harnack's analyses of Acts as the two great extremes in German Protestant research at the turn of the century; there were numerous intermediate positions between them. Still, even now the Baur school and Harnack seem to me to be the great antipodes, as is clear from a brief look at research into Acts after Harnack. Harnack's line was taken further by Alfred Wikenhauser (1921), who in his book (which even now has not been replaced) rates the historical value of Acts high, and by no less a figure than Eduard Meyer. For Meyer the authorship of the book by Paul's companion Luke is clearly demonstrated by the fact that Acts is 'one of the most significant works of history preserved to us from antiquity' (Meyer I, VIII). Volume III of his *Ursprung und Anfänge des Christentums* presents in the main a 'history of early Christianity on the basis of Acts' (for criticism see Dibelius 1924). Harnack's contribution to Acts still meets with a particular response in the Anglo-Saxon world (see the survey by Gasque 1975, 251-66). Finally in some areas of contemporary German scholarship there is a tendency to attach considerable historical value to Acts (Hengel 1979, 1983a,b; Roloff 1981 are examples); cf. also the social historians of early Christianity (e.g. Judge 1964, Theissen 1979).

By contrast, in succession to Baur there are predominantly such literary-critical works as those of Julius Wellhausen (1907, 1914), which abandon Acts as a pile of ruins and have almost lost sight of its historical value behind the traditions or sources that they have discovered. However, these books also include the works of Martin Dibelius, which successfully applied style criticism to Acts, and broad areas of North American scholarship, which under the leadership of Henry J.Cadbury, Kirsopp Lake and F.J.Foakes Jackson set up a landmark of critical research into Acts with the five-volume *The Beginnings of Christianity* (1920-1933) and in the person of scholars like John Knox (1936, 1939, 1950) and Donald W.Riddle (1940) stressed the secondary character of Acts. Mention should also be made here of the redaction-critical work on Luke-Acts (especially Acts) by Hans Conzelmann (1960, 1987) and Ernst Haenchen (1971). Though they were concerned above all with reading Luke, i.e. discovering what Luke meant by his account, by way of criticism it should be noted that contrary to the purpose of the founder of this exegetical approach – Conzelmann, at any rate, wrote a history of earliest Christianity – the redaction-critical research which has flourished up to the present in Europe (see the report by Bovon 1978) and North America (see the collections by Talbert 1978, 1984) often almost completely neglected the historical question in connection with what is reported in Acts. The reasons for this neglect were on the one hand an excessive scepticism about almost everything that Luke wrote, and the other hand the conviction that the reconstruction of history is theologically questionable and that the kerygma above all is significant. Over against this it must be stressed that since the rise of historical thinking a reconstruction of the history of early Christianity has been necessary for understanding the kerygma, and indeed is the presupposition for this understanding. As Acts itself sees itself as a historical account of early Christianity (cf. Luke 1.1-4), academic theology must constantly be concerned with its historical value (cf. the readable account by Barrett 1961).

II

In pursuit of this task the question whether the author of Acts was an eyewitness is so significant that it must be discussed here once again. If it were answered in the negative, Acts would have to be put alongside the letters of Paul as a primary source. If by contrast the author were not an eye-witness, Acts would be only a secondary source and its historical value would be generally less than the primary source, the letters of Paul, unless it had preserved its sources carefully. In so far as the letters of Paul report primitive Christian history or allow one to discover it, they are the report of someone directly involved, and in those cases where they have literary integrity (i.e. in most cases), they are a primary source, whereas in the last instance the account in Acts would have gone through at least one channel which has not been preserved (for the distinction between primary and secondary sources see Bernheim 1908, 507). There would therefore be a qualitative difference between the two sources. This observation and the consequences mentioned above could not be affected even by the fact that Paul is *partisan* and that therefore his reports may not be regarded as an *objective* source. This insight is simply a warning to treat even the primary sources critically, and forces one to concede that in some cases the secondary source can be nearer to the historical truth than the primary source. Nevertheless it is impossible to doubt the statement that if Luke was not an eyewitness, the historical value of Acts is to be estimated lower than that of Paul.

But on the basis of what criteria can we arrive at a conclusive result in the question touched on here?

One approach would be to compare the theology of Paul with that of

4

Acts (especially of Paul in Acts). If there proved to be a great difference, then the possibility that the author of Acts was a companion of Paul could probably be ruled out. (Cf. Vielhauer 1965: Luke is 'post-Pauline in his natural theology, his view of the law and his eschatology... The manifest distance from Paul in the content of his work raises the question whether the distance is not also chronological, and whether one may really see Luke the physician and travelling companion of Paul as the author of Acts', 26). However, this course must be ruled out, because theological differences between Paul and Luke are of no use in deciding this question. Moreover, we need to take into account the evidence that the theology of Paul was already regarded in extremely different ways even by the apostle's contemporaries (cf. Rom.3.8 and by contrast I Cor.6.12; 8), and in the subsequent period was understood only superficially, if at all (II Peter 3.15f.). We cannot therefore rule out *a priori* that the very un-Pauline theology of Luke's Paul was developed by a companion of the historical Paul (cf. rightly Schneider 1977, 33).

By contrast, arguments which could be used to solve the problem should be arrived at above all from *historical* considerations. In this connection it is argued against the theory that Luke was an eye-witness that he kept quiet about major conflicts which are evident in the letters of Paul. So he mentions neither the person of the Gentile Christian Titus, over whose circumcision there was a dispute at the Jerusalem conference, nor the crises in the Pauline communities to which the letters of Paul bore witness. However, even these arguments may not really hold water. The author of Acts is not writing *sine ira et studio* (for this phrase from Tacitus see Vogt 1936). It emerges even from an innocent reading of Acts that Luke knew more than he told. In other words, it is quite certain that he quite deliberately omitted some details like Paul's execution or the 'bringing' of the collection during Paul's last visit to Jerusalem, and so on, so their absence cannot be seen as conclusive arguments against authorship by an eyewitness (cf. Hommel 1955, 153).

Convincing arguments that Luke was not a companion of Paul may only be derived from such historical statements as betray a total lack of personal acquaintance with Paul on the part of the author of Acts.

Let us make a test. One of the great good fortunes of Pauline research is that the source material that has been preserved allows us to come to a certain conclusion about the number of visits Paul paid to Jerusalem. Galatians 1.15-24 says explicitly (v.20) that he was in Jerusalem only once (v.18) between his conversion (vv.15f.) and the Jerusalem conference (2.1-10). The report on the agreement over the collection (Gal.2.10) and the history of the collection in the Pauline community lends conviction to the view that after the conference Paul was only in Jerualem once, to bring the collection.

The premise of this thesis is that the making of the collection in the Pauline communities came *directly* after the agreement over the collection and had not been at a standstill for a long time (thus Georgi 1965: as a result of the incident at Antioch) before Paul, having founded his communities, implemented it as an agreement he had made several years previously. If there is a direct connection between agreement and collection, and it is possible to speak formally of a collection journey, then we can probably rule out another journey by Paul to Jerusalem before delivering the collection, on that occasion with empty hands. (Moreover reasons of finance and organization tell against this 'intermediate journey to Jerusalem.')

In other words, in Paul's Christian period there is a probability bordering on certainty that Paul went to Jerusalem only three times (cf. Lüdemann 1984, 37 n.51, 147f.; Jewett 1982, 89, 99, etc.; Hyldahl 1986, 2).

By comparison Acts reports no less than five journeys to Jerusalem (chs.9; 11; 15; 18.22; 21). The best explanation for this is to assume that Luke had no personal idea of Paul's life. Anyone who thinks to the contrary has to explain why Luke invented two additional journeys although he knew better. Regardless of the degree to which Luke gives some of the activity of Jesus and Paul the framework of a journey (see 13, below), one can hardly suppose that he committed such a major offence against historical truth. (Moreover, the three accounts of Paul's conversion in Acts 9; 22; 26 are not an analogy, since only the first is part of the narrative and the other two are parts of speeches.)

Secondly, had Luke been a companion of Paul one would have expected him to have reported more about Paul's early days.

So it is illegitimate to use the thesis that Luke was an eyewitness, however much one must recognize that even contemporary scholarship has dismissed such an assumption too quickly (Harnack 1911, 21-8 [bibliography] discusses a series of unviable reasons why Luke was not a companion of Paul; cf. also the important comments by Dibelius 1956, 136f.).

Now in the previous paragraph I already hinted that Luke knew more than he reported. Furthermore he himself writes in the prologue (Luke 1.1-4) that at least in connection with Jesus, he had predecessors whose work he evidently used in both his volumes. In other words, Luke wrote using traditions (for a definition see 9). Where did the traditions used in Acts come from? Who transmitted them to Luke? How can they be reconstructed? There are three possible answers to the question of the origin of the traditions in that part of Acts which relates to Paul:

1. Luke knew and used only the letters of Paul;
2. Luke had only traditions other than the letters of Paul at his disposal;
3. Luke used both letters and traditions.

In the interest of solving the task with which we are confronted, we must look at each possibility individually. I shall begin with the first

6

possibility and the first part of the third and ask: did the author of Acts know and use the letters of Paul?

III

The assumption that Luke knew letters of Paul is a well-founded hypothesis, which becomes the more compelling, the later Luke-Acts is to be dated. If Luke belonged to the third Christian generation, in view of the fact that he understands himself to be a pupil of Paul or – to put it more cautiously – belongs within the circle of Pauline tradition (otherwise I cannot explain to myself the detailed portrait of Paul), his knowledge of the existence of Pauline letters is (almost) certain (cf. Knox 1966). In this case the question would not be whether Luke *knew* Pauline letters but whether he *used* them to compose his work.

This can only be decided if there are sure traces of the use of Paul's letters (cf. Lindemann 1979, 65); i.e., we have to look for parallels between Acts and the letters of Paul and go on to ask whether these can best be explained on the hypothesis that Luke used Paul (cf. the survey in Walker 1985, 8f.; see also Aejmelaeus 1987, 41-73).

These are the most important reasons put forward so far by scholars in favour of the assumption that Luke used Paul's letters (cf. also Walker 1985, 8f.).

1. All the places and areas mentioned in Acts as stations of Paul's activity are named in the Pauline corpus with the exception of Caesarea, Tarsus, Cyprus and Beroea (thus Lindemann 1979, 165).

2. The stages in Paul's journeys in Acts at one point show amazing parallels to those that can be reconstructed from the letters: thus Paul travels from Philippi via Thessalonica and Athens to Corinth (cf. Acts 16ff. with I Thess.2f.).

3. The agreement between II Cor.11 and Acts 9, the reports on Paul's adventurous escape from Damascus, is all the more remarkable as both break off at the same point: Paul being lowered from the city wall in a basket.

4. The names of Paul's colleagues mentioned in Acts for the most part correspond with the information in Paul's letters.

5. Individual passages like Acts 19.21f. (cf. Rom.15.14ff.) and Acts 26.17f. (cf. Gal.1.16) or expressions like *porthein* in Acts 9.21 (cf. Gal.1.23) and *zelotes* in Acts 22.3 (cf. Gal.1.14) suggest literary dependence.

6. Luke 21.34-36 is dependent on I Thess.5.1-11 (Aejmelaeus 1985).

An examination of the above arguments produces the following result:

On 1 and 2: A large-scale identity of travel and mission stations can be explained by other theories than that of dependence. Moreover argument 1 is wrong, because e.g. Malta (Acts 28.1-10) does *not* appear in the Pauline corpus.

On 3: Here the objection is that Luke would have omitted the next passage, II Cor.12.1-10, from his account, and that would be almost incomprehensible had he made direct use of II Cor.11.32f.; moreover Acts 9.23-25 could go back to a tradition which is mediated by II Cor.11.32f. (!) (cf. Burchard 1970, 158).

On 4: The names of Paul's colleagues were, of course, part of the store of knowledge in the Pauline communities and cannot indicate any use of Paul's letters.

On 5: Galatians 1 shows that the expressions *porthein* or *zelotes* were already elements of oral tradition. The knowledge of Paul's journey in Acts 19.21f. does not conclusively presuppose use of the letters.

On 6: If I Thess.5.1-11 goes back to various elements of tradition (cf. the survey in Aejmelaeus 1985, 136), it is hard to see why the traditional view, that Luke 21.34-36 uses similar elements of tradition, is improbable. Aejmelaeus's 'utilization hypothesis' might be too simple; but cf. also his comments by way of qualification on the 'cumulative proof' of individual facts which are not in themselves plausible (136f.).

So while all the grounds cited point to significant parallels, not one of them offers compelling proof that Luke used Paul's letters. The question, therefore, is whether the evidence is not explained better, as was already evident at individual points, by the hypothesis that Luke used traditions from the Pauline mission territories, individual items in which may have come from reading the letters. In what follows, by way of a test I have presupposed the 'tradition hypothesis'.

I cannot enter here into discussion of the question why Luke did not use Paul's letters, though they (or some of them) were known to him (thus e.g. Bauernfeind 1980, 295-8). Different types of heresy hypothesis remain a possibility (for a survey see Kümmel 1975, 162f.). At present the most recent heresy hypothesis can be found in Schmithals 1982: Luke is fighting against pre-Marcionite hyper-Pauline Gnosticism which drew support from the letters of Paul. Therefore they had become suspect for Luke. However, they had 'also partially become known to him in discussion with the heretics' (16). For the presuppositions of this thesis cf. below 228f. on 20.17-38.

The simple explanation that Luke may have refrained from using the letters of Paul because they were available to anyone (in a collection?) is also worth a thorough examination. (Note the position of Acts in the canon; it can be read as an introduction to Paul's letters without the reader coming upon any repetitions in Acts worth mentioning.) Thus Tacitus refrains from incorporating Seneca's last great speech into his work because this was published later and was generally available (*Ann* XV, 63),

8

and Sallust omits a speech of Cicero against Catiline (*Cat* 31.6), probably for the same reason. In contrast to Luke, however, these authors explicitly mention their omissions.

IV

If the passages cited are not to be derived from the use of Paul's letters, then generally speaking they could be explained by the use of 'traditions', the age, origin and content of which has to be defined further. Here the term 'tradition' should be understood as widely as possible so as not to prejudice the results: in what follows 'tradition' denotes written sources, oral tradition, and also general information which Luke had (for the difficulty of using the term 'tradition' in Acts see Jervell 1984, 69).

In this connection the question of the historical value of Acts must now also be reformulated. We may not ask primarily about the historical value of Acts itself, but about the historical value of the traditions in Acts. If Luke has no personal idea of the events he describes, it would hardly be sensible (for the exceptions see 20 below) to look for the historical value of Acts on the level of his narrative. Rather, Luke's activity as a writer consists in linking traditions together, i.e. of composing a consecutive narrative on the basis of traditions. It follows from this that the *first* task is to separate redaction and tradition. The *second* task is to discover the historical value of the tradition.

Now there are considerable difficulties in discovering traditions in Acts. The reasons for this lie in the literary character of Acts and are further grounded in the fact that in contrast to the Gospel of Luke none of the material on which Acts was based has been *preserved* (apart, of course, from the Old Testament quotations and the reference back to the Gospel of Luke). Given the particular character of Acts, the classic methods of literary criticism do not always work. *Vocabulary statistics*, for example, are only rarely fruitful since Luke has fused the material he uses into his own language (vocabulary statistics are indispensable for showing that). The observation of *tensions* does not always take us back convincingly to pre-existing material, as these tensions can arise from variations made by the author (cf. Ropes 1901; e.g. the criteria of Schmidt 1910, 285, are inadequate). While I would not want to put the value of the two methodological stages in question, however, in analysing Acts the qualifications I have just made should also be noted, just as the fact that Luke has worked over traditions should again be stressed. On the other hand,

Lukan language and style do not in themselves indicate that Luke used no tradition(s).

By way of a test, I shall go on to investigate a few texts. I have deliberately taken them from the part of Acts which deals with Paul, since here we quite often have a chance to take redaction-critical and historical questions further by means of Paul's letters. The following texts or pieces of information will be analysed:

(*a*) Acts 18 (Paul in Corinth);

(*b*) Paul's journeys in Acts 16ff.; 18f.; 27;

(*c*) Acts 21 (Paul in Jerusalem).

The detailed approach I shall adopt is first to define the meaning of the redaction, then the character of the tradition and finally the historical value of individual traditions (for detailed analysis see the commentary which follows).

(*a*) Acts 18 (Paul in Corinth)

The pericope reports Paul's mission in Corinth; there he first preached week by week in the synagogue and later in the adjoining house of Titius Justus. On their way from Macedonia Silas and Timothy meet up with Paul, who is working with the married couple Aquila and Priscilla while he is in Corinth. (They had had to leave Rome because of the edict of Claudius and had come to Corinth.) It is here that the famous 'trial' of Paul before the proconsul Gallio takes place, but Gallio rejects the Jewish charges against Paul (Acts 18.12-17).

The *redactional* features in this text are obvious: numerous parallels in Acts show that Paul's preaching every sabbath in the synagogue (attaching himself to the Jews) and the positive portrait of Gallio, whose attitude is a demonstration of how the Romans (as opposed to the Jews) are to behave towards the Christians, all go back to Luke.

Elsewhere, however, the report seems to reflect *traditions*, like the apostle's employment with Aquila and Priscilla in Corinth shortly after Claudius's edict against the Jews; the arrival of Silas and Timothy from Macedonia; Paul's preaching activity in the house of Titius Justus; the conversion of Crispus, the president of the synagogue; a 'trial' before Gallio; the activity of Sosthenes as president of the synagogue. It is not linguistic reasons which lead us to suppose that Luke is using traditions but the concrete character of the above information and – more important – the evidence (which will later be laid out in detail) that a by no means inconsiderable part of the information is at least partially confirmed by Paul's letters.

It should be remarked in passing that the individual pieces of information which I have mentioned as being free of bias do not fall victim to the judgment to which Hans Conzelmann has given unforgettable expression. He applied his 'Karl May rule' to all uncritical exegesis of Acts (on this see J.Wehnert, 'Die "Karl-May-Regel" in der neutestamentliche Wissenschaft', in *Mitteilungen der Karl-May-Gesellschaft* 16, 1984, no.61, 42): 'An exact depiction of the milieu or even the large-scale use of direct speech does not prove anything about the historicity or "correctness" of the event narrated' (H.Conzelmann and A.Lindemann, *Arbeitsbuch zum Neuen Testament* [8]1985, 43). 'On that basis, in the end one can prove even the historicity of the stories by Karl May' (H.Conzelmann, review of Gasque, 1975, *Erasmus* 28, 1976, [cols 65-68] 68). For precisely this reason I am not turning to the Lukan narrative framework for a historical investigation of Acts but mainly to the individual traditions which can be recognized behind it.

In connection with the text of Acts 18 the further question immediately arises as to whether the traditions I have mentioned are given their correct chronological position here and whether they all relate to the same visit of Paul to Corinth. These two questions are to be answered in the negative for three reasons:

1. The pericope shows a jump between v.11 and v.12. Verse 11 ends with an indication of time: Paul remained in Corinth for eighteen months. After that a new passage begins, introduced by: 'Now when Gallio was proconsul in Achaea...' In other words the two units are separated even externally.

2. Verse 8 knows a Crispus as president of the synagogue, but according to v.17 Sosthenes has this function. As the office of president of the synagogue was in all probability held by only one person, both passages may indicate different points in time (as they may do even for Luke, since Sosthenes is president of the synagogue about eighteen months [v.11] after the conversion of Crispus).

3. The notes of time which are part of the tradition indicate a gap of around ten years. The expulsion of Jews from Rome presupposed in v.2 took place – as most scholars all over the world are agreed – in the year 41, whereas Gallio was in office around 51-52.

At this point, as confirmation of the analysis of the tradition which has been made, it should be pointed out that Luke reports Paul's mission by bringing together the individual pieces of information that he has in narrative form at *one* point. If Paul later visits the same place again, Luke gives a rapid account or a summary.

That is the case with Corinth (18.1ff.), though Paul spends three months here on his later journey (20.2f.); with Thessalonica (17.1ff.,), where he similarly makes a later stay (20.2); with Philippi (16.12ff.), to which he travels twice more later (20.2,3-6). The Lystra episodes similarly belong here, as only Acts 14.8-20 contains traditions, whereas Acts 14.21 gives a summary report of a journey through the place by the apostle (Acts 16.1-3 differs somewhat); cf. also Ephesus: in Acts 19 there are several traditions about Paul's activity in this city, whereas 18.19ff. is merely to be seen as a Lukan insertion into the stay in Ephesus reported in Acts 19f.

From these observations there follows the need to put the traditions that have been discovered back into chronological order. That follows from the analysis of Acts 18 made above, according to which that section contains traditions which go back to different visits by the apostle.

One block of tradition probably leads to the year 41, as Paul was working with Aquila and Priscilla on his first mission in Corinth; the other probably to 51-52, when Gallio was proconsul in Achaea.

If we go on to investigate the *historical value* of the traditions, we arrive at a positive result: Paul's close connection with Aquila and Priscilla during the visit on which he founded the community in Corinth and which is also recognizable from the letters (cf. I Cor.16.19b) is also confirmed by the report in Acts, as is the information that during the first mission in Corinth Silas and Timothy met up with him. They may have been in close contact with the brethren in Macedonia, who according to II Cor.11.9 gave Paul financial support while he was in Corinth (cf. I Thess.3.6). A further stay by Paul in Corinth in 51-52 distinct from the one during which he founded the community can be read out of Paul's letters. It belongs in the period of the making of the collection which the apostle had undertaken in connection with the agreement at the Jerusalem conference. It already follows from what has been said that the traditions in Acts 18 have considerable historical value; this would be even higher if my early dating of Paul's first mission, proposed on the basis of the work of John Knox, proved to be correct. For in that case one of the elements of the tradition contained in Acts 18 would have the chronologically correct information about Paul's arrival in Corinth; we would have to think of the time when Claudius expelled Jews – including Aquila and Priscilla – from Rome, in the year 41.

However, the same historical value cannot be attributed to Luke's redaction as to the traditions contained in Acts 18. Since for theological reasons connected with his view of salvation history – Paul's real world mission cannot have begun before the Jerusalem conference (Acts 15) because it had to be given a final 'blessing' there – Luke puts the first mission in Corinth in the period after the Jerusalem conference and reports in one narrative events which are separated by ten years, he has 'dated' Paul's mission in Greece around a decade too late. The vast majority of scholars, however, have followed him in this.

(b) Paul's journey in Acts 16ff.: 18f.: 27

Luke describes Paul's mission as a journey the destination of which is
Rome. The journeys take him from the place where he was converted,
near Damascus, to Damascus (Acts 9.8), from there to Jerusalem (Acts
9.26), then to Cilicia (Acts 9.30, 'Tarsus'), then to Antioch (Acts 11.26)
and to Jerusalem (Acts 11.30), and from there on the so-called *first*
missionary journey (Acts 13-14) via Cyprus and southern Galatia back
to Antioch. Then follows the third journey to Jerusalem (Acts 15.3f.)
followed by the so-called *second* missionary journey (Acts 15.40-18.22),
from Antioch via Asia Minor and Greece back to Jerusalem. Finally the
same stations are once again covered on the so-called *third* missionary
journey (18.22-21.15). The book ends with the dangerous sea voyage to
Rome (Acts 27f.).

Now *on the one hand* Paul's journeys are Luke's way of describing the
background of the spread of the gospel from Jerusalem to Rome. They
have a parallel in the journey of Jesus (Luke 9.51-19.28), the redactional
character of which can be demonstrated from the original in Mark. *On
the other hand* traditions can be extracted at the following three points.

1. Let us recall that it is occasionally argued from the identical sequence
of places in I Thess.2f. and Acts 16ff. (Thessalonica, Athens, Corinth)
that Luke used Paul's letters. If this theory was hardly convincing for the
reasons given, nevertheless the remarkable identity in the sequence of
stages which gave rise to it has to be explained. In my view the best
explanation is that Acts 16ff. is based on a traditional list of stages in
Paul's journey, regardless of how that may be explained by form criticism.
At this point (and at many other points in Acts) only the letters of Paul
allow us to demonstrate the existence of those traditions (cf. the similar
role played by Mark for Luke's Gospel). However, a qualification needs
to be added. Only reliable traditions can be identified through the letters
of Paul; reports which completely distort historical circumstances can
hardly be recognized as traditions on the basis of the primary sources (on
Plümacher 1984, 125).

In his admirable account of research Plümacher (1984, 120-6) unfortunately did not
report my own position correctly, probably because he misunderstood the importance
in terms of method and content of the 'reconstruction of a chronology of Paul solely
on the basis of the evidence of the letters' (Lüdemann 1984, 44-138). For it is by that
the decision whether my analysis of the tradition is correct stands or falls, and not by
the form-critical problems associated with the 'itinerary' (Plümacher 1984, 124; for
the latter cf also the comment on 22 below).

2. Acts 18f. depicts a journey from Ephesus to Caesarea, then to
Jerusalem, and from there to Antioch, Phrygia, Galatia and Ephesus.
Julius Wellhausen once described the special character of the journey like

this: ' "From Ephesus, to Caesarea, up to greet the brethren, back down to Antioch, then back through Galatia and Phrygia." All in a rush and reported in telegraphic style. No American could do it better' (1907, 14). In my view the summary character of this travel report, which covers a distance of more than 1200 miles as the crow flies, suggests the adoption of tradition at this point, since it is 'hard to see why the author should have invented the whole journey without any historical reason and then have reported it as fleetingly as that' (Pfleiderer 1902, 514f.).

3. Acts 27 depicts a dangerous sea voyage. Verses 9-11,21-26,31,33-36 (,43), which are focussed on Paul, the prophet of disaster and saviour in distress, can be bracketted off. What is left is the report of a shipwreck and its relatively happy outcome. Wellhausen's conclusion that in Acts 27 Luke made use of a literary model and enriched this with the figure of Paul (Wellhausen 1907, 18f.) seems irrefutable.

We now come to a historical assessment of the three traditions (about the journeys) that I have just reconstructed.

1. *The journey in Acts 16ff.* It can claim historical value in that the sequence of stages corresponds to the sequence which can be obtained from the letters of Paul. As I Thess.2f. shows, Paul may in fact have arrived back in Corinth from Philippi via Thessalonica and Athens on his mission in Greece. However, the chronological sequence given to this journey by Luke is open to criticism. On the basis of Paul's own testimony and – we might already add – because the expulsion of Jews from Rome and the first mission in Corinth coincide in time (Acts 18.2), the journey during which the community in Corinth was founded may have taken place ten years earlier than is indicated in Acts. If one were to preserve the pattern in Acts, it would have to be placed between Acts 9 and 11.

2. *The journey in Acts 18f.* The results here will be similar to those on Acts 16ff. The combination of Paul's own testimonies suggests that he undertook a journey to Jerusalem from Greece which corresponds to the sequence of stages in Acts 18 (cf. Lüdemann 1984, 152-6). To this degree the present tradition is historically valuable. But there are serious objections to the chronological context in which it is set. It presupposes that Paul – in the middle of his journey over the collection – made a diversion to Palestine which would have been extremely laborious, given the distance of over 1200 miles as the crow flies, and then went on to resume the collection in his communities. That must be ruled out. But the historical worth of the tradition of the journey in Acts 18f. is clear if we put it back in the historical context which can be reconstructed from Paul's letters. In that case it is an admirable account of the journey which Paul undertook from Greece to Palestine, in order to take part in the Jerusalem conference (Gal.2). (Paul's own account in Gal.2.1f. says that Paul went to Jerusalem with Barnabas. But that is no conclusive argument

14

against the thesis put forward above, since Gal.2.1f. neither tells us from where Paul and Barnabas set out for Jerusalem, nor presupposes that they had worked together immediately before the conference.)

3. *The journey in Acts 27.* The sea voyage in Acts 27 presents a different picture from the two journeys discussed under 1. and 2. Certainly it may be accepted that Paul went to Rome after his last visit to Jerusalem (I Clement 5). But the account of the sea voyage does not have any genetic relationship to Paul's journey to Rome. For Luke himself may have taken over the account of the sea voyage from a literary model. It is to be described as some of Luke's book-knowledge and therefore unhistorical. (However, that does not exclude the possibility that Luke knew that Paul was transported by ship, see below, 260.)

(c) Acts 21 (Paul in Jerusalem)

Acts reports Paul's arrival in Jerusalem. Here he finds lodging in the house of the Hellenist Mnason and is given a warm welcome by James and the elders, to whom he reports the successes of the Gentile mission. However, James advises Paul to give evidence of his loyalty to the law by performing a Jewish rite, since Christian zealots for the law had heard about the apostle to the Gentiles: 'He is teaching all the Jews who live among the Gentiles to apostasize from Moses by saying that they should not circumcise their children and should not observe (Jewish) customs.' Paul follows this advice.

The section of text which I have described shows clear traces of *Lukan redaction.* Paul has a good relationship with the Jerusalem community and its leader James. At the same time, to the last he is not guilty of any transgression of the law. Indeed, by taking part in a Jewish rite he gives evidence of his fidelity to the law.

Now two things are striking about this section of the text:

1. In v.17 the community (*hoi adelphoi*) greets Paul and his companions. However, in the sequel (vv.20-22) the many (zealous) brethren who have heard hostile rumours about Paul are distinguished from the (whole) community. (Do they not belong to the community?)

2. It is remarkable that any rumours at all are going the rounds about Paul's criticism of the law, all the more so as there is no reason whatsoever for such rumours on the basis of the description of Paul in Acts.

That leads one to conclude that both the Christians who have reservations about Paul and the report about Paul's preaching in criticism of the law are elements of a *tradition* which the author of Acts changed to match his theology but could not completely do away with. (For the

15

question whether Paul's participation in the Nazirate was part of the tradition see 234 below.)

What is the *historical value* of such a tradition? In my view it is to be rated highly, since the content of Acts 21.21 is confirmed by Paul's letters. Certainly Paul's own preaching about the law does not match the principles laid down in Acts 21.21. Paul was for everyone remaining in their state (I Cor.7.17-20), both Jews and Gentiles. But the actual practice of the Pauline communities, which were primarily Gentile Christian (cf. Gal.2.11ff.; 5.6.; 6.15: I Cor.7.19), seems to have gone beyond this noble principle. Some Jewish Christians from the Pauline communities and their children seem in fact to have been alienated from the Mosaic law by being a minority in the Pauline communities. The rumour contained in Acts 21.21 is therefore probably a historically reliable comment on what was going on in some of them. (The qualification 'some of' is important, because the rumour evidently generalizes from individual instances in a polemical way.)

However, the other element of the tradition in Acts 21, the existence of many Jewish Christians in Jerusalem who were opposed to Paul, must be reckoned historical. Paul himself points out in Rom.15.21 that the Christians of Jerusalem were possibly not well disposed to him. In addition, Paul's opponents in the communities predominantly originated from Jerusalem (cf. Lüdemann 1983, 103-65). Finally, it is remarkable that according to Luke's account Paul was not supported by Jerusalem Christians during his imprisonment in Jerusalem and Caesarea; this could be explained by his rejection on the part of the majority of the Jerusalem community.

Thus in conclusion we may say that Luke's account of Paul's arrival in Jerusalem contains some old traditional material which may be said to be historical.

V

In conclusion, after a short retrospective survey I shall make some provisional comments on the historical value of Acts.

I began with a survey of the lively history of scholarly research into the historical value of Acts. At its beginning is the radical criticism of F.C.Baur; in the middle is the return to the tradition by Adolf von Harnack; and at the present time we have on the one hand redaction critics who are not very interested in the historical question, and on the other a trend which defends the historical reliability of Acts, which is on the upturn. In retrospect it can be said that so far the Baur school and von Harnack have remained the classic antipodes in the question of the historical worth of

Acts. Therefore it was necessary to pass some judgment on the mutually exclusive positions of Baur and Harnack. To this end I first discussed the alternative arguments that the author was an eye-witness or had used the letters of Paul. Whereas the former view suggested that the historical worth of Acts was considerable, the latter view suggested that it was significantly less. But both these theses had to be rejected as improbable and replaced by the presupposition that Luke worked traditions of another kind into his work. That meant that the historical value of Acts was primarily to be discussed as a question of the historical value of the traditions incorporated into Acts. (For the question whether historically accurate traditions may have been preserved in the redaction see 20 below.) In pursuit of this task I chose three different complexes of text and each time investigated the redaction, the tradition and the historical value of the basic material. Although in this way I analysed only a small section of the text of Acts, on the basis of the result at which I arrived some general conclusions already seemed appropriate:

1. Alongside the letters of Paul Acts remains an important source for the history of early Christianity since:

2. Many of the traditions which it uses are historically reliable and enrich our knowledge of earliest Christianity in addition to the letters of Paul.

3. However, it must immediately be said by way of qualification that this verdict applies above all to the traditions incorporated into Acts, the chronological framework of which has in each case to be reconstructed from the letters of Paul. To this degree:

4. A chronology obtained solely on the basis of a critical analysis of the letters is an indispensable presupposition for the ordering and evaluation of the traditions of Acts.

5. It is now often impossible to assign the reconstructed traditions to any particular form, and in any case it is only possible to reconstruct their basic features.

6. In general it is necessary to take much more account than is usual of what Luke gathered from his reading (apart from LXX and the Gospel) when we reconstruct the traditions. This is evident from Acts 27 and may have also happened in the case of the other chapters (cf. 16.25-34; 19.13-16; 20.7-12: 28.3-6).

7. The parts of Acts not discussed above, for which there is no historical evidence in the letters of Paul, pose a special problem. We still have to analyse them, and important pointers may be expected from the way in which the traditions have been worked into the Gospel of Luke and the parts of Acts covered by the letters of Paul. However, because of the Lukan reworking throughout it seems a hopeless undertaking to reconstruct continuous sources in these passages. Here, too, it is possible only to

reconstruct individual traditions, and in many cases judgments as to their historicity have a lesser degree of probability because our possibilities of controlling them are less.

8. A critical analysis of Acts with special attention to the question of the traditions contained in it and their historical value is an important task, in view of the flood of redaction-critical studies of Acts. Nor is it without prospect of success, as has been shown clearly by the tests I made above.

Commentary on the Acts of the Apostles

Preliminary comment: The layout and method of the commentary

To carry out the programme described at the beginning I shall go on to make an analysis of the whole of Acts. Its aim is to look at each individual section to see the tradition which may possibly be contained in it and then if possible to give a reasoned judgment on its historical value. In this respect it goes against the main tendencies of modern scholarship which works on Acts (and on the Gospel of Luke) above all in order to discover the author's purpose.

Cf. especially Schneider 1982: the difficulty or impossibility of reconstructing the wording of the sources used by Luke can 'distract the exegete from his own distinctive task. He is to work through what the author "intended to say" (*quid scriptor dicere intenderit: Divino afflante Spiritu*, with a reference to Athanasius, *Contra Arianos* 154)' (5).

While recognizing the scholarly significance of this redaction-critical research into Acts (and the new literary criticism which takes it further [cf. Petersen 1978 and the bibliography]), the present work resumes the concern of the five-volume *The Beginnings of Christianity*. The editors of that volume (F.J.Foakes Jackson and Kirsopp Lake) saw that to provide an account of the beginnings of Christianity it was a priority to work out the historical facts contained in Acts (*Beg*. I, vii [the term 'fact' is not explicitly used, but it is implicit in their remarks]). They evidently planned to examine other sources, like the Gospels, for their historical value in connection with the beginnings of Christianity (*Beg*. I, viii). Though for unknown reasons the project was never continued, the aim and execution of the analysis of Acts from a historical perspective in the *Beginnings of Christianity* remain significant enough. In accord with the programme of the editors of *Beginnings* I shall again investigate what historical facts can be gained from Acts which could be the basis for assured knowledge about earliest Christianity.

Now the term 'facts' is an ambivalent one and at this point it needs to be defined more closely. Perhaps it is best to follow the remarks of J.G.Droysen (1958) here. He writes:

It is in the nature of the things with which our discipline is concerned to be mistaken if one thinks that one... is dealing with objective facts. Objective facts in their reality

19

are not accessible to our research. What happened objectively in any past is something quite different from what we call historical fact. What happened can only be understood intellectually as an interconnected happening, as a complex of cause and effect, of purpose and implementation, in short as one fact, and the same individual features could be viewed differently by others; they could be combined by others with other facts or purposes' (133f.; cf. the similar remarks by Schaff 1970; Rüsen 1983).

The distinction made by Droysen between objective facts and historical facts, i.e. the distinction between history as *res gestae* and history as *opinio rerum gestarum*, can be left out of account here. For even Droysen, despite his questioning of objective facts or history as *res gestae*, is concerned with the possibility of testing the *opinio rerum gestarum*, i.e. that account of the course of history which can best be justified. Whether such a *picture of* history is identified with history or not, the only important thing for our purpose is the objective character of facts which can be historically verified.

Droysen's other assertion is more important for our work. According to it, the objective course of events in any past is something different from what is called historical fact. For this is first understood intellectually as a complex of cause and effect, as a historical fact consisting of various details, and moreover is viewed differently and combined with other causes (e.g. effects and purposes) elsewhere.

Now in the source to be worked on here the particular event, together with its reasons, purposes, etc., which for Droysen are what together first make up a fact, occurs *first* in the Lukan framework and in the redactional parts of a particular narrative. But in my historical research neither is an object of concern; as a rule on each occasion the concern is to examine the historical value of the individual traditions – after taking away the Lukan framework and the Lukan redaction. (Only in a few cases, which will be explained in more detail, are questions asked about the historicity of the Lukan framework and/or individual information in Luke, since we cannot exclude the possibility that on occasion a tradition which can no longer be reconstructed has found its way into the redaction [cf. e.g. the summaries].) *Then*, the particular happening along with the reasons for it, its purpose or effects, can be found at the level of tradition (in the individual piece of tradition), and often these reasons will not be seen from the same perspective as that of the redaction. My aim is to investigate the reliability of each individual piece of tradition, taking into account Droysen's admonition that we no longer come upon *bruta facta* but historical facts.

At the same time it should be stressed that we shall be going on to consider not only external but also internal events as facts. For example both Peter's missionary activity in Joppa (Acts 9) and a vision given to Paul (Acts 16) can be called facts - if their historical probability can be

20

demonstrated. Similarly, in what follows the term 'fact' also describes written or oral statements by persons and their theological presuppositions, if they are historically accurate (e.g. the letters and speeches in Acts and the scriptural exegesis).

For both the more recent debate, carried on mainly by historians about the concept of fact, which was taken up in positivism and since then has become indispensable, and the problems of historiography, cf. Rüsen 1983 and bibliography, 146-54. From an earlier period, Bernheim 1908, 179-251, remains important. At the same time it needs to be stressed that each source calls for a different range of methods. According to E.Schwartz one must freely 'invent a new method for each problem... which is appropriate for precisely that problem' (K.von Fritz, *Schriften zur griechischen und römischen Verfassungsgeschichte und Verfassungstheorie*, Berlin and New York 1976, VII – cf. N.Hartmann, *Das Problem des geistigen Seins*, Berlin ³1962, 29-32). The problem discussed in the present work is how one can gain historical facts from Acts which can provide the basis for assured knowledge about earliest Christianity. Therefore a further consideration of discussions of methods in history is indispensable.

It should be stressed that the considerations about method advanced here presuppose an intensive concern with the whole text of Acts and were only written towards the end of the preparation of the manuscript, because awareness of method only follows the actual use of working methods.

The analysis which follows divides Acts into series of texts. A more refined division is worked out as a first stage. This section (I) fulfils a dual purpose. It recalls the content of the text and then gives a first insight into the structure of the text. That already indicates the connection between the sentences and clauses and thus what they set out to say. Both are the theme of the next section (II), which is an analysis of the redaction. In general what follows here is first of all a short analysis of elements of Luke's language (without any attempt at completeness) and then a dicussion of the redactional context in the text and what it seeks to convey. Following this, in each case section III raises the question of the presence of possible elements of tradition. Starting points for this are sometimes also already found under II (e.g. by indications of tensions which do not derive from redactional intent, or by un-Lukan expressions), but the possibility of tradition in any section must nevertheless be demonstrated separately. As became clear at the beginning, there is particularly good reason for assuming traditions in Acts 16-21. In addition to that, however, it may be taken as certain that the problem of the traditions in Acts 1-5; 6-12; 21-28 is different, as it cannot be extracted and controlled by a comparison with the letters of Paul (as it often can in Acts 16-21), even if in individual sections (Acts 5; 8; 12) there is information from outside Luke which can be used as comparative material. However, once again I should stress that it is possible that elements of tradition can be discovered as the basis of *individual* sections without resorting to large-scale source theories. (Of course that does not exclude the possible existence of overlapping strands of sources, but it does in part explain elements in them; cf. the detailed analysis.) Finally, I must again draw attention to my deliberately broad understanding of the concept of tradition (see 9 above).

(Exclusively) to help the reader I would like to refer here briefly to my own assumptions about the general basis for sources in Acts (apart from the Gospel of Luke, the LXX, the results of Luke's reading [see 17 above] and Luke's general knowledge). These are the presupposions and the results of the commentary which follows. (For the serious source theories put forward by scholars see also Schneider 1982, 82-103; Plümacher 1984, 120-38.)

(*a*) In Acts 15.40-21.36(?) Luke uses an itinerary supplemented by individual episodes (as a parallel cf. a journal used as a basis by Xenophon, *Anabasis*, and on it R.Nickel, *Xenophon*, Darmstadt 1979, 85f., 118). Possibly this source also partly included material from Paul's early period (Acts 9) and perhaps also the reports of the Jerusalem conference (Acts 15). For the relationship of Acts 13-14 to the itinerary see 164 below.

(*b*) Luke had an account of Paul's trial in Caesarea before Festus. This source contained information about the transfer of Paul from Jerusalem to Caesarea, the charge against Paul, the appeal to the emperor with reference to Paul's Roman citizenship, etc. However, the degree of probability of the existence of such a source is far slighter than in the case of (*a*), as it is impossible to use the letters of Paul as controls. The same goes for all three assumptions about sources which follow.

(*c*) Luke had written traditions from the Hellenist groups (Acts 6-8; 11; 13-14 [?]).

(*d*) Luke used a number of stories about Peter which he had in written or oral form (Acts 3; 5; 12).

(*e*) In Acts 1-5 Luke relied on individual oral traditions from the early period of the Jerusalem community.

(*f*) I do not know of any completely satisfactory hypothesis which covers all the 'we-passages' (Acts 16.10-17; 20.5-15; 21.1-18; 27.1-28.16). These passages are therefore analysed without any preconceived theory. A convincing partial result may at least have been achieved on Acts 27 (see 258f. below). Cf. now J.Wehnert, *Die Wir-Passagen der Apostelgeschichte*, Göttingen 1989.

Section IV subjects the reconstructed traditions in each instance to historical verification. Here too the letters of Paul play a dominant role – both in respect of individual pieces of information and also particularly in respect of the framework of Pauline chronology. It should be stressed that the historical question is raised on the basis of a hypothetically reconstructed tradition. In other words, many individual results are open to question. But as a negative generalization it should not be objected that the present commentary is too fond of hypotheses. For it is impossible to deal with Acts except by historical hypotheses, unless one limits oneself to retelling the Acts account, as unfortunately all too often happens. Rather, here too the question arises as to the best hypothesis: I shall seek

22

to arrive at this or present it for discussion for each individual section of Acts.

With the best will in the world, and despite the concession that our knowledge is partial, I cannot resolve 'in most instances to leave open' the question of historicity (Stählin 1980, 8). That is all the more impossible when the purpose of Stählin's comment becomes clear in the next sentence: 'On the other hand it must be said that there has been far too much scepticism about Luke's information and that probably a very great deal of what he reports by and large corresponds to the way things happened' (ibid.).

The subsequent analysis of Acts that I have just described in this way cannot replace the major commentaries which largely devote themselves to redaction analysis and intensive discussion of the secondary literature; nor does it seek to. Nor does it make use of translation extensively, but merely discusses translation problems in connection with individual important questions. However, it does stand on its own and is more than a supplement to more recent commentaries. It presupposes the use of a Greek text of Acts throughout and often dispenses with saying yet again what has already been said by others. Explicit discussion of secondary literature is relatively sparse. Only in individual instances, where there is a reason, is reference made to more recent literature, and relatively often to older works which threaten to be forgotten.

The introduction gives information about the place of the following analysis in the history of research. I have dropped my original plan of discussing the speeches in Acts in an appendix, as the historical results would have been relatively thin. Therefore with some exceptions the exegesis of the speeches is fairly brief. A summary at the conclusion has been dispensed with, since it would only have repeated what has been said before.

For Acts research in recent years see the well-informed article by F.Hahn, 'Der gegenwärtige Stand der Erforschung der Apostelgeschichte. Kommentare und Aufsatzbände 1980-1985', *ThRev* 82, 1986, 177-90.

Significantly, in the most recent major commentary on Acts by R.Pesch (see the bibliography), the introduction (Pesch I, 21-56) does not have a section on the historical value of Acts, though the author usually discusses it in the detailed exegesis (without making it a separate theme).

Acts 1.1-14

I Division

1.1-2: Dedication and prologue (cf. Luke 1.1-4)
3-8: Jesus' farewell actions and words of farewell
9-11: The ascension of Jesus from the Mount of Olives
12-14: The earliest community
   12: The return of the disciples to Jerusalem
   13-14: The earliest community (mentioned by name) in the upper room

II Redaction

[1-2] This section is an introduction to the second part of Luke-Acts. Lukan language is recognizable at the following places: v.1: *panton... hon, te kai*; v.2: *anelemphthe*. Verses 1 and 2 refer explicitly to the Gospel of Luke (= *protos logos*), the content of which is described as the action (*poiein*) and teaching (*didaskein*) of Jesus. The instructions which Jesus gave to his disciples before the ascension (*enteilamenos*) differ from those in Luke 24 unless it is assumed that they had been given during the farewell meal (Luke 24.41-43: thus Reicke 1957, 10). The choice of the disciples reported in v.2 took place in Luke 6.13. Reference is made to this passage here in preparation for the list of disciples which follows in v.13.

[3-8] Main examples (a selection) of Lukan language are: v.3: relative pronoun + *kai*; *parestesen* + dative (cf.9.41), *pathein* (as a designation of the suffering and death of Jesus), *legon ta peri tes basileias* (cf. Luke 9.11); v.5: *ou... pollas* (Jeremias 1980, 249); v.6: *men oun*; v.7: *eipen...pros*.
   For v.3 cf. below on vv.6f. Verse 4a (*synalizomenos* = eating together [cf.10.31]; elsewhere 'being together' is a possible translation – see the commmentaries) takes up Luke 24.41-43. Verse 4b with the command to leave Jerusalem refers back to Luke 24.49: there the disciples are already ordered to remain in the city until they are endowed with the power of the Most High. The end of v.4 (*hen ekousate mou*) is to be understood in connection with the rest of the verse as a reference back to Luke 24.49, and despite the change of person (first instead of third) is probably not an introduction to the saying in the following verse. In v.5 the Risen Christ refers to a central event of the past ('John baptized with water') and at the same time announces the imminent fulfilment of that part of John the Baptist's promise (Luke 3.16) which has yet to come to pass. This will

25

happen in Acts 2 (*ou meta pollas tautas hemeras* is a passing comment to this effect). With another reference back to Luke 24.49 (note, moreover, that according to both passages the disciples are staying in Jerusalem), Jesus recalls a saying of John the Baptist and at the same time relates it to the present by connecting it with the outpouring of the Spirit in Acts 2. Acts 11.16 then looks back to the saying of Jesus in v.5. Verses 6f. correct an imminent apocalyptic expectation (cf. Grässer 1977, 204-7; 1979). The question whether the kingdom is coming immediately (cf. 1.32f.; 24.21) is brushed aside. The kingdom is replaced by the Spirit (v.3b, Jesus' preaching of the kingdom of God, is to be interpreted in this pneumatological, ecclesiological sense). In this way the time of the parousia is shifted into an indeterminate (but not uncertain: v.11; 17.31) future. All the weight lies on v.8 (cf. Luke 24.47f.), which prefigures the preaching of the gospel throughout the world. This preaching of the gospel is the work of the Spirit, whose coming is already prophesied in v.7. Here the task of the apostles is defined as being witnesses to Jesus (see 33 below). Their work is later continued in the thirteenth witness, Paul (cf.22.15; 26.16-18 – see especially Burchard 1970, 130-5). Verse 8 has probably rightly been seen as the programme and framework of Acts (Conzelmann 1987, 7). Here the expression 'to the end of the world' denotes Rome, cf.PsSol. 8.15 and the geographical outline of Acts, which leads from Jerusalem to Rome (Hengel 1983b, 101 [bibliography] differs).

[9-11]The language of the section is that of Luke. Cf. especially v.10: *atenizontes*, a periphrastic conjugation, genitive absolute, *kai idou*; v.11: *kai* after the relative pronoun (cf. further Lohfink 1971, 186-202). Moreover the fourfold repetition of *eis ton ouranon* (vv.10, 11[3x]) in particular points to the hand of the redactor. The look forward to the parousia in v.11 is probably redactional and connects the story with vv.6f. The expectation of an imminent coming expressed in v.6 and rejected in v.7 turns into a distant expectation (not as resignation, but as hope).

[12-14] *hypostrephein* in v.12 is a favourite word of Luke's. The verse connects the story with what follows. Here the place of the ascension, the Mount of Olives, and the distance between it and Jerusalem, a sabbath day's journey, are mentioned in passing. Both pieces of information may go back to Luke; the detail 'a sabbath day's journey' serves to make a connection between the different places where the disciples are staying in Jerusalem; here the Jerusalem theme is particularly important to Luke. (The disciples are witnesses to the ascension of Jesus at a place *near* to Jerusalem and then return to Jerusalem.) For the designation 'Mount of Olives' see Luke 19.29/Mark 11.1 (Matt.21.1 omits Bethany). Luke knows from Mark that the Mount of Olives and Bethany are close together

26

or even names for the same place. So here he varies the place-name from Luke 24.50-53, where the ascension took place from Bethany. Moreover the mountain theme fits accounts of transportations (cf. the parallels in Friedrich 1978, 44).

In vv.13-14 *proskarterountes, homothymadon* and *proseuche* are Lukan language. The content is a summary description by Luke of the circumstances of the first community, which is devoting itself to prayer. This description prepares for the subsequent choice of a replacement for Judas and the further summary and edifying description of the earliest community. The mention of women who belong to the first community may go back to the redaction. But which women are meant, women followers of Jesus or wives of the apostles? The following considerations suggest that *syn gynaixin* (v.14) is meant to denote the apostles' wives (thus also Lake/Cadbury, *Beg.* IV, 11): for purely linguistic reasons it seems more likely that the women should be seen as the wives of the disciples. Were they female followers of Jesus, one would have expected the article before *gynaixin*. Moreover, when the women disciples of Jesus are mentioned in the Gospel they are almost always defined more closely (cf. Luke 8.2f.; 10.38-42; 23.49, 55; Luke 24.10 is an exception). Furthermore, in Acts Luke has no special interest in further mention of the women who had followed Jesus from Galilee, since they are not mentioned elsewhere in the book. However, if they should be meant in v.14 they are mentioned simply in order to 'check off' the theme of the 'women from Galilee' – at most for the sake of completeness. If, however, these should be the 'wives of the apostles' (thus doubtless Codex D, which has *kai teknois* in addition to *syn gynaixin*), v.14 would describe a kind of 'holy family of the earliest community', families of the disciples and the family of the Lord (built up on the chiastic pattern men [twelve apostles]/their wives – women [represented by Mary the mother of Jesus]/men [the brothers of Jesus]). If this suggestion is correct, Acts 1.14 would have to be seen in parallel to the family stories in Luke 1-2. Finally, it may have been known in the communities that the apostles had wives (cf. I Cor.9.5). Cf. also Luke 4.38 (the existence of Peter's mother-in-law shows that Peter had a wife). For an evaluation of the redactional interpretation of the women as wives see Schüssler-Fiorenza 1983, 52. From what has been said, it follows that the mention of the brothers of Jesus *at this point* is redactional and forms part of the overall picture which Luke means to give in v.14.

Excursus: Is there an interpolation in Acts 1.3ff.?

It has often been thought that a redactor intervened in the original material from v.3 on (cf. particularly emphatically Norden 1913, 311-13); Meyer I, 34-42; Bauernfeind 1980, 312ff.). The following reasons are given for this theory:

1. After the *men* of v.1 one would have expected a matching clause with *de*.

2. The account in vv.3-8 does not just take further the events narrated in Luke 24.36-53, but also goes back before them. For the time during which Jesus is with his disciples before the ascension is now extended over a period of forty days, as opposed to the one day (and a night) of Luke 24.36-53.

3. In contrast to the previous statements, vv.4f. contain direct speech.

4. The phrase *dia pneumatos hagiou* (v.2) is in the wrong place.

5. Acts 1.2, 4-9 fall on the same day (thus also Luke 24). Verse 3, which says that Jesus appeared to his disciples over forty days, has a conflicting chronology.

But none of these arguments is really convincing.

On 1: There is a *men* without a following *de* at other passages in Acts, even if not quite so striking (3.21; 4.16; 22.21). Moreover *hois kai* (v.3) matches Luke's style.

On 2: the argument holds only if Luke-Acts was originally one book. But, as emerges from Acts 1.1, that was not so. And in that case one can understand how the author begins by referring back to what he has already written and gives information about the content of the end of the first book by means of a narrative about Jesus' appearance to the disciples. This provides a better connection.

On 3: In other passages in Acts, too, there is a abrupt transition from direct to indirect speech (cf. Acts 17.3; 23.22).

On 4: Even the position of *dia pneumatos hagiou* (v.2) does not necessarily derive from an interpolator. The phrase has the function of an anticipation (an observation made by F.Rehkopf, Göttingen). In that case it relates to *hous exelexato*. (Conzelmann 1987, 3, however, connects the *dia pneumatos hagiou* with *enteilamenos*.)

On 5: 13.31 ('He appeared during many days to those who had gone up with him from Galilee, who are his witness to the people') might refer to 1.3 and thus make it probable that v.3 was always part of Acts.

III Traditions

Though we may thus rule out the theory of an interpolation in Acts 1.3ff., it is nevertheless certain that Luke worked over traditions in this section:

1. In the report Jesus' showing himself alive after his passion (v.3a) and appearing over forty days (v.3b) stand side by side. The first conception corresponds to the appearance of the exalted Jesus from heaven, which is known to Paul, and the latter is to be connected with remarks about a particular period during which Jesus was with his disciples after the resurrection; cf. eighteen months (Gnostics in Irenaeus, *Adv.haer* I 3, 2 and the Ophites [Irenaeus, *Adv.haer* I 30, 14]); 545 days (*AscJes* 9.16); 550 days (*EpJac* 2.19f.). Both conceptions here combined by Luke probably derive from oral tradition. (However, Weiser 1981, 49f., gives substantial reasons for the forty days being redactional in origin.)

2. The expectation of the kingdom for Israel as a result of the parousia of Jesus, which is expressed in the question in v.6 ('Lord, will you at this time restore the kingdom to Israel?'), is tradition which is corrected by Luke in the sense mentioned under II (p.26) above.

[9-11] Underlying this is a tradition the form of which can no longer be recognized. It reports the miraculous transportation of Jesus. Motives belonging to this are 'the cloud' and 'two men in shining garments' (cf. Luke 24.4) as interpreters of the events. (A doublet of this tradition which has been worked over even more intensively by Luke appears in Luke 24.50-53.) The tradition does not presuppose *any* chronological interval from Easter Day nor is it connected with a place. It is possible that the form of address, 'Galileans', may point to Galilee. For the details of vv.9-11 cf. in addition to the commentaries Friedrich 1978, 39-44, and Lohfink 1971, 160-2; however, Lohfink rates the creativity of Luke too highly and therefore eliminates the tradition in what are good observations throughout. For criticism cf. the important review by Hahn 1974; on vv.9-11 cf. Hahn 1974, 424f.

[12-14] Luke writes out the list of apostles (Luke 6.14-16), varying the order. The most important difference is that John is in second place in the Acts list, whereas in the Gospel list Andrew is in second place and John in third. The change may derive from the fact that in Acts Peter and John appear as a pair (cf. Acts 3-5). It should be noted, further, that Luke already mentions Peter and John together in other passages of the Gospel (in contrast to the side references): cf. Luke 22.8 (Mark 14.13: 'two of his disciples', Matt.26.17: 'the disciples'); Luke 8.51 (Mark 5.37: 'Peter, James, John'); Luke 9.28 (Mark 9.2/Matt.17.1: 'Peter, James, John').

A piece of information from the tradition about the room in which the Jerusalem community met perhaps underlies the expression 'upper room' (*hyperoon*) (cf.12.12). But on the other hand see 9.37, 39; 20.8.

The tradition that brothers of Jesus were members of the earliest community cannot be made more specific. It is part of Luke's general knowledge.

In v.14 the combination *proskarterountes... te proseuche* is traditional (see Rom.12.12; Col.4.2).

For the 'women' as part of the tradition see above under II.

IV Historical

[1-8] The account is unhistorical in its redactional form, as Luke keeps silent about the first appearances in Galilee, which he knew of from the Gospel of Mark. These earliest appearances are reflected in Mark 16.7; Matt.28.16ff.; John 21 (cf. Lüdemann 1983, 67f. [bibliography]).

Historical and unhistorical details are mixed together in the individual traditions mentioned above:

1. There were in fact appearances of the heavenly Jesus in Jerusalem

(after those in Galilee). That can be said with certainty of the vision of James (I Cor.15.7), since the Lord's brother only joined the primitive community at a *later* date. Cf. also the appearances to five hundred brethren (I Cor.15.6), the Emmaus story (Luke 24) and John 20 as evidence for a tradition of Jerusalem appearances. In their earliest form (Mark) the tomb stories in Mark 16.1-8 par. do not know of any special appearance of Jesus to the women (in contrast to Matt.28.9f.; John 20.14-18) and therefore cannot be utilized here (Hengel 1963, 251-6; Schottroff 1980, 111f. differ).

On the other hand the tradition of Jesus being with his disciples for forty days goes back to a later conception (cf. the apocryphal parallels) and is therefore unhistorical. The number 'forty' is a favourite one in biblical writing (Israel was forty days in the wilderness, Moses forty days on Sinai [and Jesus forty days in the wilderness]; cf. H.Balz, *EWNT* III, 843f.).

2. The expectation of the imminent restoration of the kingdom to Israel through the parousia of Jesus may have been shared by Jewish Christians in Jerusalem. Otherwise it is difficult to explain why influential parts of Jewish Christianity remained for years in Jerusalem or kept strict guard on its theological significance. The fact that later they only hesitantly came to an understanding with the Gentile mission (Gal.2.9) probably reflects the original expectation that Jesus' parousia would introduce a restoration of the kingdom to Israel. In this context Luke's narrative about the bestowal of the Spirit to the disciples is of course unhistorical if connected with a mission command which also includes Gentiles as a goal. The Gentile mission was only wrung out of the earliest apostles in Jerusalem by Paul and the Hellenists as a concession. They themselves, with the exception of Peter (see 132f. below on Acts 10), saw themselves only as a mission to the Jews. (For the basis of the remarks in this section cf. Lüdemann 1983, 67-102.)

[9-11] The ascension is unhistorical. It is rooted in the conceptions of the time, for which departure upwards with a cloud (Luke 24.51; Acts 1.11) was already regarded as acceptance into heaven and for which an empty tomb was already an indication of the 'transportation' of the dead. (Marshall 1980, 60, speaks on the one hand of the symbolism of the ascension and then of the historicity of what happened; he finally says that what happened lies beyond simple literal description. 'It is in this kind of way that the story of the ascension of Jesus is best understood' [ibid.]. And also other 'ascension accounts' from the ancient world?) Moreover the theological significance of the ascension of Jesus is to be separated from criticism of its historicity. However, it is wrong to go to the other extreme and assert: 'Anyone who interprets the happenings

narrated by Luke... as a simple historical event does not take them "literally" in Luke's sense. One only takes narratives of this kind "literally" when one asks very carefully about the theological purposes of their author' (Lohfink 1971, 250). For Luke was rooted in the conceptions of the time, and really thought that Jesus was carried off to heaven (his reason for that was the empty tomb).

[13-14] The framework is certainly unhistorical. The names of the disciples of Jesus are for the most part certainly historical, especially as they are supported by the synoptic parallels which are independent of one another. (However, it should be noted that unlike Luke, the list of the twelve in Mark 3.16-19 has Thaddaeus [Luke: Judas brother of James] and Simon the Canaanite [Luke: Simon the Zealot]. The existence of women disciples as members of the earliest Jerusalem community is also a historical fact, although it cannot be ascertained on the basis of vv.13-14 (see 27 above on the redactional shaping of vv.13-14).

Acts 1.15-26

I Division

1.15: Details of the situation
16-22: Peter's speech
  16-17: Introduction
  18-20: Death of Judas and scriptural proof
  21-22: The need for a replacement
23-26: The choice of the replacement

II Redaction

[15] The verse provides a *temporal* connection between what has gone before and the following episode with a Lukan phrase (*en tais hemerais tautais*). The *inner* link is the way in which Luke has just reported the harmonious prayer of the eleven apostles with other members of the community (vv.13f.). The number 'about 120' is often seen as an increase over vv.13f. However, that presupposes that the verse relates to the whole community (the women as followers of Jesus), and that is not the only possible interpretation; it is subjected to criticism on p.27.

[16-22] The address *andres adelphoi* appears in Acts without additions like *pateres*, etc., only in 23.1 and 28.17 at the beginning of a speech. *edei plerothenai ten graphen...*: the idea of the necessity of an event is certainly pre-Lukan, and was developed by the first Christians in their defence of

the passion of Jesus with reference to scripture (cf. Mark 14.21,49; for the details see Dibelius, 1971, 178-218). In v.16 the betrayal by Judas accordingly falls under the divine *dei* and as a result is given a distinctively Lukan touch (cf. also the remarks by Conzelmann 1960, 153f., on the theological use of *dei* in Luke). This prophecy is certainly taken up in v.20a (= Ps.69.26 [LXX 68.25 – not literally]). The remarks about the betrayal of Judas (v.16 end-17) refer back to Luke 22.47. The passage in vv.18-20 is largely traditional (see III below), but *kai gnoston egeneto pasi tois katoikousin Ierousalem* (v.19 beginning) reflects Lukan language (cf. 4.16; 9.42; 19.17). The end of v.20 is a transition to the choice; this part of the verse cites Ps.109.8 (LXX 108.8) where, as in this pericope, there is mention of a replacement in language which is literally the same apart from *labeto*. The figure of Judas has an important paraenetic function in the overall outline of Luke's two-volume work. After the temptation of Jesus (Luke 4.1-13) Satan had departed from him 'until the appointed hour' (*achri kairou* – Luke 4.13). The 'appointed hour' had come, when he 'entered into' Judas (Luke 22.3) and used him as an instrument against Jesus. The way in which the fate of Judas is used to show what happens to instruments of Satan in the community warns the readers of Luke-Acts not to leave any room for Satan in their own lives (cf. Vogler 1983, 75-92 and 65 below on 5.1-11). The interpretation of Ps.69.26 in terms of predestination does not go against this (see the references above to *dei*). For *dei* (v.21) cf. v.16 (*edei*). *arxamenos apo* (v.22) is Lukan language, cf. Luke 23.56; 24.27,47; Acts 8.35; 10.37 (in the New Testament only Matt. 20.8; John 8.9). *anelemphthe* refers back to 1.9 (cf. Luke 24.51). The verses are important (*a*) for Luke's understanding of the role of John the Baptist in the saving event and (*b*) for Luke's conception of the office of apostle.

(*a*) John appears in Acts in two further places, 10.37 and 13.24f. Both times the appearance of John the Baptist and that of Jesus are separated, so that the impression is given that these are two different epochs. (Cf. also the narrative of the imprisonment of John the Baptist [Luke 3.19-20], which differs from the version in Mark in that John the Baptist is imprisoned [Luke 3.19-20] *before* the baptism of Jesus [Luke 3.21-22]; in contrast to Mark 1.9 this is no longer performed by John.) The impression is intensified by Luke 16.16: here John is clearly assigned to a time which is plainly marked off from the time beginning after him (*apo tote*). Conzelmann has therefore concisely explained the position of John the Baptist in Luke like this:

'John no longer marks the arrival of the new aeon, but the division between two epochs in the one continuous story... The eschatological event does not break out after John, but a new stage in the process of salvation is reached, John himself still belonging to the earlier of the two epochs which meet at this point' (1960, 22f.)

This theory probably cannot be carried through as smoothly as Conzelmann thinks. For in Acts 1.22 the baptism of John is the starting point of the life of Jesus, sharing in which is the qualification for the witnesses; i.e. John here belongs in the 'time of Jesus' (against Conzelmann 1960, 22 n.3). Moreover it is not certain whether Luke 16.16 *mechri Ioannou* is to be understood inclusively (he belongs in the period of the law and the prophets – thus Conzelmann) or exclusively (he does not belong in this period). For the two reasons mentioned it is hardly possible to assign John the Baptist exclusively to one period or the other (on this problem see the balanced accounts by Kränkl 1972, 88-97 [bibliography], and Schneider 1977, 89f.).

(*b*) An apostle is someone who has gone in and out with Jesus from the baptism of John (Luke 3.7[?], 21) to the ascension (without interruption: Luke deletes the flight of the disciples in Mark 14.50; all Jesus' friends are present at the cross in Luke 23.49) *and* – by divine determination – a witness of his resurrection (v.22). (For Luke's concept of witness see Burchard 1970, 130-5.) The number of the apostles is evidently limited to 'twelve' and implicitly excludes Paul (but see 14.4, 14). In the election which follows, the apostles are made up to the number twelve by the choice of Matthias, before the outpouring of the Spirit. (But note that after the death of James the son of Zebedee in Acts 12 there is no longer any mention of a replacement! In Luke's account the era of the twelve apostles ends with ch.12; James takes their place [12.17] along with the presbyters [15.2 etc.].)

[23-26] *kaloumenon* (see on 8.10) and *epeklethe* in v.23 are Lukan language. In v.24 the (motive of) prayer is redactional (cf. earlier 1.14 and later the community prayer in 4.24-30). Verse 25 refers back to vv.17-18 (both times mention is made of *tes diakonias tautes*). The mention of the eleven apostles in v.25 presupposes Luke's concept of the twelve apostles (see on 1.22).

III Traditions

Judas

The name Judas Iscariot and the fact that he was a disciple of Jesus can be regarded as tradition, as probably also can his betrayal of Jesus. Without any doubt the narrative of the death of Judas (vv.18-20) in Peter's speech (vv.16-22) goes back to tradition. There are further narratives of the end of Judas, of which Matt 27.1-10 and a fragment of Papias preserved by Apollinaris are the most important. (The text of the Papias fragment appears in Kürzinger 1983, 104f.; Körtner 1983, 59-61; Körtner comments on the fragment mentioned in 137-44 [with bibliography]. In what follows I presuppose, with Körtner, that Papias [or his source] did *not* know Acts.)

Matthew's version differs from the Acts and Papias versions in reporting Judas' repentance and therefore making him give back the money and commit suicide. By contrast, Luke and Papias depict the horrible manner in which a traitor dies (for details see below). The connection betwen Judas and a plot of land is common to all three accounts; here Matthew and Acts are particularly close in that they call the plot of land 'the field of blood' - though they explain this in different ways. (The transmission of the Aramaic designation *hakeldamach* for field of blood in Acts 1.19 is phonetically correct, see Hengel 1983b, 108.) According to Matt.27.7 the high priests buy a field with the thirty pieces of silver which Judas returns (v.7: *agros kerameos* – v.8: 'called "the field of blood" to this day', because it was bought with 'blood money' [v.6]); according to the Lukan version Judas buys a field (*chorion*) for himself with his reward (Mark 14.11/Luke 22.5 do not know its exact amount – the number 'thirty' in Matt 26.15 is taken from Zech.11.12f.), on which he evidently hastens to his fearful end (which is why it is called field of blood). Papias tells how Judas dies an equally gruesome death on his own land (*en idio chorio*) and how the stench from his putrefying corpse spread all around. The accounts by Papias and Luke come close on two points: (*a*) Acts reports that Judas bursts apart (as the result of a fall) and his entrails come out. According to Papias, Judas swells up to an enormous size and – one may add – as a consequence he bursts, so that his entrails come out. (*b*) In the Papias story the description of the fearful swelling up of Judas's body seems to be connected with Ps.109.18 [108.18 LXX]: 'He loved the curse – so may it come upon him. He put on the curse like a garment, and it came like water into his entrails.' This swelling up of Judas's body and even his eyelids was so bad that he went completely blind. The announcement of the blindness of the godless can again be read in Ps.69.23/68.23 LXX: 'May their eyes be darkened that they no longer see.' As both Ps.109 and Ps.69 are used in the Acts version of the Judas story the question arises whether the two Psalm passages were associated with the story of Judas at the pre-Lukan stage (in connection with this see Schweizer 1958).

While the comparison of the Judas traditions made above indicates that the three narratives belong together generically, it is impossible to speak of a rounded story of the death of Judas as the basis of the three versions. What have emerged are only elements of tradition (fearful death, a field as the place of death, with an elaboration from Psalm passages).

34

The Twelve – the apostles

The designations of Jesus' followers as the Twelve and/or the apostles in this section are also from the tradition. The Twelve as recipients of a christophany appear in I Cor.15.5, and also outside this passage in the synoptic lists of the Twelve (Mark 3.16ff.; Matt.10.2ff.; Luke 6.14ff.) and Acts 6.2. The apostles appear in I Cor.15.7 as an element of tradition, and then in Gal.1.18 – on each occasion as a designation of the great figures in Jerusalem. Both groups appear in combination first in Mark 6.7,30, and Luke accordingly gives them the place described above in the context of Luke-Acts.

Joseph Barsabbas and Matthias

The names of the two candidates, Joseph Barsabbas and Matthias (v.23), might also go back to traditions.

Lohfink 1975a has even supposed 'that in Acts 1.15-26 an old Palestinian narrative of the election of Matthias has been worked over' (24). As support for this he refers to the phrase *edokan klerous autois* (v.26). *edokan*, he says, is a Hebraism and *autois* a *dativus commodi*. From secular Greek and LXX linguistic usage the following sentence would have been expected: *kai ebalon klerous kai epesen ho kleros epi Matthian* (248). We must imagine the lot-process as involving two lots, one inscribed 'for Matthias' and one 'for Joseph' being put in a vessel; 'the first lot that came out when the vessel was shaken (or less probably, the first to be drawn out) revealed the man willed by God' (248), cf. Lev.16.8.

IV Historical

The remarks made above about the traditions of the death of Judas have brought out the fragmentary character of the tradition. The constants which can be picked out are: 1. the disciple Judas Iscariot (Iscariot simply means 'the man from Kariot'); 2. his betrayal of Jesus; 3. his death at a particular place.

In what follows I shall go through the elements of the tradition individually. 1. The disciple Iscariot is without doubt a historical person (Schläger 1914, 52f. [bibliography] still differs: Judas is to be related to Judah). 2. It has been conjectured that the concept of treachery should not be made as narrow as it is in the Gospels. E.g. Peter also betrayed Jesus (if his denial of Jesus is historical). In other words, a 'traitor' could still remain a member of the community even after the resurrection (thus Vogler 1983, 24-30). But this does not give a convincing explanation why a member of the Twelve was regarded as an enemy of Jesus at a particular time. In that case the best thing would be to assume that: Judas, a disciple of the Lord, made a decisive contribution to delivering Jesus into the hands of the Jewish authorities. The 'betrayal of Judas will be a historical fact because it would be completely incomprehensible as a legend' (Wrede 1907, 132). 3. As the death of God's enemy is a standard theme of ancient literature (cf. Nestle 1968, 567-98), we may not regard the sudden violent death of Judas as an assured historical fact. We simply do not know what happened to this disciple after his betrayal and death of Jesus.

But what about Judas' membership of the Twelve? Before we attempt an answer to that, we must first discuss some problems relating to the apostles and the Twelve.

The existence of a group of twelve in the earliest period of the first community is attested by I Cor.15.5. Paul mentions it here only because he is repeating the tradition which he had handed on in his sermon when the Corinthian community was founded. He himself has no personal knowledge of the Twelve as such. Certainly during his first visit to Jerusalem he meets Cephas, the dominant figure of the Twelve. But apparently at that time the apostolic college had already become the leading body in the Jerusalem community (cf. Gal.1.19), and this might have contained at least some of the Twelve. There are traces from Paul's perspective of traditions about the Twelve, who disappeared surprisingly quickly, in lists of the Twelve in the Gospels which are probably independent of one another (Mark 3.16ff./Matt.10.2ff./Luke 6.14ff.), and in the logion 19.28, which goes back to Q. (The theory of Trilling 1978, 213-20, that we cannot conclude with sufficient certainty that the logion is addressed to the Twelve, is improbable.) The logion illustrates the concept of the group of the Twelve. They will sit on thrones in future glory and judge the twelve tribes of Israel. But in that case the expression *hoi dodeka* 'was not a purely numerical designation of twelve individual personalities, but signified the group of the representatives of the twelve tribes in the end time' (Jeremias 1971, 234). It is a fixed entity.

Those who argue that this group came into being after Easter have problems with chronology. If they were right, the group would have had to have lost its significance not long after it was formed, or even have disappeared (see the evidence in the Pauline corpus). Therefore it is more probable that it should be attributed to Jesus (cf. most recently also Sanders 1985, 98-106). In that case Peter would have reorganized the group of twelve founded by Jesus in Galilee and would have brought them with him to Jerusalem. In due course it was replaced by the group of apostles, which was constituted by a christophany (I Cor.15.7: the Jerusalem apostolate).

A considerable body of scholarship has energetically denied that Judas was one of the Twelve, referring to I Cor.15.5. Had Judas been a member

36

of the Twelve, it is stressed, Paul or his tradition could only have spoken of an appearance of Jesus to the Eleven (thus some secondary textual witnesses), for after his betrayal he would no longer have belonged to the Twelve. So the fact that I Cor.15.5 speaks of the appearance to the Twelve would prove that Judas cannot have belonged to them (cf. following Wellhausen 1911, 138-47: Vielhauer 1965, 68-71; Klein 1961, 34-8, etc.). However, the arguments are not convincing because the Twelve is a fixed entity (see above). If a member fell out, the group continued and the vacancy was not necessarily filled immediately. The ancient historian E.Meyer refers to an illuminating parallel from antiquity: 'Anthony and Octavian remain *triumviri* even after Lepidus has been deposed' (Meyer I, 297 n.2). Meyer's comments on the Twelve on 291-9 are generally acceptable.

In positive terms it should be said that the pre-Markan tradition Mark 14.10 already speaks of Judas as one of the Twelve (cf. also Mark 14.20,43 parr.). So it is historically probable that Judas was one of the Twelve and that this group derives from the period before Easter – as is further confirmed by what has just been said.

When it comes to the election of Matthias we are fumbling in the dark historically as we have no means of checking anything. It should also be noted that despite the existence of a group of Twelve it was not necessary – as Luke imagines – for it to be made up again immediately. Finally, what is perhaps the rapid disappearance of the Twelve must be recalled. In addition to that there would be the difficulty of explaining how such a tradition could have preserved the election of Matthias to the Twelve anyway, had this only been of short duration. One is therefore inclined to challenge the historicity of the election of Matthias (against Lohfink 1975a; Weiser 1981, 72). This does not mean, though, that the Jerusalem Christians Matthias and Joseph were not historical figures.

For Judas see now the exhaustive study by H.-J.Klauck, *Judas – ein Jünger des Herrn*, Quaestiones Disputatae 111, Freiburg, Basel and Vienna 1987.

Acts 2.1-13

I Division

2.1-4: The glossolalia of the disciples assembled in a house in Jerusalem on the first Pentecost

    1: Details of time and place

2: The glossolalia through the descent of the Spirit
5-13: The language miracle
  5: The presence of Jews from all lands in Jerusalem
  6-13: The language miracle and the reaction of the Jews

II Redaction

[1-4] This section reflects the following elements of Luke's language and style (a selection): v.1, *en to* + infinitive (cf. Jeremias 1980, 28), *sympleroushthai* (in the NT elsewhere only in 8.23; 9.51 [the wording matches 2.1]), *pantes, epi to auto* (cf. 1.15 etc.); v.2, *aphno, echos, pnoes eplerosen*, periphrastic conjugation; v.3, *diamerizomenai, hosei, hena hekaston*; v.4, *eplesthesan, pantes, pneumatos hagiou, erxanto, heterais*. *Pentekoste* in v.1 appears in 10.16 in a redactional context and will also be Lukan here. It takes up the forty days mentioned at 1.3. The use of *kai* seven times in a row will also be Luke's work. It serves to move on the account and from v.5 is replaced by *de* (vv. 5,6,7,12,13). The evidence that Luke often replaces *kai* with *de* in the Gospel does not tell against this, as the *kai* in vv.1-4 is an imitation of LXX (cf. the similar situation in Luke 1.57-66; 2.22-39). Two further observations support the view that Luke worked over the present section:

(*a*) Verses 2 and 3 have an almost completely parallel construction:
A: And suddenly there came from heaven a rushing
A1: And there appeared to them divided tongues
B: like a mighty wind
B1: like a fire
C: and it filled the whole house where they were sitting
C1: and it sat upon each one of them.

(*b*) The manner of expression in vv.2f. is assimilated to the descriptions of the Sinai theophany (cf. Ex.19.16-19; Deut. 4.11f.). (For vv.3f. cf. especially Num.11.25.) Luke also imitates the LXX in other passages (cf. Plümacher 1972, 38-50, 69-72). The unit of text culminates in the sentence: 'And they began to speak in other tongues (*heterais glossais*) as the Spirit gave them utterance' (v.4). The context indicates that the phrase 'other tongues' refers to the fact that those present could understand the spirit-filled disciples; cf. v.1: 'How do we hear speak in our tongues (*tais hemeterais glossais*) the wonderful works of God?' (cf. vv.6,8). Thus v.4 is the expression of a language miracle and its context is developed in the narrative in the following verses.

[5-13] The section contains elements of Luke's language and style (this is

38

a selection): v.5, periphrastic conjugation, *katoikountes, andres eulabeis* (cf.8.2 – for the adjective cf. Luke 2.25; Acts 22.12), *hypo ton ouranon* (Luke 17.24; Acts 4.12; cf. Col.1.23); v.6, genitive absolute, *synelthen, to plethos*; v.7, *existanto, ethaumazon, idou*. The direct speech in vv.7-11 has been shaped by Luke. (Each time it is introduced by *existanto... legontes*, vv.7,12.) In this way Luke creates a lively scene (cf. 1.4-12; 5.1-11; 25.12,22; 26.32). Also Lukan usage is: v.11, *ta megaleia* (cf. Luke 1.49 [variant reading] and the verb *megalyno*: Luke 1.46,58; Acts 5.13; 10.46; 19.17); v.12, *existanto, dieporoun*; for *ti thelei touto einai* cf. 17.20.

The section is skilfully connected to the previous unit. Verse 6 refers back to v.2 (*phone* takes up *echos*). Verses 6,8,11 take up v.4 and show that the event is a language miracle. A list of the various peoples is framed within the unit vv.5-13 by *akouomen* (vv.8,11). The way in which the reaction of the hearers is described twice (vv.12 + 13) is in accordance with Lukan narrative style (cf. 17.32f.; 28.24).

The function of vv.1-13 in context

With the account of the receiving of the Spirit by the disciples, 1.8 (cf. Luke 24.29) is fulfilled. The somewhat ponderous indication of time, 'when the day of Pentecost was fulfilled', shows that what is to come is the fulfilment of the promise made by Jesus in 1.8. It is no chance that the ensuing speech of Peter (vv.14-40) begins with the receiving of the Spirit (vv.17-18). From now on the receiving of the Spirit is constitutive for being a Christian (cf. esp.8.14-24; 19.1-7). However, its specific effects have still to be defined in each case (cf. the survey by Jervell 1984, 96f.).

It may be Luke's purpose, as well as describing the receiving of the Spirit, also to depict the Pentecost event as a miracle of language. The fact that on the very day on which the Christian religion is founded the Holy Spirit equips the members of the new movement with the languages of all other peoples already expresses Luke's conviction of the universal nature of Christianity, as Zeller 1854, 114, rightly saw. (Later Luke can neglect the question of languages and take it for granted that everyone understands the preachers – see Dibelius 1956, 178f.) The objection should not be made to this that Luke did not want to stress the idea of the world-wide extension of the gospel here (thus Roloff 1981, 39), since this is precisely the notion that is already stressed at 1.8. However, the universalism of the preaching of the gospel is not yet expressed in this passage in terms of the Gentile mission, since the pericope describes the audience as Diaspora Jews. Here 'these Diaspora Jews are to some extent regarded as representatives of the nations of the world who are at least potentially present in them' (Schneider 1980, 251); e.g. the Levite Barnabas is *Kyprios to genei*

(4.36; cf.11.20); cf. also *apo pantos ethnous* (2.5) and *te idia dialekto* (2.8).

III Traditions

The last two sections made it clear that the pericope is a self-contained unit. The investigation of traditions will first of all demonstrate the breaks which are nevertheless there and attempt to identify the elements of tradition which result from them.

1. The event depicted in vv.1-4 takes place in a house (v.2), but the sequel (vv.5-13) is evidently in the open air.

2. Verses 9-11 interrupt the argument and may go back to a source. As the list of peoples nevertheless fits very well in vv.5-13, this may be an indication of Luke's redactional work.

Excursus: The list of peoples in Acts 2.9-11

Preliminary comment: The position of Judaea between Mesopotamia and Cappadocia (v.9) is remarkable. Moreover Judaea itself is out of place in such a list. How could the Palestinian Jews not have understood the Galilean disciples of Jesus? Therefore we shall have to see 'Judaea' as a post-Lukan correction of an original reading like 'Armenia' (see the reading attested by Tertullian and Augustine [in part]) or 'Galatia'. Still, Judaea would seem obvious to readers of the Bible. (Perhaps the correction even goes back to Luke.)

Weinstock 1948 made a decisive contribuion to the traditio-historical clarification of vv.9-11 (cf. Brinkman 1963 – the arguments to the contrary by Metzger 1970 are not convincing). Weinstock demonstrated the great similarity of the list enumerated in vv.9-11 to an astrological catalogue of Paulus Alexandrinus (fourth century CE). Paulus lists: Aries/Persia; Taurus/Babylon; Gemini/Cappadocia; Cancer/Armenia; Leo/Asia; Virgo/Hellas and Ionia; Libra/Libya and Cyrene; Scorpio/Italy; Sagittarius/Cilicia and Crete; Capricorn/Syria; Aquarius/Egypt; Pisces/Red Sea and India. Of the nations mentioned by Paulus Alexandrinus we also find in Acts 2.9-11, though in a different order, Cappadocia, Asia, Libya, Cyrene, Crete, Egypt. Others correspond in substance though the name is not the same (the difference in nomenclature reflects different political constellations): Persia corresponds to the Parthians, Medes and Elamites (v.9a); Babylon corresponds to Mesopotamia; Italy corresponds to Rome; the Red Sea and India roughly correspond to Arabia; Armenia certainly does not correspond to Pontus, but the two lands are neighbouring states in northern Asia Minor. Moreover in the fourth century the province of Armenia Minor or the provinces of Armenia I and Armenia II were part of the diocese of Pontica (Irmscher 1985, 456). – So the above comparison shows amazing similarities. Of the list in Paulus Alexandrinus only Hellas/ Ionia and Syria (see the reading attested by Jerome in v.9 for *Ioudaian*) have no parallel in Paulus Alexandrinus. For in the fourth century the provinces of Pamphylia and Phrygia belonged with Asia to the diocese Asiana (according to Irmscher 1985, 456). The hypothesis of a genetic relationship is therefore

40

very probable. Paulus's list might be taken from a geographical list. Luke may have taken the list inserted into vv.9-11 from a similar source. It was important for him to mention as many lands as possible in which Jews lived in order to give support to v.5 ('now there were in Jerusalem Jews living, pious men, *from every nation under heaven*'). To this end he used the list contained in vv.9-11. To confirm the reference to Judaea (cf.v.5) Luke may have added 'Jews and proselytes' (v.11).

The disparity between vv.1-4 and 5-13 to which I have drawn attention can be intensified at one point. Verse 4 says that the disciples spoke in 'other tongues'. If we regard 'other' (*heterais*) as redactional, then a language miracle would become speaking in tongues, i.e. glossolalia, which we know from I Cor.14. In that case the tradition contained in vv.1-4 (and v.13?) reports an ecstatic experience in a house of a group of disciples, and it was Luke who would first have interpreted this tradition as a language miracle in order to prepare for the idea of world-wide mission. This suggestion is supported by the evidence that Luke probably no longer knew the original glossolalia. In 19.6 he identifies it with prophecy (cf. 10.46). This makes easier 'the synthesis with the language miracle' (Conzelmann 1987, 15). So a distinction needs to be made between glossolalia (1-4) and language miracle (vv.5-13) in the framework of the analysis of the tradition.

Glossolalia is generally an incomprehensible ecstatic speech (cf. G.Dautzenberg, *RAC* XI, 225-46). Of the Corinthian glossolalia in particular it can be said with certainty that it was not speaking in foreign languages. It had to be translated (I Cor.14.5); not, however, because it was a foreign language (thus Haacker 1970, 127) but because it was incomprehensible (cf. I Cor.14.19,23) – in Paul's world-view, it was the language of the angels (I Cor.13.1 [cf. II Cor.12.4]).

In analysis of the tradition of the language miracle (vv.5-13) attention should be paid above all to the rabbinic notion of a language miracle at Sinai, in which the voice of God divided itself into seventy world languages and the law was made known to all nations, but only Israel accepted it (cf. Weiser 1981, 84).

It is also worth noting that the redactional themes of the theophany in Acts 2.1-4 also have a parallel in descriptions of the Sinai event.

Cf. Philo, *Decalogue* 46 (on Ex.19.16ff.): 'Then from the midst of the fire that streamed from heaven there uttered a voice... for the flame became articulate speech in the language familiar to the audience, and so clearly and distinctly were the words formed by it that they seem to see rather than hear them.'

'In this presentation the stress on the interconnection of fire, voice and language is particularly striking' (Weiser 1981, 84); this matches Luke's account of Pentecost in Acts 2.1-4. And finally the redactional indication of time, 'Pentecost' (v.1), fits the Sinai complex of motives to which I have referred, if in Luke's time the feast of Pentecost was already understood as the feast of concluding of the covenant (cf. Conzelmann 1987, 16 [text and literature]; Sanders 1977, 378 n.31).

Summary of the analysis of the tradition

Traditions that can be extracted are: 1. The story of the ecstasy of the disciples in a house in Jerusalem (perhaps v.13 also belongs to this). 2. The list of peoples. – The language miracle is not an independent tradition, but Luke has composed it on the basis of knowledge of the Sinai tradition (his interest in the language miracle is already evident from his adoption of the list of peoples).

The other possibility, that the language miracle is the bedrock of the tradition (thus apparently Conzelmann 1987, 15, etc.), is improbable. In that case it would have to be assumed that the report of the glossolalia had already grown up at the stage of the tradition (as was demonstrated above, Luke no longer has any idea of it), and the proposal would be based on a second-degree hypothesis.

IV Historical

Two recent opinions may be put at the beginning of this section:

Reicke 1957 writes: 'But even someone who claims to think in purely empirical and rationalistic terms should not doubt that at the first Pentecost something extraordinary happened to the Christian community; for it is very understandable that the cheerful feast of Pentecost should have increased the joy of the disciples at the resurrection of Jesus to the pitch of an extraordinary enthusiasm' (28).

Roloff 1981 explains: 'We come upon a small but firm historical nucleus which is determined by the factors "Pentecost" and "being filled with Spirit". Here in all probability is recollection of an experience of the disciples of Jesus at the first Pentecost after his death, which they understood as being overwhelmed by the Holy Spirit' (39).

In my view both scholars are wrong in presupposing that the term Pentecost belongs to the tradition. Moreover both views are historically rather vague, very formal, and general or edifying.

The first question to be raised here is whether the account of the ecstasy of the disciples in a house in Jerusalem is credible. Now Paul himself attests the phenomenon of glossolalia. He claims that he himself speaks more in tongues than the Corinthians (I Cor.14.18), and I Thess.5.19 seems formal encouragement to his converts to practise glossolalia, since v.20 speaks of prophecy (see the order in I Cor.14.1-5). Regardless of how the Gentile Christian Corinthians understood glossolalia, it would seem plausible that Paul saw it as an 'eschatologically given possibility of praising God with the angels, and of experiencing or repeating the mysteries of heaven (I Cor.14.2)' (Dautzenberg, *RAC* XI, 237). In it he was using the language of the angels (I Cor.13.1). We find kindred phenomena in *TestJob* 48.2; 49.1; 50.2. Similar phenomena are to be conjectured in Palestinian Christianity for the daughters of Philip who prophesied. So we may certainly regard a happening of the kind described by the tradition behind vv.1-4 as very possible (cf. Dunn 1975, 189-93).

At various times it has been suggested that 'Pentecost' should be identified with the appearance to five hundred brethren (I Cor.15.6). However it has been objected to this that: 'The development from a christophany (sc. like I Cor.15.5) to this theophany is really not conceivable, because in the older version of the Easter christophany the Spirit is not mentioned' (Conzelmann 1987, 16). Against this, John 20.21f. shows the connection between christophany and the bestowal of the Spirit (on the passage see Kremer 1973, 224-8), and the features of a theophany in Acts 2 were probably only introduced by Luke, if the glossolalia can be seen as the substratum of the tradition in the story. I therefore regard it as at least possible that the appearance to 500 brothers has a genetic connection with the tradition behind Acts 2.1-4. In this case, however, we are to assume traditio-historical links which would among other things explain the contradiction between the large number 500 and the scene of the phenomenon 'in the house', which allows only a far smaller number, and the forking of the tradition (a christophany on the one hand and the bestowing of the Spirit on the other).

Acts 2.14-47

I Division

2.14-40: Peter's speech
  14a: Note of framework
  14b: Address
  14c: Appeal to the audience
  15f.: Assertion of a misunderstanding among the hearers (underestimation of the apostles) and its removal
  17-21: Argument from scripture: Joel 3.1-5/2.28-32 (LXX)
  22a: New address and new appeal to hearers
  22b-24: Christological kerygma
  25-31: Argument from scripture with interpretation (v.29: third address)
  32f.: Continuation of the interrupted christological kerygma

34f. Resumption of the argument from scripture (in the same scheme as 25-31)
36: The one crucified by the people of Jerusalem is the Christ (as the culmination of the indicative comments by Peter)
37: Interjected question from the hearers
38: Call to repentance and proclamation of salvation
39: Explicit focus of the message on the hearers
40: Conclusion of discourse
41: Note of success
42-47: Summary

II Redaction

In Peter's speech (vv.14-40) it is striking that the three Old Testament quotations are each marked off by a quotation formula and a renewed form of address (vv.16/22; vv.25/29; vv.34/36). The first quotation in the discourse (vv.17-21) at the beginning gives a further explanation of the preceding Pentecost miracle and the second part of it then prepares for the christological section (vv.22ff.).

The first part of the Joel quotation (vv.17-18)

It is preceded by a refutation of the assumption that those who are seized by the Spirit are drunk: it is only the third hour. The verb *apophtheggesthai* (v.14) is picked up from v.4 (it occurs in only one other passage in the NT, Acts 26.25) and thus shows that Peter's speech belongs with what has gone before. It should be noted that it is not those among the foreign peoples who lay the charge of drunkenness, but evidently only those who are not addressed by the Pentecost event. The mockery that the people are drunk will therefore not reflect Luke's interpretation of the Pentecost event. Rather, it is a means of bringing the composition to life, which picks up an element that was perhaps part of the basic material of the Pentecost tradition (v.13) and takes the action further (cf. Schneider 1980: 'The standard theme of misunderstanding on the part of the hearers is also used as a literary means in 3.12 and 14.15' [267]).

The Joel quotation corresponds with the LXX version apart from four divergences.

1. Verse 17 reads 'in the last days' instead of 'after these things' (thus also codex B). Perhaps B has the older reading (cf. esp. Rese 1969, 51f.); even if it does not, the result is insignificant for the question of redaction because the phrase 'in the last days' has already been smoothed over (e.g. II Tim.3.1). So it can only be said with qualifications that the outpouring of the Spirit is connected with 'a fulfilment of a promise of *God* for the *end time*' (Schneider 1980, 268).

44

In that case a better comment is: 'However, Luke understands "the last days" as a lengthy period... What is taking place with the outpouring of the Spirit, above all the prophetic gift, is the characteristic feature of the "time of the church" which has now dawned' (Schneider 1980, 268, cf. also Kränkl 1972, 190-3).

2. Verse 17 also has the sequence 'young-old' instead of "old-young'. This may be just an improvement in the expression.

3. Verse 18 twice inserts a *mou* ('my') after 'servants' and 'handmaids'. Here representatives of a particular social group become servants and handmaids of God (cf. Roloff 1981, 53).

4. Verse 18 adds 'and they will prophesy' to the Joel quotation. This assertion was very important to Luke, since it already appears in the Joel quotation (v.17c). With it he interprets the Pentecost event as the capacity for prophecy (cf. 19.6), an understanding which does not contradict Luke's description of the Pentecost event as a miracle of tongues (2.5-13).

The second part of the Joel quotation (vv.19-21)

This matches the LXX literally apart from the addition of *ano, semeia, kato*. Apparently Luke leaves out the half-verse which follows the quotation (Joel 3.5b/2.32b [LXX]) deliberately: '...for on Mount Zion and in Jerusalem he will be saved, thus says the Lord, and they whom the Lord has called will hear the good news.' This *a priori* makes clear that the Gentiles are included in salvation (cf. Resc 1969, 50; Dupont 1967, 393-419).

The characterization of the church as being governed by the Spirit (vv.17-18) is followed in vv.19-20 by the transition from the present 'to the apocalyptic future', which 'corresponds with the picture in Luke 21' (Conzelmann 1987, 20). With v.21, which again includes the present, the point of the quotation is reached (Roloff 1981, 5). 'Anyone who calls on the name of the Lord (sc. Jesus) will be saved.' So the offer of salvation is universal. There should be no question that the 'apocalyptic part' of the Joel quotation already leads on to the christological kerymatic part (vv.22b-24). The expressions *semeia* (added to the LXX text) and *terata* are deliberately taken up there (v.22b).

Roloff 1981 evidently differs: 'Possibly in the case of the "wonders in heaven above" Luke was thinking of the coming of the Spirit from heaven (v.33) and in the "signs on the earth below" again of the miracle of speaking in tongues performed through the Spirit. We should hardly think in terms of a reference to the miracles of Jesus' (53). The parallelism in expressions tells against that.

Verse 22a is the second address after v.14b and in the analysis has the function of indicating a redactional division. In v.22b the mention of the *dynameis, terata* and *semeia* refers back to the Gospel. There the miraculous proofs of the prophet Jesus are decisive for the christology. 'In the account in Luke 4.16ff., and also in the rest of the narrative, it is

Jesus' deeds which prove that scripture is being fulfilled' (Conzelmann 1960, 190). For the understanding of miracle in Luke see also Busse 1979 and bibliography.

'The part played by miracle in Luke is not adequately explained by reference to a "seeking for wonders". It is true that this is a feature of the age, which Luke shares, but we must not overlook the fact that he seeks to include the christological aspect of miracle within the framework of his general conception. Jesus' deeds are for Luke the evidence of the time of salvation, which has "arrived" with Christ' (Conzelmann 1960, 192).

The passion takes place (v.23), in keeping with Luke's theology, in accordance with God's plan (Conzelmann 1960, 151 n.2, see ibid., 151-3). The verse corresponds with Luke 23.18-25 (the Jews bring about the condemnation of Jesus by the Romans). Cf. also the variation in the statements about the passion in 3.15; 4.10; 5.30; 7.52; 10.39 (on this see Wilckens 1974, 109-37).

Verse 24: 'God has forced death to surrender Jesus' (Stählin 1980, 46). (The conception of the death of Jesus as a positive act of salvation [cf. 20.28] is remote from this.) In this way the plan of God, which is described more closely in the following verses, comes into being.

The quotation in vv.25-28 matches the LXX completely (Ps.16 [15]. 8-11). Verse 13, the conclusion, takes up v.27. The meaning for the redaction is as follows: David already spoke with a view to (*eis*) the person of the Messiah Jesus. God assured him that his soul would not remain in Hades nor would he himself be delivered over to corruption. (In 13.35f., by taking up the quotation again, Luke makes clear the *difference* between David and Jesus at this point.) This provides the scriptural proof for v.24.

Therefore God has raised him from the dead, of which the apostles are witnesses, and has raised him to his right hand. From here *Jesus* has received from the Father the promise of the Holy Spirit and poured this out, as Peter's hearers can themselves see and hear (vv.32-33). In this way Luke provides a link back to 1.4 and makes specific the statement there that the disciples are waiting for the promise of the Father (= the outpouring of the Holy Spirit) as they have heard it from Jesus.

Verses 34-35 take up the scriptural proof in the same schema as vv.25-31. This runs: the prophecy was not fulfilled in David, so someone else is meant. Therefore the scripture announces Christ, since in him the prophecy is fulfilled.

Verse 36, which relates to the hearers, apparently concludes the speech, in order to make possible the interjected question (v.37). The interruption is a literary device (cf. 10.44). For *ti poiesomen* cf. Luke 3.10,12,14 (note the context of the repentance as in v.37).

Peter's answer in v.38 contains Luke's view of how one becomes a

Christian, namely by repentance, baptism for the forgiveness of sins and the bestowing of the Holy Spirit (Conzelmann 1960, 229).

Verse 39 is Lukan in that the author alludes indirectly to Joel 3.5b/2.32b (LXX), which has been omitted in Peter's speech – with the addition of Isa.57.19. The sense then is that the universalization of the mission to the Gentiles must be safeguarded. In this way the verse is linked to Peter's speech.

The statement that Peter addressed the crowd 'with many other words' (v.40) is a literary device and therefore redactional: it 'gives the author freedom to record those words of the speaker which fit in with the author's plan, but at the same time to indicate to the reader that these words do not exhaust what the speaker said' (Dibelius 1956, 178; ibid., examples from Polybius, Xenophon and Appian). The *sothete* in the concluding appeal in v.40b ('Save yourselves from this perverse generation') picks up the last word of the Joel quotation (*sothesetai*, v.21).

[41] *men oun* is a favourite particle of Luke's. *apodechesthai* occurs in the NT only in Luke-Acts (twice in Luke and five times in Acts); *prostithemi* and *hosei* are similarly Lukan language. The number 3000 comes from Luke's imagination and is meant to bring out the magnitude of the event. The number of Christians has risen enormously from 1.15 ('about 120').

[42-47] The verses are a Lukan summary which has a parallel in 4.32-35 and 5.(11,)12-15(,16)(cf. as a summary Zimmermann 1982, 251-66). Verses 42-47 are predominantly redactional in language and refer to what has been reported previously (cf. *terata, semeia* [v.43] with vv.19,22, *apostolon* [v.43] with v.37, *prosetithei* [v.47] with v.41), and their content also makes good redactional sense. (For *epi to auto* [v.44] see above, 38 on 2.1.) Here the earliest community appears in a bright light. In the readers' mind's eye on the one hand the nature of the Jerusalem community is developed timelessly in a generalized and typical way, and in addition recollections of Greek ideals are prompted (see the examples on 61 and Mönning 1978, 74-86). On the other hand, the summaries serve as paraenesis (see below 61f. on 4.32-37). So they are an important descriptive means for Luke.

III Traditions

In what follows I presuppose that the speeches in Acts in their present form come from Luke's pen, as redactor. First indications of this could already be seen in the redaction-critical analysis above. This does not exclude the possibility that the scheme of the speeches, which is not usually discussed (the Areopagus speech is an exception, 192f.),

47

and individual elements in them, derive from traditions. (Here the remark about the resurrection in v.24 is deliberately bracketted off, as in other speeches; on this see M.Rese, *NTS* 30, 1984, 335-53 and bibliography.) Two elements of the speech in particular probably existed before Luke.

1. The use of Joel 2.32 (LXX)/3.5 in v.21. Paul uses the same passage in Rom.10.13 and can call Christians generally 'those who call on the name of the Lord' (I Cor.1.2). As the natural use of this expression in the last-mentioned passage shows, Joel 2.32 (LXX) may already have been used as an interpretation of the Christ-kerygma before I Cor.1.2 (on Rese 1969, 64, with Bultmann 1952, 125).

2. The use of Ps.109 (LXX)/110 in the framework of christological discussion is part of the tradition in vv.34f., as the parallels show (I Cor.15.25; Mark 12.36, etc.). In addition, *lysas tas odinas tou thanatou* (v.24) in connection with the saying about the resurrection (ibid.) may derive from tradition because of the correspondence with Polycarp, II Phil.1.2 (Polycarp probably does not know Acts).

For *prospexantes aneilate* (v.23) see the remarks on 5.30 at 71f. below.

In the summary vv.42-47, v.42 may go back to tradition (thus also Roloff 1981, 6f.; in addition he regards v.43 as part of the tradition), cf. Rom.12.12f. Moreover *koinonia* does not appear elsewhere in Luke-Acts, and v.42 is partly taken up again in v.46 (*proskarterountes, klontes arton*). Such thematic duplication within the summary is unusual and does not appear in the other summaries. Here Luke has worked in information from the tradition which reported the fellowship of the first Christians, their meals together and their instruction by the apostles. For historical reasons (apostles, see IV below) its origin might be sought in Jerusalem. However, we cannot completely exclude the other possibility, that Luke, like Paul (Rom.12.12f.), is using paraenetic traditions from the Pauline mission sphere and prematurely transferring them to the Jerusalem community.

The basis in the tradition of the statement about selling possessions (v.45) may be reports like 4.36f.; 5.1ff. which came down to Luke.

IV Historical

The Acts account of the events of Pentecost is certainly unhistorical in its present form. Peter did not make a speech on the first day of Pentecost in Jerusalem, certainly not with the sort of content that is reproduced in Acts 2. Nevertheless, four historical facts may underlie this section.

1. Directly after the death of Jesus and the appearances, Peter took a leading role in the Jerusalem community (cf. Lüdemann 1983, 67-73).

2. At a very early stage Joel 2.32 (LXX) was a proof text in early Christianity.

3. Ps.109 (LXX) was already used in christological discussions at a very early stage.

4. The Jerusalem community assembled and stayed together in common breaking of the bread. Perhaps we may combine the two and say that fellowship was realized in particular at the shared meal (the continuation of the table fellowship of Jesus with his disciples or the regular repetition of Jesus' last meal with his followers, or an ordinary Jewish meal). But it is impossible to make any statement which is even half probable as to whether the death of Jesus was a focal point of the meals and/or even whether the Lord (of the cult) was thought to be present at them as the giver of bread and wine, as in the Pauline communities (cf. on this problem the balanced reflections of Weiss 1959, 56-66). The meeting places are the houses of individual members of the Jesus community like Mary's house (Acts 12.12).

The instruction by the apostles is also to be accepted as historical, since in the early period of the Jerusalem community the apostles had a leading role. So Paul can speak of those who were apostles before him (in Jerusalem!, Gal.1.17).

If the other possibility about v.42 considered under III should be true, then the historical considerations just advanced are, of course, groundless.

Acts 3

Preliminary comment: The segment really extends from 3.1 to 4.37 (between two summaries). Because it is so large, I shall deal with it by chapters, but without losing sight of its unity.

I Division

3.1-10: The healing of the lame man in the temple (for a more subtle division see 53 below)
11: (transition) The lame man with Peter and John in the hall of Solomon. Amazement of the people
12-26: Peter's speech
  12a: Address
  12b: A misunderstanding removed

13-15a: Scriptural quotation and assertion of the guilt of the people of Jerusalem for the death of Jesus
15b: Resurrection of Jesus and witness of the apostles
16: Reference back to the healing of the lame man
17: Further address and theme of ignorance
18: The testimony of the prophets
19-21: Call to repentance and eschatological prospect
22-26: Scriptural argument to induce repentance

II Redaction

[1-10] The miracle story which follows does not appear here by chance. Though in its immediate context it may be an explanation of 2.43, in particular it is meant to attest the miracle of the outpouring of the Spirit (*dynamei* [3.12] is a reference back to 1.8 and 2.22).

Verse 1 shows the apostles in Lukan fashion as Jews who are loyal to the law, who observe the hours of prayer (for the indication of the time of prayer 'around the ninth hour' cf. 10.3, 30, 'the ninth hour'; 10.9, 'the sixth hour'). The mention of John here, as in vv.3,4, etc. (8.14), is redactional. John is a bystander throughout and the verbs in v.4 (*eipen*) and v.7 (*egeiren*) are in the singular. Luke needs *two* witnesses later before the Supreme Council. Moreover he has a preference for mission in pairs (see Luke 22.8 [Mark 14.13 is different] – Schille 1983, 136, overlooks this passage in his protest against the above thesis; for the whole issue see also Weiser 1981, 108). Verses 4f. are perhaps totally redactional (*atenisas* [v.4] and *epeichen* [v.5] are Lukan language). The redactional seam would be *labein* (v.3 end and v.5 end.). But it is equally possible that Luke only began to work on a model, say by the addition of 'with John' and 'look at *us*', instead of 'look at *me*'. In v.6 the phrase 'silver and gold have I none...' may refer back to the situation over possessions depicted in 2.44f. (cf. also the echo of v.6 in 20.33 [by Paul]), and at the same time prepare for 4.32ff. Verse 8b takes up v.8a: *exallomenos* and *periepatei*. The praise of God from the healed man (*ainon ton theon*) refers back to 2.47, where the same thing is said of the community. The three participles at the end are a feature of Luke's narrative style. Since in addition part of the verse prepares for the redactional v.11, we should attribute it wholly to Luke. Verses 9-10 have individual traces of Luke: cf. *ainounta ton theon* as a link to v.8, which itself refers back to 2.47.

[11] This verse is a transitional sentence which links the previous scene of the miracle with the speech by Peter which follows. *ekthamboi* takes up *thambous* (v.10). In what follows we find ourselves in the hall of Solomon,

which Luke evidently thinks is within the temple precinct, with the 'Beautiful Gate' of v.2 as an entrance to it.

Luke does not distinguish different areas within the temple 'and conceives of the "Beautiful Gate" as located in the outer enclosure. After passing through it one arrives at the hall of Solomon' (Conzelmann 1987, 26; cf. Hengel 1985, 36). The Western text offers an 'emendation'. According to it Peter and John leave the temple and (only then) find themselves in the Hall of Solomon; cf. Dibelius 1956, 102-4.

The theory 'that Luke... has no... knowledge of the place' (Conzelmann 1987, 26) remains apt, since 'he does not distinguish between the various areas in the inner part of the temple' (ibid.), suggestions of which at least would have been expected in his detailed description of events in the temple at Jerusalem (Acts 3-5; 21-22). He is, however, at least concerned to give some local colouring (see 17.16-34; 19.23-49), though one should not expect of him the topographical curiosity of later pilgrims (on Hengel 1983b, 104; Hengel also rejects the opinion of Conzelmann cited above because our own knowledge of the temple of Herod is too fragmentary to allow a decision here). The real question is whether Luke's information has to be proved to be true or rather whether it is only false if it can certainly be shown to be so. Hengel always seems to assume the latter and Conzelmann the former. However, Hengel, 1983b, 104, will be right in maintaining that the designation 'Beautiful Gate' is part of the tradition (see 53f. below).

[12-26] *idon... laon* in v.12a links the speech which follows to v.11. The address *andres Israelitai* corresponds to 2.22a. Like the Pentecost speech (2.15), v.12b rejects a misunderstanding after the address. Even more clearly than 2.23, vv.13-15a are a reference back to Luke 23.16, 18-25 (cf. the detailed demonstration in Wilckens 1974, 128f.). *pais theou* (v.13) appears as a designation of Jesus in v.26; 4.27, 30; in addition we have only Matt.12.18 (quotation) in the NT (on this see Kränkl 1972, 125-9; Wilckens 1974, 163-7).

Like 2.24, v.15b contains an announcement of the resurrection and attaches the Lukan theme of witness to it (cf.2.32 and 33 on 1.22 for the twelve apostles as witnesses).

Verse 16 is an artificial reference to the miracle story. 'Luke adds that there is no miracle without faith. Incidentally the reference looks like an appeal to the hearers' (Schille 1983, 28). For the name of Jesus as a mode of the presence of the exalted Christ cf. Kränkl 1972, 177-80.

According to Wilckens 1974, the passage 'is formulated so ponderously and unskilfully that it is hard to accept that it was written by Luke' (40). But cf. Schneider 1980, 320f. Furthermore, according to Roloff 1981, 75f., there is no mention of the faith of the person who is healed, but only of Peter's faith. No, the over-loaded formulation only shows Luke's difficulties in shaping the tradition to his theology (cf. the miracle stories in the Gospel which are interpreted in terms of the concept of faith in 5.20; 7.9, 50; 8.48; 18.42).

kai nyn in v.17 is a sign of division (cf. on 20.22, 25). The theme of ignorance in connection with the passion is Lukan (cf. Luke 23.34 [if it is original]; Acts 13.27). According to Luke's theology the suffering of Christ is in accordance with the scriptures (v.18, cf. Luke 24.26f., etc.); the testimony of the prophets also appears in v.21b and v.24. Verse 19 is a Lukan call to repentance, which if heard brings with it the forgiveness of sins (cf. earlier 2.38). Verses 20f. look like an alien body in a polished context which can be said to be redactional. The verses evidently presuppose – in an un-Lukan way – an inner connection between repentance and the realization of future salvation. The future time of salvation is ushered in by the conversion (of the Jews, cf. II Peter 3,12); *hopos an* here has strictly final significance. If in this passage, too, Luke is writing under the influence of tradition (see further in III below), the redactional meaning may be as follows: despite their killing of Jesus the Jews have a further possibility of repentance before the parousia. Certainly the suffering of Christ was scriptural, but that is also true of the preaching between resurrection and parousia (Luke 2.44-47) and of the parousia itself (the times of *apokatastasis*, v.21). To this degree everything is still part of the salvation history which is foretold. In v.21 Luke also seems to presuppose a delay of the parousia (however, it will come on the appointed day, cf. 1.7). The statement about the prophets who prophesied the suffering of Christ (v.18b) or the (future) times of the restoration of all things (v.21b) is the framework of the call to repentance and the eschatological prospect.

Verses 22-26 also offer a kind of retrospect (in contrast to the prospect in vv.20-21) on the historical Jesus, with scriptural proof and an admonition to repent. Verses 22-24 belong together. The *men* after Moses (v.22) is taken up by the *de* after *pantes* (v.24). Here Moses is counted among the prophets. It follows from this that he also is one of the prophets mentioned in vv.18 and 21. Their proclamation refers to 'these days' (v.24). 'Here scripture is not used in the prophecy-fulfilment scheme' (Rese 1969, 69). Genesis 22.18 (LXX) probably underlies v.25. Here Luke, minor details aside, has changed *panta ta ethne tes ges* into *pasai hai patriai tes ges*. This change was necessary because in the context of Acts the speech was addressed only to Jews, and in Acts *ta ethne* means the Gentiles. The expression *patriai*, however, includes the Jews. As *proton* in 3.26 shows, theirs especially is the blessing. In this way Luke has adapted the quotation to the context of Peter's sermon to Jews (cf. Rese 1969, 73).

In conclusion it should be stressed that Peter's speeches in Acts 2 and 3 belong together: 1. In the quotation in 2.21 the message of grace was already promised to all who call on the name of the Lord; according to 3.23 the threat of destruction falls on those who do not accept the message (cf.2.21: *kai estai* + offer of salvation; 3.23: *estai de* + threat. The phrase in 3.23 probably deliberately refers back to 2.21). 2. According to Acts 2 the result of repentance is the gift of the Holy Spirit (v.38 [33f.]); according to Acts 3 it is fulfilment in the parousia of Jesus (vv.20f.). 3. Both speeches make use of scriptural proof; both Joel and the other prophets spoke of the present time. If one likes, both speeches of Peter are therefore one large speech.

III Traditions

Verses 1-10 contain a complete miracle story with a unified style. Verses 1-2 provide the introduction, with information about the place ('Beautiful Gate'); v.3, the action of the lame man, introduces the main part (vv.6b-8), and here the dialogue in vv.3-6a is, from a form-critical point of view, an addition. Verses 6b-8, the main part, with the miraculous action and the healing itself, contain the following stylistic elements: word of healing (v.6b), gesture of healing (v.7a), the immediate occurrence of healing (v.7b), demonstration (v.8a). Verses 9-10 form the conclusion. This depicts the effect on the crowd present (v.8b is completely redactional, see above under II).

The parallels which the story has, especially with Acts 14.8-10 (healing of a lame man in Lystra by Paul) and Luke 5.17-26 (healing of a lame man by Jesus), are very illuminating in an analysis of the tradition. See the synopsis in Schneider 1980, 307, and the exegesis of Acts 14.8-10 (158ff., below). Whereas the basis of the parallel between this story and Luke 5.17-27 (Mark 2.1-2) is probably the analogous situation, there are so many verbal parallels with Acts 14.8-10 that we have to posit a genetic relationship (cf. the detailed comparison with 14.8-10 on 159f. below). Moreover, it is striking that the motive of faith is not explicitly contained in Acts 3.1-10 and that therefore 3.16 is added by Luke, whereas both 14.9 and Luke 5.20 are part of the narrative. Luke may be the author in both cases, having already found it in Mark 2.5.

As the two healing stories in Acts 3 and 14 have such a parallel construction and show many verbal points of contact, there may be a genetic relationship between them. The Peter story is probably original, as it does not yet contain the Lukan theme of faith (this clearly tells against the thesis that Luke created Acts 14 and Acts 3 on the basis of Mark 2, which would otherwise be possible) and presumably this is already indicated by the detail of the 'Beautfiul Gate'. In favour of this assumption is the fact that we cannot identify this gate (cf. Hengel 1983b, 103). Perhaps the detail from the transitional v.11, 'the hall of Solomon', is also part of the traditional element in the story. At all events this has Jerusalem as its location. Harnack (1908, 146) regards this as a part of the Pentecost story which competes with Acts 2. But this theory presupposes the correctness of Harnack's division of the sources (see the critical comments on this in Conzelmann 1987, xxxvii).

[**12-26**] Peter's speech is a Lukan composition which might reflect traditions at the following points:

In v.13 the designation of Jesus as *pais theou* will not derive from Luke, despite the vocabulary statistics (see above under II), as the broad dissemination of *pais theou* in early Christian writings up to the middle of the second century cannot be explained in this way (for details see Wilckens 1974, 16; Kränkl 1972, 125f.). Verses (19,)20-21 are unique in that they see the conversion of Israel as the prerequisite of the arrival of eschatological salvation. Furthermore, the parallelizing of the coming of times of refreshment (cf.Heb.9.20) with the coming of Jesus is striking. The whole passage is to be termed a primitive Christian conversion tradition which had its context in a Jewish-Christian community the faith of which was strongly orientated on the future (for the definition of the tradition see Hahn 1979, 129-54; for the connection between repentance and the time of salvation in Judaism cf. Bill I, 162-5, 519). The interpretation of the seed of Abraham in terms of Jesus which is made in v.25 already appears in Gal.3.16. The following explanations for this are conceivable: 1. Paul and Luke go back quite independently of one another to a tradition. 2. Luke is using Gal.3.16. 3. Luke is using a tradition from the Pauline mission sphere which goes back to Gal.3.16.

IV Historical

There is no historical nucleus to the tradition of the miracle story in vv.1-10. Those who are lame from their childhood are (unfortunately) not made whole again. But the story reflects the existence of a Christian community which reported great things of Peter's activity in Jerusalem and/or miracles performed by him.

The development of the tradition will have to be imagined as having taken place in the first ten years after the crucifixion of Jesus, when Peter took over the leadership of the community in Jerusalem and probably also did 'wonders' there (see the commentary on 5.1-10), or even at a later time, when Peter was regarded as one of the leading figures of early Christianity (in that case the place-name 'Beautiful Gate' would have been supplied by Luke).

For v.13 see the comments under III.

In view of the significance of the idea of the parousia and the role of the Jewish people in the tradition, vv.19-21 can best be connected with the earliest Christianity in Jerusalem. Another possibility is to see vv.19-21 as a reflection on the delay of the *parousia* which would have led to an intensified call upon Israel for repentance. In this case the origin of the tradition would be open and its development later than in the case of the possibility mentioned first.

The tradition of the christological interpretation of Gen.22.18 (v.25) is in any case pre-Lukan. As it is orientated on the LXX, it fits a Greek-speaking community. How old it is thought to be depends on the decision as to which of the three possibilities mentioned under II is preferred (in my view this should be the third).

Acts 4.1-31

I Division

4.1-3: Imprisonment of Peter and John in the evening by the priests, the captain of the temple and the Sadducees
4: The great success of the sermon: the community grows to 5000 members
5-22: Before the Supreme Council
    5-7: The next morning: Peter and John are taken before the council and asked about their authority by the Jewish authorities
    8-12: Peter's testimony
    13-22: Peter and John are forbidden to preach, but they refuse to obey. The apostles are set free because of the people, who are praising God because of the healing of a man lame from birth who is over forty years old
23-30: Return of the disciples and reaction of the community
    23-24a: Peter and John go to the assembled community
    24b-30: Community prayer
        24b: Address to and predicate of God
        25a: Introduction of quotation
        25b-26: Psalm quotation
        27f.: Exegesis of the quotation in terms of the passion of Jesus
        29: Prayer for boldness to preach
        30: Prayer for a miraculous sign
31: Summary report: earthquake, being filled with the Holy Spirit, preaching of the gospel with boldness

II Redaction

The action comes to a climax. After the lame man has been healed and Peter has addressed the people, there is resistance. The apostles are arrested.

[1-3] Verse 1a attributes Peter's previous speech (in the Lukan genitive absolute) to both apostles. Verses 1b-3 are redactional in both language and style: cf. v.2, *dia to* + infinitive; *kataggelein*; v.3, *epebalon tas cheiras* (as a fulfilment of Luke 21.12 [which differs from Mark], cf. 5.18; 12.1; *ethento*. The section contains the exposition for the trial to follow. All three parties (the priests, the captain of the temple, the Sadducees) take offence at Peter and John teaching the people. But Luke already indicates here that the resistance of the Jewish groups to the Christians is not unanimous; only the Sadducees are disturbed that the apostles are proclaiming the resurrection of the dead (cf. a similar redactional connection in 23.6).

[4] The growth of the community is continuing in a miraculous way. After 120 (1.15) or approximately 3000 (2.41) believers, 5000 are now attributed to the community. When Paul greets James on his last visit to Jerusalem (21.20) there are even more: tens of thousands.

[5-22] Verses 5-7 are the redactional introduction to the hearing. For the introductory *egeneto* + accusative with infinitive cf. Radl 1975, 403. Verse 7 refers back to 3.12, 16 (cf.3.6), and puts the question to the apostles in such a way as to compel them to make the speech which follows: 'In what power and in what name did you do this?' The readers already know the answer. Peter's speech which follows in vv.8-12 combines in a redactional way the miracle reported in Acts 3 and the Christ kerygma. In addition, with a reference to Ps.118.22 there is a scriptural argument not previously used in Acts (cf. Luke 20.17/Mark 12.10 – perhaps a deliberate reference back to this scene). Verse 8, the introduction to Peter's speech, is completely Lukan in language. Verses 9f. refer to the healing story; here the following word-for-word parallels with it and the previous narratives are to be noted: *gnoston esto* (= 2.14); 'in the name of Jesus Christ the Nazorean' (= 3.6); 'whom you crucified' (= 2.36); 'whom God has raised from the dead' (= 3.15). Verse 11 gives the scriptural proof for the kerygma, taking up Ps.118.22 (see III below). Verse 12 links back to the situation of the address. Verses 13-22 come to a climax in the apostles' refusing to obey the ban on their preaching (because they cannot). The keyword *parrhesia* in v.13 also appears in the following verses 29 + 31, a sign that Luke has one fact in view: the freedom of proclamation from Jewish intervention. (It has a parallel in the freedom to preach in the Roman state – cf. the end of Acts.) It is striking that the accusers only now discover the close relationship between the disciples and Jesus (*epeginoskon*). That is similarly fiction (cf.4.1f.), as is their amazement at the apostles' lack of education (v.13a). This lack of education is in contrast to Peter's spirit-filled speech, while the discovery

of the link with Jesus intensifies the drama (the accusers finally discover what is really at stake). Verse 14 (*anteipein* is perhaps a reference back to Luke 21.15 [which is redactional]) serves to link the scene to 3.1-11; it already prepares for the report of the subsequent action against the apostles. The man who was healed there stands by the apostles and as it were provokes the subsequent actions of the Jewish authorities against them. Verses 16f. once again make the present deliberations – at which the apostles are not present (cf. v.15) – seem to have been caused by the miracle previously reported; v.16b puts the insight intended by Luke into the mouth of the Jewish authorities (in Lukan language; notice also the solitary *men*, cf. 1.1): through the apostles a sign has taken place which is clear to all the inhabitants of Jerusalem. In vv.17f. the prohibition against preaching is given only in order not to be obeyed. *phtheggesthai* refers back to 2.4,14 (*apophtheggesthai*). 'Whether it is right before God to obey you more than God is something that will decide itself' (v.19, cf. 5.29) contains an allusion to Socrates, who in a similar situation had said to his judges: 'I will obey the god rather than you' (Plato, *Apology* 29d). In this way Luke shows his Greek readers his own Hellenistic education (cf. Plümacher 1972, 18f.). At the same time he demonstrates the necessity of the mission in Jerusalem. Verse 21 confirms vv.17f.: the Jewish authorities want to prevent the preaching of the gospel but cannot. Verse 22 rounds off the whole scene begun in 3.1 by stressing once again the miraculous nature of the healing: the lame man was more than forty, i.e. had had the affliction all that time.

[23-30] Verses 23-24a have Lukan colouring (*apolythentes, apeggeilan hosa, homothymadon*). They link the previous unit with vv.24b-30, the community prayer. *despota* in v.24b is an address to God which occurs in the NT also in the prayer of Simeon, Luke 2.29, and at 6.10. The conception of God the creator of heaven and earth and sea comes from the Old Testament. (For the possible derivation of v.24b from tradition see III below.) Verse 25a is corrupt.

On Schneider 1980: his attempt at restoration is hardly convincing; he writes: 'The grammatically overloaded construction of v.25a is possibly the result of Luke's intent to qualify the following quotation as a divine promise. The introduction of the quotation contains the following individual elements: *ho eipon* (i.e. God's own statement is cited); also, God speaks at the same time "through the mouth of our father David", who was "God's servant", and "through the Holy Spirit" (357). That comes to grief on the grammar. Cf. also Rese 1969: 'The restoration of the original text at this point seems as impossible as the attempt is vain to explain the origin of the corrupt text' (94). Haenchen 1971, 226 n.3, thinks that there are two additions in v.25a which crept in later: *tou patros hemon* and *dia pneumatos hagiou*.

Verses 25b-26 quote Psalm 2.1f. (LXX) literally and will therefore derive from the redaction. Verse 27 introduces the interpretation with the verb *synechthesan*, which comes from the quotation. Three of the four groups mentioned in the quotation (*ethne, laoi, basileis, archontes*) are interpreted in the light of the Lukan passion narrative as follows: Herod Antipas is a representative of the *basileis*, Pilate of the *archontes* and Israel of the *laoi*. Therefore the *ethne* may refer to the Roman soldiers. Verse 27 is a redactional reference back to Luke 23.12. 'However, the general tone is different from that in Luke's passion narrative. There Pilate is exonerated in an apologetic manner whereas here, in line with Luke's fundamental view of salvation history, Pilate's guilt is stressed' (Conzelmann 1987, 35). *Both* approaches are Lukan. For *paida sou* (see also v.30) cf.the commentary on 3.13.

In addition, vv.25-27b have a chiastic construction. They are framed by the *ethne* and *laoi*, then the *basileis* (= Herod Antipas) and the *archontes* (= Pilate); the Lord (= God and his anointed) is in the centre. Because of the literal quotation of the LXX and the artistic chiastic construction the composition of vv.25b-27 is to be attributed to Luke, though this does not exclude an underlying tradition.

Verse 28 is Lukan in language and content. On the language: *cheir sou* and *boule sou* (Luke 7.30; Acts 2.23; 13.36; 20.27) are Lukan expressions. In content, the idea of God's plan is redactional: 'A striking example is provided by the many compounds with *pro*' (Conzelmann 1960, 151; cf. ibid., the whole section 151-4). Verse 29 brings the prayer back to the present distress of the community: *kai ta nyn* is a Lukan transitional phrase: in the NT it occurs elsewhere only in 5.38; 20.32; 27.22 (17.30: *ta nyn*; 20.22,25: *kai nyn*). God's attention is drawn to the threats of the Jewish authorities made in vv.17,21. Verse 30 points back to the healing and the miraculous actions which took place in the name of Jesus: *iasis* refers to the particular healing of the lame man, *semeia* and *terata* to the mighty acts reported since Acts 2, which for their part continue the miracles narrated in the Gospel of Luke (cf.Acts 2.22). The fulfilment of the wish in the prayer is reported summarily in 5.12; 6.8.

[31] After the introductory Lucan genitive absolute this verse describes the hearing of the prayer, which takes the form of a shaking of the place, and reports a kind of second Pentecost. All (Christians) are filled with the Holy Spirit.

To sum up, stress should be laid on the redactional shaping by Luke throughout vv.23-31.

III Traditions

[11] Psalm 118.22 is an element of earliest Christian apologetic against the Jews from the tradition: see Mark 12.10 par. (cf. Lindars 1973, 169-86).

[24b-30] The theory advanced in various forms that vv.24b-28 are part of an old community prayer (thus most recently Roloff 1981, 85) comes to grief on the fact that here it is not the style of prayer but that of exegesis (of Ps.2.1f.) which predominates. That is not to dispute that the prayer corresponds fully to the scheme in Jewish and Old Testament scriptures (cf. Tobit 3.11-15; 8.5-7 and esp. Isa.37.16-20) and therefore may have pre-Lukan Christian predecessors.

'First God is addressed in praise as the Lord and Creator of heaven and earth. Then he is reminded of the promise he gave to the fathers, to which Christian prayer adds fulfilment through Jesus. The phrase *kai ta nyn kyrie* introduces the particular prayer of the suppliant and asks God for his miraculous help' (v.d. Goltz 1901, 235).

Here it is worth while (against v.d.Goltz, ibid.) describing the prayer as a Lukan composition because of the redactional features mentioned above.

Nevertheless it is sensible to ask whether individual elements of the prayer shaped by Luke can be derived from tradition. That seems necessary in one case, since the interpretation of Ps.2.1f. in terms of Herod and Pilate probably underlies the prayer – cf. similarly Luke 23.6, a scene which has even been composed on the basis of an already existing interpretation of Ps.2.1f. in terms of Herod and Pilate (cf. Dibelius 1915; Wilckens 1974, 230f. [with bibliography]). The different portrayals of Pilate do not affect this theory, against Kränkl 1972:

'The discrepancy between Acts 4.25-27 and the rest of Luke's work can be understood more easily if we assume that here the author has taken up a piece of tradition which is in tension with his own composition' (110).

IV Historical

[11] The use of Ps.118.22 as an element of early Christian apologetic is already pre-Markan. But this interpretation cannot be convincingly attributed to Peter, as it is not an element of the tradition.

[25b-28] The use of Ps.2.1f. in the framework of the passion narrative is singular in the early Christian texts known to us (but cf. above on

Luke 23.6ff.). It derives from Luke's scriptural exegesis (or that of his community) and probably does not go back to the first generation.

On Luke's general knowledge in Acts 3-4.31

Despite what is in other respects the negative result of the historical analysis of the traditions in Acts 3-4.31, the question remains whether Luke's general knowledge of this period of the earliest community is of historical value. We should probably answer this in the affirmative, because his depiction of the conflict between the earliest community and the priestly nobility rests on correct historical assumptions. For the missionary activity of the earliest community in Jerusalem not long after the crucifixion of Jesus may have alarmed Sadducaean circles (cf. the action of the Sadducee Ananus against James in 62 CE [Josephus, *Antt* XX, 199-203]), so that they might at least have prompted considerations about action against the Jesus community (cf. Roloff 1981, 80). That means that while the narrative *details* of Acts 3-4.31 are in other respects historically worthless (on Judge 1964, 63), the narrative framework is based on some accurate historical foundations, i.e. on facts. Its origin can probably no longer be discovered. (Or did Luke himself construct it on the basis of the Gospel of Mark?)

Acts 4.32-37

I Division

4.32: The unity of the community
33: The testimony of the apostles to the resurrection and the grace that rests on all of them
34-35: The selling of goods and the distribution of the proceeds by the apostles
36-37: The example of Barnabas

II Redaction

[32] This verse stresses the unity of the community. *plethos* and *hyparchonta* are Lukan in language, *pisteusanton* and *hapanta koina* refer back to 2.44. Verse 32b evidently presupposes that individual members of the community continued to have possessions (no one called any of his

possessions his own), but that the owners resigned their rights of ownership to the community, so that they had everything in common (*autois hapanta koina*). In this verse Luke combines biblical expressions ('one heart and one soul', cf. Deut.6.6) with Greek ideals (for *hapanta koina* cf. *koina ta philon*, Aristotle *NE* IX 8,2 – this ideal probably goes back as far as Pythagoras, see Epicurus in Diogenes Laertius X 11 and Timaeus, ibid., VIII 10) for the purpose of depicting the earliest community. But as the idea of sharing with those not of equal rank is more Jewish than Greek, at this point we have more than the use of knowledge gained from reading, namely the Jewish-Christian interpretation of a Greek ideal (cf. on this the survey by Klauck 1982, 48-52; Klauck's investigation is, moreover, a full and valuable contribution on the question of earliest Christian 'communism').

[33] Verse 33a interrupts the description of the earliest community and in good Lukan style stresses the apostles' testimony to the resurrection of Jesus. This was given with great power. Verse 33b explains how great grace (viz. of God) took hold of all the Christians. That leads back to the internal description of the earliest community begun in v.32 and taken up again in v.34.

[34-35] Verse 34a ('No one was in need among them', cf. Deut.15.4) is the basis (*gar*) of the statement made in v.33b that a great grace had come upon the Christians. We may hardly infer different sources from the interruption in v.33 and the resumption of v.32 in v.34a. Luke wants to depict the internal life of the earliest community, and at the same time describe the special function of its apostles.

In contrast to v.32, vv.34b-35 seems to presuppose a total surrender of possessions on the part of the members of the Jewish community. Those who had lands or houses sold them and laid the proceeds at the feet of the apostles, who distributed them to each according to need. But we do not have to presuppose that the owners sold *all* their possessions, so that the difference from v.32 would simply be one between *the surrender of possessions* (v.34f.) and *resignation of the right to possessions* (32). However, Luke's point does not lie in petty details of this kind, but in defining the purpose of the action: *kathoti an tis chreian eichen*, v.35 (cf.2.45), and showing that Old Testament and Greek ideals were being realized in the Jerusalem community (cf. above on v.32).

Perhaps Luke's meaning can be discovered further in the following observation: vv.35 and 37 say in the same way that the Christians or Barnabas had laid what they had sold (for the benefit of the community) at the apostles' feet. The same phrase is taken up again in 5.2 and 5.10 (variant reading), and this might suggest its redactional character.

Schille 1983, 145, differs: 'The threefold (vv.34, 37; 5.2) repetition seems to show that "laid at the apostles' feet" is already being used as a formula.' However, Schille overlooks 5.10. The redactional explanation is simpler, and moreover Schille has to answer the question where Luke got this formal phrase from. Even Horn 1983, 40, thinks that 'only the pre-Lukan tradition is interested in the laying of money at the apostles' feet'. However, his reference to the lack of this phrase in Acts 2.44 (ibid.) is hardly an adequate reason. For the matter is presupposed in Acts 2.45.

The first two positive and the next two negative examples indicate Luke's concern: this is the selling of the possessions of those with goods for the benefit of the poor, whereas before in 2.45 the apostles have the task of distribution. Here we can see part of 'Luke's concrete social utopia' (Schottroff/Stegemann 1978, 149), according to which those with possessions renounce so much 'that there are neither rich nor needy in the community' (153; cf. generally ibid., 149-53, and Horn 1983, 39-49. Despite individual differences, in my view both works are rightly agreed in stressing the paraenetic purposes of the summaries against a one-sided idealistic view [cf. e.g. Conzelmann 1960, 14, 209-15, etc.]. For the literature see Horn 1983, 300f. n.49).

kathoti an tis chreian eichen in v.35b corresponds word for word with 2.45c and reflects the thrust of Luke's concern which has just been mentioned (for the above phrase see Horn 1983, 43, 45, 48f.). 'Luke projects what he expects of his community in paradigmatic fashion back to the time of the earliest community' (Horn 1983, 43).

[36-37] *apo ton apostolon* is certainly redactional. So far in Acts the Jerusalem perspective is still dominant. Here, as later in 11.22, Barnabas is assigned by the redaction to Jerusalem. In v.37 *hyparchontos* is Lukan language, and echoes the Lukan *hyperchon* (v.34). For the redactional phrase 'lay at the apostles' feet', cf. 4.35; 5.2,10 (variant reading).

III Traditions

For the elements of 'tradition' in the summary see the comments on 2.42-27, above 47.

[36-37] Luke may have had a tradition (oral) that Barnabas had sold a field in favour of the Jerusalem community. (The reason for this is that the Lukan framework generalizes, while the information about the sale of one field is specific and is in tension with the framework.) Similarly the designation of his origin, 'Cypriot' (*Kyprios to genei*), is an element of tradition. It means either that Barnabas comes from Cyprus (cf. 15.39, where Barnabas and John Mark travel to Cyprus), or that (only) his family comes from there (cf. 11.20; 21.16, Mnason the Cypriot). It is impossible

to decide whether tradition underlies the derivation of the name Barnabas, 'son of comfort'. Its derivation is also uncertain (see the commentaries).

IV Historical

There can hardly be any doubt about the historicity of Barnabas' sale of a field in favour of the Jerusalem community. Even at a later period the Jerusalem community was dependent on gifts from the Gentile Christian communities. Perhaps Barnabas' action is one of those gifts of love. However, it is impossible to decide when the sale of the field for the community was made. It may have been in the early period, but it could also have been after the conference, when the Antiochene and Pauline communities undertook a collection.

Acts 5.1-11

I Division

1-2: Exposition: The sale of a piece of land and the keeping back of part of the proceeds by Ananias and Sapphira
3-6: Ananias and his punishment
7-10: Sapphira and her punishment
11: The effect on the crowd

II Redaction

[1-2] *aner de tis onomati* in v.1 is a Lukan phrase. *epolesen ktema* links back to 4.37, where the same verb is used in connection with Barnabas' sale of the field. 'At the apostles' feet' (v.2) already appears at 4.35,37 (cf. later 5.10 [variant reading]). With this redactional phrase Luke indicates that 4.32-37 belongs with 5.1-10 and refers to the same matter.

[3-6] The term 'Holy Spirit' in v.3 may come from Luke, because he pays special attention to it. Verse 4 is Lukan throughout. In form it stands outside the framework as an explanation for readers. In content it rejects the idea of any obligation to renounce possessions and stresses the voluntary nature of the sale of the property and the handing over of

the proceeds (cf. Schneider 1980, 375). The clause v.4c (*ouk epseuso anthropois alla to theo*), moreover, recalls Peter's saying (which is Lukan) in 5.29 and the advice of Gamaliel in 5.38f., which is also redactional. Both times (as in 4c) the concern is with a commitment to God rather than to men.

[7-10,11] Verses 7-10 seem to be a redactional composition on the model of the previous episode, in order to add emphasis to the statement made there. (Or *both* episodes are a negative illustration of 4.32-37.) The figure 'three' in v.7 is redactional. In v.8 Peter asks whether the contribution given was the whole amount. As he knows that the two sums are not identical, the question has the same aim as in vv.2-3 and makes the embezzlement clear. The beginning of v.9, *ti hoti*, refers back to v.4b. The statement in v.10 that Sapphira fell at Peter's feet plays on the thrice-repeated phrase 'at the apostles' feet' (4.35, 37; 5.2). This rhetorical device may derive from the narrator Luke. 'In v.11 the term *ekklesia* (here the individual community in Jerusalem) which occurs here for the first time in Acts, but in view of 8.1; 9.31 was surely chosen deliberately, reveals the hand of Luke' (Weiser 1981, 146). The verse repeats v.5b but adds 'the whole church' (*holen ten ekklesian*). Perhaps this means that the episode 4.32-5.11 is important for Luke's church (cf. Schmithals 1982, 57). Certainly at the narrative level *ekklesia* denotes the Jerusalem community, but at the redactional level the whole church (including that of Luke) might be meant.

Acts 5.1-11 is relatively closely connected with 4.32-37. For after 4.34, 36f., Luke is here reporting a third case, as the proceeds of the property sold are laid at the apostles' feet. Here, by the example of Ananias and Sapphira, there is a demonstration of what would happen to those who went against the Holy Spirit. However, this story is not an instruction of how Luke's community should act, but a didactic example from the earliest Christian period. But the narrative also shows Luke's real concern: not the renunciation of property as a principle but undivided, unhypocritical commitment to God, or not cheating God. Ananias and Sapphira are not punished because they did not give up all their possessions or put only part of them at the disposal of the community, but because their actions were a sham and they thus showed an impure disposition. 'So according to Luke the sin of Ananias and Sapphira consists in dealing selfishly with material possessions' (Weiser 1981, 146). By introducing an example of behaviour which damages the community, Luke subsequently sheds even more light on the exemplary conduct of Barnabas and the community (cf. Horn 1983, 42).

64

III Traditions

The analysis of the redaction showed that Luke did not just add the tradition in v.4 but worked over the whole story. Elements of tradition are the names Ananias and Peter, the verb *nosphizomai*, and the death of Ananias as a result of an action directed against him by Peter. The tradition might hypothetically be described as a punitive rule miracle. Ananias had acted against a rule of the Christian community and had to pay for it with his life, through the instrumental action of Peter. The verb *nosphizomai* might (thus Weiser 1981, 144) come from the story of Achan (Josh.7), who had stolen property which was devoted to God and under the ban. The story may have been told in the early-Christian Jewish world with a reference back to that. In content it corresponds to Jewish rule miracles.

'In the Jewish rule miracles the issue is almost always one of life or death. Breaches of the law lead to death; observance of the law preserves from death. The law does not chastise; it kills. This seems to us archaic and inhuman, especially in the case of unimportant transgressions, but is a sign of great seriousness about the observance of the divine will: in the presence of God the issue is one of life and death' (Theissen 1983, 110).

Against what did Ananias actually offend? That can hardly be specified now. It is Luke who illustrates the 'embezzlement' by the context. If we leave this aside, all that is left is an offence against the rules or the holy law of a community. The transgression was probably to do with finances, but it need not have been as Luke portrays it. Be this as it may, there are parallels from early Christianity for offences against sacred law. At the end of a section concerned with the community, Paul writes: 'Cast out the evil one from your midst' (I Cor.5.13b). This quotation from Deut.17.7 (cf. Deut.19.19; 21.21; 22.21, 24; 24.9 [LXX]) and its use in Paul illuminate the milieu of the tradition in Acts 5.

Paul had been concerned with an incestuous person in the same context (I Cor.5.1-5) and concluded that he should be handed over to Satan (cf. Acts 5.3: the Satan) – for the destruction of the flesh so that his spirit should be saved on the day of judgment (I Cor.5.5b). Certainly the tradition here, in contrast to I Cor.5, does not reflect the future fate of the sinner, and we are not explicitly told that Peter handed him over to Satan. But the context of the idea is the same. A 'holy' man, Peter or Paul, executes sacred law on a sinner which results in his death. At the same time this implies that Peter is an element of the tradition.

Roloff 1981 differs: on the basis of content and form there is no Peter legend. 'Certainly there is stress on his central position in the community and on his miraculous knowledge, but in the last resort the narrator's interest is not in him' (92).

IV Historical

The tradition probably came into being in the Jerusalem community, at its earliest period, when Peter was its leader. Because of the parallel to I Cor.5 an analogous event seems to underlie this as a historical nucleus. A member of the community had offended against sacred law and was therefore cursed and expelled by the head of the community (Stählin 1980, 85, however, regards such an action, with fatal consequences and no offer of repentance, as incompatible with the Spirit of Jesus and Paul. But I Cor.5 makes one think!). Whether he died, though, is uncertain (Reicke 1957, 89, differs). But it is certain that according to sacred law he should have died. So the 'heightening of the event to the point at which it becomes a judgment of God with fatal consequences' may accord with the 'rules of popular tradition' (Roloff 1981, 93). (For the historicity of a cursing which results in death cf. the examples in Remus 1983, 93f., with reference to Walter B.Cannon's ethnological studies.)

Finally, it should be stressed once again that the exact crime of Ananias is no longer quite clear. And the pericope is in no way 'clear evidence' for the sharing of goods in the earliest community, as Jeremias (1969, 130 n.19) thinks. (Jeremias, ibid.: 'The sin of Ananias was not his lie, but the withholding of something that had been dedicated to God.')

Acts 5.12-16

I Division

12a: The apostles' signs and wonders
12b: Peaceful attendance of Christians (in the temple) in the hall of Solomon
13: The attitude of the world around to the Christians
14: The constant growth of the community
15: The healings by Peter's shadow
16: The healing of all the sick from around Jerusalem

II Redaction

The section depicts the miraculous power of the apostles and the constant influx of people into the Christian community, and is the last extended summary in Acts. In fact in its description of the apostles' miracles it puts all the other summaries in the shade.

The pericope shows a number of tensions: there is no intrinsic connection between vv.12a and 12b, and the same is true of vv.13a and 13b. Verse 13a says that none of the others dared to join the community, but according to v.13b they seem to have praised the Christians. Verse 15 is introduced with *hoste*, which seems to refer back to v.12a and is unconnected in the present context. Does this evidence not suggest that sources or traditions have been worked into the pericope? But both the language and the content tell against this. (So there will be neither section III nor section IV here.)

[12a] *semeia kai terata polla* is Lukan language. The verse refers back to 2.19,22,43; 4.30 and thus once again states the miracles of the apostles in summary form.

[12b] *homothymadon* is Lukan language. The report that the Christians frequent the hall of Solomon in harmony is a variant on the idea of Christians being together in the temple in harmony which is already known from 2.46. (According to Luke, the hall of Solomon, already mentioned in 3.11, is in the temple.)

[13] *kollasthai* is Lukan language, as is *emegalynen*. By describing the fear of the population Luke makes a link back to the pericope 5.1-11; cf. esp. 11b: 'Great fear fell upon all who heard of it.' On the other hand the high regard for the Christians among the people is used in the next episode (cf. esp.v.26).

[14] *prosetithento, pisteuontes, plethe* and the mention of the men and especially the women are frequent in Luke. In content, the note about the growth of the community logically follows the report of the attitude of the public to it.

[15] The verse shows the effect of the event described in vv.12-14 (*hoste* does not relate to *mallon* [v.14] but to vv.12-14). Verse 15a + b corresponds to Mark 6.56, a passage which the author passes over in the Gospel of Luke and inserts here. Verse 15c, the report of the miraculous shadow of Peter, has a parallel (which the author will have intended) in 19.12, the note about Paul's handkerchiefs.

[16] *synercheto* and *plethos* are Lukan language. The verse introduces a further report about the spread of the preaching of the gospel. Whole cities outside Jerusalem (as in Luke 6.17, Luke is thinking of the far-

distant cities of Judaea) come to the capital for their sick to be healed. With this statement Luke prepares for the next chapter, in which the gospel is borne 'outside' (cf.1.8). 'The mention that the people stream in from the surrounding "cities" is fully in accord with the social and cultural milieu from which and in which *Luke* sees the activity of Jesus, the apostles and missionaries as a *city* mission' (Weiser 1981, 150). (Judge 1964, 12f., evidently thinks v.16 historically reliable!)

Acts 5.17-42

I Division

5.17-18: Exposition: The apostles are arrested by the high priest and the Sadducees
19-21a: The miracle of their liberation and the command
   19: Liberation of the prisoners by an angel of the Lord
   20: Instruction to teach the people in the temple
   21a: The instruction is carried out
21b-40: The apostles before the Sanhedrin
   21b: (After the Sanhedrin has assembled) Instruction to bring in the prisoners
   22: The servants cannnot find the prisoners
   23: Report to the Sanhedrin
   24: The temple captain and the Sanhedrin at a loss
   25: Report that the prisoners are teaching in the temple
   26-27a: The apostles brought before the Sanhedrin
   27b-40: Legal hearing
      27b-28: Accusation
      29-32: Defence: Speech of Peter and the apostles
      33: Furious reaction by the audience
      34-39b: Gamaliel's speech
      39c: Assent to Gamaliel's speech
      40: The apostles are punished and released. (Further ban on preaching the gospel)
41-42: Joy of the apostles over suffering in the name of Christ and further preaching in the temple

II Redaction

The episode is a variation on the theme of Acts 3-4. The Jewish authorities take offence at the proclamation of Christ, forbid the apostles to preach and the apostles then continue all the more undeterred (cf.4.18-20).

[17-18] *anastas, eplesthesan, epebalon tas cheiras epi, demosia* are Lukan

in language. The section gives the reason for the arrest of the apostles as the *zelos* of the Jewish authorities. What is in mind is their displeasure at the success of the apostles' preaching. Cf. the parallel 4.2, where the Jewish aristocracy takes offence at the teaching of the people (*diaponoumenoi*). The account of the imprisonment in 5.18 is also parallel to 4.3.

[19-21a] The story of the freeing of the apostles from prison by an angel has no parallel in Acts 4. Instead of this there are parallels with the miraculous releases in 12.4-10 and 16.23-24. However, we should note that in comparison to chs.12, 16, the account of the miraculous liberation remains relatively pale. At most the text might therefore have *individual* features of a miraculous release which Luke introduced into the narrative context here in order to demonstrate from the start God's intervention on behalf of the apostles. There is no reference to the miraculous release in the sequel. Rather, at the hearing the high priest refers back to the ban against teaching in the name of Jesus in 4.8. The account of the miraculous release is therefore at a different level from the narrative level, namely that of the author and the reader (on this see further on vv.38f.).

[21b-40] This section is totally Lukan. Cf. the following selection of indications of Lukan authorship in language and content: v.21, *paragenomenos*; v.22, *paragenomenoi, apeggeilan*; v.23, the direct speech makes the account lively; v.24, the potential optative with *an* occurs similarly in 10.17; v.25, *paragenomenos, apeggeilen, idou*; for the anxiety about the people in v.26, cf. similarly 4.21. Verse 27a is a transitional note (*agagontes* takes up *egen* in v.26). The accusation is that despite the ban (cf.4.18) the apostles had taught the people in the name of Jesus Christ (v.28a), indeed that they had filled Jerusalem with Christian teaching (v.28b). The remark which is attached, namely that they wanted to bring the blood of this man (viz. Jesus) upon their (i.e. the members of the Sanhedrin) head (v.28), heightens the narrative tension. At the same time 'the reader's attention is drawn to the consequences of the Sandherin's mode of action. Indirectly the Sanhedrin is burdened with both the killing of Jesus and the proceedings against the apostles as guilt to be punished by God' (Schneider 1980, 34). Verse 28 can already be shown to be redaction by the fact that it is based on 4.18. The subsequent speech of Peter and the apostles in vv.29-32 refers to Acts 4, as does the previous section. Cf. v.29, 'We must obey God rather than men', with 4.19, 'Is it just before God to obey you more than God?' Verses 30-32 expand this clause of Peter's (v.29), which recalls Socrates (cf. Plato, *Apol* 29D), with a christological section; it contains predicates which already appear in the previous chapters: v.30, the statement that the Jews are the main agents in the crucifixion of Jesus (cf. 2.23; 3.14f.; cf. also the word-for-word agreement between v.30b and

10.39 end: *kremasantes epi xylou*); the announcement of the resurrection (cf. 2.24; 3.15); v.31: the designation of Jesus as *archegos* (cf. 3.15: *archegos tes zoes*); the exaltation of Jesus to the right hand of God (cf.2.33).

The role of the exalted Jesus to give or bring about repentance and the forgiveness of sins (v.31) does not appear again in Acts in this form. It has therefore occasionally been thought that a traditional formulation can be found here since (as 11.18) 'repentance is thought of as the gift of salvation' (Conzelmann 1960, 228 n.2), whereas elsewhere repentance is the first action on the human side. But these distinctions are probably over-subtle. I regard the present phrase as also being redactional, since 1. repentance and forgiveness are a Lukan pair; 2. v.31 corresponds in content to 2.33: the Jesus who is exalted to the right hand of God pours out the Holy Spirit (as a gift!).

Verse 32a, the apostles' witness, is Lukan; cf. the same statement in 2.32; 3.15 (in connection with a christological formulation). *rhematon touton* refers back to the saving acts of God (= resurrection, ascension, the offer of repentance through Jesus), i.e. *rhema* here, as often in Luke, means 'thing' (cf. Schneider 1980, 37). In verse 32b the conception that the Holy Spirit is a further independent witness alongside the apostles is singular in Luke. Granted, according to Conzelmann 'the juxtaposition of the testimony of the apostles and of the Spirit is explained by 2.32-39 and Luke 24.48-49' (1987, 42: he is followed by Schneider 1980, 317). But there is no parallel in the passages mentioned (with Schille 1983, 12). The furious reaction of the crowd (v.33) is a stylistic reaction to the speech of the apostles. Verses 34-39 are to be understood in terms of the redaction. Moreover v.34 matches Acts 4.15: in both cases the apostles have to leave the room before the discussion. Gamaliel's advice (vv.38f.) contains Luke's apologetic programme (Conzelmann 1987, 43). That the Christian plan is 'from God' has of course long been clear to the readers. 'By his miraculous intervention (in the story of the release) God has made the proclamation of the apostles by word and deed his cause' (Kratz 1979, 454). Here Luke makes the Pharisees resemble the Christians, since both, in contrast to the Sadducees, teach the resurrection from the dead (cf.23.6-9). Therefore the Sadducees appear as enemies and persecutors of the Christians. Gamaliel's advice is supported by two historical examples, the rebellions of Theudas and Judas. In this passage they certainly derive from Luke. Theudas only emerged after 44 CE (cf. Josephus, *Antt* XX, 97-99). Luke takes Gamaliel's speech as the occasion for providing historical allusions. But if these are recognized as redactional additions, at this point the person of Gamaliel must also be attributed to Luke. However, the mediating role of the 'Hillelite' Gamaliel well fits the advice attributed to him. Still, apart from the difficulties of the historical conception of Gamaliel, against this is the evidence that (at the Lukan narrative level) Gamaliel's pupil Paul was evidently not disposed to the tolerance which is attributed to his teacher. So the fact remains that the person and speech of Gamaliel at this point are a Lukan creation (for attempts to find a historical nucleus in 5.38f. see IV below). Verse 40 relies for language on 5.28 and 4.18. It is striking that despite the assent of the Sanhedrin to Gamaliel's advice, the apostles are flogged. This tension can best be explained in terms of the redaction. The suffering of the apostles has the character of a model for the time of Luke (cf. also the next verses 41-42).

[41-42] In language and content these verse are wholly Lukan. They depict once again the roots of the earliest community in Judaism (cf. the preaching in the temple) but then interpret the present dimension of the Lukan church and Christian existence in it by the motto of suffering (the *dei* of the suffering in 14.22 is a joy in suffering).To sum up, apart from the miraculous release (vv.19f.), Acts 5.17-42 is a variation on Acts 3-4. There the apostles Peter and John are arrested because of their miracles and preaching, brought before the supreme council, but set free again after a warning because there are insufficient legal grounds. Luke achieves a stage beyond this in ch.5 by having *all* the apostles again arrested by the Jewish authorities because of their successful activity, but miraculously released by God, who can intervene on behalf of his missionaries at any time. In another hearing before the supreme court it is shown that no human prohibition can effectively oppose the divinely-willed proclamation of the apostles in the name of Jesus Christ. Gamaliel stresses programmatically that no *theomachos* can defeat the Christian cause (this is on the author-reader level). The scene ends with an indirect look at the suffering *and* the constant proclamation of the good news (cf. Kratz 1979, 457).

III Traditions

For the reasons mentioned, Luke has inserted into the action elements from a miraculous release which has parallels with the miraculous releases in Acts 12 and 16. It is not in its original place here, nor is any reference made to it in the action which follows. Moreover the whole scene proves to have been composed by Luke, while the elements of the liberation miracle, as is shown by a comparison with Acts 12, Acts 16 and non-Christian parallels (see 182f. below), derive from tradition.

Verse 30 is an allusion to Deut.21.22f. (LXX), a passage which in the pre-Christian period, in contrast to its original meaning (there it describes the hanging up of a corpse after stoning), could be related to crucifixion (cf. Temple Scroll, col.64.6-13). The allusion hardly goes back to Luke's own reflection on the death of Jesus (though cf. Luke 23.39 [Mark differs]), but is part of the tradition connected with the death of Jesus (cf.

Gal. 3.13). However, this is not a theologoumenon of the community but a counter-argument of the synagogue (for details see Dietzfelbinger 1985, 36f. [literature]; Friedrich 1982, 122-30, differs).

The information about Theudas and Judas derives from Luke's reading or from oral information (for this question see Dibelius 1956, 186f.). The person of Gamaliel was known to Luke from the tradition on Paul's pre-Christian period (22.3) or was part of his general knowledge.

IV Historical

The elements of the tradition of the miraculous release were first woven into this passage by Luke. They have nothing to do with a historical nucleus.

It follows from what has been said above about the character of v.30 as tradition that – on the basis of a historical judgment – the Jewish reference to Deut.21.22f. was a counter-argument to the Christian thesis of the messiahship of Jesus, and that the Christian reference to the resurrection of Jesus represented the Christian answer to this. In addition it can be presupposed that Paul himself in his pre-Christian period (the Christian period is not relevant) would have known Deut.21.22f. as an anti-Christian argument from the synagogue. If this hypothesis should be correct, it would explain the sharpness and the contours which the theology of the cross has in Paul (for a thorough justification see Dietzfelbinger 1985, 30-42 [with bibliography]).

Roloff has recently claimed a historical nucleus in Gamaliel's advice in 5.38f. on the basis of careful arguments (cf. also Hengel 1976, 82). As such an assertion would be highly significant if it were right, we must look at it further here. Roloff writes:

The 'Gamaliel speech could hardly have come into being without the use of tradition. Certainly in its present form it has all the characteristics of a speech composed by Luke; however, it is hardly conceivable that he would have created a speech which was as exposed as this by its position in the context and by its content without any support in the tradition, and would go against what we can establish throughout. At the least we must assume that in the Jerusalem community there was a view of the respected Pharisee Gamaliel, who counselled the toleration of Christians, and was cited in controversies with Jewish opponents as positive evidence from a known Jewish authority. Here we must think specifically of vv.38f. Gamaliel the elder was one of the leading figures in Pharisaic Judaism between 25 and 30 CE. As the grandson of the famous Rabbi Hillel, like him he represented a liberal devotion to the law and was committed to the spirit of tolerance and humanity... It is in accord with the spirit of that liberal Pharisaism to warn against over-hasty proceedings against a group recognized as heretical for fear of God's supremacy over history' (1981, 100f.).

On this it should be observed:

1. The assumption that Luke could not himself have composed a significant speech is questionable in view of Paul's speech at Miletus, which is clearly redactional.

2. Unfortunately we do not know (we no longer know!) as much about the historical Gamaliel I as Roloff thinks. Gamaliel was not the grandson of Hillel (Simon, the middle link here, probably never existed, see Schürer 1979, 367f.), nor is there sufficient proof of a link between Hillel and Gamaliel I (see Neusner 1971 [Vol.1], 375). Moreover Roloff's characterization of Hillel as a representative of a liberal devotion to the law indebted to the spirit of tolerance and humanity goes back to a pre-critical use of rabbinic writings which, despite its great popularity among New Testament scholars, is no longer acceptable in that form; cf. the important survey by Neusner 1971 (Vol.III), 320-68 (cf. especially 338-40 on the liberal Hillel committed to humanity). Finally, it is possible to point to a statement similar to 'Gamaliel's advice' in Acts 5.38f., from the rabbinic writings: MAboth 4.11: 'R.Johanan, the Sandal-maker (a pupil of Akiba), says: Any assembling together for the sake of heaven shall in the end be established, but any that is not for the sake of Heaven shall not in the end be established' (cf. MAboth 5, 17).

Conclusion: because the context of Acts 5.38f. is certainly Lukan and because of the historical impossibility of verifying 'Gamaliel's advice' from rabbinic writings, the conclusion drawn above that Acts 5.38f. is to be seen as redactional is confirmed. The chronological transposition of Gamaliel's advice to the period of Agrippa's persecution to which Roloff (1981, 101) resorts does not make the Lukan account any more credible.

Acts 6.1-7

I Division

6.1: Exposition: The problem of the neglect of the Hellenist widows
2-6: Solution of the conflict: The choice of the Seven
7: Summary and note about priests joining the community

II Redaction

A new section in Acts begins with chapter 6. 'The narrative is introduced by the report of the appointment of deacons in 6.1ff., which continues the description of the communistic organization of the community in 2.44f.; 4.32-5.11' (Meyer III, 154). The mission which had previously been limited to Jerusalem now (after the hints in 5.16) reaches out to the surrounding areas through the preaching of the Hellenists. The next section (6.1-8.3) centres on the person of Stephen, as does 8.4-40 on the figure of Philip. On the one hand Luke depicts their (and the Hellenists') understanding with the Jerusalem church leaders. On the other hand he cannot completely explain away a conflict which existed between the people of Jerusalem and the Hellenistic community (see III below).

[1] The introductory phrase 'in those days' is Lukan. This assumption is supported by the genitive absolute as the introduction to a new episode (cf. 4.1 etc.) and the parallels to the general indication of time (cf. Luke 2.1 etc.; Acts 11.27; 12.1; 19.23, etc). Verse 1 refers back to 4.35b. From 4.35 the reader knows that the apostles looked after the needs of individuals (cf. v.2).

Probably no basis for tradition comes through vv.1-2a (against Roloff 1981, 107, etc.). The reasons cited for this thesis ('disciples' as a designation of the community, 'the Twelve' instead of 'the apostles') are not convincing. So here Luke is probably talking of the Twelve instead of the apostles because he is going on to talk of the Seven. Granted, the expression 'disciples' is not used in the first five chapters of Acts, but after that it is very frequent (twenty-eight times). Moreover the expression from Mark is frequent in Luke. This criticism of Roloff does not mean that Luke is not reporting under the influence of tradition but that he is not following any source material in vv.1-2a. (For v.1b as an element of the tradition see 78 below.)

The conflict reported in v.1 is intrinsically plausible. Many pious Jews settled in Jerusalem in the evening of their lives in order to be buried in the holy city. Therefore the care of their widows was a problem which came up relatively frequently. Now Judaism in the first century knew two different ways of supporting the poor, *tamhuy* and *quppah*: 'The *tamhuy* was distributed daily among wandering paupers and consisted of food (bread, beans and fruits, with the prescribed cup of wine at Passover). The *quppah* was a weekly dole to the poor of the city and consisted of food and clothing' (Jeremias 1969, 131; cf. also Bill.II, 643-7 and esp. Krauss 1912, 68f.).

Seccombe 1978 disputes not only the historical weight of the evidence produced by Jeremias (MKet 13, 1-2; MPes 10,1; MShek 5, 6 [in my view Jeremias should also have cited MPeah 8,7]), but also the presence of an institution for care of the poor in

Jerusalem and in the Jewish Diaspora in the first century – this is probably a somewhat exaggerated assertion.

Jeremias observes: 'The daily distribution of aid (viz. in Acts 6) indicates the *tamhuy*, and the fact that local people (especially widows) were helped indicates the *quppah*' (ibid.).

Now first of all it should be stressed that there is some connection between the Jewish institution of aid for the poor and the care of the widows reported in Acts 6, however it may be explained, since the content of Acts 6 is a happening which took place in the first half of the first Christian century within a Jewish Christian group in Jerusalem. But in that case an explanation has to be found of the contradiction that a kind of welfare was practised for a local group of poor which elsewhere applied only to travellers in need.

Proposed solutions

Possibility 1: (put forward among others by Jeremias 1969, 131f.; Haenchen 1971, 261f.; Schneider 1980, 424; Roloff 1981, 109; Reicke 1957, 117-19): the Christians were no longer included in the Jewish community's care of the poor.

This theory is sometimes developed in detail in the following different ways:

(*a*) 'In the early period the community had probably not yet developed a similar concept which made possible longer-term welfare and security. That on each occasion people distributed the food that was available on a day-to-day basis without any great planning accords with the enthusiastic character of the sharing of goods' (Roloff 1981, 109).

(*b*) 'The "*daily* provision" coped with the lack of any more long-term welfare. People deliberately lived from hand to mouth, as Jesus had commanded them in the Lord's Prayer (Luke 11.3 = Matt.6.11) and in the prohibition against "concern for the morrow" (Matt.6.34)' (Hengel 1983a, 16).

(*c*) 'We will probably have to suppose that these widows of the "Hellenists" were overlooked, i.e. not paid attention to, in the distribution of community food to those in need. And there was probably no malicious intent here. The fact that these widows belonged to the "Hellenists" means, rather, that they belonged to a Jerusalem group of people which – in principle – was not included among the needy' (Schottroff and Stegemann 1978, 152).

Criticism: In criticism of the general thesis that the Christians were no longer included in the Jewish community's care of the poor it has to be said that there is nothing to indicate a separation of the Jerusalem church from the Jewish community in the earliest period. The fact that the primitive community remained in Jerusalem when the Hellenists fled also tells against this possibility.

75

The following individual points may also be made against the various detailed explanations of the theory above:

On (*a*): The reference to the sharing of goods does not apply, as this is clearly a redactional statement.

On (*b*): If one combines an observation on Jesus' prohibition about care with Acts 1, the question arises how only one particular group was negatively affected by it.

On (*c*): The presupposition that the widows of the Hellenists are not to be counted among the needy is hardly correct when put as generally as this, despite the fact that on average they were probably economically better off. (Moreover we are not told how the 'murmuring' arose. Redaction?)

Possibility 2: The conflict is a creation of Luke himself, who did not have any exact knowledge of Jewish welfare. Therefore the conflict over the feeding of the Hellenistic widows is completely redactional. Luke took the material for describing the conflict from vague knowledge of the Jewish welfare system (ignorance of Jewish customs is not an isolated matter in Luke-Acts – cf. Luke 2.22; Acts 9.1-2; 16.3; 21.26f.; 22.30). Provisionally I regard this explanation as the right one, and we shall see whether it holds up in the analysis which follows. (For the question why Luke describes a conflict between Hebrews and Hellenists here at all, see 78f. below.)

[2-6] Verse 2a seems to presuppose the constitution of the Lukan church. Two leading bodies stand over against each other, the leaders of the community – here the Twelve – and the full assembly. The leaders of the community summon the full assembly and make proposals to it (cf. Roloff 1981, 109). *(plereis) pneumatos kai sophias* in v.3 appears subsequently (v.10) as a description of Stephen. The description of the task of the Seven, to see to the care of the widows, uses a phrase which picks up the summaries in 2.45; 4.35. While it was said there that the apostles (!) distributed the resources of the earliest community *kathoti an tis chreian eichen*, from now on the Seven (and no longer the apostles) will see to this task (*tes chreias tautes*).

Schille 1983 differs: the phrase *diakonein trapezais* does not refer to material care but to cultic service at the eucharist (cf. also Neudorfer 1983, 92-4): 'With Did.11.9 (*trapeza* = eucharistic table) we may think of the eucharistic, in principle the cultic, function' (Schille 1983, 169). Against Schille, in Didache 11.9 *trapeza* does not mean the eucharistic table but the simple table from which one eats one's fill (see the context of Didache 11).

Verse 4 presupposes the Lukan conception that the Twelve were concerned with prayer and preaching the word (for both see 2.42; 4.29 – for the expression *diakonia tou logou* see Luke 1.2: the eye-witnesses as the servants of the Word = the twelve apostles). *proskarterein* appears 6 times in Acts, 10 times in the NT as a whole. Verse 5 refers back to v.2, and like that verse presupposes the constitution of Luke's church; the proposal made by the Twelve (= leaders of the community) meets with the assent of the mass of disciples (= full assembly). Luke may be responsible for the order of the list in v.5, which is probably from the tradition. He puts Stephen at its head, as he will be mentioned soon. It is not fortuitous that Philip occupies second place, as he will be the main figure fom 8.4 on. The proselyte Nicolaus occupies the last place. That may be tradition, but it is also redactional. In the latter case Luke would be showing that he knows about the difference between a proselyte and a (full) Jew. In v.6 the laying-on of hands is Lukan. It also appears in 13.3 (14.23), in the entrusting of someone with a special task (cf. I Tim.4.14).

[7] Verse 7a is a Lukan summary. The note about the growth of the word of God and the increase in the number of the disciples is a link back to v.1 ('...while the disciples were multiplying'; cf. 5.14 earlier). After indicating the numbers (2.41,47; 4.4) by the general statements mentioned, Luke stresses that the process of growth in the community continues constantly (cf. Lohfink 1975b, 52). In v.7b the report that many priests had joined the community indicates a further development, since previously only parts of the Jewish people had become Christians. This report makes it particularly clear that they are gathered fom all the people (cf. Lohfink, ibid.). 'Perhaps the note is meant to show that they adopted a new attitude to the temple or that the "Christian" attitude to the temple (cf. the charges against Stephen, 6.11, 13f.) could be reconciled with their service' (Schneider 1980, 430).

III Traditions

The bedrock tradition of this section is the list of the Seven in v.5. 'All the Seven have Greek names: this makes their "Hellenist" provenance clear: Stephen, Philip, Prochorus, Nicanor, Timon, Parmenas and Nicolaus' (Schneider 1980, 428; cf. ibid. on the individual names). The number seven is a sacred number (cf. Bauer 1979, 306), and was probably already part of the tradition. The reference back to this passage from Acts 21.8 (where Philip is called one of the Seven) need not tell against that. Possibly the number seven is meant to express the character of those named as leaders. In that case it would have a parallel in the seven members ('The Seven') of a city which was the local authority for Jewish communities (cf. Bill.II, 641). However, the number seven can also quite generally express the particular significance of the persons included in it; cf. just the seven wise men (Diogenes Laertius I, 40f. – on this see generally Lesky 1963, 180f. [sources and bibliography]). See also Conzelmann 1987, 45;

he refers to ancient councils (*septemviri*; *hoi hepta*). Cf. also Neudorfer 1983, 126-32 ('Survey of the various interpretations of the number Seven' [largely curiosities]).

Do other elements in 6.1-6 belong to the tradition in v.5? In my view that is also true of v.1b. For the dispute between the Hebrews and the Hellenists is introduced abruptly. In my view the list in v.5 and the *abrupt* introduction of Hebrews and Hellenists best suggest a written tradition, which reported a conflict between two groups in Jerusalem. (We shall have to go on to see whether this tradition also underlies vv.8ff.)

[7] For *hypekouon te pistei* cf. *hypakoe pisteos* (Rom.1.5). Here there is influence from Rom.1.5 or a tradition from the Pauline missionary sphere.

IV Historical

There is an almost universal consensus among scholars that the Hellenists are Greek-speaking Jews and the Hebrews Aramaic-speaking Jews of Jerusalem. However, this assumption *cannot* appeal to terminology (in Phil.3.5 and II Cor.11.22 'Hebrew' in no way denotes Aramaic-speaking Jews – the expression also appears in Greek and Latin inscriptions [cf.Bauer 1979, 213] – though in the Diaspora *hebraios* often refers to origin in Palestine and thus presupposes a knowlege of Aramaic as a first language; cf. Solin 1983, 649-51 [with bibliography]), but the theory above is probably based on the nearer and wider context of Acts 6. So the Seven, as has already been mentioned above, have Greek names (Acts 6.5) in contrast to the predominantly semitic names of the twelve apostles (only Andrew and Philip are the exceptions here). Furthermore 'the only word of a kindred root which Luke uses, the adjective *Hebrais*, can support "Hebrew" as being used predominantly in a linguistic sense. The adjective occurs exclusively in the phrase *te Hebraidi dialekto* (Acts 21.40; 22.2; 26.14)' (Schneider 1980, 407 n.10), cf. John 5.2; 19.13, 17, 20 (for the history of research see Neudorfer 1983, 219ff.). There was some controversy – if not over the care of widows (this is to be seen as a Lukan toning down of another conflict, see below) – between the two parties in Jerusalem in the early period of the primitive community, although no further information about the nature of the conflict is available on the basis of the tradition contained in vv.1-6. But should there be a genetic connection between the elements of tradition in the present section and those underlying Acts 6.8-7.1, one could make a reasoned guess at the occasion for the conflict: Aramaic-speaking Christians who were strict observers of the law fell out with Greek-speaking Christians over the question of the law, and the language barrier added a further element to

78

the dispute. This dispute took place in the early period of the primitive community in Jerusalem, since Paul was already persecuting members of this group of Hellenists outside Jerusalem and no longer found them in Jerusalem during his first visit (cf. also on 118f. below). Acts 9.29 differs.

E.Schwartz's thesis that 'the Seven' is a title like 'the Twelve' is an attractive one. He thinks that they were a council in the earliest community like the latter: 'what the Twelve were for Israel the Seven were to be for the proselytes. They did not carry on a mission only to their Jewish "fellow countrymen", and would not have been numerous enough for that: according to I Cor.15.7 the number of missionaries who had been legitimated by the risen Lord himself must have been very much greater, even before Paul's conversion. But it may be supposed that the institution of the Seven arose out of the mission, which made progress among the proselytes and soon required a central authority alongside the Twelve, which had had to find a place in this development' (1963, 146f.; similarly Wellhausen 1911, 11; Meyer III, 155). Schwartz's theory is possible, but it cannot be verified on the sole basis of Acts 6.1-7, since 'the Twelve' in this passage probably also derives from Luke (see 74 above).

For further details about the criticism of the law and the person of Stephen, a member of the group of Hellenists, see on 6.8ff.

Acts 6.8-15

I Division

6.8: Summary description of the miracles of Stephen among the people
9-14: Two charges against Stephen
   9-10: The unsuccessful attack by the members of the Hellenist (synagogue) communities through disputations
   11-14: The attack by false witness, its impact on the people, the elders and the scribes and the proceedings before the Sanhedrin
15: Description of Stephen's face

II Redaction

[8] The language of this verse is Lukan; cf. *pleres, charitos, dynameos, terata kai semeia... en to lao* (see 5.12). This last combination of words also makes it clear that Stephen's activity corresponds to that of the apostles. At the same time v.8 is a transition to the following episode. 'Stephen is not depicted "serving tables" but in public, nor in "serving

the word", but being effective through miracles; only in v.11 is his proclamation of the word mentioned, and then *indirectly*' (Weiser 1981, 171).

[9-14] Verse 9 is a kind of prelude to the conflict which follows and which ends in Stephen's death. 'Stephen's adversaries will hardly have taken offence at his miracles (v.8). The presumption is that Stephen carried out a mission among them in Jerusalem' (Schneider 1980, 436). The designation of Stephen's opponents is unclear. Does *synagoge* here mean 'community', 'synagogue', or both? Furthermore are one, two, three, four or five synagogues mentioned here?

Cf. the history of research in Neudorfer 1983, 158-63; for his own solution see 266-9: Luke 'had no exact knowledge about their interconnections in Jerusalem... and therefore gave only a vague report' (269).

Now the repeated article *ton* after *tines* divides the members listed into two groups (cf. Schneider 1980, 435 n.19). Certainly Luke's text, strictly speaking, makes only the first three synagogue members, and not the rest (cf.24.19), but this only confirms the remark made above about the obscurity of the text, and Luke seems only to have been concerned with a global opposition to Stephen on the part of the circle of Hellenistic Jews. That explains his vague mode of expression. The tension between an obscure form of expression and the wealth of precise information indicates tradition. (For the question whether *synagoge* means community and/or synagogue see below on III and IV.) The attempt of the Hellenistic Jews to defeat Stephen with arguments comes to grief on the wisdom and the spirit in which he speaks. As early as 6.3 'wisdom' and 'spirit' are characteristics of the seven Hellenists among whom Stephen belongs. This make it clear that in v.10 Luke is referring back to v.3, and this links the two pericopes vv.1-7 and vv.8-15 together.

For the content cf. also Luke 21.15 (which differs from Mark, Matthew): 'For I will give you a mouth and wisdom (*sophia*), which none of your adversaries will be able to withstand (*antistenai*) or contradict!'

The parallels between Luke 21.15 and Acts 6.10 show that Luke sees the statement of Luke 21.15 realized in the trial of Stephen. However, this does not rule out the possibility that Luke has taken both terms (*sophia, pneuma*) from a tradition which is genetically connected with Stephen, though their tone is redactional. After the failure of the first attack against Stephen, v.11 introduces a second. Its authors, the members of the Hellenist (synagogue) communities mentioned in v.10, make use of underhand means because otherwise they would not have been able to get at Stephen. They induce men to say: 'We have heard him speak blasphemies against Moses and God' (for the history of research into the

80

accusation cf. Neudorfer 1983, 172-182). Verse 12 describes the success of their action. Even the people, which hitherto was on the side of the Christians (cf. also v.8), is influenced, as – less amazingly – are the elders and scribes, who had already been involved in actions against the earliest community in Jerusalem (Acts 4; 5). The hearing before the Supreme Council heightens the drama in the narrative, as now the official Jewish authorities are taking note of events. As in the first accusation (v.11), witnesses are produced who are said to have/heard Stephen make certain statements. Verse 13 says explicitly that the witnesses were false (*martyras pseudeis*), whereas in v.11 they were still described neutrally as 'men' (*andres*). However, in v.11 doubt was cast in advance on what they said by Luke's narrative, which spoke of incitement (to testify: *hypoballein*). According to Luke, the statement made by the men/false witnesses is therefore wrong in both cases. In terms of content the accusation in v.13 is not completely identical with that in v.11. Verse 11 speaks of blasphemy against Moses and God, whereas v.13 speaks of attacks on the holy place (= temple) and the law.

It has occasionally become customary for scholars to say that vv.13f. are redactional (cf. most recently Weiser 1981, 171-3), thus giving the impression that the focus of Luke's interest lies in what is said in vv.13f., especially as the subsequent speech by Stephen (which is redactional) develops the theme of the temple, which is addressed in vv.13f. (cf. 7.48-50). The frequently made observation that v.14a is formulated on the basis of Mark 14.58 helps us to grasp Luke's intention. Cf. Mark 14.58: 'We heard (Jesus) say, "I will destroy this temple that is made with hands (and in three days I will build another, not made with hands)."' A further reason for assuming a genetic relationship between v.13 and Mark 14.58b is provided by the observation that both in v.13 and in the immediate context of the Mark passage false witnesses appear (Mark 14.56 : 'For many bore false witness [*epseudomartyroun*] against him'). If there is a genetic connection between Mark 14.58 and v.13, it is important to note that Luke did not take up the second part of the false witness in Mark 14.58 ('and in three days I will build another, not made with hands'), but replaced it with the statement 'and will change the customs which Moses delivered to us'. Luke is probably deliberately avoiding any statement about the rebuilding of the temple, as he is writing after its destruction. The remark about changing the customs of Moses is a way of making the words against the law at the end of v.13 more specific. *ethe* (ten of the twelve instances in the NT come from Luke-Acts, and seven from Acts) in Luke relates to individual commandments (thus Acts 15.1 to circumcision and 16.21; 21.21; 26.3; 28.17 to the Jewish law generally – similarly Luke 1.9; 2.42). Stephen's speech as written by Luke gives the lie to this criticism (or rejection) of the law. For in it (7.53) Stephen accuses *his opponents* of not observing the *torah*, from which it emerges that *he* observes it.

Criticism

First of all it must be said quite positively that in Acts there is a genetic connection between Jesus' saying about the temple in Mark 14.58 (which is from tradition) and Acts 6.14b. But an explanation in terms of redaction criticism cannot really explain why Stephen's remarks in Acts 6.13 are presented as false witness. If the explanation given above is correct, one would have to assume that Luke connected the accusations in vv.13f. with Stephen *and* at the same time declared them to be false witness about Stephen. This latter course seems to me to be possible only if Luke had a tradition rooted in Stephen, the content of which corresponded to the position behind Acts 6.(11,) 13f. Why should Luke attribute to Stephen what he dissociates from Jesus in the Gospel? (There is certainly *no* parallel here.)

The difficulty over the redactional-critical explanation of vv.13f. to which I have just drawn attention leads to the assumption that in basic content the verses are part of the tradition. *Luke* represented the criticism of the law which becomes evident in them as false witness. For him Stephen's criticism of the law was too radical.

Similarly Walter 1983: 'That in 6.13 Luke is handing down a tradition which in truth is historically accurate, precisely because the points in the charge against Stephen reported there indicate too revolutionary an attitude' (371). Cf. similarly Wellhausen 1907: 'The link between Stephen and Jesus's radical saying about the destruction of the temple and the cult, which while it is not formal is nevertheless clear (6.13; 7.47-50), cannot have been invented by Luke, as he does not want to have anything to do with blasphemy against the temple by Jesus in the Gospel. So Stephen opens up a wound which the earliest disciples would have liked to see healed' (12).

Closely connected with this, the conception of the unity of the Jerusalem community *a priori* prohibits Luke from allowing any criticism of the temple and the law. Therefore the basic elements of vv.11, 13f. may go back to tradition, and not be redactional.

[15] The language suggests that this derives from Luke: *atenisantes; synedrio; hosei.*

III Traditions

An element of tradition appears in the designation of those with whom Stephen has a disputation in v.9: 'People from the so-called synagogue of the Libertines and of the Cyrenians and of the Alexandrians and of the inhabitants of Cilicia and Asia Minor.' Here first of all answers must be given to the two questions raised under II above: 1. the meaning of *synagoge* (= community and/or synagogue) and 2. the number of the communities/synagogues.

1. *synagoge* should be translated 'synagogue community', as in one case the existence of national synagogue communities can be demonstrated by archaeology. A Greek inscription found in Jerusalem shortly before the First World War indicated, among other things, that the synagogue had been built by the priest and synagogue president Theodotus, son of Vettenus, and that a guest house and water supply for pilgrims had been connected with it. Perhaps this inscription is a reference to the Libertini (a Latin loan word, which denotes freed Jews) mentioned in 6.9. The father of Theodotus has a Roman name, Vettenus, which he may have adopted after being freed, because he owed his freedom to a Roman member of the *gens Vettena*. In that case his family may have belonged to the synagogue of the Libertini in Jerusalem (for the inscription see further Deissmann 1927, 438-41 [picture, text, translation and commentary]; Hengel 1983a, 17f.: Cadbury 1955, 88f.).

Bihler 1963 objects to the conclusions drawn above: 'What does the name *libertinos* mean? Have we to understand it to mean freemen? Since Schürer put forward this view and tried to defend it, this interpretation seems to have become commonplace. But it completely fails to explain what connects the "Freedmen" with the Alexandrians and Cyrenians, as in 6.9 they are evidently thought to belong to the same group. We should not overlook the fact that a synagogue is being talked about here. Even if Luke took over this designation, that does not mean that he must have used it in the original sense. He may have used this expression as an assumed name. One can hardly say more or be more precise' (212). Bihler falls into the error of mixing redaction and tradition (see 80 above).

So there are good reasons for assuming that 6.9 reflects the tradition that there were one or more such synagogue communities in Jerusalem (cf. also Acts 24.12). In Rome there is evidence of at least eleven such synagogues (Leon 1960, 135-66).

On 2. I said above under II that by the repeated article *ton* after *tines* Luke is suggesting that the members listed are two groups. So between one and five synagogues may have been mentioned in the tradition as Luke had it.

In v.10 Stephen is portrayed as a preacher, in other words quite differently from what might have been expected from the share of work assigned to him in 6.2, which distinguishes him from the apostles. If one follows Luke's account through, one might even ask whether the daily care for the widows could have improved at all under such conditions (cf. Walter 1983, 370). It follows from this that the understanding of Stephen in v.10 is quite different from that in vv.1-7. Therefore despite the Lukan peculiarities of language indicated above, this verse will derive from tradition. Verse 11 reflects elements of Stephen's preaching at the stage of tradition, as will vv.13f., since the redaction-critical explanation cannot give a conclusive explanation of the theme of the false witnesses, etc. Rather, with this motive Luke domesticates Stephen's criticism of the law and interprets it by individual features in Stephen's speech (cf. esp.7.53).

Wellhausen 1914 notes a tension between v.11 and vv.12f.: 'An attempt is made to find room for v.11 alongside vv.12,13 by saying that this talks of men who were urged to stir up *the people*, whereas here they are witnesses before *the Sanhedrin*. However, there is no difference; the men in v.11 are witnesses (accusers) and are thought to be before the Sanhedrin. So v.11 anticipates the content of vv.13, 14 and is inconsistent with it. In v.12 the elders and scribes are distinguished from the Sanhedrin, and similarly in 5.21. The witnesses are called lying witnesses in 14, after Mark 14.57; in 11 that is avoided, and the accusation also reads differently' (12). Jackson/Lake argue similarly in *Beg.* II, 148f.: they claim that vv.9-11 and 12-14 are doublets which would be continued in 7.54-58 and 7.58-60 respectively (see further below). However, there are hardly adequate criteria for such a division of sources.

On the question whether the tradition underlying vv.8-16 was an element of a traditional report of Stephen's martyrdom see below, 93.

IV Historical

Stephen was not a deacon (v.8) but a preacher filled with the spirit (cf. most recently Dietzfelbinger 1985, 16-20).

The tradition of the presence in Jerusalem of the groups named in v.9 has a good deal to be said for it historically. At that time Jerusalem was a prized dwelling place for the (Hellenist) Jews of the Diaspora. As an example of the presence of Diaspora Jews in Jerusalem see Simon of Cyrene and his two sons Alexander and Rufus (Mark 15.21 par.: see the important literature on Cyrene in G.Schneider, *EWNT* II, 810f.). The existence of Jews from Cilicia in Jerusalem is illustrated by Paul's sister (Acts 23.16).

However, it is not certain whether all the different national groups were organized into synagogue communities, however much the probability of the existence of a synagogue of the Libertines has been increased by the historical support of the Theodotus inscription. (Moreover it is the earliest evidence for a synagogue in Judaea, see Cohen 1984, 152.) I would want to draw analogies from that for the other communities.

It is historically improbable that all the Hellenistic Jews mentioned in v.9 were involved in the disputation with Stephen, as Luke suggests on the redactional level. Rather, the dispute will have arisen in one Hellenistic synagogue community to which Stephen belonged (for a similar possibility in Rome see Lüdemann 1984, 188 n.68). The issue was Stephen's critical view of the law, to which his opponents took offence. This dispute was initially verbal and then became physical. How remote Luke already is from the historical Stephen is evident from the fact that he presents the information about Stephen's criticism of the law as untrue. We may assume that Stephen combined faith in Christ with an understanding of the law in a way that was unacceptable to the members of the Hellenistic synaogue. At any rate it was regarded as blasphemous, and led to the action hinted at in v.12 and described in vv.57f. (for these verses see 91f. below). Stephen's view of the law led not only to a fateful dispute in the Hellenistic synagogues (or a Hellenistic synagogue) but also, as Acts 6.1f. depicts indirectly, to a split in early Christianity. We may also say that another consequence of the dispute was a partial separation of Judaism and Christianity in Jerusalem, as the Hellenists were expelled from the capital (see 93f.).

Stephen's understanding of the law

According to Acts 6.11 Stephen spoke against Moses and God, i.e. he criticized the law. Furthermore according to 6.14 he criticized the temple and the law with reference to Jesus. I said on p. 82 above that Luke could hardly have both connected the criticism of the law with Stephen in vv.11, 13f. and at the same time described the testimony about it as false witness. Rather, the tradition about Stephen which is twice presented by Luke as false witness has a historical basis. 'The formula that Jesus *will change* the customs handed down by Moses does not suggest total abrogation of the law. Regardless of what the difficult future tense may mean here, we must cautiously conclude that Stephen criticized the law and the temple, starting from Jesus. Perhaps like Jesus he announced the destruction of the temple and criticized at least points of the law in the light of God's eschatological will' (Luz 1981, 88). Others go further and think that Stephen and the Hellenists 'declared that the law was abolished in principle' (G.Klein, *TRE* X, 1982, 81). However, such a theory cannot be put forward conclusively on the basis of the tradition(s) in vv.11, 13f., and despite the pogrom, the expulsion from Jerusalem, the Gentile mission carried on by the Hellenists who were driven out of Jerusalem (see below 136, on 11.20) and the persecution of Hellenistic communities by Paul, it is only a remote possibility.

Acts 7.(1,)2-53

I Division

(7.1: Transition to the speech)
2-38: The history of Israel from Abraham to Moses
    2-8a: The Abraham story
    8b: Transitional note: from Isaac to the twelve patriarchs
    9-16: The Joseph story
    17-38: The Moses story
39-50: Israel's apostasy: idolatry and building of the temple
    39-43: Idolatry
    44-50: Building of the temple
        44-47: The tent of meeting and the building of the temple for the house of Jacob
        48-50: Polemic against the view that God dwells in the temple
51-53: The guilt of Israel (Deuteronomistic polemic against the audience)

II Redaction

In what follows I shall identify only the clearly redactional features (for detailed analysis see the commentaries; for v.1 see 89 below).

[2-38] Verse 2a is Lukan; the beginning of the speech corresponds word for word with the beginning of Paul's speech in 22.1. In vv.2-4, against the biblical account (Gen.11.28-12.1), it is stressed that God appeared to Abraham before he came to Haran, in Mesopotamia. Then v.4 tells how Abraham left Chaldaea to dwell in Haran. But Mesopotamia is on the way fom Chaldaea to Haran. Either the author has confused the geography, or there are signs here of the influences of different traditions. Moreover it is striking that repeatedly changes of place or place details are stressed: cf. 'in Mesopotamia, before he dwelt in Haran' (v.2) and the whole of v.4. The end of v.4 (*eis ten gen... katoikeite*) is redactional because it refers to Stephen's hearers. The end of v.5, *ouk ontos auto teknou*, certainly derives from the author. This is suggested by the genitive absolute, *eimi* + dative and the classical negative *ou* in the participle instead of *me* (see Storch 1967, 26 n.9). In v.7c *oro* (LXX) is changed by the redactor to *topo*, probably to focus the report on the theme of the temple. For the story of Abraham in vv.2-8a cf. the summary in Bihler, 1963, 38-46.

Verse 8b confirms that Joseph, who is to be discussed next, is a descendant of Abraham.

Redactional narrative elements in vv.9-16 are the two sets of sentences divided by *kai* which stand at the beginning and the end of this section. Because they diverge from the biblical passage, v.10a, the rescue from all tribulations, and v.10b, the gift of wisdom to Joseph, are probably redactional. 'Our fathers' in vv.11f. focusses on the audience. 'Abraham' in v.16 refers back to vv.2-8a, cf. similarly v.17.

The account of the life and activity of Moses in vv.17-38 is divided into three sections each of forty years (cf. vv.23,30,36), which makes it very schematic. This is the work of Luke, who has got the three periods from Deut.34.7 (Moses was 120 years old at his death). Verses 20-23 contain a tripartite scheme which the author of Acts also uses with Paul in 22.13. The description of Moses, 'He was mighty in words and deeds', certainly goes against Exod.4.10, but exactly matches the description of Jesus in Luke 24.19: Jesus was 'a man, a prophet, mighty in deed and word before God and before the whole people'. At this point there is a Moses-Jesus typology which derives from Luke and has a parallel in 7.35f., which is also redactional. In v.25 content and vocabulary suggest Lukan authorship. What Luke says here of Moses he stresses elsewhere with reference to Jesus. The Jews did not recognize that God wanted to create salvation for them through Jesus (cf. 3.17: 4.10-12; Weiser 1981, 175 – see what is said on vv.20ff.). The Moses-Jesus typology which is already visible in vv.20-23 is again expressed in *archonta* (of Moses, v.35), cf. *archegos* (of Jesus) in Acts 3.15; 5.31; for *lytroten* (of Moses) cf. *mellon lytrousthai Israel* (of Jesus), Luke 24.21. The twice emphasized *touton* is picked up by the triple *houtos* in vv.36-38. The latter echoes the form of the encomium (cf.Norden 1913, 164f., 222ff.). Moses did miracles before the people (v.36) like Jesus and the apostles (5.12: see what is said above on the Moses-Jesus typology). In v.37 Deut.18.15 is used in a christological argument from scripture (as it is already in Acts 3.22).

[39-50] For *hoi pateres hemon* in v.39 see vv.11,12,15(,19),44,45. Verses 39-41 cite the story of the golden calf as an example of the Israelites' idolatry (the first). In vv.42f. the statements about idolatry are further intensified. God gave the Israelites over to the worship of the host of heaven as punishment for their worship of the golden calf, as Amos 5.25-27 (LXX) shows (Luke alters 'Damascus' to Babylon in the quotation and thus adapts the prophetic forecast to what really happened [the Babylonian exile]).

The language of the whole section vv.44-50 is strongly influenced by Luke (cf. the details indicated by Storch 1967, 98-100). *skene (tou martyriou)* in v.44 picks up *skenen (tou Moloch)* in v.43 by the use of a key word. The strange feature of this verse is that on their wandering in the wilderness the Israelites took a second tent with them (in addition to the tent of Moloch, v.42), the *skene tou martryriou*. Conzelmann 1987,

55, and others see this as the result of using sources. By contrast, Roloff (1981) argues: 'Whereas v.43 was about the cult which was actually practised by Israel in the wilderness, v.44 speaks about the divine claim on Israel in respect of the cult. Israel brought along the tent at the settlement and had it constantly up to the time of David...' (124). *skenoma* in v.46 recalls *skene* (vv.43, 44). On text-critical grounds we should probably read *to oiko Iakob* (instead of *to theo Iakob*: for the reason see Storch 1967, 94f.). This stresses that the temple is built for the house of Jacob. This statement is far from making any criticism of the temple.

On the presupposition that Luke shaped Stephen's speech we would not have expected any criticism of the temple, as Luke connects early Christianity closely with the temple. Cf. Luke 2.21-39; 2.41-51. 'Jesus is deliberately portrayed as the redeemer of Israel who gathers his holy people, begins his activity in the holy city of Jerusalem in the temple (Luke 2.41f.; 4.9ff.), and ends it again there' (Luz 1981, 131). The earliest community meets in the temple for prayer (Luke 24.53; Acts 2.46; 5.42). During his last visit to Jerusalem Paul takes part in a ceremony in the temple (Acts 21.26f.). 'So Luke could not have depicted the temple as a product of apostasy if he tells his readers all this about the temple. Jesus could not have spent decisive periods of his ministry in the "house of idols"' (Storch 1967, 102).

Verses 48-50 are polemic against the view that God dwells in the temple built for the house of Jacob (cf.17.24). In this way Luke gives a reason why Gentile Christians are independent of the temple (cf. Storch 1967, 103).

[51-53] These verses indicate Israel's guilt and bring the speech to a climax with the accusation. (The call to repentance which features in the other mission sermons in Acts is missing from Stephen's speech.) The whole history of Israel was characterized by rebellion against the will of God: 'You always rebelled against the Holy Spirit, like your fathers before you' (51). In other words, the guilt of the Jews, culminating in the murder of the righteous one (v.25), has 'a prehistory in the behaviour of their fathers. But the speaker cannot stress all this too strongly without at the same time distancing himself from this conduct. Now he speaks of "your fathers" and "you" whereas in vv.2-50 he usually spoke of "our fathers"' (Bihler 1963, 77). At the same time the behaviour of the Jews was a failure to observe the law which they had received through the instruction(s) of angels (v.53 – cf. Gal.3.19), i.e. the law comes from God. Cf. already similarly v.38: Moses received 'living words' on Sinai. The covenant of circumcision (v.8a) as an assurance of the promise has been broken (*ouk ephylaxate*) by the repudiation of Moses, whose appearance brought the fulfilment of the promise (v.17).

Retrospect on the redactional shaping of Stephen's speech

Stephen's speech, the longest sermon in Acts, stands at a turning point in Acts. Through the mouth of the first Christian martyr, Luke tells his readers that on the one hand Christianity is rooted in the Old Testament ('*our* fathers') but that on the other the Jewish authority condemned by Stephen, which has always resisted the Holy Spirit (v.51), has parted company with the Christian community. In this way Luke is preparing at the narrative level for the separation of Jews and Christians, which had not yet taken place in the first five chapters of Acts.

Individual themes of the speech are related by Luke to the accusation, for example the assertion that the Jews had not observed the law although it was willed by God (vv.38, 53) or the statement that Solomon had built a temple for Jacob (!) (v.47). With both these remarks Luke shows the falsity of the charges made against Stephen that he had preached against the law and the temple (6.11, 13f.). (Cf. the redactional transition in v.1.)

But Luke also uses Stephen's speech to describe his view of the true place of piety, which is justified at length elsewhere (Acts 17.22-31). By limiting the validity of the temple to the Jews, Stephen's speech at the same time serves to elaborate and give further justification for his distinctive theory of salvation history.

There is probably no single conception behind Stephen's speech. At best one could see vv.2-38 as a unity, following the pattern 'promise – oppression in Egypt – fulfilment by Moses'; here the story of the idolatry of Israel (vv.39-43) would follow closely on the Moses story (vv.20-38). Verses 44-50 cannot be connected directly with vv.39-43, while vv.51-53, unlike the preceding verses, relate to the accusation. I shall not discuss here whether there was a basis for all Stephen's speech in the tradition. However, as further analogies for outlines of history reference should be made to the following passages, parts of which at least Luke knew: Deut.6.20-34; 26.5-9; Josh.24.2-13; Neh.9.6-31; Judith 5.6-18; I Macc.2.52-60; Ps.78; 105; 106; 136; Wisdom 10; Sirach 44-50; III Macc.2.2-12; IV Ezra 3.4-36.

For the reasons given above there are no sections III and IV.

Acts 7.54-8.3

I Division

7.54-8.1a: Stephen's martyrdom
   54: The Sanhedrin's reaction to Stephen's speech
   55-56: Stephen's vision
   57-60: The stoning of Stephen
      57-58a: The Sanhedrin's reaction to Stephen's vision: the stoning
      58b: The behaviour of the witnesses: they lay down their garments before Saul
      59-60: The stoning of Stephen and his behaviour
   8.1a: Saul's joy at the killing of Stephen
1b-3: The persecution of the Jerusalem church
   1b: The expulsion of all but the apostles
   2: The burial of Stephen
   3: The persecution of the church by Saul

II Redaction

[**7.54-8.1a**] *akouontes de... dieprionto* corresponds to 5.33. *kardiais* is perhaps a resumption of v.51. As Stephen's hearers are uncircumcised in hearts and ears, they become angry in their hearts (v.54) and in v.57 stop up their ears. That illustrates Stephen's charge against his audience on the author-reader level, and this is all the more probable when in v.55 they have been given the answer about the true place of God (see what follows).

The language in vv.55-56 is Lukan: *hyparchon, pleres pneumatos hagiou, atenisas eis ton ouranon* (cf.1.10), *doxan, ek dexion tou theou*. The report of the vision in v.55 and the announcement of the vision in v.56 may have been shaped by Luke, since the verses seem to be dependent on Luke 22.69 ('from now on the Son of Man will sit at the right hand of the power of God'). Here in this sentence from his account of the passion Luke has omitted the statement 'you will see' from Mark 14.62, because he wanted to express the fact that the vision of the exalted Christ was not granted to the opponents, but to the believing witness. Luke now demonstrates this with Stephen in Acts 7.55. Finally, the remarks about the 'opened heaven', the 'glory of God' and 'Jesus at the right hand of God' are very closely connected with the preceding Lukan verses 48-50; they give the answer to the question of the true place of God.

Verse 57 contains elements of Lukan language: 'they cried with a loud voice' (cf. v.60); 'they rushed together upon him' (cf. 19.29 and the way in which Luke constructs riot scenes in the Sanhedrin [cf. 5.33; 23.7-10; see also Luke 4.28f.]). Here v.58a is in accordance with Jewish legal ordinances (cf. Lev.24.14; Num.15.35; MSanh 6.1), according to which the stoning had to take place outside the 'camp'. Similarly, the stoning of Stephen may not take place in Jerusalem. First, therefore, he has to be dragged out of the city.

The observation in v.58b that the witnesses lay down their garments at the feet of the young man Saul serves to link the martyrdom of Stephen with the story of Paul which follows. In this way the great missionary first appears on the scene as a bystander. 'That the witnesses lay down their clothes (as at some sports event) is presumably the result of a Lukan misunderstanding' (Schille 1983, 189). The Jewish legal ordinance (MSanh 6.3) which Luke probably wanted to weave in here called for the condemned person to be stripped.

Verse 59a resumes the thread of the narrative which was interrupted by v.58a – as is visible from the repetition of *elithoboloun*.

Against Wellhausen 1914: 'Verse 58 cannot remain behind v.59 because a stoning cannot take place twice and may not be reported twice' (14). But *elithoboloun* is repeated because the note about Paul is between the two occurrences.

The report of the death of Stephen in v.59b is strikingly close to the Lukan narrative of Jesus' death and is therefore also redactional. According to Luke 23.46 Jesus' last word is 'Father, into your hands I commend my spirit.' This corresponds almost word for word with Ps.30.6 (LXX), a passage which in Judaism was used as an evening prayer. In contrast to Luke 23.46, Stephen's exclamation ('Lord Jesus, receive my spirit') is addressed to Jesus, whom he has seen as the exalted Lord. The introductory phrase *theis de ta gonata* in v.60 is Lukan in language and content; cf. Luke 22.42: in Gethsemane Jesus falls on his knees (Mark differs). In this way Luke may have drawn a further parallel between the martyrdom of Stephen and that of Jesus. The calling out with a loud voice again recalls the passion of Jesus (Luke 23.46). At the same time the petition 'Reckon not this sin to their charge' is close to Jesus' saying: 'Father, forgive them, for they know not what they do' (Luke 23.34 – but perhaps text-critically this verse is secondary).

Verse 8.1a goes back to Luke, who wants Saul to be involved in the execution (cf. also the climax to the remark in v.58, where Saul functions as a guard for the clothes: in v.1a he is already delighted at the killing of Stephen, and then 8.3 depicts him as an active persecutor).

[8.1b-3] *pantes* in v.1b is a Lukan generalization. The account of the burial of the martyr in v.2 is often taken as an element of a tradition (cf. only Schneider 1980, 257f.; Roloff 1981, 130, thinks that at the level of the tradition the 'godfearing men' would have been members of the Aramaic-speaking community, but Luke thought in terms of pious Jews;

cf. finally Schille 1983, 198; see also Neudorfer 1983, 212-15: excursus 'The Burial of Stephen'). At least *eulabes* is Lukan; it denotes Symeon (Luke 2.25) and Ananias (Acts 22.12). Furthermore the report of a burial of Stephen hardly fits with the expulsion of the Hellenists from Jerusalem. Cf. also the redactional portrait of Joseph, who buries Jesus, as *agathos kai dikaios* (Luke 23.50f. [Mark 15.43 differs]). In v.3 *eisporeuomenos, andras kai gynaikas* reflect Lukan traces. The verse takes up 8.1a (which is redactional) and heightens the statement made there. At the same time it prepares for the story of the conversion of Saul, which is told later (cf. the way in which 8.3 is picked up in 9.1-2).

III Traditions

The analysis of the redaction showed that Luke tried to make the trial and execution of Stephen an orderly procedure carried out by the Supreme Council (cf. 6.12b-14; 7.1; 7.58b). In so doing he made the mistake of describing the stoning as different from what was customary in Jewish legal ordinances (see above on v.58b). If we begin from the presupposition that Stephen was killed in Jerusalem, it is probable that the account of a riot over Stephen has a basis in tradition, and that as a consequence of this he fell a victim to lynch law. On this presupposition we must assume that the tradition has been completely overlaid by Lukan language and shaping, particularly in the scene of the riot in v.57. Stoning remains possible as the manner of his death, as lynch law often made use of it (cf. Philo, *Spec* 1, 54-57). Cf. the summary judgment of Wellhausen:

'There is no sentence, and Stephen is stoned without a verdict. The stoning is an act of popular justice... There is no sign of the Sanhedrin. It could not carry out capital sentences, only the Roman occupying forces could, and there is no mention of them anywhere in the first part of Acts – this needs to be stressed. So Baur is right in asserting that Stephen fell victim to a riot and that there was no legal proceeding against him' (Wellhausen 1914, 14; the remark in Baur to which he refers is 1845, 54; cf. most recently Neudorfer 1983, 186-96).

The report that supporters of Stephen had to leave Jerusalem following his martyrdom was probably also part of this tradition.

On the question of a genetic connection between the tradition which became visible behind vv.54ff. and 6.8-7.1

In support of an original connection is the fact that in v.54 there is no further mention of the name 'Stephen'. Otherwise a mention would have been expected after the long speech. This therefore supports the assumption that underlying Acts 6-7 is a tradition according to which the criticism of temple and law by Stephen and the Hellenists caused a popular uprising in which Stephen suffered martyrdom and as a result his followers had to leave Jerusalem (cf. already Meyer III, 158, and especially Burchard 1970, 26-31).

If the theory that there is a connection between the traditions contained in 6.8-7.1 and 7.54ff. is correct, a further assumption is at least possible, that the tradition lying behind 6.1-7 belongs to the block of tradition that has just been discovered and probably introduced it. Similarly Walter 1983: the tradition in 6.1ff. would fit as the introduction to the Stephen tradition: 'At all events the Stephen narrative might well have been preceded by a report about the beginnings of the group on which he made such a mark' (372). The objection to such a theory, that seven Hellenists are mentioned in vv.1-6 and afterwards only one, carries some weight, but is probably not enough to put it seriously in question.

IV Historical

E. Zeller 1854 succinctly summed up the historical elements in the tradition of Acts 6-7: 'The death of Stephen is beyond dispute the clearest point in the history of Christianity before Paul. With this event we first find ourselves on undeniably historical ground. Evidence for that would already be the one decisive fact which was occasioned by the persecution of Stephen, namely the conversion of Paul, if any further proof were needed of the fact of an event which according to all sides had such a visible effect on the development of the Christian cause' (146). As I explained in more detail earlier, Stephen's criticism of law and cult are to be regarded as historical. The expulsion of those of like mind from Jerusalem is the best reason for such an assumption. For the circumstances of Stephen's death see the remarks by Wellhausen quoted on 92 above.

Acts 8.4-25

I Division

8.4: Generalized note about the travel and preaching of the expelled Hellenists
5-8: The success of Philip's preaching in Samaria
9-13: Simon Magus is bested by Philip

II Redaction

[4] This verse is a Lukan transitional note which is a close parallel to 11.19: cf. *hoi men oun diasparentes dielthon euaggelizomenoi ton logon* (v.4) with *hoi men oun diasparentes apo tes thlipseos tes genomenes epi Stephano dielthon... lalountes ton logon...* (for the question whether we can argue from this to the use of a Hellenist source cf. on 11.19). *men oun* appears frequently in Luke; *diasparentes* takes up the *diesparesan* of v.1. Moreover the verb *diaspeiro* occurs only in these two passages anywhere in the New Testament. The phrase 'proclaim the word' is redactional (cf. 15.35) and should be compared with other Lukan expressions for preaching (cf. Conzelmann 1960, 218-24).

[5-8] These verses are a summary account of Philip's preaching success in Samaria. The language of the section shows Luke's influence: v.5, *katelthon, ekeryssen... ton Christon* (cf. 9.20; 19.13, both times with Jesus as object). It cannot be demonstrated by vocabulary statistics that *proseichon* in v.6 is redactional, but that is probably the case because it is used again in vv.10, 11; *homothymadon* and *en to* + infinitive (cf. Radl 1975, 433) are Lukan; *semeia* is taken up again in v.13. The threefold use of forms of the adjective *polys* (twice in v.7 and once in v.8) is part of Luke's narrative technique which in this way stresses the magnitude of the success. *paralelymenos* (= lame) occurs in the NT only in Luke (twice in the Gospel and twice in Acts); the verb occurs in the NT at Heb.12.12. *chara* in v.8 is a favourite Lukan word (cf. Harnack 1908, 207-10). In content vv.5-8 serve to prepare for what follows and the section is an exposition of it (see the way in which *prosecho* and *semeia* are picked up in vv.9-13).

[9-13] The first sub-section (vv.9-11) refers to the time before Philip's arrival and depicts the prehistory of Simon's activity in Samaria, which we need to know in order to understand what comes next. Luke's redactional hand is more than clear in language and style.

aner de tis onomati (v.9) as elsewhere in Luke introduces a person by name (cf. Luke 10.38; 16.20; Acts 5.1; 9.10, 36; 10.1, etc. – cf. Schneider

1980, 489). *proyparcho* occurs in the NT only at Luke 23.12. The verb *existano* appears in this section only in vv.11, 13. It is as Lukan (cf. Jeremias 1980, 101 [cf. Luke 2.47]) as is the word-play with *dynamis megale* (vv.10, 13); *legon einai tina heauton megan* is a Lukan anticipation of the acclamation in v.10b ('this man is the great power of God'); here the formula recalls 5.36. For the phrase *apo mikrou heos megalou* in v.10 cf. 26.22. The qualification of 'great power' by *tou theou* is a Lukan pleonasm (cf. Jeremias 1980, 208f. [on Luke 11.49]); *kaloumene*: Luke uses the present participle passive to give a person, thing or place the name or surname that they bear (thus Bauer 1979, 399): cf. Luke 10.39; 19.29; 21.37; Acts 1.12. Even a superficial comparison with Acts 19.28, 34, shows that in respect of the form of acclamation in this pericope Luke is not primarily concerned with techniques to enliven the narrative (therefore the form probably derives from tradition, see 98 below). *hikano chrono* in v.11 is a variation on a favourite Lukan phrase (cf. Luke 8.27 [Mark differs]; 20.9 [plural; Mark differs]; 23.8 [plural]; Acts 14.3; 27.9). Here as already in v.9, Simon's activity is connected with magic and is thus defamed (cf. similarly 13.6, 8: Elymas the magician). By contrast with this, Philip does wonders and signs. (For the fluctuating reputation of the *magos* in Hellenism cf. Nock, *Beg.* V, 164-88.) Whether the defamation was also a demotion depends on investigation of the tradition and historical analysis.

The second sub-section (vv.12-13) depicts the superiority of the Christian miracle-worker and preacher Philip to Simon. Verse 12 links directly to vv.5-8 and reports the baptism of the population: the phrase in v.12 ('preach about the kingdom of God and the name of Jesus Christ') corresponds to v.5 ('preach Christ'). Both phrases are Lukan (cf. Conzelmann 1960, 105). For the redactional *andres* and *gynaikes* cf. 5.14; 8.3; 9.2; 17.12. *proskarteron* in v.13 appears six times in Acts and four times in the rest of the New Testament. Simon's envy and amazement at the mighty acts of Philip will correspond in the next episode to Simon's desire to convey the Holy Spirit by the laying on of hands in the same way as the apostles. Therefore v.13b has a redactional motivation.

The significance of Acts 8.4-13 for Luke

If we disregard the redactional interlocking of vv.4-13 and compare the portrait of Philip with that of Simon, we can see a striking parallelism (cf. Beyschlag 1974, 101, who has produced the following comparison):

Philip	Simon
1. comes into the city (v.5),	1. is already in the city (v.9),
2. proclaims Christ (and the kingdom of God, vv.5,12)	2. designates himself a man of power (v.9),

3. does manifest signs (or 'great acts of power'), vv.6f.,13;	3. does magic publicly and is allegedly 'the great power' (vv.9-11);
4. the whole people hears him, sees his actions and 'follows him' (vv. 6, 12)	4. the whole people is 'beside itself' and 'follows him' (vv.9,11).
5. Great joy in the people, faith and baptism of all (vv.8, 12).	5. Simon sees the mighty acts of power by Philip and is 'beside himself' (v.13).

It emerges from this comparison (= *synkrisis* – for the phenomenon see Berger 1984, 222f.) that Luke wants to depict the superiority of Philip's power to that of Simon. In this connection Philip's signs and wonders are as superior to Simon's magic as his proclamation of the word is superior to the self-glorification or self-divinization of the latter. At the narrative level, Acts 14.8ff. provides a parallel to Simon's deification of himself (thus rightly Beyschlag 1974, 102).

The presence of the Jerusalem apostles Peter and John develops the action which ends when Philip vanquishes Simon, since two questions had been left open: 1. the failure to bestow the Holy Spirit; 2. the role of Simon. Could it really be that the famous/notorious Simon remained a member of the Christian community?

[14-24] Verses 14-17 depict the bestowal of the Holy Spirit on the Christians in Samaria. The whole section is redactional in both language and content.

Here is a selection of features of redactional language and style: v.14, *dedektai (he Samareia) ton logon tou theo* (cf. Luke 8.13 [Mark differs]; Acts 11.1; 17.11); v.15, *katabantes, proseuxanto*; v.16, the use of the periphrastic pluperfect (cf. Radl 1975, 443); *hyperchon*; v.17, *epetithesan tas cheiras* (Luke 4.40 [Mark differs]; Acts 6.6; 8.19; 9.12, 17; 13.3; 19.6; 28.8).

As to content: the redactional significance of the narrative is clear from a look at 11.22-24:

'Both passages are concerned to sanction the move of the Hellenists by Jerusalem and draw closer the threads between the earliest community and the Hellenists, which otherwise threaten to tear apart because of the suspicious independence with which the narratives about the Hellenists and Peter run side by side in chs. 6-12' (Overbeck 1870, 123).

So vv.14-17 provide the endorsement of the Samaria mission by the Jerusalem apostles. To this end Peter and John are 'smuggled into' the story of Philip (Schwartz 1963, 144 n.2). The separation of baptism and the bestowal of the Holy Spirit which elsewhere coincide in Luke (cf. 2.38, etc.) is best explained by Luke's purpose, mentioned above. It is an *ad hoc* construction as in 10.44-48 (the bestowal of the Holy Spirit before baptism) or 19.1-7.

Dietrich 1972 differs: the explanation given above is unsatisfactory, 'because it hardly explains why the two apostles merely bestow the Spirit and do not themselves make the decisive breakthrough in Samaria' (247). Dietrich comes to the untenable conclusion that in the early period of the Jerusalem community there was a rule 'that the bestowal of the Spirit was reserved for the apostles. On this basis Philip respected the privilege of the apostles' (249f.). Against this is the fact that Dietrich's explanation conflicts with the Spirit-filled activity of the Hellenists which is clearly expressed in the traditions used by Luke.

Verses 18-24 answer the other question raised by vv.5-13, namely whether the notorious Simon remained in the Christian community. Their redactional character emerges mainly from arguments relating to content and from the link between the episode and its context. The following linguistic characteristics are Lukan: v.18, *didonai to pneuma* ([Luke 11.13;] Acts 5.32; 11.17; 15.8); v.19, *ho ean, epitho tas cheiras*; v.20, *eipen pros, dorea*. For the Lukan language in vv.20-24 see Koch 1986, 71f. n.21.

For the negative use of the theme of money in vv.18f. cf. below 249 on 24.24-26. The idea that money does not secure salvation occurs, as in 8.18f., in Peter's remark in 3.6:

'Silver and gold have I none, but what I have, I give to you: In the name of Jesus Christ the Nazorene, arise and walk!' – For the whole problem see the valuable article by Barrett 1979, 281-95.

So the section expresses the fact that the Holy Spirit is not to be bought but is a gift of grace (on *dorea tou pneumatos* cf. 2.38; 10.45; 11.17). Simon Magus was a welcome example which Luke could use to impress these ideas on his readers.

One might also ask why Luke has left the end of the story so relatively open that it is not clear whether Simon is saved or damned. Why does Luke not report an inglorious end for Simon, as he did in the case of Judas, or Ananias and Sapphira? Did he have to reckon with the fact that his readers knew different stories about Simon's effectiveness *in his time*, and/ or did the end of the story hint at the possibility that (Simonian) heretics could be converted or at least not excluded (cf. Klein 169, 287-99, esp. 295)?

[25] The verse is part of the Lukan framework and takes Peter and John back to Jerusalem. On their way back they preach the word of the Lord (4.29; 6.2), also to the people of Samaria. This fulfils the second part of

1.8. Because the verse is redactional throughout, there is no need to analyse it under III and IV below.

III Traditions

[5-8] The foundation of this is the tradition of a spirit-filled activity of the preacher Philip in Samaria (see what is said above on the Hellenists).

[9-13] Here Luke has summarized a tradition which, like the accounts by Justin, Irenaeus and Hippolytus (see below, 100ff.), was an ingredient of the early Christian tradition about Simon Magus. It reported the great power of Simon and its effectiveness in Samaria. The designation 'great power' for Simon is confirmed by other testimony in the early Christian tradition about Simon Magus (cf. Lüdemann 1975, 47), and in both passages denotes the God of the Simonians who had a great following in Samaria. It should be noted that in all probability the acclamation is part of the tradition (see above, II). It can be described as a soteriological type of speech (Norden 1913, 188) and might have corresponded to a proclamation made by Simon about himself in the tradition. But in that case the question still remains how this should be specified more closely. Are these the words of a man who identifies himself with God (= great power)? (For formulae of identification see Bultmann 1971, 225 n.3.) Or are these the words of a Gnostic redeemer-figure who appeared as a human being and who claims to be such with the formula (formula of recognition, see Bultmann, ibid.)? Only historical considerations can decide, as the evidence from the tradition is not clear.

The question whether Simon's miracles are part of the tradition has certainly often been answered in the affirmative (cf. most recently Koch 1986, 70), but it too can be decided only in the context of historical considerations. It is hardly possible to arrive at a positive answer from an isolated redactional analysis of the text of Acts.

I think it probable that the tradition about Simon Magus underlying vv.9-13 is part of a written or oral tradition from Hellenist circles which reported the clash between the supporters of Simonian and Christian religion. (Whether it was an individual tradition, and what form it may have taken, can no longer be decided with any certainty because of its fragmentary character, but one attractive conjecture is that the basis was a cycle of stories about Philip, see below 104f. – The other possibility, that Luke was the first to take the figures of Philip and Simon from different traditions and work them together in the present story, is improbable because in that case he could have arranged an immediate confrontation between Peter and Simon Magus.) In that case, the Hellenist tradition would have contained not only an account of the successful mission to the Gentiles in Samaria but also an account of the victory over the god of the Simonians. Here the nature of the controversy between Philip and Simon can be left open: miracles and/or the gift of the Spirit or whatever.We shall probably never know (cf. the reconstruction by Haenchen 1971, 306f., and the report by Koch, 1986, 73f., on Haenchen's different positions on this question).

[14-24]As demonstrated above, the present passage is a Lukan composition. Schille's assertion (1983, 207) that the tradition originally narrated a clash between Peter and Simon cannot explain why in that case Philip was introduced at all. ('The whole prehistory with the picture of the exorcistic competition for the soul of Samaria is a literary exposition of what follows' ([ibid., 204]). In my view this explanation is not at all illuminating. The information in vv.18f. that Simon wanted to buy the capability to bestow the Holy Spirit by the laying on of hands does not reflect a tradition, but is closely connected in the redaction with v.20.

Koch 1986 discovers a difference between v.19 and v.20 and sees here a 'reference to material from the pre-Lukan tradition' (76). The 'difference' consists in the fact that according to v.19 Simon wants to buy the capacity to bestow the Holy Spirit by the laying on of hands, whereas v.20 speaks of 'acquiring the gift of God'. In other words, it is not clear whether *dorea tou theou* ('gift of God') refers to the capacity to bestow the Spirit or to the Spirit itself. However, such a differentiation is over-sharp, and is no use for dividing redaction from tradition, especially as the theme of the Spirit dominates the section vv.14-17 which Koch also sees as redactional, and the special theme of the laying on of hands and the bestowal of the Spirit fits smoothly with vv.14-17.

Now Koch reconstructs the following hypothetical wording of the tradition underlying 8.5-25: 'A certain man called Simon was in the city of Samaria. He performed magic and amazed the people of Samaria (v.9). All hearkened to him, both small and great, and said, "This is the great power [of God]" (v.10). But when Peter came into the city and the community had assembled, they were filled with the Spirit (cf. vv.14-17). Now when Simon saw that, he brought money and said: "Give the Holy Spirit to me also" (cf. vv.18f.). But Peter said to him, "May your money perish with you, because you have believed that you can earn the gift of God with money" (v.20)' (1986, 77f.).

By way of criticism: 1. Koch's treatment of the Philip section (vv.5-3) begins from the presupposition that Luke 'otherwise... had no specific material for Philip's missionary activity' (78). That is questionable, since the next story (8.26-40) demonstrates the opposite. There are therefore good reasons for assuming that Philip and Simon were the object of a tradition deriving from Hellenistic circles and underlying vv.5-13. 2. The motive of the Spirit fits well with what we know about the Hellenists and tells against taking Philip out of Koch's hypothetical tradition. 3. The theme of money which Koch attributes to the tradition is a favourite theme of Luke's (see above in the text). 4. Koch's treatment of the question of the historical Simon Magus suffers from an isolation of the theme from the early-Christian Simon Magus tradition. Koch claims to be drawing a relatively accurate historical picture of Simon on the sole basis of Acts 8, which consists in his performing miracles and being revered as the great power of God since – and here Koch's presupposition is in my view misleading – a 'completely inaccurate picture or one relating only to incidentals would *a priori* have robbed the tradition of its effect' (81). Now as a rule controversies of a religious kind are usually meant to convince or fortify one's own followers and not the opposition. How else are the discrepancies between self-explanation and polemic against others to be explained? And Koch should have investigated in particular the Simonians' own understanding of the basis of the early-Christian Simon Magus tradition, instead of abruptly framing the New Testament polemical fragments as a historical statement. At any rate the fact that in the authentic tradition of the early Christian Simonians there is no mention of the possession of the Spirit and of miracles must make us think. In other words, in no way can either of these have had the significance that Koch attaches to them. (This objection is independent of the question whether a Gnostic doctrine already underlies Acts 8.) – This criticism does not detract from the merits of Koch's impressive analysis of Acts 8.

However, tradition is visible behind *epinoias tes kardias sou. kardias* refers back to *kardia* in v.21. But *epinoia* is surprising. The term does not occur elsewhere in the New Testament, but it does so in LXX (for the phrase *epinoias tes kardias* [which does not occur in the LXX] see *ennoiai tes kardias* [Heb.4.12]). On the other hand, *epinoia* or *ennoia* in the Simon Magus tradition is Simon's female partner, for whose salvation he has come into the world (see also Jacquier 1926, 263). Cf. Justin, *Apol* I 26, 3: *prote ennoia*; Hippolytus, *Ref* VI, 19: *epinoia*. If *epinoia* refers to Simon's female partner, then Luke already knew about her from the tradition; in that case he would have been making Peter allude ironically to *epinoia* (cf. Schmithals 1982, 82). The Hellenist tradition already worked on in vv.5ff. is a possible origin. However, we cannot completely exclude the possibility that Luke had some literary knowledge. In this case the original would no longer have contained *epinoia*, but Luke would have contributed this figure from his *own* knowledge of the Simon Magus tradition (as the result of his reading).

IV Historical

The mission in Samaria carried on by the Hellenist Philip is in all probability a historical fact. However, it is not completely clear whether this took place among the Samarians (= the Gentile population of Samaria) or the Samaritans (= members of the religious community). As in all probability Simon appeared among the Samarians, the same is also likely for Philip, but that does not mean that a mission among the Samaritans must be ruled out. (It is even probable.) Chronologically, the mission in Samaria by Philip probably lies in the 30s, after the expulsion of the Hellenists from Jerusalem, on the occasion of the martyrdom of Stephen, but a more exact *terminus ad quem* cannot be ascertained.

Similarly, the encounter of the Hellenists with followers of the Simonian religion in Samaria might be a historical fact. Anyone who set foot there inevitably clashed with the followers of Simon (or Simon himself, see below), for in the middle of the second century Justin, who was born in Flavia Neapolis (Shechem), and probably knew the area (cf. Harnack 1913b, 60), reports that almost all the members of his people worship Simon as the supreme God (*Apol* I 26, 3). Here Justin has been accused of 'excessive exaggeration' (Hengel 1983b, 207 n.133). Nevertheless it seems probable that Simon had a significant following in Samaria in the second century. This sheds light on the question of the circumstances of the Hellenist mission in Samaria. The Hellenists had to clash with Simonians sooner or later. Therefore the tradition which Luke works on in Acts 8 is reliable in this detail.

The question now arises as to what form of Simonian religion Philip came up against. On the presupposition that the remarks above about the character of *epinoia* as tradition (v.22) are right, the Simonian religion was already Gnostic when Philip came into contact with it. For the two essential foundations of the Gnostic system which is first attested in Justin (not first in Irenaeus [against Roloff 1981, 137], cf. Lüdemann 1975, 55f.) were already present: the god Simon and his syzygos, *epinoia*. Granted, it would still be possible that the two elements mentioned are to be derived from philosophical speculation and not a Gnostic myth (cf. the evidence in Lüdemann 1975, 55f.). But that is improbable, since Justin presupposes a fully developed Gnostic myth among the Simonians (note that Justin, *Apol* I 26,3, knows the harlot Helen, whose saviour Simon is, as an ingredient of the Simonian 'system' alongside the *prote ennoia*). According to the comments made above, Simon's proclamation of himself which can be inferred from Acts 8.10b can be described as a formula of recognition.

If the insertion of *epinoia* derives from Luke's knowledge acquired through reading, the conclusions drawn above would be uncertain. Nevertheless in this case the composition of Luke-Acts would be the *terminus ad quem* of the Gnostic stage of Simonian religion.

If the Gnostic interpretation advanced above is correct, then Luke's account (and perhaps also that of the Hellenists) would partly have degraded Simon by depicting him one-sidedly as a magician, though magic and Gnosticism could come close together (cf. Mark [Irenaeus, *Haer* I, 13-15]) and in this case may have been connected (at all events, apart from the hint in v.22, the text is silent about Simon's Gnostic teaching).

As to the question of the historical Simon, first it must be stressed that the bedrock of the tradition about him in Acts 8 is the worship of Simon as a god and the existence of *epinoia* as his syzygos. Simon can have been a prophet, teacher or miracle worker to whom a Gnostic interpretation was attached, or who had himself developed one – it could have been connected with a Zeus cult on Gerizim (cf. Lüdemann 1975, 52-4). In that case he would have called himself Simon Zeus (cf. the parallel Menecrates Zeus) or would have been called on as such.

For Acts 8.4-25 see my article 'The Acts of the Apostles and the Beginnings of Simonian Gnosis', *NTS* 33, 1987, 420-6.

Acts 8.26-40

I Division

8.26-28: Dual exposition: command of the angel to Philip to travel along the road from Jerusalem to Gaza; Philip does so. Return of the Ethiopian eunuch from Jerusalem and his reading of the book of Isaiah
29-35: Encounter of Philip with the eunuch and preaching of the gospel, starting from Isa 53.7f.
36-38: Baptism of the eunuch by Philip
39: Transportation of Philip after performing the baptism; joyful return of the eunuch
40: Philip in Ashdod. After preaching the gospel, Philip arrives in Caesarea

II Redaction

[26-28] In v.26, *anastethi* (cf. *anastas* in v.27), *poreuou, katabainousan* are Lukan language. The angel motive may be redactional: Luke often has angels appearing and giving commands to people in direct speech (Luke 1.11-25, 26-28; 2.8-20, 21; Acts 5.19f.; 12.6-17). *kata mesembrian* is either an indication of direction ('southwards') or more probably, like 22.6, a note about time ('towards midday'). The phrase 'from Jerusalem to Gaza' fits 'Luke's concept of mission; after Samaria in the north has been missionized, the message now turns southwards: as Luke understands it, "Jerusalem" once again recalls the starting point of the gospel' (Weiser 1981, 209).

haute estin eremos is a redactional explanation (cf. 16.12b; 17.21; 23.8) which refers to the road between Jerusalem and Gaza (cf. Bauer 1979, 149). From Gaza a caravan route leads to Egypt. Cf. Arrian, *Anabasis* II, 26: 'This (i.e. Gaza) is the last place on

102

the road from Phoenicia to Egypt. After it the desert begins.' So at this point Luke has accurate knowledge of Palestine (cf. Hengel 1983b, 112).

The phrase *anastas eporeuthe* in v.27 is redactional in language, as are *kai idou, proskyneson eis Ierousalem* (cf. the verbal parallel in 24.11); cf. *eis* for *en* also in Luke 4.23; 11.7; Acts 7.12; 19.22 (see W.Elliger, *EWNT* I, 965-68). The Candace motive may be 'an adornment of the story with mysterious features, but on the other hand it may be connected with the fact that the chamberlain is a eunuch and explain why this is so. Here a piece of contemporary educational material is used to make the range of the Christian mission universal and to take the reader in imagination into a magical world into which the news of the fulfilment of the Isaiah prophecy has penetrated' (Dinkler 1975, 94; cf. Plümacher 1972, 12). *hypostrephein* in v.28 is a favourite Lukan word; for Luke's periphrastic conjugation cf. the list in Radl 1975, 431. *ton propheten Esaian* is a reference forward to vv.32f. Cf. the similar structure of Jesus' inaugural preaching in Nazareth which is shaped by Luke: Luke 4.17 (Jesus is given the book of the prophet Isaiah)/4.18f. (quotation of an Isaiah passage which is to be understood christologically). The co-ordination of Philip's meeting with the eunuch by an angel of the Lord (v.26) or by the Spirit (v.29) may be redactional, since in the subsequent stories of the conversion of Paul (Acts 9) and Cornelius (Acts 10f.) the courses of two people (Paul/Ananias, Cornelius/Peter) are similarly brought together. However, at this point the motive is at its weakest. Nevertheless, from now on the readers know how God acts and co-ordinates the actions of human beings through commands.

[29-35] *to pneuma* in v.29 is a Lukan variant for *aggelos kyriou* (in v.39 we have *pneuma kyriou* instead). *kollaomai* appears five times in Acts, twice in Luke, and five times in the rest of the New Testament. The paronomasia *ginoskeis/anaginoskeis* (v.30) is Lukan (cf. earlier v.26f.: *gaza* [the city]/*gaza* [treasure]). The potential optative in v.31 occurs in the New Testament only in Luke: Luke 1.62; 6.11 (Mark differs); 9.46 (Mark differs); 15.26; Acts 5.24; 8.31; 10.17; 17.18; 26.29 (cf. further Schneider 1980, 504 n.49). Verses 32-34 are probably completely redactional: like Luke 4.18f. the verses are Isaiah testimonies interpreted christologically. By contrast the narrative in the tradition is about Philip's *proclamation* of Jesus, as v.35 shows (cf. Schneider 1980, 504). Moreover v.35 attaches smoothly to v.31.

However, Rese 1969, 97-100, thinks that vv.32f. were an element of pre-Lukan tradition *and* that this also contained Isa 53.8d (*apo ton anomion tou laou mou echte eis thanaton*). Luke 'deliberately omitted this sentence in order to avoid saying anything about the atoning power of the death of Jesus' (98). But Isa.53.8d says nothing about the atoning power of the death of Jesus. Luke seems, rather, to have left out v.8d 'because it is anticlimactic, if *airein* is understood as referring to the exaltation' (Conzelmann 1987, 68).

For *anoixas to stoma* in v.35 cf. 10.34. *archomai apo* is frequent in Luke (Luke 24.27, 47; Acts 1.22; 10.37), as is 'proclaim Jesus'.

[36-38] For the phrase *ti kolyei me baptisthenai* in v.36 see the almost identical redactional phrase in 10.47 (cf. 11.17). Verse 37 is secondary from a text-critical point of view (on this see von Campenhausen 1972, 226). For *katebesan* (v.38) cf. v.26.

[39] The sentence 'the eunuch went on his way rejoicing' (v.39d) does not fit well as a reason why he no longer saw Philip (cf. Weiser 1981, 211). This tension with the preceding sentence and the evidence that *poreuomai* and *chairo* are favourite Lukan words demonstrate that v.39d is redactional and v.39a-c is an element of the source material.

[40] This verse is a pragmatic addition by Luke (Dibelius 1956, 15) and tells the readers where Philip will be (later), in Caesarea (21.8).

Azotus (Ashdod), like Gaza, is one of the five former Philistine cities and also by the sea (about twenty miles north-east of Gaza). So here Luke is displaying geographical knowledge which may rest on traditional material from Hellenist circles (cf. Hengel 1983b, 110-5).

With Acts 8.26-40 Luke adds a second story about Philip to his narrative about the Hellenist mission outside Jerusalem. It should be noted that he does not report that the Spirit was bestowed on the eunuch (but cf. the secondary reading of Codex A on v.39 to this effect). In this way Luke has remained faithful to his principle which became evident in the first story about Philip (8.5-25), not to connect the bestowing of the Spirit with the Hellenist preaching and to suppress reports to this effect. Analysis subsequently shows that this is a further reason for the assumption made above that Acts 8.4-25 is based on a tradition about Philip and not Peter.

III Traditions

If we extract the certainly redactional features from the text – a process which is often methodologically problematical – then following Weiser 1981, 208, we get the following elements of tradition: v.27b, 'an Ethiopian, a eunuch'; v.38, 'and both descended into the water, Philip and the eunuch, and he baptized him'; v.39, 'now when they came up out of the water the Spirit of the Lord carried off Philip, and the eunuch saw him no more'. Though we may have doubts about the exact length of the tradition, the evidence is enough for a form-critical classification: the tradition used by Luke is a conversion story which probably had paradigmatic significance for the mission to the Gentiles in Hellenist circles (Harnack 1908, 150f., attributes the tradition to Philip himself, but that is not conclusive; however, cf. Dinkler 1975, 88). Whereas Luke has deliberately left the religious status of the eunuch in the air – 'Apparently he did not venture to describe him as a proselyte because of what he found in his sources; he could not let him appear as a Gentile, because the Gentile mission really begins in chapter 10' (Conzelmann 1987, 68) – the tradition not only presupposes the latter but also reports that the Gentile was a eunuch. That further emphasizes the statement that the gospel had gone beyond the bounds of Judaism. Perhaps in these circles the story was seen as the fulfilment of Isa.56.3b-5:

'Let not the eunuch say, "Behold, I am a dry tree." For thus says the Lord: "To the eunuchs who keep my sabbaths, who choose the things that please me and hold fast my covenant, I will give in my house and within my walls a monument and a name better than sons and daughters; I will give them an everlasting name which shall not be cut off."'

The story gives the impression of being an old one (but Schille 1983, 213, differs) and is probably part of a cycle of stories about Philip, two of which Luke worked into ch.8 and from which he will have taken the report about Philip and his prophesying virgin daughters which is given later (21.8). The style is legendary throughout (a mixture of the edifying, the personal and the miraculous, cf. Dibelius 1956, 15).

IV Historical

The legendary conversion story reflects the historical fact that the conversion of an Ethiopian eunuch was one of the missionary successes of the Hellenists and Philip. The possibility of this arises out of what is known about the Hellenists, the probability of such a verdict because of the specific character of the tradition contained in Acts 8 (Ethiopian, eunuch) and the tension between this story and Acts 10. Chronologically we should think of the 30s or 40s of the first century.

Acts 9.1-19a

I Division

9.1-2: Saul active as a persecutor (exposition)
3-9: The christophany to Saul near Damascus
   3a: Travel note with information about the location
   3b: Appearance of light
   4a: Saul falls down
   4b-6: Conversation between Jesus and Saul
   7: The reaction of the companions
   8-9: The effect of the phenomenon on Saul
10-19a: Ananias's vision of Christ with the commission; he carries it out
   10a: Introduction of the figure of Ananias with information about locality
   10b: Information about the form of perception (*horama*)
   10c-16: Conversation in the vision and command
   17-19a: Laying on of hands, which leads to the regaining of Saul's sight and his baptism by Ananias

II Redaction

[1-2] The following phrases or terms are redactional in language: v.1, *eti, mathetas tou kyriou*; v.2 *hopos ean, andras te kai gynaikas*. In content both verses are redactional exposition: Luke is connecting the redactional episodes, previously reported, of Saul's involvement in Stephen's martyrdom (7.58; 8.1a) and his subsequent activity as a successful persecutor (8.3) with a story about the conversion of the persecutor before Damascus, by making this happen on the way from Jerusalem to Damascus and giving as a reason for the journey that Saul is travelling to Damascus on the orders of the high priest in order to arrest Christians there and have them brought to Jerusalem. This skilfully makes a contrast between the zealous persecutor of Christians and the convert.

There is in fact no support in the tradition for a journey from Jerusalem to Damascus with such a motive. One may add that should against all probability the opposite be the case, this journey with its alleged purpose would nevertheless be unhistorical, since the jurisdiction of the Sanhedrin did not extend as far as Damascus, but was limited to Judaea. Against this, reference has been made to the 'letter' from the Roman consul Lucius to king Ptolemy which is preserved in I Macc.15.16-21 (thus e.g. Lake/Cadbury, *Beg.* IV, 99): Lucius reports the renewal of the alliance and friendship between the Romans and the Jews which has just taken place (under the high priest Simon) and asks Ptolemy: 'If any pestilent men have fled to you from their country, hand them over to Simon the high priest, that he may punish them according to their law.' But the letter does not refer to synagogues, as in Acts 9.1f., but to non-Jewish authorities to whom the Jews had fled and – quite apart from the question of the authenticity of the letter (which is open) – it is uncertain whether the order was still in force two hundred years later. Cf. also Conzelmann 1987, 71; Goldstein 1976 points out, with reference to I Macc.2.44 and Deut.4.25-28, that the high priest Simon probably did not intend to pursue apostates outside the promised land (497). Schürer 1979, 198, 218f., confirms the above understanding, although he then leaves the historicity of Acts 9.2 in the air. For the whole problem see Burchard 1970, 44f. n.15. (Judge 1964 wrongly speaks of an 'extradition agreement' between the republic of Damascus and the Jewish government of Jerusalem [21]).

[3-9] It is best to introduce the redactional analysis of vv.3-9 with a synoptic comparison of the parallel reports in Acts 9; 22; 26. As all three accounts relate to the Damascus event and are genetically interconnected, a close comparison may further the redactional question and prepare for the traditio-historical analysis. Acts 9 will serve as the guiding thread.

Synoptic comparison of the three accounts of the conversion of Paul (cf. the synopsis which is Appendix I in Löning 1973)

In general: Acts 9 is a report in the third person singular, while Acts 22 and 26 are in the first person singular. In 22.3-16 Paul is delivering the temple speech to his own fellow-countrymen, while in 26.4f., 9-18 he is speaking to Agrippa, Festus and Berenice. Both speeches are apologias.

We begin with 8.3, because that section is the prehistory to the conversion and is taken up in all three accounts.

8.3 corresponds to 22.4 and 26.9-11. All three passages say that Saul has Christians put in prison (*phylake*). 26.10b (which is perhaps a specific instance for 22.4) intensifies this by saying that Paul was involved in death sentences ('If they were to be executed, I gave my consent'). 26.11b intensifies the matter yet further by extending Paul's acts of persecution to the cities outside Jerusalem.

9.1-2 corresponds to 22.5b and 26.11b-12. In both 9 and 22 there is mention of letters which Saul asks for from (9.2) or has been given by (22.5b) the high priest or the Sanhedrin. 26.12 asserts that Paul travelled to Damascus with the authority and permission of the high priest (cf. already v.10b). Whereas 9.2 and 22.5b limit Saul's activity as a persecutor to Damascus (Saul wants to bring the Christians there to Jerusalem to be punished), 26.12 omits this detail. (Here Saul is travelling to Damascus with the authority of the high priests.) The above detail can no longer be reported because in 26.11b Saul is already depicted as someone who had persecuted the Christians as far as the cities outside Jerusalem. Chapter 26 therefore presupposes 9 and 22 and heightens the statements made there.

9.3-9 has a parallel in 22.6-11 and 26.12-16a:

9.3 corresponds down to its vocabulary with 22.6. 9.3 contains no note of time, while 22.6 speaks of *peri mesembrian* and 26.13 similarly of *hemeras meses*. The appearance to Saul is described in all three accounts as light (*phos*: 26.13 again intensifies this by saying that the light is brighter than the rays of the sun). Each time it takes place from heaven (twice *ek tou ouranou, ouranothen* [26.13]), 9.3 and 22.6 make the phenomenon take place suddenly (*exaiphnes*). In 9.3 and 22.6 the light shines (only) round Saul; according to 26.13 it shines round Saul *and* his companions.

According to 9.4; 22.7, Saul falls to the ground; in 26.14 this is Saul and those with him; in contrast to the parallel accounts the light also shone round Saul's companions. All three narratives again agree that Saul hears a voice which says to him, 'Saul, Saul, why are you persecuting me?'; however, 26.14 has two significant additions: 1. the voice speaks in Hebrew; 2. the question to Saul as to why he is persecuting the speaker is supplemented by the comment: 'It is hard for you to kick against the pricks.' The two additions must be seen as Lukan expansion. The first addition (the speaking in Hebrew) explains the form of the name of Saul, which is to be found in all three versions. Moreover the encounter between persecutor and persecuted forms a solemn and dramatic scene. However, the fact that in the second addition the persecuted Jesus then uses a Greek proverb does not fit the Hebrew language (cf. Conzelmann 1987, 210f.). Here in fact the writer Luke is speaking; on the one hand he wants to demonstrate the total dependence of Saul on Jesus and on the other to show off his own reading.

9.5 corresponds almost completely with the parallels 22.8; 26.15: when Saul asks who is speaking, he is told 'I am Jesus (the Nazorene) whom you are persecuting'. In connection with this 22.9 contains the observation that Saul's companions had (seen the light, but) not heard the voice which spoke to Saul. By contrast, 9.7 a little later says quite the opposite: Saul's companions heard the voice.

9.6 is closely parallel to 22.10: Saul is to rise, go to Damascus, and there he will be told what to do. 26.16a contains only the order to rise, but no command that Saul is to go to Damascus. It is only logical that ch.26 also has no information about Ananias. Rather, 26.16b immediately describes the real command to Saul to preach, which the parallel versions give only later (see below on 9.15; 22.14). Therefore in what follows, only the first two versions of the Damascus event are to be compared.

9.7: cf. above on 9.5/22.9.

9.8 corresponds to 22.11: Saul cannot see anything and his companions lead him by the hand to Damascus.

9.9 has no parallel in 22. The observation that Saul could not see anything and did not eat or drink anything for three days is perhaps a redactional addition. At all events 'three' is a round (Lukan) number. The fasting significantly precedes the healing and the gift of the Holy Spirit (cf. v.17).

9.10-17, the Ananias episode, has only a partial parallel in 22.12-13. 9.10-17 depicts a vision of Christ by Ananias. He is told that Saul is in Damascus, living with Judas in the Straight Street and praying (v.11). In a vision Saul has seen Ananias coming (v.12). Verses 13f. contain an objection by Ananias which is grounded in Saul's previous actions against the Christians. The prehistory of Ananias's encounter with Saul which has just been described has no parallel in ch.22. In 22.12 Ananias is introduced as 'a pious man after the law, in good standing with all the Jews there'. Immediately after this the text depicts the healing of Saul by Ananias (v.13), which in ch.9 is only narrated later, in v.17. The introduction of Ananias in 22.12 without further explanation of the prehistory of his intervention is abrupt and can only be introduced into the narrative because the readers have already learned something about him in ch.9. At the same time that means that the report in ch.22 refers back to ch.9. (Chapter 26 continues the abbreviation of the account of the conversion of Saul begun in ch.22 and completely passes over the Ananias episode.)

9.15-16 has a parallel in 22.14-15 and 26.16b. But different accents are clear: 9.15 describes Saul as *skeuos ekloges*, who will bear the name of the Lord before the peoples, kings and sons of Israel. Verse 16 gives the reason for this statement: 'I will show him how much he is to suffer for my name.' Without anticipating the subsequent redactional analysis, it can already be said that here Saul is depicted (at least primarily) as a martyr. The situation in ch.22 and esp.26 is different from this: 22.14 has a different subject from 9.15: (Not Christ, but) God has chosen Saul in advance to know his will, to see the holy one and to hear a voice from his mouth. The verb 'choose beforehand' (*procheirizesthai*) similarly appears in 26.16b and its content may match that of (*skeuos*) *ekloges*. The second part of v.14 ('to know his will and to see the righteous one and to hear the voice from his mouth') has no direct parallel in 9.5 or 26.16. But there is a parallel with 26.16 in connection with seeing Jesus.

22.15 has a close parallel in 26.16b. Cf. the 'for you shall be a witness for him (sc.Christ) to all men of what you have seen and heard' (22.15) with 'I appeared to you for this purpose, to appoint you to serve and bear witness to what you have seen and what will be shown you' (26.16b). So according to both versions Saul is a witness. The special task of the witness seems to be developed following 26.16b, i.e. in vv.17-18, which has no parallel in ch.22. Cf. vv.17-18: 'And I will deliver you from the people and from the Gentiles to whom I send you to open their eyes, that they may turn from darkness to light and from the power of Satan to God, that they may receive forgiveness of sins and a place among those who are sanctified through faith in me.' This expresses the call of Saul to be missionary to the Gentiles, a theme which was probably not contained in ch.9 and only indirectly in ch.22.1-16 (however, it appears in the immediate context, vv.17-21).

9.17-19 depicts the healing of Saul by Ananias which in ch.22 was already reported in v.13. We should not read an explanation for Saul's blindness out of v.18a ('Then there fell like scales fom his eyes...'), and then contrast this with 22.11, where it is explained by the radiance of the light, and then regard the two explanations as mutually exclusive. For 'scales from his eyes' is a metaphor, and in 9.8 the blindness is also in fact caused by the radiance of the light (cf. 9.3b, against Hedrick 1981, 431).

The result of the synoptic comparison

All three accounts belong genetically together. At the redactional level the second account in 22.12 presupposes the first, just as the third version can be understood as an abbreviation of the two previous ones. In it the contrast between Paul's pre-Christian and Christian periods (cf. the elaboration of Paul's activity as a persecutor) is heightened and the conversion of Acts 9 is understood as a call to the Gentile mission. (The second account in ch.22 occupies an intermediate position. But the theme of the Gentile mission is indicated in it by the immediate context [22.17-21].)

In view of the many correspondences, the difference between 9.7 (Saul's companions heard the voice) and 22.9 (Saul's companions did not hear a voice) should not be interpreted in terms of different sources. However, we can hardly regard the difference as carelessness on Luke's part (on Schneider 1982, 22 and n.1), since the fact that in interrupting the dialogue between Jesus and Saul 22.9 deliberately refers back to 9.7 (note the alternation between hearing and seeing) tells against that; here the readers are given an additional piece of information about the conversion of Saul (cf. Hedrick 1981, 431). The question left open in 9.7, whether Saul's companions had seen (a) light, is thus answered in the affirmative. (9.7 had only denied that the companions had seen anyone [= Jesus].) Moreover the statement in 22.9 that Saul's companions had not heard a voice sounds like a Lukan correction of the pre-Lukan statement to the contrary in 9.7. Here Luke wants to exclude the possibility that Saul's companions took part in the revelation, which was solely reserved for Saul (cf. Hedrick 1981, 430f.).

My statement above that the third version is an abbreviation of the first two is not a conclusive demonstration that individual motives in it are not original and that the tradition which underlies all three reports was the story of a conversion or a call. Here, too, it is uncertain whether Ananias was part of this tradition.

[3-9] The introduction (v.3a) *en de to poreuesthai...* has Lukan features. Luke introduces an episode in a similar way in Luke 18.35; 19.29; Acts 10.9. Verses 4b-6 have been described by G.Lohfink (1965; 1967, 53-60) as an appearance conversation which was part of the sources for the three accounts of the conversion of Saul in 22.7-10/26.14-16 alongside vv.4-6 (cf. 9.10f.) and has analogies in the Old Testament: Gen.31.11-13; 46.2f.; Exod.3.2-10. The Old Testament form is tripartite: 1. Address or call; 2. Answer with question; 3. Introduction with charge. It has been imitated by Luke, so that vv.4b-6 are to be regarded as redactional. But against this conclusion stands the occurrence of the same form in JosAs 14 and TestJob 3; in these passages we should expect not an imitation of the LXX but the use of a narrative schema (for criticism of Lohfink's thesis see Burchard 1970, 88f.).

However, the question whether vv.4b-6 in their present form are redactional or part of the tradition is not decided by the derivation of this scheme. Nevertheless, the observation that it also occurs outside this text in a redactional context (9.10f.; 10.3-5) arouses the suspicion that it originates from Luke. This assumption is confirmed on two further grounds: 1. vv.4b-6 can be dispensed with in the action. 2. Luke has a predilection for shaping scenes with dialogue. (For the question whether individual elements of vv.4b-6 are part of the tradition see III below.)

Redactional features in this section can be demonstrated in two further passages: v.4, the duplication 'Saul, Saul' has an analogy in the duplication

110

of the address in Luke 8.24 (Mark differs); 10.41; 22.31. The number 'three' in v.9 is certainly redactional.

[10-19a] In v.10a the introduction of Ananias (*tis... onomati*) is Lukan in language. In v.10b the proclamation of divine decisions by a vision (*horama*) is an important literary device for Luke (cf. Acts 10f. etc). (Note that vv.3-9 do not report a *horama* but a christophany – for this see further below, III.)

In the analysis of the redaction, particular note should be taken of the context in which vv.10c-16 are put. The narrative is connected with the previous pericope (8.26-40) about Philip and the Ethiopian eunuch and the subsequent story of Cornelius (10.1-11.18) in that each time the actions of two people are connected or co-ordinated. In the Cornelius story this comes about through duplicate visions, as it does in the present story – however, with the significant difference that Saul's vision (in contrast to that of Ananias) is not developed in narrative form but is presupposed (9,12). By contrast, 8.26-40 only report the appearance of an angel of the Lord to Philip, who is sent by this angel to the eunuch. In contrast to the second figure in the narratives in Acts 9 (Ananias) and Acts 10f. (Peter), the eunuch himself has not received a corresponding vision. This may make it clear that the three stories in question belong together (cf. already Baur 1866, 81, though he stressed only the close connection between Acts 9 and Acts 10f.) and have been arranged by Luke towards a climax. This suggests that Luke was the first to give the vision of Ananias narrative status in order to incorporate the story into the wider narrative complex. That is all the more probable since the christophany to Saul (9.3-4) really does not fit the type of story that appears in chs.8; 10f. (However, Luke does mean to understand it as such in this context, cf. 9.12.) The instructive examples of duplicate visions from Graeco-Roman literature in Wikenhauser 1948, 100-11, are certainly fine illustrations of the narrative style, but they do not contain *any* parallels to 9.3-9.

So Haenchen 1971 must be regarded as correct: the community tradition did not yet contain 'the two curious corresponding *horamata*' (328).

Verses 13-14 are a redactional retrospect on 8.3; vv.15-16 are Lukan (the most recent to differ is Dietzfelbinger 1985, 80) – on grounds of language and content.

On language: the phrase '(the Lord) spoke to him' is redactional. The verb *poreuesthai* occurs 'frequently in Luke, but the imperative form *poreuou* is particularly characteristic of him... In *skeuos ekloges* the Hebraizing qualitative genitive stands for an adjective, as elsewhere in Luke. For *estin moi* cf. . . . Luke 5.10; Acts 19.31; and in wording Acts 18.10... The infinitive with the preceding *tou* is particularly

Lukan' (Radl 1975, 70), similarly *to onoma*, above all in Acts. *enopion* is characteristic of Luke/Acts (but equally of Revelation). The juxtaposition of *ethne* and *basileis* appears in Luke 22.25 (Mark 10.42; Matt.10.25 differ). The particles *te*, and *te...te* and *te...kai* appear often in Acts, as does *Israel* linked with *hyioi*. Verse 16 begins with *ego gar*, cf. Luke 1.18; 8.46; 21.15. Moreover *dei, hyper tou onomatos* and *pathein* are redactional.

As to content, the stress on the name of Jesus seems to point to the redaction. As many instances show, according to Acts 'the whole realization of faith is linked with the concept of the name' (Conzelmann 1960, 178 n.1) and the effect of the name may even be described as 'the specifically Lukan way of depicting the presence of Christ' (Conzelmann 1960, 178); cf. 3.16; 4.12; 8.12. Moreover, 'here we have the contrast between Jews and Gentiles which is... characteristic of Luke. Furthermore in connection with this there is mention of Paul the confessor – even before Israel – and Paul the sufferer, although Paul was primarily a missionary. Finally, the *dei* of the need to suffer is above all in Luke a... periphrasis for the divine plan' (Radl 1975, 72.)

Verse 15 is often understood as a comment about Saul's missionary activity (thus most recently Hedrick 1981, 420f.). In reality, however, we already have a intimation here of the theme of suffering, for *bastazein to onoma enopion tinos* does not mean 'carry the name to someone' but 'bear the name before someone' (cf. Lohfink 1967, 83f.; Burchard 1970, 100f.; Radl 1975, 7f.). This solves the old problem of the relationship between v.16 and v.15, and *gar* in v.16 can be translated 'namely'.

apelthen... eiselthen in v.17 is a redactional word-play (cf. 1.21, 35c.). *epitheis ep'auton tas cheiras* and *plesthes (pneumatos hagiou)* are Lukan in language. The verse extends the charge of healing Saul given to Ananias in v.12; in addition Saul is filled with Holy Spirit. Verse 17 seems to clash with v.18, the account of Saul's baptism (after the bestowing of the Holy Spirit in v.17). Verse 19a rounds off the story.

III Traditions

[3-9] After the removal of the redaction the following elements of tradition can be detected. 1. Saul, the persecutor of Christians, is near Damascus. 2. A heavenly light shines out and Saul falls down. 3. His companions, who have heard the voice speaking to Saul, take him (blinded?) to Damascus. – Reconstructed in this way the tradition can be described as a legend of the punishment of one who despises God (there are examples in Nestle 1968, 567-98). But it should be noted that such a method of

reconstructing the tradition (namely that of subtraction) is uncertain. Who can rule out the possibility that vv.4b-6 – which in this form are certainly redactional – do not still have a foundation in tradition? This is all the more probable, since at the stage of tradition v.7 certainly refers back to the voice which has spoken to Saul. Moreover, who can discount *a priori* the possibility that Luke deleted elements? The definition of form will change, depending on what one decides to substitute. In what follows I shall speak of a christophany in order to express two things: 1. vv.3-9 are not about visions like those in 9.10-19a; 10f. 2. The subject of the event before Damascus is the persecuted Christ. Such a definition of form thus allows the story to be classified as the story of a conversion *or* call. Historical considerations (see IV below) will help here.

One might go on to consider whether the basis of the tradition in Acts 9.3-9 comes from Damascus. Further, one may see the starting point of the tradition in Gal.1.23 ('he who once persecuted us now proclaims the faith that he tried to destroy'). But it is not worth making too exact a reconstruction of the history of the tradition because of the uncertainties mentioned above.

[10-19a] The basis of this section in tradition is even harder to define than that of the previous section.

At all events it would not be correct to say: 'But Luke must at least have had a simple *horama* of Ananias, since Ananias' actions must have been motivated (the unmotivated appearance in 22.12 is possible only because knowledge of 9.10ff. is presupposed)' (Burchard 1970, 123). For the motive of the vision comes from Luke and the 'unmotivated' appearance of Ananias in 22.12 does *not* suggest tradition but merely presupposes on the *redactional* level that Luke had already spoken of him.

In my view only the existence of the disciple Ananias is an element of tradition (Luke will hardly have added this name to the tradition; see the negative characterization of others who bear it: Acts 5.1ff.; 23.2). The tradition will also have recorded that he lived in Damascus, healed Paul there (for the reason for this see Trocmé 1957, 176) and perhaps also baptized him (9.18). Whether the house of Judas on Straight Street is genetically part of the tradition is unclear. Luke himself is interested in 'lodging' (see Cadbury 1926, 305-22 – cf.16.14f.; 21.8, 16; 28.7, 16, 23, 30) and may therefore have elaborated the story with local Damascus colouring. The elements of tradition mentioned above were either the basis of a story along with the basis of vv.3-9 or Luke himself put them together.

Hedrick 1981, 422, revives Trocmé's theory that at the stage of tradition Acts 9.1-19a goes back to a healing story bound up with a christophany. There is a parallel to this in the Acts of Peter (Pap.Ber.8502 pp.135-8, English translation in Hennecke-Schneemelcher-Wilson, *New Testament Apocrypha* II, London and Philadelphia

1965, 277f., 'The story of the rich Ptolemaeus and the virgin daughter of Peter'). By way of qualification it should be noted that: 1. The story in the Acts of Peter has been composed on the basis of Acts (!) and therefore cannot be regarded as an independent parallel form of Acts 9.1-19a. 2. Paul's 'sickness' (Acts 9.8) is the consequence of the christophany on which the main weight lies, despite the individual features of the topic of miracle in vv.10-19a.

IV Historical

[3-9] The tradition behind vv.3-19a reports, in agreement with the letters, that a particular event made the persecutor a proclaimer, the enemy of Christ a disciple of Christ (cf. Gal.1). Furthermore, the information that the conversion or calling took place in or near Damascus is also historically accurate. Galatians 1.17 says that after Paul's conversion he went to Arabia, after which he returned to Damascus. So he must have been near or in this city soon after his conversion.

The tradition further agrees with Paul's own testimony in reporting a christophany. In support of this: in I Cor.9.1f. Paul speaks in Easter language (cf. John 20.18,24) of seeing the Lord, as he does in I Cor.15.8 of Jesus showing himself (cf. Luke 24.34; I Cor.15.3-7). Both passages reflect one and the same event: I Cor.9.1 the (active) perception of Jesus for which I Cor.15.8 is the presupposition. Now the striking point of difference between Acts 9.3-9 and I Cor.9.1f.; 15.8 is that here Acts does not speak explicitly of seeing the Lord but of hearing his words (vv.4b-6) – if this derives from the tradition at all – and of the appearance of light from heaven and Paul's falling down. At all events vv.3-9 say nothing about Saul seeing the Lord. Over against this, however, reference should be made to 9.17c where, looking back on vv.3-9, Ananias describes the appearance of the light before Damascus as a showing (*ophtenai*) of Jesus to Saul (cf.26.19), and to 9.7 (Saul's companions did not see anyone); here it is presupposed that Saul saw someone (i.e. Jesus, cf. Jacquier 1926, 286; Burchard 1970, 97 n.153 differs).

Therefore there is probably no conflict in the mode of Jesus' appearance between the tradition behind 9.3-9 and the letters of Paul – both in fact attest that Paul has seen the Lord (cf. the somewhat vulnerable but probably quite correct remarks by Benz 1969: 37, 327, etc.). However, in another respect differences seem to be unbridgeable. Paul himself stresses that the christophany before Damascus marked his calling to be a missionary (cf. esp. Gal.1.15), but this is not contained in Acts 9, because that is about the way in which Jesus overcomes the persecutor of the Christians. On the other hand, the call of Paul the persecutor of Christians (to be a missionary) introduces a conclusive shift which is described in Acts 9 (cf. similarly Dietzfelbinger 1985, 97). Therefore it is quite possible

114

that what Luke narrated in Acts 9 and 26 in two stories with different focal points in fact took place historically within a short space (as we have seen above, Acts 22 comes in the middle). In that case Acts 9 and 26 contained just two different aspects of one and the same event (for the consequences for the analysis of the tradition see below). Finally, it should also be pointed out that probably neither Luke nor Paul mention the real inner aspect of the Damascus event in their accounts, if the statement 'The one who is cursed by the law is the Son' (Dietzfelbinger 1985, 81f.) was the content of the conversion/call. In this case the basic insight lying behind the doctrine of justification would have been the content of the Damascus event, although it is not described in that way in *any* of the accounts by Paul or Luke.

[10-19a] It is hardly possible to make any well-founded historical judgment on the person of Ananias and his involvement in the conversion/call of Saul. However, it is illegitimate to cite Gal.1.12, that Paul does not have his revelation from a human person, against any involvement of Ananias in whatever form. For this information hardly excludes the involvement of Ananias, as it would not put in question the particular character of the conversion/call (cf. I Cor.11.23ff.).

A retrospect on the analysis of the tradition in 9.1-19a, taking into account the historical reconstruction

I said above that it was possible to make final comments as to whether the tradition narrates a conversion or a call only after historical considerations. Now the most important result of the historical reconstruction was that the tradition essentially corresponds with Paul's own testimony. It reports a christophany and depicts the circumstances which go with it (aspect of conversion). Certainly no call to mission can be found in Acts 9. But we can *ex hypothesi* attribute its absence to the redactor Luke because of the other parallels between tradition and Paul, since in Luke's plan for Acts the mission of Paul is not yet a theme in Acts 9 (cf. Maddox 1982, 74). Luke probably deliberately interpreted the tradition of the story of a calling of Paul (cf. Acts 22 + 26) as a conversion story and put it in a series of three conversion stories (8.26-40; 9.1-19a; 10.1-11.18 - cf. also what is said about the duplicated visions in the three conversion stories on 111 above). The proposal argued for here thus conflicts with that of Burchard 1970. Burchard thinks that in Acts 9.3-19a Luke is reproducing essentially unchanged the tradition of a conversion story, whereas in Acts 22 and Acts 26 he interprets this as a call to mission in order to put Paul on a level with the twelve apostles as the thirteenth

115

witness. Since Paul himself regards the Damascus event as a call, Luke's account, which is later in time, has a higher historical value than the tradition given in Acts 9 (for this thesis cf. esp. Maddox 1982, 72-5). No, the tradition of the Damascus event which Luke had was a call story, which essentially corresponds with Paul's own testimony. Luke has told it three times for literary purposes and in Acts 9 takes it one stage further from historical truth by interpreting the call as a conversion.

Acts 9.19b-30

I Division

9.19b-25: Saul in Damascus
    19b-20: Saul's preaching in the synagogue of Damascus
    21: Astonished reaction of the hearers (reference to Saul's activity as a persecutor)
    22: More powerful preaching by Saul
    23-25: Saul leaves Damascus because of the plans of the Jews to kill him
26-30: Saul in Jerusalem
    26: Saul seeks in vain to make contact with the disciples in Jerusalem
    27: The role of Barnabas as mediator
    28-29a: Saul's dealings with the disciples in Jerusalem, preaching and controversy with Hellenistic Jews
    29b-30: Saul is brought by the brethren via Caesarea to Tarsus, because the Hellenistic Jews want to kill him

II Redaction

[19b-25] Verses 19b-20 may derive from the redaction in their entirety. The note of time, 'some days' (v.19b), is indeterminate, and the approach to the Jews first in v.20 follows from Luke's known pattern. Verse 20 (Saul 'proclaims Christ that he is the Son of God') is a remote recollection of Gal.1.16. Either Luke is citing here again what is known of Paul in the community tradition or (though probably this is not to be understood as an alternative) here he is showing his knowledge of Pauline tradition and is deliberately becoming Pauline (cf. similarly 13.38f.; 20.33). Verse 21a is Lukan in language (*existanto, pantes*). Verse 21b puts what had already been said (8.1,3; 9.1,14) in direct speech as a question; here by using the word *porthein*, which he has not used before, the writer is indicating that he knows Pauline tradition (cf. Gal.1.13,23). The end of v.21 takes up

116

9.2. Verse 22 is redactional in language: cf. *sygchynno* (this appears only in Acts in the NT – four times), *katoikeo*, *symbibazo*. The verse describes the preaching of Paul (Jesus is the Christ – cf. 18.5,28) who, according to the Lukan pattern, turns to the Jews (of Damascus). In its description of the Jews' plan to act against Paul, v.23 is redactional (cf. 20.3,19). It is introduced by a Lukan note of time: (*eplerounto*) *hemerai hikanai*. In v.24 *egnosthe* + dative is like Luke 24.35; *paratereo* is relatively frequent in Luke, cf. Luke 6.7; 14.1; 20.20 (in the NT elsewhere only in Mark 3.2; Gal.4.10). For the pleonastic use of *labon* in v.25 see the Lukan parallel in 16.3; see also Luke 13.19,21. For the difficult *autou* cf. the commentaries (in my view this is not original).

[26-30] In v.26 Luke gives a very rapid report. 'In v.26, Paul is in Jerusalem, as though the basket which lowered him down from the city wall of Damascus touched ground in Jerusalem' (Burchard 1970, 145). As the crow flies, the distance between Jerusalem and Damascus is about 125 miles. For Saul to try to see the disciples in Jerusalem after his conversion is a requirement of the redaction. The Jerusalem community is the base in salvation history for Luke's church. Of course the main figure in the second part of Acts must make contact with it, in the interest of the idea of the church. Since the disciples' fear of Saul (like the fear of Ananias earlier) is all too understandable, in *narrative* terms it makes sense to insert a mediator at this point. In v.27, Luke may have inferred from the later tradition of the collaboration between Paul and Baranbas (Acts 13-14) that Barnabas introduced Paul to the Jerusalem community (cf. the parallel instance 11.25f.). To describe this individual feature as 'mediatizing' (Klein 1961, 164) is to overinterpret a narrative combination which arose out of the historicization. (In the next chapters, Barnabas and Paul are partners in mission.) Verse 27b sums up the conversion of Saul which was narrated previously (vv. 3-9) and his preaching activity in Damascus (v.20) (apparently Barnabas is the spokesman). Verse 28 has Saul conversing with the Jerusalem apostles (for the phrase *eisporeuomenos kai ekporeuomenos* cf. 1.21, *eiselthen kai exelthen*), preaching in Jerusalem (*parrhesiazomenos* [v.28] takes up the same verb in v.27) and disputing with the Hellenists. 'Paul is doing in Jerusalem, in company with the Twelve, precisely what he had already done in Damascus before he made their acquaintance' (Burchard 1970, 149). In v.29 the apostle fills the gap which was made by Stephen's death. *laleo* and *syzeteo* are used here and in 6.9f. to describe the arguments of the Hellenistic Jews with Stephen/Saul. Of course they want to murder Saul (*anelein*), as the Jews of Damascus planned to murder him (v.23, *anelein*) and as they had previously acted against Stephen (6.11-14: accusation on the basis of false

witnesses to bring about Stephen's execution). The threat against Saul (v.30) explains why he is sent to Tarsus.

III Traditions

[19b-25] The report that Paul preached in Damascus is very probably part of the tradition. However, the assumption is only indirectly supported by the present text, which has a redactional stamp throughout, and arises mainly out of historical considerations (see IV below). The note about the flight from Damascus (vv.24b-25) is part of the tradition. That follows first for literary-critical reasons: vv.23-24a are a kind of exposition which depicts the Jews' plan to murder Paul (and derives from Luke, see below). The seam between v.24a and v.24b is visible in the concreteness of what follows (cf. Burchard 1970, 151). The reconstructed tradition then has a striking parallelism with II Cor.11.32f.:

'The two texts, which are quite different at the beginning, run together in *pareterounto*, Acts 9.24b/*ephrourei* II Cor.11.32, and from there on are amazingly similar right to the end; both break off with the lowering of Paul down "through" the wall (leaving aside the Pauline note of success in v.33b which has no parallel in Acts). It is clear that Luke here is using tradition. This must have been just as brief as II Cor.11.32f.; had Luke had a longer story, he would hardly have been able to arrive at such a compact version (even had he wanted to)' (Burchard 1970, 151).

We need to keep in mind (against Burchard 1970, 52) that the Jews as persecutors of Paul in this story may still derive from Luke as redactor. Burchard will be right about the origin of the tradition: the basis of Acts 9.24-25 is a piece of Pauline personal tradition which is already based on II Cor.11.32f. (Burchard 1970, 158).

[26-30] The analysis of the redaction showed that this passage was composed by Luke – without any support from tradition rooted in Paul's first visit to Jerusalem.

The contrary is often asserted: cf. e.g. Burchard 1970 (similarly Weiser 1981, 232 – following Burchard). However, Burchard's learned but tortuous remarks demonstrate only the opposite, cf.: 'Here (sc.vv.26-30) as elsewhere Luke could have used questionable tradition' (153). 'Nor do I see why Luke should have invented a controversy with Hellenists. Whether Luke had the tradition thus detectable at the beginning and end of the pericope in one piece is difficult to say, especially as in its present form v.27b is Lukan and the general summary information in v.28 could also come from him. But it is probably simplest to assume that in 9.26-30 he used a continuous piece of tradition' (154).

Anyone who sees tradition behind vv.26-30 can connect this with the version that Paul's opponents in Galatia perhaps advanced against him, namely that he had been

118

in Jerusalem for some time and had shown himself dependent on the apostles in Jerusalem (cf. Linton 1951, 84f.) Moreover the proximity of such an explanation of the tradition to the redactional explanation by G.Klein (1961, 162-6) and others is illuminating.

The concluding note about Paul's journey (v.30) can come from the tradition, cf. under IV.

IV Historical

[19b-25] The traditions contained in this section correspond with Paul's own testimony that he had to escape from Damascus. The real reason for his flight was the interference from the ethnarch of King Aretas IV of the Nabataeans (who reigned between 9 BCE and 39 CE). (Jewett 1982, 30-3 thought that the action was to be connected with the political rule of the Nabataeans over Damascus between 37 and 39CE; but against Bauer 1979, 218, the term *ethnarches* does not denote the governor but the head of an ethnic group, and there is no evidence whatsoever for Jewett's theory [cf. Burchard 1970, 158. n.100].) The reasons for the action against Paul are not clear. This action should not be exploited as a historical rehabilitation of Luke's account (the Jews as Paul's persecutors) by attributing the interference by the Nabataean ethnarch to the prompting of the Jews (thus Wikenhauser 1921, 186; against this rightly Burchard 1970, 158f. n.100).

[26-30] Finally, the account in v.30 that after his stay in Jerusalem Paul travelled in the direction of Tarsus is also historical. It corresponds to what Paul himself says, namely that after visiting Cephas he went to Syria and Cilicia (Gal.1.21). Tarsus lay in Cilicia, and after 44 CE Syria and Cilicia formed one province. At the time of the composition of Galatians (between 50 and 53), in Gal.1.21 Paul may simply have adopted the usual terminology (cf. Lüdemann 1984, 117 [and bibliography]).

Acts 9.31

The verse (introduced with the Lukan *men oun*) is a redactional summary which provides a kind of interim balance sheet. Because of the conversion of the persecutor, the persecution has collapsed, and the church, which is no longer limited to Jerusalem, as in 5.11, but includes Judaea, Samaria and Galilee (see Lohfink 1975b, 56), has peace, walks in the fear of the Lord and is strengthened by the Holy Spirit.

It is interesting that there are reports of the existence of communites in Galilee of which we have not heard previously in Acts and of which we shall not hear again. It is almost impossible to decide whether Luke knew of traditions from the area of Galilee. It is clear that had he known them he could hardly have made use of them (cf. his suppression of the Galilean resurrection tradition in Luke 24.6).

The sequence 'Judaea, Galilee, Samaria' gives the impression that Luke imagines Judaea and Galilee as being adjacent; cf. similarly (in the opposite direction) Luke 17.11: Jesus 'went through (*dia meson*) Samaria and Galilee' to Jerusalem; cf. Conzelmann 1960, 68f. Hengel 1983b regards such an interpretation of Luke 17.11 as an over-interpretation, and thinks that we cannot know what the author was thinking here (100). But he passes over Acts 9.31. The discussion of Luke 17.11 in Hengel 1983b, 97-100, hardly does justice to Conzelmann and in strident polemic only indirectly makes it clear that the *decisive* references to the geographical 'knowledge' of Palestine in Luke-Acts in the context of that time appear in Conzelmann 1960, 19 n.1; 69 (cf. Hengel 1983b, 98f.).

Acts 9.32-43

I Division

9.32: Peter's tour of inspection
33-35: The healing of Aeneas in Lydda
36-42: The resurrection of Tabitha in Joppa
43: Peter's stay in Joppa with Simon the tanner

II Redaction

[**32**] *egeneto de* is a Lukan introductory phrase (cf. 4.5; 9.37,43; 10.1 etc.); *dierchesthai* also occurs in 8.4; 19.1. Similarly, *panton* can be attributed to Luke – in that case it probably refers to the communities in the previous verse. However, here *panton* seems very clumsy and is left hanging. But this evidence should not be referred to in support of the hypothesis of earlier material (thus, however, Lake/Cadbury, *Beg.* IV, 108). *hagious* is picked up again in v.41.

[**33-35**] *onomati* is redactional; similarly the relative pronoun *hos* is frequent in Luke (cf. Radl 1975, 420). *paralelymenos* denotes a lame

120

person only in Luke (cf. 8.7). Elsewhere in the cross references we find *paralytikos*. For the word of command in v.34 cf. 14.10 and Luke 5.24. But the differences in the two passages do not allow us to infer tradition (variation). *pantes, katoikein* and *epistrephein* in v.35 are favourite words of Luke's.

[36-42] *tis... onomati* in v.36 is redactional; the expression 'alms' corresponds to 10.2 and is a favourite word of Luke's. Moreover the description of Tabitha (for the name see below III on v.40) – that she is full of good works – and the reference to the pieces of clothing that she made for others (v.39c) is redactional. For this is how the woman is meant to be shown worthy of the miracle (cf. Luke 7.2-5; 7.12; Acts 10.2,4). 'In those days' (v.37) is a Lukan indication of time. Verse 38 connects the previous miracle story with this one. By mentioning the distance between Lydda and Joppa and reporting Peter's stay in Lydda and the sending of two men, Luke links the two narratives together.

'The artificiality of this connection is also evident from the fact that according to v.43 Peter does not return to Lydda, from which he has suddenly been removed and only because of a single piece of aid, but remains in Joppa' (Weiser 1981, 241).

Joppa is about twelve miles from Lydda. The note in v.38 therefore reflects an accurate knowledge of the geography of the coastal region (cf. rightly M.Hengel 1983b, 116f., and see already Conzelmann 1960, 69).

In language, v.39 is Lukan: *anastas, synelthen*, the replacement of the demonstrative pronoun with the relative pronoun (cf. 19.25), *anegagon*. The motive of prayer in v.40 and the kneeling down are redactional (cf. Luke 22.41 [Mark differs]/Acts 7.60; 20.36; 21.5). *anekathisen* corresponds exactly with Luke 7.15. According to Schille 1983, v.41 is 'unfortunate, as the person who has been raised is already alive and sitting up. The touching of hands still indicates the old theme of the establishment of a magical contact which of course would have to be made before the miracle (thus Mark 5.41)' (240). However, it should be noted that the girl only sits up (*anekathisen*) in v.40b. So the miracle is not yet complete and further help is needed. *hagious* refers back to v.32, and *cheras* to v.39. The phrase *parestesen auten zosan* recalls 1.3. *kai episteusan polloi epi ton kyrion* in v.42b is a striking parallel to v.35b (*hoitines epestrepsan epi ton kyrion*). Luke probably formulated the concluding sentences of the two stories in the same way deliberately, in order to make the two accounts parallel for the reader.

On the whole we have to accept the influence of the Old Testament resurrection narratives in I Kings 17.17-24 and II Kings 4.32-27 for vv.36-42 (cf. similarly Luke 17.15). This form probably derives from Luke's reading of the Bible and not from tradition. Of course that makes the reconstruction of the basis in tradition considerably more difficult (cf. the comparison of Acts 9.36-42 with I Kings 17 and II Kings 4 in Weiser 1981, 238).

The redactional position of the miracle stories in Acts 9.33-35; 9.36-42

The two miracle stories bring Peter to Caesarea and stress that Peter, the representative of the twelve apostles, is continuing Jesus' activity, including his miracles (cf. Schmithals 1982, 99). At the same time he establishes the connection between the communities of Lydda and Joppa and the mother community in Jerusalem (cf. 8.4) by the tour of inspection (v.32).

III Tradition

[33-35] The basis of this section is a miracle story, but it has been considerably compressed by Luke. It has no situation (v.32 is part of the redactional framework), and no real conclusion. For v.35 does not contain 'the *effect on the observer*, following the style of the miracle story' (Conzelmann 1987, 76), but only the consequences (Schille 1983, 238 is correct). The narrative is a distant recollection of the healing of the man sick of the palsy (Mark 2.1-12 parr.).

[36-42] On the whole the story gives the impression of being a miracle story with a developed style. It begins with the introduction of the person of Tabitha and confirms her death. The miracle worker is brought, and the weeping women (widows) in v.39 provide a contrast to his appearance (v.40). In accordance with the form the resurrection follows the miracle worker's command. Verse 41 contains the demonstration of the miracle. Because of the way in which it begins, this story may have come to Luke in isolation.

It has a parallel in the story of Jairus's daughter (Mark 5). 'Tabitha recalls the Talitha in Mark 5.41; vv.39,40 so correspond with Mark 5.40,41 that we cannot think the two stories independent of each other' (Wellhausen 1914, 19; cf. further the weeping women or widows on each occasion). If Wellhausen is right, we might suppose that the two narratives had been assimilated at a pre-Lukan stage. Similarly we must not dismiss the other possibility that Luke has formulated the whole story on the basis of Mark 5. Cf. also Roloff 1973, 190. Roloff similarly refers to the parallelism between Mark 5 and Acts 9, but stresses the absence of the motive of faith in Acts 9. But this is no argument against dependence, as the theme of faith is dispensable here for the reasons mentioned (p.121).

122

[43] The information that Peter lodged in Joppa at the house of Simon the Tanner is regarded by many as being too specific not to be based on tradition. Cf. Weiser 1981: the report that Peter stayed in the house of Simon the tanner comes from a local tradition (241). Against this see Wellhausen 1914: 'In contrast to the Gospels of Mark and Matthew, names are given, even for the area in Joppa. But the names do not guarantee the reliability of what is reported, any more than do those in the Third and Fourth Gospels' (19). Cf. further Luke's interest in lodging places (see Cadbury 1926). For the novellistic interest in names see Bultmann 1968, 241f. In Luke 8.41, Luke himself 'invents' the name of the person who remains anonymous in Mark 5.22. The conclusion to be drawn is that the specific information given by Luke in v.43 need not go back to tradition.

IV Historical

[32-42] The historical basis of both accounts is a stay of Peter in Lydda and Joppa. As these are markedly Jewish places (cf., comprehensively, Hengel 1983b, 116-19), we may see Peter's journey as a historical basis for his mission to the Jews (cf. Gal.2.7), as was agreed or endorsed during the visit by Paul to Cephas (Gal.1.18; for the reasons see Lüdemann 1983, 72f.). From this the time between the visit of Cephas (33/36) and the conference (48/51) can be defined as the period during which Peter travelled to the two places mentioned and there visited or even founded communities. However, by way of qualification it should be stressed that the reconstruction above rests on more than one uncertain foundation.

Loisy 1920, 431, differs. He explains the setting in Lydda and Joppa merely in terms of a pragmatic purpose to bring Peter near to the next scene, Caesarea.

Furthermore it is a fact that miracle traditions are attached to leading figures of early Christianity: 'that stories of this kind tended to be attached to various people and places in the tradition where any occasion offered itself as a point of contact is a well-known phenomenon of all sagas' (Pfleiderer 1902, 492). The further question whether the miracle traditions were developed in the places mentioned by Luke or were only connected with them by Luke himself cannot now be answered. But Aeneas may have had a connection with Peter which can no longer be discovered. The same is true of Tabitha – though in her case that is less probable.

[43] Peter's stay with Simon the tanner is, like that of Paul with Judas in the Straight Street, only a historical possibility.

Acts 10.1-11.18

I Division

Acts 10

10.1-8: Cornelius's vision
  1-2: Description of Cornelius
  3-6 Vision
    3a: Time and place of the vision
    3b-6: Conversation in the vision and command to Cornelius
  7-8: Cornelius obeys
9-16: Peter's vision
  9a: Link between vv.1-8 and vv.9-16
  9b-10a: Information about time, place and more specific circumstances
  10b-16: Vision
    10b-12: Vision
    13: Audition
    14: Peter's objection
    15: Further audition
    16a: Reference to the event being repeated three times
    16b: End of vision
17-23: Encounter between Cornelius's messenger and Peter
  17a: Peter at a loss
  17b-18: Arrival of Cornelius's messenger
  19a: Peter reflects on his vision
  19b-20: Order by the Spirit to go with the messenger
  21: Peter introduces himself and asks why the messenger has come
  22: Report of Cornelius's vision
  23a: Cornelius's messenger welcomed warmly by Peter
  23b: (The next day) Peter departs for Caesarea with Cornelius's messenger, accompanied by some brethren from Joppa
24-48: The events in Cornelius's house in Caesarea
  24-33: Encounter between Peter and Cornelius
    24a: Arrival of Peter in Caesarea
    24b: (Retrospect:) Preparation for the meeting by Cornelius
    25: Welcoming of Peter by Cornelius with prostration and proskynesis
    26: Repudiation by Peter
    27: Conversation between Peter and Cornelius, they enter the house and meet many people
    28-29: Peter explains why he is entering a Gentile house and asks why Cornelius has summoned him
    30-33: Report by Cornelius about his vision and declaration of his readiness to obey the order given to Peter
  34-43: Peter's speech
    34-36: Introduction to the situation
    37-43: Recapitulation of Luke and Acts

37-41: Body of the speech
37-39a: Jesus's public activity
39b-41: Death and resurrection of Jesus
42-43: The commission to the apostles to preach
44-48: Outpouring of the Holy Spirit on Peter's audience and their baptism
 Reaction of people of the circumcision

Acts 11

1-18: Peter in Jerusalem
  1: The Jerusalem apostles and brethren in Judaea hear that the Gentiles have
     accepted the word
  2-3: (When Peter is in Jerusalem:) objections to Peter's dealings with non-Jews by
     the people from the circumcision
  4-17: Peter's speech (retrospect on ch.10)
     4: Introduction
     5-10: Peter's vision in Joppa
     11: The arrival of Cornelius's messengers
     12a: The order by the Spirit to go with the messengers without hesitation
     12b: The journey (with six brethren) and the arrival in Cornelius's house
     13-14: Cornelius's vision
     15: Descent of the Holy Spirit on Cornelius's house
     16: Reference back to Jesus's word about the baptism with the Spirit (1.5)
     17: Peter could not resist the working of God
  18: Reaction of the hearers: praise of God

II Redaction

Excursus: The Cornelius Story and the Narrative about the Centurion
from Capernaum

The first part (vv.1-8) is very reminiscent of the Lukan version of the story of the
centurion of Capernaum (Luke 7.1-10 par Matt.8.5-13; the Johannine version in John
4.46-53 certainly has close genetic connections with the synoptic version – cf. Dauer
1984, 39-44). Whereas Matt.8.5 simply describes the centurion as a Gentile who turns
humbly and in trust to Jesus and is heard by him, Luke 7.2-5, while representing him
as a Gentile, in addition stresses through the elders of the Jews who entreat Jesus on
his behalf that he loves the Jews and has had a synagogue built for them. This
description matches that of Cornelius in Acts 10: he is similarly portrayed as a Gentile,
but is a godfearer and has given much alms to the Jewish people. Luke 7 and Acts 10
are further similar in that Jesus is entreated by the centurion, as Peter is by Cornelius,
through messengers sent to his house (Luke 7.3/Acts 10.7f.), whereas Matt.8.6
contains what is probably an original feature of the story (cf. Luke 7.6), that Jesus
does not want to go into the centurion's house (cf. Zeller 1854, 429f., 508; Muhlack
1979, 39-54). Certainly Luke 7.1-10 and Acts 10 are basically different in that one

story narrates a miracle (the centurion's servant is healed) and the other a conversion. Therefore although we need not assume a doublet, the parallels just mentioned between this story and Luke 7, i.e. the description of Cornelius's positive attitude to Judaism and the statement that he was a centurion, may be regarded as redactional. For the first Gentile to be converted by Peter to be a centurion fits Luke's apologetic too well to be traditional (cf. Lüdemann 1984, 18). The information that Cornelius was a member of the Italian cohort also serves the same purpose in this connection. The information is historically incorrect (the Italian cohort only existed from 69 CE into the second century, and in Syria; see Broughton, *Beg.* V, 441-3: Schürer 1973, 375) and can be understood as arising out of Luke's concern to give particular people a context in world history (there are other examples in Lüdemann 1984, 19).

Hengel 1983b thinks any dispute over the historicity of the existence of the Italian cohort in Caesarea in the time of Cornelius pointless. The reason that he gives is that Luke's information 'may be an anachronism but need not necessarily be so. Auxiliary cohorts could be posted anywhere in the Roman empire according to need, cf. Josephus, *Antt* 19, 364-6' (203 n.111; cf. Wikenhauser 1921, 314f., who is still positive about Luke's information). But according to what we know about the composition of the cohorts, it is extremely improbable that a cohort consisting of Roman citizens from Italy should have been stationed in Caesarea in 40 CE (cf. Schürer 1973, 365). Remarks by Hengel which recall our too scanty 'knowledge of Roman troops in Syria and Palestine' (1983b, 203 n.111), as the learned author himself knows, cannot seriously shake the judgment on probability made above on the basis of knowledge currently available. Discussion with Hengel (which is always worth while) ends up in the question at what point information in Luke may be deemed to be false (cf. above, 51, on Acts 3.2).

[1-8] *aner de tis, onomati, kaloumenes* in v.1 are Lukan language. The characterization of the centurion (v.2) matches the way in which Luke elsewhere describes people who are thought worthy of special divine interventions: cf. Luke 1.6 (Zechariah and Elizabeth); 2.25 (Symeon); 2.37 (Hannah); Acts 9.36 (Tabitha). For *phoboumenos ton theon* see 155f. on 13.43; for the *oikos* formula see 182 on 16.15. Perhaps the details of time are redactional. Cf. the mention of the Jewish times of prayer in Luke 1.10; Acts 3.1; 10.9,30. For the conversations in the visions (vv.3b-6) cf. 9.4f. Cornelius's question in v.4 is like that of Saul in 9.5. Verse 6 picks up 9.43 (Peter with Simon the Tanner). *proskarterounton* in v.7 is redactional in language, as are *exegesamenos, hapanta* in v.8.

[9-16] The following characteristics match Lukan language and style: v.9, the genitive absolute (on which see Radl 1975, 432), the information about the time of prayer (cf.v.3), the theme of prayer; v.10, *egeneto ep',* *ekstasis*, v.11, *theorei, kathiemenon.* For the theme of the opening of heaven see 7.56; v.12, *hyperchen*; v.13, *egeneto phone, anastas +* imperative (cf. Jeremias 1980, 55), *thyson*; v.16, *anelemphthe.*

The verses contain a vision of Peter the aim of which is to show the distinction between impure and pure foods to be of no significance. Peter later refers to this vision (v.28) and takes it to mean that restrictions on contacts between Jews and Gentiles are done away with (the Gentiles are from now on no longer unclean). That means that Peter's vision in vv.9-16 has a metaphorical significance for Luke. The abolition of the tabu over food in effect means the abolition of restrictions between Gentiles and Jews. In future Jews will be allowed unlimited fellowship with Gentiles (Luke presupposes the latter in the Pauline part of Acts).

[17-23] The language used in the description of Peter's perplexity in v.17a recalls 5.24. For the redactional *idou* cf. Radl 1975, 413. Verses 17b-18 link the Peter episode and the Cornelius episode. Cornelius's messengers appear at the door. Verse 19a is a link, in the redactional genitive absolute, with v.17a (the description of Peter's perplexity; cf. the connection by the keyword *horama* [v.19a/v.17a]). In vv.19b-20 it is remarkable that the Spirit speaks to Peter again. The instruction by the Spirit does *not* relate to the previous vision. For *idou* in v.21 cf. v.17a. Verse 22 summarizes Cornelius's vision (vv.1-8). *xenizo* (v.23, cf.v.18) is frequent in Luke, as is the theme of lodging (cf. Cadbury 1926). In addition, this part of the verse explains the divine instructions given explicitly later (v.28), which in Luke's understanding were already contained in vv.10-16. The journey of the group from Joppa to Caesarea (v.23b) makes possible the encounter between Peter and Cornelius which is mentioned next; by introducing the Jewish brethren (cf.10.45), at the same time it prepares for the debate in 11.1-18.

[24-48] In v.24, *te de epaurion* (cf.v.23b), *prosdokon*, the periphrastic conjugation (cf. Radl 1975, 431), *sygkalesamenos* are redactional, as are *synantesas* and *tou* + infinitive (cf.Radl 1975, 432f.) in v.25. For v.26 cf. 14.15. *eiselthen* in v.27 picks up *eiselthein* in v.25. Verses 25 and 27 are in tension, since according to v.25 Cornelius is already in the gathering (thus already Wellhausen 1914, 20, similarly Dibelius 1956, 113 – cf. the harmonization by Codex D). *heuriskei, synelelythotas* are Lucan in language. Verses 28-29 contain Luke's interpretation of Peter's vision (vv.10-16). From now on there is no longer any difference between Jew and non-Jew; one may no longer call anyone common and unclean (as Peter still did before his vision). Verses 30-33, Cornelius's speech, are a Lucan repetition of vv.1-8. The redactional v.33b leads into Peter's speech (vv.34-43). Cornelius's house wants to hear what the Lord has to say to them through Peter.

For the linguistic shaping of the speech in vv.34-43 cf. Weiser 1981, 258f. Verses 34f. pick up the portrait of Cornelius in the previous story. The statement that in every people those are acceptable to the Lord who fear him and act justly certainly applies to Cornelius. He had been portrayed as a godfearer and one who had given much alms (10.2, 22).

127

Verse 36 is syntactically difficult or even corrupt (cf. the commentaries ad loc. and Burchard 1985, 292f.: Burchard stresses the links between Luke 2.10ff. and Acts 10.36). But the sense is to some extent clear if v.36 can be interpreted in connection with vv.34f. (cf. the way in which *panti* [v.35] is picked up by *panton* [v.36]): as the messenger of peace for Israel Jesus is called Lord over all (including the non-Jews mentioned in vv.34f.). Verse 36 is at the same time the heading for the next section (vv.37-43). Cf. also the parallel formulation of vv.36b, 42b and the way in which *panton* (v.36) is picked up by *pantas* (v.38) and *panta* (v.43). In vv.37-43 Peter recapitulates Luke and Acts (cf. the extensive explanation by Schneider 1985, 276-9) at the author-reader level. In v.37 *hymeis oidate* is occasionally regarded as a reference to pre-Lucan tradition (cf. just Dibelius 1956, 111 n.5), since the address has nothing to do with the situation and does not fit Cornelius and his house. However, we should not yet conclude a tradition from this, for those addressed are the readers of Luke and Acts (cf. similarly Dibelius 1956, 111). For *holes tes Ioudaias* see Luke 4.44; 23.5; *apo tes Galilaias*, Luke 4.14,16; 23.6; *meta to baptisma... Ioannes*, Luke 4.14; 16.16; cf. Acts 1.2 (*arxamenos*). For *echrisen... pneumati hagio* in v.38 cf. Luke 4.18,14. For *euergeton* cf. Luke 22,25; Acts 4.9; for *iomenos*, Luke 5.17; 6.19; for *tous katadynast-euomenous hypo tou diabolou* cf. Luke 6.18f.; 1.42. For the testimony of the apostles (v.39) cf. Acts 1.21 (see further there); for the death of Jesus on the cross cf. on Acts 5.30. For vv.40-41 cf. Luke 24-Acts 1; for v.42, cf. Luke 24.47; for v.43, Luke 24.44. Further evidence also indicates a redactional origin for the speech throughout. Peter's speech in Caesarea offers far more information about the earthly career of Jesus than Peter's other speeches. That takes account of the composition of the audience. Another feature which fits the situation is that there are no explicit quotations from the Old Testament in Peter's speech as in his speeches in Acts 2; 3. In this way careful notice is taken by the redaction of the particular audience, which is between Judaism and the Gentile world. Nevertheless the speech alludes to the testimony of scripture (v.43) in contrast to the purely Gentile sermons in Acts (14.15-17; 17.22-31). For the character of the speech see the remarks by Schneider 1982, 63f. and Schneider 1985, 273-9 (here there is also a report and criticism of various hypotheses about a tradition behind Acts 10.37-43; particular attention should be paid to it).

Verses 44-48 demonstrate in Lukan fashion the consequence of the acceptance of the gospel by the Gentiles. The Spirit falls upon all who hear Peter's speech. Indeed, like the disciples at Pentecost they speak in tongues (v.46) and are baptized. The apparent break in the speech in v.44 is a device of Luke's (cf. Luke 22.40 [Mark 14.72 differs]); Luke 8.49 [= Mark 5.35]; Luke 22.47 [= Mark 14.43], since all that needs to be said has been said. *existemi* and *synerchomai* in v.45 are favourite Lukan words. For *dora tou hagiou pneumatos* cf. 2.38. The verse describes the reaction of the believers from the circumcision (*hoi ek peritomes pistoi*) to the bestowal of the Spirit on the Gentiles and thus prepares for what follows (cf. 11.2, 'the people from the circumcision'), where Peter will explain the significance of the Cornelius episode to the community in Jerusalem (11.4-17). Verse 46 makes it clear that Cornelius's people shared in the same gifts as the first Pentecost community. The account of the baptism after the receiving of the Spirit in vv.47-48 only apparently contradicts Luke's theology, which suggests the bestowing of the Spirit after baptism (cf. 8.16; 19.5f.). Here as in 9.17f. (end) the bestowal of the Spirit comes before the baptism only for reasons of narrative technique.

[**11.1-18**] In v.1 the author recalls 8.14; cf. 'the Gentiles have accepted the word of God' (v.1) with 'Samaria has accepted the word of God' (8.14). In both cases the Jerusalem community hears the news and makes a decision.

With the key words 'enter in' (*eiselthein*) and 'eat with' (*symphagein*) the reproof of the people from the circumcision ('You went in among uncircumcised people and ate with them') in vv.2,3 refers to 10.27 (*symphagein* probably corresponds to *synomilein* or points back to Peter's stay with Cornelius which is presupposed in 10.48). At the same time the theme 'eat' may be an allusion to 10.10-16. Thus vv.2f. draw together the theme which is Luke's concern in what follows.

Verses 4-17 describe what has happened so far by repeating it and thus give the events heightened emphasis. The small deviations should not lead to the wrong assumption that different sources have been used here (11.14/10.5,32: the latter passage does not mention the goal of Peter's speech, namely the salvation of Cornelius and his house; 11.15/10.44: in one passage the Spirit falls at the beginning of the speech [if *archomai* in 11.15 does not have a weakened meaning, as it does in 1.1] where the speech is not taken further, and in the other towards the end, where it is). In connection with this last point Dibelius has aptly explained: 'A speech can obviously be regarded by the author as an assertion or addition which does not necessarily affect the course of the narrative' (1956, 110; Trocmé 1957, 171 n.1, rejects this without giving a reason). The first deviation mentioned (11.14/10.5,32) is connected with the narrative style. 'The legend itself does not at this point disclose what is to be the outcome, so tension arises when, in the re-telling of the story, both the message and the ultimate purpose of the angel's appearance are included' (Dibelius 1956, 110). Verses 15f. once again (after 10.46) link the Gentile Christian experience of the Spirit with the beginning of Acts.

To sum up, following Dibelius we may say the following about the significance of the Cornelius story for Luke:

'Luke wanted to show how the will of God was made known to Peter in the conversion of Cornelius; it was because of this same will that the Gentiles were called, and just how this came about Luke proposed to relate immediately afterwards (11.20f.) in several examples concerning (named) people in Antioch. Here, however, the classic example was to be described, the decisive first manifestation of this will. This is how Luke regards the story of Cornelius, and as such he makes Peter quote it (*aph'hemeron archaion*, 15.7) and James (*kathos proton ho theos epeskepsato*, 15.14). Therefore, right at the beginning of the story of Cornelius, God must speak words of authority to Peter, telling him to go to the Gentiles' (Dibelius 1956, 117f.)

As Acts 15.7 shows, this story points the way ahead for the subsequent period. Luke has stressed the significance of this event – quite apart from the length of the episode and the repetitions – by effectively making the conversion of Cornelius the last in the series of three conversion stories and by giving it the most developed co-ordination of individuals through visions.

But Luke may have associated a subsidiary purpose with the Cornelius story. He knows from his sources that at the Jerusalem conference which he reports in ch.15 the right to carry on the mission to the Gentiles had to be fought for by Paul, and that a strong group in the Jerusalem community accepted the compromise there only hesitantly, if at all. Therefore he brings the conflict forward and attributes its resolution to an announcement of the will of God given to Peter, which can be presupposed at the conference as a fact.

So at the historical level we may not ask why the events of Acts 15 were possible after those of Acts 10f., and explain them as an intensified nomism on the part of the Jerusalem community (thus Jervell 1984, 23). That is a premature historicization which does not do justice to what Luke means to say.

III Traditions

A retrospect on the analysis of the redaction, with special reference to the question of tradition

The above analysis of the redaction has indicated the Lukan character of the language and content throughout the Cornelius pericope. As the story stands, it can be assigned verse by verse to Lukan narrative style and theology. Nevertheless the following observations already made in the text suggest that we can argue back to material used by Luke: v.19b (the instruction of the Spirit) makes the vision narrated previously seem superfluous and does not once refer to it. On the other hand it is not clear why the instruction of the Spirit is given *after* Peter's vision. For the heavenly voice had spoken unambiguously (10.15: 11.9). Probably the best explanation of the evidence is to assume that vv.10-16 go back to tradition which Luke has introduced in this context (for the reasons see 127 above). He has toned down the tension which thus arises between vv.10-16 and v.19 by v.17 (Peter in perplexity) and v.19a (Peter's reflection on the vision).

Verses 27-29a also derive from Luke, since here (v.28) Peter refers to the vision of vv.10-16. The assumption that vv.27-29a are redactional is confirmed by a literary-critical observation: vv.25 and 27 are in tension with each other (according to v.25 Cornelius is at home, according to v.27 he is only going in – Haenchen 1971 differs: v.25 refers to going into the gateway and v.27 into the house proper [350])). The tradition which is interrupted in v.26 and is broken off by the 'interruption to the narrative' (Dibelius 1956, 113) of vv.27-29a then runs on in v.39b (for v.39b as tradition cf. 71 on 5.30).

After these reflections and on the basis of the analysis of the redaction we can conjecture the following traditions in the Cornelius narrative.

A. Luke had before him a story about the conversion of the Gentile Cornelius by Peter in Caesarea. The narrative described in detail how Cornelius, prompted by an angel, had Peter brought from Joppa; Peter, instructed by a voice from heaven, accepted the invitation. Peter preached to Cornelius and his house, and they were baptized and received the Holy Spirit.

It must be stressed once again that we can reconstruct only the outline of a tradition. To reconstruct more and to claim greater certainty would be all the less compelling because of Luke's work of redaction; individual features like e.g the invitation of Peter (Acts 10.7f. – cf. the parallel in Luke 7.3) may also go back to Luke.

In form-critical terms the narrative can be compared with the conversion story of the Ethiopian eunuch which comes from Luke (Acts 8.26-39). But the narrative is not a foundation legend for the community in Caesarea in which there is stress on Peter as founder (cf. Schille 1983, 254), since Cornelius – and not Peter – is at the centre.

What has been said above largely follows Dibelius 1956, 109-22; Haacker's objections are helpful in raising problems, but end up by being apologetic: 'There is really... nothing against the view that reports of the event – as Acts 11.1 asserts – came to Jerusalem, provoked criticism there and possibly resulted in an authentic account which is put on the lips of Peter in Acts 11.4-7' (1980, 249). For the same question see also section IV and the views discussed there.

B. The vision in 10.10-16 is derived from tradition. It serves as a norm by explaining that the difference between different foods is irrelevant.

Luke inserted it as it is associated with the theme of Gentiles and Jews. It does *not* seem that it should be attached to the sphere of tradition relating to the 'incident at Antioch' (on Dibelius 1956, 112; Weiser 1981, 262). Eating with Gentiles was usual in Antioch. To end it would have required the revelation. Moreover in Antioch Peter is following (for the moment) a custom which was already in existence. It is better to regard the association of the vision with Peter at this point as redactional and perhaps assign 10.10-16 conjecturally to a Hellenistic Jewish Christianity which had emancipated itself from Jewish food laws (cf. Mark 7.15; Rom. 14.14).

C. In recent years the conjecture has repeatedly been made that the rebuke against the table-fellowship with the uncircumcised practised by Peter (10.45; 11.2f.) comes from the pre-Lukan tradition (cf. Bovon 1970, 34f.; Haacker 1980, 249). Weiser 1981 seeks to support it further by the following arguments:

'One consists in the observation... that in his account of the apostolic age Luke does not himself create any scenes of conflict but rather avoids them. The second consists in the fact attested by Gal.2.12-14 that Peter practised table fellowship with uncircumcised Gentile Christians in Antioch, but changed his attitude "for fear of those of the circumcision" who had come from James from Jerusalem' (262).

On 1: Lukas transfers the news of the objection of the Jewish Christians to the acceptance of Gentiles, which he knows from the traditions of the conference, in order to tone them down in the context of the Cornelius story (see the shifting of the collection forward from ch.21 to ch.11 and the observations on 130f. in the framework of the analysis of the redaction). Consequently we may not argue from here that this tradition belongs to the Cornelius story.

2. For the reasons mentioned above, the incident at Antioch may not be brought in here.

However, it is the case that *hoi ek peritomes* (cf. on this Ellis 1978, 116-28) is a traditional designation of Jewish Christians who strictly observe the law. Luke knows the designation either from Gal.2.12 or – more probably – from a tradition (cf. also Col.4.11; see further Titus 1.10 [however, these are probably not Jewish Christians but Jews]). At all events Luke has skilfully woven this designation from the tradition into the narrative complex at this point.

IV Historical

The historical nucleus of the Cornelius tradition, which is markedly legendary, is that Peter had been involved in the conversion of a Gentile called Cornelius in Caesarea. Certainly Peter had gone primarily to Jews, as Gal.2.7 makes clear for the 30s and as emerges from his activity in Lydda and Joppa. But the possibility cannot be excluded that, as with Jesus, so too with Peter, there were non-Jews among the audience, and it was all too understandable if Gentiles took note of the leader of the church which was carrying on a mission to the Jews and gradually also to the Gentiles. Cf. also his reputation in the predominantly Gentile Christian community of Corinth (I Cor.1.12) and in the Roman church.

On the other hand it must be conceded that the tradition, the basic features of which are described above, has already moved one stage away from history and only came into being at a time when Jewish Christians of Petrine origin were carrying on a mission predominantly to the Gentiles (cf. as an analogy for Jewish-Christian groups which were increasingly becoming open to the Gentile mission the communities behind Q, Matt and John). If that is correct, we need to ask whether we cannot also see in the development of the tradition a tendency to make Peter rather than Paul the founder of the Gentile mission and/or make the Gentile mission begin before Paul. The historical nucleus of the Cornelius tradition probably goes back to the period between Paul's visit to Cephas and the Jerusalem conference, i.e. the years between 33/36 and 48/51 CE. Peter moved outside Jerusalem and undertook attempts at mission among the Jews which were evidently crowned with success, in the wake of which a Gentile, Cornelius, was also converted.

The tradition in 10.10-16 may be historical in that it once served to legitimate a Jewish-Christian community in emancipating itself from Jewish food laws. Unfortunately we know nothing about who received the vision or where.

For the historicity of the tradition in 10.39b, see 71 on 5.30.

Acts 11.19-30

I Division

11.19-21: Spread of the preaching of the gospel to Antioch. Notice of success (v.21)
22-24: (After this event is noted by the Jerusalem community) sending of Barnabas to Antioch. Notice of success (v.24b)
25-26: Barnabas brings Saul from Tarsus to Antioch. They work together there for a year
26d: Passing remark about the origin of the name Christians
27-30: Prophecy of a general famine by Agabus and the taking of a collection from Antioch to Jerusalem by Barnabas and Saul

II Redaction

[19-21] Verse 19a corresponds word for word with 8.4a, where there is a reference back to 8.1. The verse is not a continuation of the interrupted statement 8.4a, *hoi men oun diasparentes..., dielthon...* (Bultmann 1967, 422, etc.), but a redactional link to it. Luke wants to depict the continuation of the Hellenist mission, the external stimulus to which was the murder of Stephen, having in the meantime also created the intrinsic presuppositions for it. 'After the conversion of Paul, a delayed intermezzo, and after the missionary journey of Peter, a contrafact [sic!] to that of Philip, there is a reference back to ch.8' (Wellhausen 1914, 21). In vv.19b-20 the phrases 'proclaim the word' (cf.4.29,31; 8.25; 13.46; 14.25; 16.6, 32) and 'preach the Lord Jesus' (cf. similarly 5.42) are redactional. Verse 19b brings out the fact that the mission of the Hellenists was only to the Jews. That is in contrast to v.20 which follows, according to which members of the Hellenists also preached to the Gentiles (*hellenas* – however, important manuscripts read *hellenistas*, though the context tells against this). Also underlying vv.19f. is the scheme 'to the Jews first – then to the Gentiles', which also holds for Luke's Paul (cf. 13.5,14; 14.1; 16.13; 17.1f.,10,17). The phrase 'the hand of the Lord was with them' (v.21) has a parallel in Luke 1.66 and is probably a Septuagintism (cf. II Sam.3.12). The note about success (v.21b – cf. later v.24 end) is redactional in language and content (cf. Zingg 1974, 35f.).

[22-24] The section is to be derived from Luke in language and content. For the language: v.22, *eis ta ota* (cf. Luke 1.44; cf. Isa.5.8 [LXX]), *exapesteilan*; v.23, *hos* at the beginning of the sentence, *paragenomenos*, *charin/echare* (paronomasia); v.24, *pleres pneumatos hagious, prosetethe, ochlos, hikanos*. The link between the Jerusalem community and the incident in Antioch derives from Luke: the community hears of the success of the mission as in 8.14 and as in that passage (cf.15.22) sends a delegate. However, Barnabas does not inspect, 'but simply joins the Hellenists and remains in Antioch' (Wellhausen 1914, 21). The characterization of Barnabas in v.24a is Lukan and has a parallel in Luke 1.6; 23.50; Acts 6.3; 9.36; 10.2, 22. Verse 24b is a typical Lukan notice of success (cf. 2.47b; 5.14; 9.31; 11.1b; 16.5).

[25-26c] Here Luke introduces the future protagonist and has him brought by Barnabas from Tarsus to Antioch. Verse 26b is difficult. Wellhausen thinks even the meaning of *synachthenai* unclear (1914, 21). For the construction *egeneto de autois* cf. 20.16. In Acts *synago* denotes a gathering of particular people, usually Christian meetings (4.31; 14.27; 15.6,30; 20.7). Then v.26b reports that Barnabas and Saul met with the

community of Antioch over the space of a year and instructed them (cf. Blass/Debrunner/Funk, *Grammar*, § 332 ³; Zingg 1974, 215f.).

[26d] At this point where he gives a summary report, Luke introduces an interesting detail about the emergence of the name 'Christian', albeit not within the narrative but at the author-reader level.

[27-30] 'In those days' is a general Lukan indication of time; cf. Luke 23.7 and (with a different positioning of the *tautais*) Luke 1.39; 6.12; 24.18; Acts 6.1. For *anastas de*/subject/*onomati* in v.28 cf. Acts 5.34. *hole(n)* is redactional in langueage, as is *hetis* (cf. Radl 1975, 420). The famine 'extending over the whole world was as universal as Quirinius's census' (Wellhausen 1914, 21). In both passages Luke is generalizing from limited local phenomena. There were many famines in the reign of Claudius, but these were as local as the census. It is possible that Luke generalized from the famine in Judaea which probably took place betwen 46 and 48 CE (Josephus, *Antt* XX 51,101 – Suhl 1975, 58-62, however, transfers the said famine to the years 43-44).

In addition to the famine in Judaea mentioned above, the following famines are known during the reign of Claudius: 1. a famine in Rome at the beginning of Claudius's reign; 2. a famine in Greece in 49; and 3. a famine in Rome in 51; cf. Schürer 1973, 457 n.8; Wikenhauser 1921, 407-9 (who sets out the sources in question). Remarkably, Meyer III, 165f., regards the famines mentioned as confirmation of Luke's information – as does Wikenhauser, ibid.

The observation that the famine prophesied by Agabus took place under Claudius arises out of Luke's concern to root the events of salvation history in secular history (cf. Lüdemann 1984, 19). Verses 29-30 describe how the daughter community of Antioch shows solidarity with the mother community of Jerusalem. Barnabas and Saul are sent from Antioch to Jerusalem to bring a collection. (Here as often in Acts Judaea stands for Jerusalem.) The formulation doubtless derives from Luke. This is indicated primarily by the content (only *horisan* in v.29 is certainly Lukan in language, and the constitution of the Lukan church is reflected in *presbyterous* [v.30]). The author establishes a close connection between Antioch and Jerusalem through the note about bringing the collection in order to show their continuity in salvation history. The saving event is continued by the action of the Antiochene community. Its future vehicles, Barnabas and Paul, are therefore emphatically present in vv.29-30.

All in all the summary nature of the account in comparison with 10.1-11.18 is striking. (Weiss even thinks that the section 'does no great credit to the narrative art of the author' [1897, 19].) Not a single story is told, but a relatively large number of facts is set side by side. So we are probably not to take the whole passage as an extract from an Antiochene source (Trocmé 1957, 166f., argues against that – in my view rightly), but as the redactional deployment of individual items which Luke found gathered in the communities and/or in one or more sources (cf. also the instructive commentary by Dibelius 1956, 10f.).

[19-21, 22f.] The report of the Hellenist mission to Phoenicia, Cyprus and Antioch is part of the tradition, since here we have concrete information without a bias. A visit in or journey through Phoenicia is mentioned again in 15.3, but probably does not go back to tradition there (see ad loc.). The material about Cyprus is more extensive: 4.36 depicts Barnabas as a Levite, born in Cyprus; 13.4-12 relate the missionizing of Cyprus by Barnabas and Paul; and 15.39 reports that after separating from Paul, Barnabas went with Mark to Cyprus, evidently to carry on the mission there. The sources about the Hellenist mission on Cyprus were probably reports about Barnabas – himself a Greek-speaking Jewish Christian and active in the Antioch community (v.22; cf. 13.1) – which Luke used for his information in 11.19 (for 13.4ff. see ad loc.). Luke had most material from Antioch (cf. 11.26d; 13.1-3; 15.1-2, etc.), so that there certainly had to be a mention of Antioch here in last place, all the more since from 13.1 Antioch will come into the foreground of the narrative.

The note about the mission to the Gentiles in v.20 is tradition, since it does not fit into Luke's view of history. But by itself it means that the Hellenists were the first to take the step to the Gentile mission, and not Peter through the conversion of Cornelius. For *Kyrenaioi* cf. 13.1 (Lucius the Cyrenaean); 6.9.

Underlying vv.22f. is a tradition the content of which is the activity of Barnabas in the Antioch community (cf.13.1-2). We can also recognize that the link between Barnabas and Jerusalem (cf. earlier 4.36; 9.37) is a Lukan fiction from the fact that the next verse seems to forget that he was sent by the Jerusalem community (v.22b) and gives no reason for his stay in Antioch. This expresses the link in the tradition between Barnabas and Antioch.

[25-26c] For Tarsus cf. 9.30. The activity of Barnabas and Paul in Antioch for the period of a year is probably part of the tradition, since it is a specific

136

unmotivated report in a context where there are scattered elements of tradition (see on v.26d).

[26d] The information about the origin of the name of Christians in Antioch might go back to an isolated tradition which Luke has inserted here. The information stands here without any relationship to context.

[27-30] Verse 27 contains an interesting detail about the activity of prophets in Jerusalem and Antioch. So generally speaking it might be tradition, although we have specific information only in the next verse. The prophet Agabus (v.28) also appears in 21.10, where he prophesies Paul's end. If his appearance there is redactional, he may in fact have his original place in the tradition in the context of 11.27-30. In that case his prophecy would relate at the level of tradition to a famine in Judaea under Claudius. However, the opposite assumption is even more probable, namely that he belonged in the source about Paul's last visit to Jerusalem (cf. Lüdemann 1983, 97). The information about a collection for Jerusalem does not appear elsewhere in Acts, but it does so often in Paul; there it is also designated *diakonia*: I Cor.16.15; II Cor.8.4; 9.1-13; Rom.15.31. For that reason it might not only be tradition, but also have a genetic connection with Paul's collection.

What has just been said relates to Schille 1983: 'We should be careful not to identify this information too quickly with the Pauline information and appeals about the collections for Jerusalem in order in this way to arrive at a collection journey for Paul (v.30). We should keep open the possibility that our action does not correspond with those either in time or in the group of recipients (here only for Judaea?)' (267; following that, Schille mentions the decisive argument to the contrary that in Paul, as in this passage, the collection is called *diakonia*).

The journey made by Barnabas and Paul to Jerusalem (v.30) appears elsewhere in Acts only in 15.1-4, and in Paul in Gal.2.1. The question whether at the level of tradition it can be connected with the bringing of a collection can only be decided on the basis of historical considerations.

IV Historical

The traditions behind vv.19-26 are without doubt historical, namely that the Hellenists began the mission to the Gentiles in Cyprus, Phoenicia and Antioch (cf. H.Balz, *EWNT* I, 264 [bibliography]). Their beginnings might lie in the middle of the 30s. Perhaps the reconstructed elements of tradition also allow the historical judgment that Paul and Barnabas 'originally distinguished themselves from the Hellenists around Stephen and only combined with them in Antioch' (Wellhausen 1914, 21). The tradition that Paul and Barnabas worked together in the Antiochene mission for a period has a higher degree of probability. In the framework of this mission, in the middle of the 30s, they undertook a missionary journey together to southern Galatia (Acts 13-14) and also went later as former mission companions to the Jerusalem conference (Gal.2.1). I Corinthians 9.6 also reflects their former work togeher. In all probability, however, they were only active in Antioch itself for one year (Acts 11.26) (see Weiss 1959, 204).

The information about the origin of the name Christian is historically valuable. The ending -anoi is a Latinism and denotes the supporters of a person (Pompeians, Herodians, etc.). In the second century names of sects were formed in an analogous way (Valentinians, Simonians, etc., cf. Blass/Debrunner/Funk § 5[12]). For this reason it is uncertain whether the name Christian denotes *political* following of Christ (thus Wengst 1987, 73). The tradition is right in that the name Christian, like the other parallels, is a term used by outsiders (cf. in the NT also Acts 26.28; I Peter 4.16 [?!]). The 'Christians' only used the name themselves in the time of Ignatius (IgnEph 11.2; IgnRom 3.2; IgnMagn 4); by contrast it is used by Pliny the Younger (*Ep* X, 96f.) and by Tacitus (*Ann* XV, 44: the people called the victims of Nero's persecution *Chrestiani* [= popular form of *Christiani*]). For the whole problem see Harnack 1924, 424-33; the argument that *Christianoi* was originally a self-designation, which has recently been renewed (Zingg 1974, 217-22), collapses on the non-Christian evidence.

Even if the information about the emergence of the name Christian is reliable, one certainly cannot say whether Luke has put it at the right chronological point. Since he probably had no opportunity of providing this information in the narrative of Acts, it was natural for him to insert it here, where he is giving a summary report about the Antiochene community.

A journey with the collection at this point is ruled out by the Pauline chronology (Lüdemann 1984, 13f.). Luke apparently took over the motive of the collection from the traditional material used in Acts 21 (see 236f. below) and probably also the figure of the prophet Agabus. It is striking that he avoids the theme of the collection in Acts 15-21. Luke may have duplicated the joint journey of Barnabas and Paul from the complex of tradition about the Jerusalem conference which he had at his disposal and transferred it here.

Less probable, but not to be ruled out, is the possibility that at this point we have historically reliable evidence of the tradition of a collection made by the community at Antioch for the Jerusalem community. At the conference, indeed, not only did Paul commit himself to making a collection for the people of Jerusalem but Barnabas did

138

the same on behalf of the Antiochene community (cf. Gal.2.10 and the commentary in Lüdemann 1984, 77-80). The tradition would then reflect the making of the collection by the Antioch community for the Jerusalem community.

Moreover Acts 11.19-30 reflects the historical fact that the Antioch community and the Jerusalem mother community were in close contact from the earliest period. From the beginning both churches worked together. The ecumenical movement was not a late fruit.

Acts 12

I Division

12.1-2: Execution of James the son of Zebedee on the orders of Herod Agrippa I
3-17: Imprisonment and release of Peter. Peter in Mary's house
  3-4: (Framework) Occasion and point in time of Peter's imprisonment (future plans)
  5-17: Imprisonment and release of Peter
    5a: Peter in prison
    5b: The unceasing prayer of the community for Peter
    6: Peter asleep in the night before the trial with strengthened guard
    7-10: Miraculous release
    11: Peter's recognition that the lord has sent his angel and snatched him from the hand of Herod and all the expectation of the Jews
    12-17: Peter among the Jerusalem Christians gathered in Mary's house
      12: Peter goes to Mary's house
      13-16: Peter is admitted only after overcoming the doubts of the Christians
      17a-d: Peter's description of his release and instructions to the community
      17e: Peter leaves Jerusalem
18-19: Punishment of Peter's guard on the orders of Herod Agrippa I
20-23: Death of Herod Agrippa I in Caesarea
24-25: Summary. Return of Barnabas and Saul from Jerusalem to Antioch

II Redaction

This chapter is interwoven with the previous episode, which reports the collection by the Antioch community for Jerusalem. Those who bring the collection, Barnabas and Saul, are thought of as being present in Jerusalem during the persecution – without being integrated into the story – and return to Antioch once Peter has been released from prison and gone to 'another place' (v.17e). The technique of inserting another story between the sending and the return of messengers is also used in Mark 6.7-13.30 (par. Luke 9.1-9) and may have inspired Luke to compose this scene (cf. similarly Schneider 1982, 101).

The present story is one of several narratives about the release of apostles/missionaries; cf. 4.1-22; 5.17-42; 16.19-40. By repeatedly taking up the theme, Luke stresses that no resistance of any kind can hinder the implementation of God's plan of salvation. A summary note about growth in v.24a, as in 9.31, stresses that the enemy of the Christians can do nothing against the word of the Lord. Lukan redactional elements can be recognized in what follows.

[1-2] The note 'at that time' in v.1 has a parallel in 19.23 and Luke 13.1; the phrase 'lay on hands' also appears in 4.3; 5.18; 21.27 (cf. Luke 20.19; 21.12).

[3-17] 'When he saw that it pleased the Jews' is probably a piece of Lukan pragmatism to motivate the transition to a further attack on a leading figure of the earliest community. In that case v.11, in harmony with v.3, depicts Herod and the people of the Jews as enemies of the Christians from whom Peter must be saved. The change in the mood of the people cannot be understood historically, but is part of the redaction.

Even about twenty years later the attack on James the brother of Jesus was still so unpopular that the person responsible for it, Ananus, lost his office as a consequence (cf. Lüdemann 1983, 99-101).

The execution of James the son of Zebedee (v.2) and the attack on Peter (v.3) correspond to the hostile action against Stephen (Acts 6f.), and the portrayal of the people of Jerusalem tends to be predominantly negative after Acts 6 (cf. 9.29; 12.3f.,11; 21.27,30, 36; 22.22; 23.12,20f.) and in the Diaspora (13.45,50 etc. – for the evidence above cf. Lohfink 1975b, 55, and already Overbeck 1870, 181f.). The fact that there is no replacement for James son of Zebedee shows that in terms of salvation history the phase of the earliest community is over. The future bearers of the mission to the Gentiles have already appeared on the scene.

Verse 3 gives an interesting note about time: Agrippa has Peter arrested during the days of unleavened bread. But that is in tension with the remark in v.4b that Agrippa is thinking of presenting Peter to the people after the Passover. For traditionally the days of unleavened bread (15-21 Nisan) follow the passover (= 14 Nisan), cf. Ex.12.6-15. Now Luke identifies the days of unleavened bread (as already Mark 14.1,12) with the feast of the passover (cf. Luke 22.1,7; Acts 20.6 – the same is probably true of popular Jewish terminology, cf. Josephus, Antt XIV, 21 and H.Patsch, EWNT III, 117-20). The meaning of v.3 then is that there is a parallel between the arrest of Peter on the feast of the passover and that of Jesus at the same time (Luke 22.7). So Peter's fate is prefigured in that of Jesus.

etheto in v.4 similarly appears in 4.3 (there too in connection with 'lay hands on someone'). The information about the military guard and the planned presentation prepares for the statements in the subsequent story about the guarding of Peter by the soldiers (v.5f.) and the presentation itself (v.6). Verse 4 is therefore a redactional anticipation of the following narrative (cf. Conzelmann 1987, 93). *men oun* in v.5a is redactional; v.5b as a whole gives the impression of being a Lukan addition. According to vv.12 + 17 the community, which is presented as being at prayer, has not yet completely assembled. So in v.17 Peter first asks the Christians assembled in Mary's house to report his release to other members of the community (James and the brethren). The mention of Herod in v.6 derives from the framework (v.1). For the formulations in v.7a cf. Luke 2.9. *pataxas* has been deliberately chosen; it is a negative counterpart to v.23. As indicated by the keyword *patassein*, in both cases the angel of the Lord initiates the rescue or the punishment. Verse 9b-c are resolved in the redactional v.11. The event is unbelievable – Peter thinks he is seeing only a vision – yet true. Therefore v.9b-c is also redactional. Verse 11 depicts Peter's recognition, subsequent to v.9b-c: 'Now I know for certain that the Lord has sent his angel and snatched me from the hand of Herod and all that the Jewish people were expecting.' The substance of Peter's recognition is derived from the previous story (+ redaction). For the negative characterization of Herod and the people of the Jews cf. the remark above on v.3. The direct speech enlivens the scene and stresses the significance of the sentence which is spoken in direct speech (cf. similarly 25.12; 26.32). In the next sub-section vv.12-17 the hand of Luke is evident in the language at the following points: v.12, periphrastic conjugation, *hikanoi, proseuchomenoi*; v.13, *onomati*; v.14, *epignousa, charas, apeggeilen*; v.15, *eipan* (+ *pros*); v.16, *exestesan*; v.17, *kataseisas, diegesato*. Moreover there is a Lukan intervention in v.12 (the mother of John Mark). With this observation Luke prepares for v.25. (However, we should not conclude from this that Luke is responsible for the whole of v.12 [cf. Conzelmann 1987, 94 against Hanechen 1971, 384f.].) Moreover the artistic composition of the recognition scene (vv.13-16) may derive from Luke on the basis of a simpler report. Finally, the remark in v.17c ('Tell this to James and the brethren') also derives from Luke. In that way he introduces the new leader of the Jerusalem Christian community (though that he is only becomes clearly visible in ch.21).

[18-19] The section as a whole derives from Luke. The litotes in v.18, *ouk oligos*, is frequent in Luke, as is the introductory genitive absolute; for the formulation 'there was not a little unrest' cf. 19.23. In v.19 the note about the killing of the negligent guard will have to be attributed wholly

141

to the redactor as it stresses the miracle on the one side and Herod's cruelty on the other. Verse 19b is a transition to the next episode.

[20-23] Here Luke works in a tradition about the death of Agrippa in order to depict this as a punishment for his acts of violence against members of the earliest community. (This redactional purpose emerges out of a consideration of vv.20-23 in the context of Acts 12.)

[24-25] Verse 24 is a summary which is meant to show the growth of the word of God despite of and in the persecution (cf. Zingg 1974, 20-40); the parallel passages in Acts appear in the margin of the Nestle/Aland text on Acts 2.47. Verse 25 reports the return of Barnabas and Saul to Antioch with reference to 11.30 (*hypostrepho* is a favourite Lukan word). From now on, after an interlude with Barnabas and the description of the Jerusalem conference, Paul is at the centre. His taking of John Mark with him was already prepared for by v.12 (Peter comes into the house of Mary, the mother of John Mark).

Text-critically v.25 causes perplexity as to whether we should read *ex Ierousalem* or *eis Ierousalem*. If *eis I.* is to be preferred (thus Nestle/Aland[26]), it is to be connected with *plerosantes*. In any case it is clear that here Luke was thinking of a return to Antioch (cf. Lüdemann 1984, 182 n.27).

III Traditions

[1-2] Luke has taken the report of the killing of James the son of Zebedee on the orders of Herod Agrippa from a tradition. It is impossible to decide whether the redactor abbreviated an extended report (martyrology) or whether the news of the death of James under Agrippa I had come down to him without further description.

For various attempts to explain the brevity of the note see, from an early period, Overbeck 1870, 181f. Schille 1983 recently explained the sparseness of the verses by saying that Luke knew only of two people being arrested (268).

It is often suggested that there is a genetic relationship between the tradition behind vv.1-2 and Mark 10.38f. Since E.Schwartz 1963, 48-50, there should no longer be any room for doubt that the passage mentioned is a *vaticinium ex eventu* which looks back to the violent death of the sons of Zebedee. The theory developed by E.Schwartz (ibid.) and others (most recently Suhl 1975, 316-32) about this is that the sons of Zebedee both suffered martyrdom under Agrippa. Luke deliberately did not mention John in Acts 12. The significance of this theory for the history of earliest Christianity is as follows: in that case we would have a *terminus ad quem* for the Jerusalem conference in which, according to Paul (Gal. 2.9), John son of Zebedee took part. It would have then taken place before 44 (and not around 48). But Gal.2.9 itself tells against such a theory. For this passage mentions only John, the brother of James, the son of Zebedee. If we take it with the tradition in Acts 12.2, Gal.2.9 seems to presuppose the death of James. The observation that in Gal.2.9, in contrast of Gal.1.19, Paul no longer needs to explain the name of James the brother of the Lord, leads to the same assumption. Cf. rightly Georgi 1965, 91-2; Suhl's reply, that Gal.1.19 has suffcent clarified whom Paul is speaking about (1975, 319 n.21), applies only to Paul's first visit to Jerusalem and not to the conference which took place fourteen years later. Finally, there are virtually no convincing reasons why John's name should be omitted in Acts 12.2.

Suhl 1975, differs: the special significance of John alongside Peter in Luke and Acts led to the deletion of his name in Acts 12.2 (317f.).

Attractive as Schwartz's proposal on Acts 12.2 is, for the reasons given above it must be rejected as improbable. There is probably no genetic connection between Mark 10.38f. and Acts 12.2.

[3-17] The analysis of the redaction above showed vv.3-4, 5b-6a, 9b-c, 11, 17c to be Lukan. In addition, the recognition scene in vv.13-16 shows Lukan features. The possible existence of the tradition thus arrived at by subtraction can be made more probable by the following considerations.

1. The tradition contains echoes of Hellenistic miraculous releases which speak of fetters falling off as in v.7 and doors opening by themselves as in v.10 (instances in Weiser 1981, 284f.). However, the appearance of this motive is not in itself enough to provide sufficient evidence of a tradition.

2. The beginning and the end of the tradition can be defined. Verse 5a is the beginning because v.4 may be a redactional look forward. Verse 17d will contain the end of Luke's source material because Luke himself would hardly provide such an insignificant note (in Acts 15 Peter is again in Jerusalem), and it fits the story well, which has no interest in details nor any reference to the release.

Overbeck 1870, 186, differs; as an analogy for v.17 he points to the fleetingness of the note in 12.2 and to 28.31, 'where the story of Paul is dropped as abruptly as the story of Peter here. The author has only introduced Peter very incompletely here, in order to prepare for Paul, and he is not interested in his further history here, where the stage is set for the appearance of Paul as the apostle to the Gentiles. Nor is it of interest in the present narrative.' But 28.31 is not a parallel, because it is the end of the book.

3. The local colouring (cf.v.10), the precise personal details (Rhoda the

maid and Mary) and the information about the place where the Christians meet (Mary's house) favour the acceptance of tradition. (But that does not mean that Mary's house is a house church of the Hellenists in Jerusalem [on Schüssler-Fiorenza 1983, 166].)

The tradition behind Acts 12.5-17 reports the imprisonment of Peter in Jerusalem, his miraculous release, the meeting with amazed members of the community in Mary's house and his departure from Jerusalem. Form critically it has some proximity to the miraculous releases. But it is not exhausted by these, as a simpler form of recognition scene was probably an ingredient of the tradition. (The attempt to derive the miraculous release and the recognition scene from two originally different traditions, though intrinsically possible, leads to more difficulties than the above assumption.) It may have been narrated by Jerusalem Christians, in recognition and praise of the miraculous release of Peter, the disciple of the Lord, from prison in Jerusalem.

Verse 17c contains an element of tradition ('James and the brethren') which will have come to Luke by word of mouth, cf. I Cor.15.7 (already cited by Paul as a tradition, see Lüdemann 1983, 78-84).

[20-23] These verses contain a tradition about the death of Agrippa I. It begins with an account of a conflict between the people of Tyre and Sidon and Agrippa and the role of the chamberlain Blastus as mediator. Without being given any further detail about the settlement, we are also told that Agrippa made a speech to them (i.e. probably to the people of Sidon and Tyre) in a royal robe, whereupon the people exclaimed: '(That is) the voice of a God, not a man.' An angel of the Lord then smote King Agrippa because he did not give God the glory and he died, devoured by worms.

The existence of a tradition worked over by Luke in vv.20-23 follows from the many details, from the reason (which diverges from that in Luke) given by the tradition for the death of Agrippa (he did not give God the glory) and from a parallel tradition about the death of Agrippa in Josephus, *Antt* XIX, 343ff. The Lukan version seems to be an abbreviation of that of Josephus. Many details in the context of the tradition reproduced by Luke are unclear (e.g. the position of Blastus, the role of the garment), or are difficult to discover (the intrinsic connection between Agrippa's controversy with the people of Sidon and Tyre and Agrippa's speech). Luke will himself have abbreviated a written source. Common to both versions is the fact that death follows the appropriation of divine honour. Here the Jewish starting point for the formation of the tradition becomes clear (cf. II Macc.9.5ff.). The statement that Agrippa died from being devoured by worms (12.23) or that he died after violent pains in his entrails (Josephus) is a variant of the widespread theme of the fearful death of those who despise God (cf. Acts 1.18; evidence in Nestle 1968, 594 [there is an illuminating table there]).

IV Historical

[1-2] The killing of James the son of Zebedee on the orders of Agrippa is probably historical. Agrippa (for whom see Schürer 1973, 442-54) feigned a strict Judaism in Jerusalem. James the son of Zebedee, on the other hand, was no longer alive at the conference a few years later, as otherwise he would have been mentioned in Paul's account in Gal.2.9. Now there is a *vaticinium ex eventu* about the martyr death of him and his brother (Mark 10.38f.), so it is natural to make Agrippa's opportunism responsible for the killing of James (cf. Lüdemann 1983, 74).

[3-17] The historicity of Agrippa's measure against James is illuminating for any assessment of the historical value of the subsequent miraculous release. First it needs to be stressed, with Baur (1866, 188), that the miraculous release bears within itself its own historical refutation. However, we may still presuppose a historical nucleus in it, namely that Agrippa had Peter arrested. This assumption is plausible on the presupposition of Agrippa's previous action against James, because at that time Peter was (still) the leading man in the earliest community in Jerusalem. Moreover the legend seems to have preserved a historical nucleus to the effect that Peter left Jerusalem. This alone explains why some years later James was the leader of the earliest community at the conference and Peter was only in second place (cf. Lüdemann 1983, 73-84).

Now if Peter was to be able to leave Jerusalem at all, he first had to be got out of prison. The views of scholars differ as to the manner of the release – where this question is raised at all; some assume that the question cannot be answered because vv.7-10 are strongly marked by the theme of miraculous releases in antiquity (cf. Weiser 1981, 290). By contrast, Roloff conjectures 'that the apostle managed to escape from prison in dramatic circumstances and that afterwards the group around Mary and her son John Mark supported him in his secret departure from Jerusalem' (1981, 187). However, such a proposal is simply a paraphrase of the account in Acts. I would prefer to revive Baur's old proposal that Agrippa himself released Peter once the unpopularity of his action against James had become clear (1866, 184f.).

Baur conjectures that the high priest Matthias was deposed by Agrippa I (Josephus, *Antt* XIX, 342) for similar reasons to those behind the deposition of the high priest Ananus by Agrippa II (*Antt* XX, 203). Both acted against Christians and in both cases the unpopularity of these measures cost them their office. (Apparently Baur presupposes that Agrippa acted against James on the prompting of the high priest Matthias.)

It is historically probable that Mary and her maid Rhoda were members of the Jerusalem community (the link between Mary and John Mark in v.12 was shown to be redactional at 142 above). Similarly, Mary's house in Jerusalem is probably a historical fact.

In v.17c we have the historically correct statement that after the departure of Peter, James became leader of the earliest community (see above).

[20-23] Nowhere else is there evidence of the conflict between Agrippa and the people of Tyre and Sidon. However, from the Old Testament (I Kings 5.23; Ezek.27.17) we can demonstrate a degree of economic dependence of Phoenicia on Palestine, which fits in with the information in v.20 (for this cf. Wikenhauser 1921, 323). Therefore the conflict and the desire for peace between the people of Tyre and Sidon and the role of Blastus the chamberlain as mediator may be historical.

The tradition about the death of Agrippa in Caesarea is confirmed by Josephus's report, even if we need to be critical of the legendary details.

Acts 13.1-3

I Division

13.1-3: The sending out of Barnabas and Saul by the church of Antioch
  1: The five prophets and/or teachers in the community of Antioch are mentioned by name
  2: The instruction of the Spirit to send out Barnabas and Saul
  3: Barnabas and Saul take their leave after fasting, prayer and the laying on of hands

II Redaction

[1-3] For *ousan* in v.1 see 5.17; 28.17. The position of Barnabas at the head of the list and that of Saul at the end may be intended by Luke. In this way emphasis is put on the two protagonists of the next chapter. The three persons thus framed by Barnabas and Saul are in each case described further, as they are not yet known to the readers (in contrast to Barnabas and Saul). The genitive absolute in v.2 and the conception that the Holy

146

Spirit speaks (cf.8.29; 10.10) derive from Luke. For v.3 cf. 6.6; in both places hands are laid on a particular group with prayer, but in v.3 there is also fasting. Both prayer and fasting appear in connection with the appointment of presbyters in 14.23 (which is redactional); cf. also Luke 2.37. Because of the parallel with 14.23, we should regard *nesteusantes* in v.3 as redactional.

III Traditions

The five names and the mention of the place (Antioch) go back to tradition. The more detailed descriptions of Symeon, Lucius and Manaen confirm this assumption, as does the observation that elsewhere in Acts prophets are portrayed as itinerant (11.27f.; 21.10). But it is uncertain whether Luke had a list of five or whether this is his own work (that he interfered with it is clear from the position of Barnabas and Saul, see above under II). The first possibility is perhaps supported by the fact that the number five is unexpected (cf. Schille 1983, 282f.). Moreover the designation of the individuals as 'prophets and teachers' may be part of the tradition; here it is no longer possible to decide which persons are teachers and which prophets (Harnack 1924, 349 n.2 [cf. Wendt 1913, 201] had thought that the particle sequence *te...kai, kai...te* made it probable that the first three persons were prophets and the last two teachers, but the framework 'Barnabas-Saul' derives from Luke). Teachers do not appear elsewhere in Luke, and we also find the connection between prophets and teachers in Didache 13.10-12 (and especially 15.1) and I Cor.12.28 (together with apostles). This last passage certainly derives from tradition; perhaps it comes from Antioch (cf. Zimmermann 1984, 92-113: the use of the formula is a concession to Peter's ecclesiology [112]). See also Eph.4.11 and for the analysis of further examples from early Christianity Zimmermann 1984 and Harnack 1924, 332-79. The information about fasting (v.42, *nesteuein*) in connection with *leitourgein to kyrio* goes back to tradition. The latter phrase probably denotes prayer, but it cannot be limited to that and should be rendered comprehensively as 'serve the Lord'. The activity of prophets and teachers in Antioch evidently presupposes that the community is relatively settled (Agabus, for example, is a different matter).

The question whether the tradition also gave information about the sending out of Barnabas and Saul (vv.26f.) and whether a continuous source begins in the verses can only be answered after the analysis of Acts 13-14 (see below, 165).

IV Historical

In all probability the underlying tradition reflects historical circumstances. The five persons mentioned will have been active as prophets and/or teachers in the Antioch community (cf. above 137f. on Paul's relationship to the Antiochene community and to Barnabas). For the moment they were attached to that place, but at any time could be delegated by the Spirit. This fluctuation between settled churches and itinerants matches the later evidence in Paul. He travels and nevertheless remains for lengthy periods with his communities. Moreover in his understanding of the apostolate there are elements of both itinerancy and a local apostolate (in Jerusalem, cf. Lüdemann 1983, 82).

Acts 13.4-12

I Division

13.4-5: Journey of Barnabas and Saul from Antioch via Seleucia to Cyprus. Preaching in the synagogues of Salamis. Note about John's assistance

6-12: Successful preaching before the proconsul Sergius Paulus in Paphos and the besting of the magician Barjesus Elymas

6-7a: Meeting with Barjesus and Sergius Paulus

7b: The wish of Sergius Paulus to hear the word of God

8: The attempt of Elymas the magician to seduce Sergius Paulus from the faith

9-11: Peter's curse against Elymas

12: Sergius Paulus becomes a believer

II Redaction

[4-5] *ekpemphthentes hypo tou hagiou pneumatos* in v.4 picks up v.2b. The content of v.5 is based on Luke's scheme of going to the Jews first; *logos tou theou* as the object of preaching appears in this chapter in vv.7c, 44,46. The expression 'synagogues' (plural!) of the Jews is evidence of the summary character of v.5.

[6-12] The following expressions or phrases certainly derive from Luke: v.6, *pseudopropheten*; v.7, relative linking the clause, *proskalesamenos, akousai ton logon tou theou*. Verse 8b is a Lukan explanation that *magos*

148

is a translation of Elymas (Zahn 1921, 412f.; Bauer 1979, 253, differs, and regards Elymas as a translation of Barjesus). *magos* picks up *magon* in v.6. Luke regards Barjesus and Elymas as one and the same person (cf. also the address 'Son of the devil' [v.10] as a negative description of Barjesus = son of Jesus/Joshua). *diatrepsai* and *pisteos* are Lukan in language. The way in which the name of Paul is introduced in v.9 has a parallel in the way in which Luke 6.14 introduces the name of Peter: 'that it only derives from the author of the whole work is shown by the unbroken regularity with which previously the apostle had been called only Saul and subsequently is called only Paul' (Zeller 1854, 517). Luke associates the change of name from Saul to Paul externally with the figure of the proconsul Sergius Paulus. The intrinsic reason for this is probably that from now on Luke thinks the use of the apostle's Roman name advisable, because Paul has begun the mission to the Gentiles (cf. Cadbury 1927, 225). The change of name from Saul to Paul corresponds to that from Barjesus to Elymas (cf. Holtzmann 1882, 373). Verses 10-11 are obviously formulated on the basis of 8.20-23. Apart from *rhadiourgia*, all the words of v.10 appear in LXX; in v.11 *achri kairou* and *parachrema* stand out as being Lukan. For *idon... to gegonos* in v.12 cf. Luke 8.34 (Mark differs).

Observations on the structure of the pericope make Lukan editorial work seem even more marked than has already been demonstrated in the previous investigations. The story has no exposition and conclusion. After v.6 (Paul and Barnabas come with a magician, a false prophet), one would expect the description of a controversy with this figure, but the reader is disappointed. Instead of this, the relative clause explaining the 'false prophet' (v.7a) introduces a new figure, Sergius Paulus, who summons the two missionaries so that he can hear the word of God from them. After that the Barjesus who has been previously mentioned under his other name, Elymas, is introduced, but the identity between Barjesus and Elymas is not explicitly made clear. When Barjesus Elymas attempts to seduce Sergius Paulus from the faith, in a solemn curse Paul ordains that his adversary shall be blinded for a certain period (*achri kairou*). Thereupon the proconsul believes, overwhelmed by the teaching about the (!) Lord. With the keyword *didache tou kyriou* Luke makes a link back to *ton logon tou theou* in v.7 and thus on the one hand brings out the close connection between word and demonstrations of power (here punitive miracles, cf. Schneider 1982, 124). On the other hand the stress on the element of teaching in Christianity marks it out from magic, since such a misunderstanding might arise after Paul's curse and its effect.

The conclusion to be drawn from these observations on the course of the story is that Luke has either totally broken up a story in the tradition or inserted notes into a story which had rather scanty details (see below under III).

In any case the intention is clear. The author is concerned once again after ch.8 to distinguish the Christians from rival contemporary religious groups. To this end he defames Barjesus Elymas as he did Simon ('Magus'), making him a magician (cf. also the demotion of Barjesus Elymas to being a false prophet in v.6; for the connection between magic and being a Jew see 16.20f.; 19.13 and 181). By restricting Elymas's blindness to a period, Luke seems to have left open the possibility for rival groups to be converted, as he already did in ch.8 (cf. Klein 1969, 281-7).

But demarcation from rivals is only one aspect of Luke's purpose. His other aim focuses on the person of the proconsul Sergius Paulus. Lukan apologetic is again clear in the latter's conversion to Christianity, and is so in a massive way, as here not only a centurion like Cornelius in Acts 10 but even a Roman proconsul accepts the faith. That was not in the tradition, as otherwise Luke would have gone on to report the baptism of Sergius Paulus and the outpouring of the Spirit (on Jacquier 1926, 388f., who regards the conversion of Sergius Paulus as historical because of v.12 [as does Judge 1964, 52]).

III Traditions

The names and designations of the activities of Sergius Paulus and Barjesus Elymas are elements of the tradition; because of the name Barjesus, the Jewish origin of the latter might be part of the tradition and both his names might relate to the same person (Dibelius 1956, 16, and others, differ). The link between the proconsul and Barjesus Elymas may also be part of the tradition (cf. the close connection between the emperor Tiberius and the astrologer Thrasyllus [see Nock, *Beg.* V, 183f.] and the frequent links between the Roman nobility and astrologers, magicians and philosophers). But this individual feature may also go back to Luke. However, it should be stressed that at the level of tradition there is no recognizable genetic relationship between Paulus and the two persons mentioned (see below II). (Most recently Weiser, 1985, 314, again differs: 314 is a paraphrase of the tradition – arrived at by a process of subtraction.)

Paul's mission on Cyprus will probably have no support in tradition. Luke has created it from elements in the tradition like the origin of Barnabas from Cyprus, his mission with John Mark on Cyprus and the collaboration between Barnabas and Paul (cf. Loisy 1920, 518).

The two names of the apostle to the Gentiles, Saul and Paul (v.9), derive from tradition, as does the report in v.6 that he took John Mark with him), though neither Paul nor Mark are genetically connected with the story.

150

IV Historical

The question whether there was a proconsul Sergius Paulus and (among his followers) a prophet Barjesus Elymas on Cyprus is probably to be answered in the affirmative, although outside Acts there is no clear evidence to link a proconsul Sergius Paulus with Cyprus (see the analysis of Lake, *Beg.* V, 455-9, and previously Wikenhauser 1921, 338-40 [lit.] – only to be used in conjunction with Lake). At the same time the qualification should be made that there is no way of dating the persons mentioned. Barjesus Elymas was a prophet and magician (in the positive sense). Elymas is probably derived from the Arabic *'alima* = 'gain insight into something' (cf. Bauer 1979, 253), or is the Greek transcription of the Aramaic word *haloma* = interpreter of dreams (cf. Weiser 1985, 312f. and bibliography). Perhaps in v.11 with the superfluous *me blepon ton helion* Luke is hinting that observation of the Helios, etc., was an activity of Barjesus Elymas (see *Papyri Graecae Magicae* III, 198ff. [prayer to Helios]; for the phenomenon of prophecy/magic cf. Aune 1983, 23-48). In that case there would be a parallel to the ironical allusion to the *epinoia* of *Simon* in Acts 8.22.

The tradition of the double name of the apostle, Saul/Paul, may be historically reliable. (Leon 1960, 107, cites twelve examples of Semitic/ Latin dual names from Roman Judaism.) Saul (Josephus knows several Jews who bear this name) is the Graecized form of *Sha'ul* and is plausible as a name for the apostle, because he was a Benjaminite (Phil.3.5), as was his famous forebear, the king Saul (I Sam 9.1.). The apostle's Roman name, Paul, is historical, since it appears in the letters. It is rare in the East.

The theory that the apostle took the cognomen Paulus only after his encounter with the Roman proconsul Sergius Paulus on Cyprus (Dessau 1910, cf. similarly Meyer III, 197) is improbable, because Paul's mission on Cyprus is a redactional construction. (Or is there a valuable tradition behind the redaction which can no longer be verified? Sergius Paulus does not necessarily belong on Cyprus.) Cf. also 241 below on the name Paul.

The traditions of the collaboration of Barnabas with John Mark are certainly unhistorical in the present context, but generally derive from the historical fact of a mission of Barnabas and John Mark on Cyprus (cf. 15.39). For the history of the collaboration of Barnabas with Paul see 137f. above.

Acts 13.13-52

I Division

13.13-14a: Journey from Paphos via Perga to Pisidian Antioch. John Mark leaves
14b-15: Paul and Barnabas in the synagogue at Antioch
    14b: Entry into the synagogue on the sabbath
    15: Invitation to speak
16-41: Paul's speech
    16a: Paul's gesture as a speaker
    16b-25: Salvation-historical outline from the Exodus to Jesus
        16b: Address
        17-22: The Old Testament salvation history: Exodus, conquest, Samuel, Saul, David
        23-25: John the Baptist
    26-31: Jesus' suffering and death as the fault of the inhabitants and rulers of Jerusalem and the fulfilment of Scripture. Jesus' resurrection and appearances as the action of God
    32-37: Scriptural proof
    38-41: Application to the hearers
        38-39: Proclamation of the forgiveness of sins
        40-41: Salvation-historical warning to the Jewish audience
42-43: Success of the sermon among Jews and proselytes
44-52: (On the next sabbath) Masses come but the Jews resist and Paul and Barnabas turn to the Gentiles
    44: The whole city wants to hear the word of God
    45: Envy and blasphemy of the Jews against Paul
    46: The repudiation of the preaching of the word of God by the Jews is the basis of Barnabas's and Paul's move to the Gentiles
    47: Scriptural proof
    48: Praise of God by the Gentiles
    49: Information about the spread of the faith
    50: Barnabas and Paul driven out by the Jews
    51: After symbolic actions, journey on to Iconium
    52: The disciples (in Pisidian Antioch) are filled with joy and Holy Spirit

II Redaction

[**13-14a**] *apochoresas* and *hypestrepsen* are Lukan language. In the phrase *hoi peri Paulon*, which is singular in Luke, and the pre-eminence of Paul which it implies (Barnabas is tacitly reckoned to be a follower of Paul), we have emphasis on the significance of Paul which has been expressed since v.9. The note about John Mark (13b) refers back to v.5c. *paregenonto* in v.14a is Lukan in language.

[14b-15] The entry into the synagogue is based on the redactional pattern of linkage. Verse 15 contains the correct information that a sermon could follow the reading of the Torah and prophets in synagogue worship. However, the information that presidents of the synagogue (in the plural) had asked for a word of admonition is based on an error, since there was only one president of any one synagogue at that time (cf. Lüdemann 1984, 185 n.52 [with bibliography]).

[16-41] Paul's speech in Pisidian Antioch has a parallel within the structure of Luke-Acts in Jesus' inaugural sermon in Nazareth in Luke 4.16-30 (cf Wellhausen 1914, 25f., and at length Radl 1975, 82-100). For in both cases they stand almost programmatically at the beginning of the activities of Jesus and Paul.

In what follows I shall cite only what can certainly be said to be Lukan (for the details see the commentaries and Buss 1980).

For *anastas* and the gesture of the speaker in v.16 see 12.17; 21.40; 26.1. For further features see v.17, *exelexato*; v.18, *hos* (cf. v.20); v.23, for Jesus as Son of David see (in addition to the genealogies in Matt.1 and Luke 3), Luke 1.32f.; 18.38f.; 20.41; Acts 2.30 (but see Rom.1.3 as pre-Pauline evidence of Jesus as son of David). *prokeryxantos* and *eisodou* in v.24 certainly derive from Luke, though this is the only time they appear in Acts (cf. Luke's predilection for composite verbs with *pro-* and his conception of the activity of Jesus and Paul as a journey, see Lüdemann 1984, 13f.). For *panti to lao* cf. (*baptisthenai*) *hapanta ton laon* in Luke 3.21 (Mark differs). For *dromos* (v.25) cf.20.24. Otherwise, like v.24b the verse is a reference back to Luke 3.15-20 (for the readers). For the role of John the Baptist in salvation history in Luke see above on 1.22. As in v.38, *andres adelphoi* in v.26 introduces a new section. In this way the author himself presents the decisive points: v.26 (christological part)/v.38 (application to the hearers); v.27, for the 'inhabitants of Jerusalem' cf.1.19; 2.14; for 'their leaders' cf. 3.17: Luke 23.35. The theme of ignorance also appears in 3.17 (however, there it is presented as an excuse and here – v.27 – it is an accusation). The reading of scripture on the sabbath appears in Luke 4.16. For v.28, cf. 3.13f. The first half of v.29 corresponds to Luke 2.39, the second reports the burial. Thus the time between death and resurrection is filled in from a narrative perspective (cf. I Cor.15.4a); for v.30 cf. 3.15; 5.30; 10.40. Verse 31 links back to Acts 1: *hemeras pleious* takes up the 'forty days' (1.3); for *martyres autou* cf. 1.22. *euaggelizesthai* and *epaggelia* (v.32) are frequent in Luke. Cf. also 26.6 for the 'promise given to the fathers'. For vv.33-35 see III below. For v.36 cf. 2.27. For God's plan (v.36) cf. Conzelmann 1960, 151-4 and the concordances s.v. *boule*. Verses 36-37 correspond to 2.29-31 (note the keyword *diaphthora*). *gnostos* (v.38) is Lucan language, as are *andres adelphoi* (cf. on v.26); *kataggelletai* (see Conzelmann 1960, 220). The keyword 'forgiveness of sins' appears often in Peter's speeches (2.38; 5.31; 10.43). Verses 38f. are striking, in that as later in the Miletus speech (20.18-35) Luke makes use of Pauline terminology:

'Let it be known to you therefore, brethren, that through this man forgiveness of sins is proclaimed to you, and by him everyone that believes is freed from everything from which you could not be freed by the law of Moses.'

However, to say that does not mean that Luke 'understood' Paul's doctrine of justification. For the righteousness of faith is not clearly formulated in antithesis to righteousness by works (on Lindemann 1979, 59f. n.62). 'Anyone who did not know the Pauline doctrine of justification and the law previously would certainly not perceive it from this fleeting intimation' (Zeller 1854, 292). Despite these qualifications it is clear that with vv.38f. Luke wants to give the first extended sermon by Paul in Acts a touch of Pauline authenticity. If he wanted to show his readers his own familiarity with Paul's preaching, Paul's first sermon gave him the opportunity to do so. (Lindemann 1979 exaggerates: 'through 14.38f. Paul is presented once for all as the theologian of justification' [56]).

On the relationship of the speech at Antioch to the other Pauline speeches it should be noted here that on each of the three great journeys which start from Antioch Paul gives an extended speech: on the first journey, to the Jews (sermon in Pisidian Antioch); on the second, to the Gentiles (Acts 17); and on the third, to the Christians (Acts 20) – for this problem cf. already Overbeck 1870, 189.

[42-43] These two verses look like doublets. Each begins with a note of time ('going out'/'when the assembly broke up') and contains a reaction of the audience to Paul's sermon (invitation to further preaching/meeting with Paul and Barnabas). But the whole passage can be explained as redactional, with v.42 introducing a general version and v.43 making it specific.

Many Jews and pious 'proselytes' (however, this translation is uncertain, see the next excursus) followed the missionaries, who admonished them to remain in grace (*prosmenein te chariti tou theou* is Lukan language). This positive portrayal of the Jews makes an effective contrast to what follows. The expression *polloi ton Ioudaion kai oi sebomenon proselyton* evidently refers back to vv.16, 26, where Paul addressed the audience as follows: *andres Israelitai kai hoi phoboumenoi ton theon* (v.16) and *andres adelphoi, hyioi genous Abraam kai hoi en hymin phoboumenoi ton theon* (v.26). There are no difficulties over understanding the first part of the address. On each occasion it refers to the Jews. But

154

what is the relationship between the *phoboumenoi ton theon* (v.16 + 26) and the *sebomenoi proselytoi* (v.43)?

Excursus. On the relationship between 'Godfearers' and 'Proselytes' in Acts (for the literature cf. Solin 1983, 618-21; Kraabel 1981; Wilcox 1981; and the Aphrodisias inscription which has meanwhile been published with a commentary: J.Reynolds and R.Tannenbaum, *Jews and Godfearers at Aphrodisias*, Cambridge Philological Society, Supplementary Volume 12, Cambridge 1987, especially the remarks made on 48-66)

Luke uses *phoboumenos ton theon – sebomenos (ton theon)* with a purpose. Otherwise it would be impossible to explain why he uses the former expression in 10.2,22,35; 13.16,26 and afterwards only the latter; see 13.43,50; 16.14; 17.4,17; 18.7 (for an evaluation see Cadbury 1926: *sebomenos* is less semitic than *phoboumenos*, *sebomenos* is more appropriate for the Gentile Christian environment in which the mission of Paul is taking place [225]) – *proselytoi* appears in Acts only at 2.11, 6.5 (singular) and 13.43. That Luke's formulation in using this term is also deliberate is evident from the order both in 2.11 (Jews and proselytes) and in 6.5 (here the proselyte Nicolaus stands at the end of a list of the Seven). Scholars find it least difficult to understand the term 'proselyte'. It denotes the Gentiles converted to Judaism who, receiving their credentials by circumcision (which was not carried out on women), immersion and (before 70) sacrifice in the Jerusalem temple, had become (full) Jews, although certain restrictions remained (thus e.g. women proselytes could not marry priests). This partially lower status is also expressed in the order in Acts 2.11; 6.5. If the expression 'proselyte' is a technical term in Jewish writings in the above-mentioned sense, the same can hardly be said of *sebomenoi/phobomenoi ton theon*. It should be stressed that no evidence has yet been found of either expression in the Greek inscriptions (cf. Siegert 1973, 151; Solin 1983, 619; Kraabel 1981, 116; though see now the Aphrodisias insription, even if it needs further discussion [see already Kraabel 1981, 125f. n.26; Meeks 1983, 207f. n.175 and the valuable commentary given by the editors of the Aphrodisias inscription]) and that it remains quite questionable whether the *metuens deum* which appears in inscriptions is a Latin equivalent for *phoboumenos/sebomenos ton theon* (see Siegert 1973, 161). Moreover it is uncertain whether the rabbinic *yere shamayim* is to be understood as a technical term and can at least indirectly give the desired support for a technical use of 'godfearer' (cf. rightly Siegert 1973, 110-19). Finally it is certain that the adjectives *sebomenos, phoboumenos* and *theosebes* could be applied to Jews (cf. Solin 1983, 619).

If the theory that 'godfearer' is a technical term is therefore questionable, it cannot seriously be questioned that the Gentiles interested in Judaism were often designated by this predicate: cf. Josephus, *Antt* XIV, 110: 'It should not surprise anyone that such great riches were in our temple, since the Jews and godfearers from all over the world (*panton ton kata ten oikoumenen Ioudaion kai sebomenon ton theon*), and finally also those from Asia and Europe, had contributed to it for a very long time.' They were not Jews, but felt drawn to the Jewish communities, took part in their synagogue worship, partly accepted the Jewish moral and ceremonial law and in many

155

instances supported the Jewish communities. (The distinction made by Siegert 1973 between godfearers [= those seriously interested in the Jewish religion] and sympathizers [= those who imitated some Jewish customs or were well disposed politically to the Jews] may be left aside here.) Luke's stress on them in the environment of the synagogue as conversation partners of Paul is based on a historically plausible judgment. However, the historical value of individual details must be determined separately.

The expression *sebomenoi proselytoi* in v.43 remains a difficult problem. Possible solutions are: 1. At this point proselyte has a non-technical significance (Siegert 1973, 139). 2. It is a 'careless expression' of Luke's (Conzelmann 1987, 106). 3. Proselyte is a gloss (Conzelmann 1987, 106). In my view none of these proposals is satisfactory, though each remains possible. Perhaps the key to a convincing solution lies in the observation that up to 13.26 Luke uses *phoboumenos ton theon*, whereas afterwards he prefers *sebomenos (ton theon)*; he uses it specifically for the first time in v.43. In this way he seems to express the fact that for him *phoboumenos ton theon* is identical to *sebomenos proselytos* and this in turn means the same thing as *sebomenos ton theon*. In this case he would have attached a different sense to the term 'proselyte' to that in the Jewish terminology of the time, but this would not be intrinsically impossible. However, against this proposal is the unique use of 'proselyte' at this point. It is in fact 'inadvisable to draw far-reaching conclusions from this singular passage' (Siegert 1973, 139f), even in terms of the redaction. The problem in 13.43 is therefore still unresolved.

[44-52] These verses are redactional throughout. They merely express in narrative form the implementation of Luke's programme that the Jews have rejected the gospel and that therefore Paul and Barnabas are going to the Gentiles.

The expression *pasa he polis* in v.44 recalls 21.30; 19.19; *logos tou theou* also appears in this chapter at vv.5,7,44,46. Luke has not noted that the whole city cannot find room in the synagogue. In v.45 the following language is redactional: *idontes de* + subject and object; *ochloi* (plural!); for *eplesthesan zelou* cf. 5.17 (for features of Lukan language in v.45 see Radl 1975, 86). In content the negative characterization of the Jews is typical of Luke (cf. 17.5; 18.6, etc.). For the Jews as the first to have the preaching addressed to them (v.46) cf. 14.1; 16.13; 17.1,10,17; 18.4,19; 19.8. In this verse Luke introduces his idea of the Gentile mission, which is grounded in v.47 by a scriptural proof; here Isa.49.6 is related to the mission, while in Luke 2.32 it still refers to Jesus. In v.48 *echairon, edoxazon, logon tou theou* are Lukan in language. In content the verse carries forward vv.46f. The further definition in v.48b ('who were destined for eternal life') probably does not reflect any predestination in Luke's theology but is only meant to indicate that not everyone believes. Verse 49 is a summary notice of success and for Luke often comes at the end of scenes which report a mission. The leading women in v.50 and the first people of the city are a redactional theme (cf.17.12); so too is the occasion for the persecution of the preachers by the Jews (v.45; 17.5, etc.). Paul's and Barnabas's reaction in v.51, to shake the dust of their feet off against the Jews, accords with Jesus' instruction which Luke already picked up from Q (Luke 10.11; for the Lukan character of the language in v.51 and already in v.50 cf. Radl 1975, 87f.). However, here Luke gets entangled in the contradiction – to be explained in terms of redaction – that there is already a Christian community in the city whose dust the missionaries shake off their feet. The motives of the Spirit and joy are Lukan, as is *eplerounto*.

III Traditions

[13-14, 50-51] The above travel stations, Perga (v.13), Antioch (v.14) and Iconium (v.51), may go back to tradition, along with the names of the missionaries Barnabas and Paul (Paphos [vv.6,13] is no longer part of the tradition, see 148f. above. Moreover one could not travel by ship from Paphos to Perga, as Luke presupposes). Cf. also the tradition of Paul's missionary activity in Iconium and Antioch in the Acts of Paul, which is probably independent of Acts (see Hennecke-Schneemelcher-Wilson, *New Testament Apocrypha* II, London and Philadelphia 1965, 353-7, 360-4). The report of the perseuction in Antioch in v.50 may also go back to tradition, however much it makes sense redactionally. For II Tim.3.11 speaks of the 'persecutions, my sufferings which I experienced in Antioch, in Iconium, in Lystra'. If II Tim.3.11 were independent of Acts 13.50 (Easton 1947 differs: he claims that II Tim.3.11 is the first certain quotation of Acts in Christian literature [67]), the same tradition underlies both passages (cf Lüdemann 1984, 180 n.2).

[33-35] The quotation from Isa.55.3 in v.34 is so fragmentary as to be incomprehensible. Perhaps Luke already found it combined with what follows (from Ps.16.10). For Ps.16.10 cf. also 2.27.

IV Historical

The tradition of a journey by Barnabas and Paul to Perga, Antioch and Iconium does not have *any* explicit support in the letters of Paul. From them it is possible only to infer a missionary activity of the apostle in Syria and Cilicia immediately after the first journey to Jerusalem (Gal.1.21). But this evidence is not enough to rule out the historicity of that missionary activity. (Paul's letters do not reflect all the places to which Paul travelled.)

Rather, the combination of the reliable information we are given suggests that this mission in southern Galatia is historical.

In support of this: first of all, there is a high degree of historical probability about the tradition of a collaboration of Paul with Barnabas (cf. Gal.2.1,11ff.; I Cor.9.6). Then we should note that southern Galatia is on the way from Syria and Cilicia to Greece. Moreover, the theory that a mission there among the Gentiles followed that in Syria and Cilicia, in which Paul was accompanied by Barnabas, is very likely. (For the question of the historicity of Paul's suffering in Antioch, Iconium and Lystra [13.50] see below on 14.19f., 165f.)

[33-35] There are no criteria for discovering the age of the tradition. Like the resurrection tradition (vv.30f., see on this 48 above on 2.24), it gives an insight into the life of faith of the Hellenistic communities in the first century.

Acts 14

I Division

14.1-7: Activity of Paul and Barnabas in Iconium and their flight
  1: Successful preaching in the synagogue of Iconium
  2: The Gentiles are stirred up by the unbelieving Jews
  3: The activity of Paul in Iconium accompanied by signs and wonders
  4: The population split into two camps between the Jews and the apostles
  5-7: Because of the plan of the Gentiles and Jews to stone Paul and Barnabas, flight to Lystra, Derbe and surroundings. Preaching there
8-10: Healing of a lame man in Lystra by Paul
11-13: Reaction: desire of the people of Lystra to offer sacrifices to Barnabas and Paul as Zeus and Hermes
14-17: Speech of Paul and Barnabas
18: The people maintain their purpose (despite the speech of Paul and Barnabas)
19-20a: Stoning of Paul in Lystra by the people at the incitement of Jews from Antioch and Iconium
20b-28: Return of Barnabas and Paul to the starting point of the journey, Antioch on the Orontes, via Derbe, Lystra, Iconium, (Pisidian) Antioch, Perga and Attalia

II Redaction

[1-7] Verse 1a contains the Lukan scheme of going to the Jews first; v.1b, with the remark that the preaching in the synagogue led a large mass of Jews and Greeks to believe, similarly appears in 18.4 (cf. also the formula 'Jews and Greeks', 19.10, 17; 20.21). For v.2, cf. 13.45. Verse 3 is a summary note which, like v.1, reports the success of the preaching. This took place with signs and wonders at the hands of Paul and Barnabas. The verse is Lukan in language and content. Verse 3b appears almost word for word in 20.32; vv.3c-d have a close parallel with the summary of the healing in 5.12; cf. 19,11. Verse 4 sums up what has been said so far; the crowd (see on v.1b) in the city divides; some follow the (hostile) Jews and the others the apostles (cf. the similar formulation 'some-others' in 17.32, 28.24).

A number of exegetes (most recently and emphatically Roloff 1981, 211) have regarded the expression 'apostles' (plural!) as an indication of the use of a source. Roloff writes that the evidence in v.4 (and in v.14) 'goes so fundamentally against Luke's terminology that the formulation of this verse cannot come from him' (ibid.). But such a theory is not the only possibility. Luke knows the term 'apostle' and may have used it here too in a wider sense. '*apostoloi* are primarily the leaders of the Jerusalem community; but evidently *apostoloi* can also be used of those who preach the gospel among the Gentiles. That the term is not used later in connection with Paul accords with Lukan terminology; Paul now only appears as an individual, but Luke always speaks of *apostoloi* in the plural' (Lindemann 1979, 62). Moreover it is generally not a good thing to attach too much weight to one expression as evidence for the existence of a consecutive source, especially as everything else has a Lucan colouring, down to individual details.

For vv.5f. cf. 164 below under III. The periphrastic conjugation is typically Lucan; the idea of the mission is called for by the narrative.

[8-10] The narrative of the healing of the lame man has a parallel in 3.2-8 which in more recent literature is often explained as the 'typical style of miracle stories' (Conzelmann 1987, 109). But typical style is a far cry from a number of verbal points of contact. There are verbal points of contact at the following points (cf. already Baur 1866, 108f., and more recently Schneider 1980, 307 [table]).

1. 'A man, one lame from birth' (v.8/3.2).
2. The miracle worker 'looks' at the lame man (v.9/3.4 *atenizein*).
3. The lame man 'leapt up and walked around' (v.10 [parataxis]/3.8 [hypotaxis]).
4. There is also a parallel in the motive of faith. In Acts 14 it is integrated (v.9), whereas in Acts 3 it appears in an interpretative framework (v.16).

Schneider 1980, 307f., stresses the parallelism of the two accounts Acts 3/14 with Luke 5.17-26 (the healing of a lame man by Jesus). But it should be observed that the above parallels 1-2 do not appear in Luke 5, so that the particularly close contact between Acts 3 and 14 must be evaluated in its own terms. That is not to dispute that for Luke 'there is also a parallelism and continuity between Jesus's miracles and the acts of the apostles' (Schneider 1980, 306f.).

The verbal parallels mentioned above and the parallelism of the miracles of Peter and Paul elsewhere (cf. Schneider 1980, 304-10) allow the following conclusion:

The story of the healing of a lame man at this point is redactional (the explanations of Weiser 1985, 344f., suggest the same conclusion, despite the author's theory to the contrary), and has been developed on the basis of the story narrated in Acts 3 – first in order once again to make a parallel between Paul and Peter, and secondly, as shown by the way in which the story (vv.11-13) runs into the subsequent preaching to the Gentiles without a break (vv.15-17), to distinguish the proclamation of the one God from idolatry.

[11-13] These verses derive wholly from Luke. Lukan words and phrases, however, can chiefly be found only in v.11: *ochloi* (plural, cf. v.13), *eperan ten phonen, katebesan*. The section runs on without a break from the previous episode. Paul's miracle is the occasion for the subsequent development, in which Barnabas and Paul are taken as an incarnation of Zeus and Hermes. Since the inhabitants of Lystra identify Barnabas and Paul with gods in the language of Lycaonia and the latter do not understand that language, they can only raise objections later (cf. Cadbury 1955, 21f.). This gives Luke the narrative possibility of developing a vivid scene in v.13 and subsequently (vv.15-17) distinguishing Christian preaching from the worship of idols all the more clearly. The inhabitants of Lystra are to turn away from their useless idols (like Zeus and Hermes) and worship the living God.

Now we may certainly ask whether the remarkable detail that Paul and Barnabas are worshipped as Zeus and Hermes tells against the assumption of redaction. For we must join F.C.Baur in asking 'why of the many miracles which the apostles are said to have performed, only this one had so striking a consequence; why this scene of divinization had to take place in Lystra in particular, why the people here went so quickly from one extreme to another that the very apostles to whom they wanted to offer sacrifices... as to a god are immediately thereafter driven out of the city with stones and left for dead because of the insinuations of some Jews from Antioch and Iconium' (1866, 112). A last feature which also seems to tell against the redaction hypothesis is that this episode has a remote parallel in the legend reproduced by Ovid (*Met* VIII, 620-774), according to which Jupiter, Zeus and Mercury/Hermes visited the old couple Philemon and Baucis. Indeed this parallel (and/or the evidence that Zeus and Hermes appear together on inscriptions in this area [see the commentaries ad loc.]) could be taken as examples of the credibility of the report in Acts. Against that Baur already objects:

Instead of 'taking such sagas as confirmation of the historical truth of the facts narrated here, we should reverse the position and ask whether the alleged fact is not itself to be seen merely as an imitation of that old mythical situation' (1866, 114) – not at the level of tradition but at that of redaction. Luke himself (with Baur) seems to take up that theme and to demonstrate yet again that he is a writer with a literary education. In that case here is a further result of his reading.

Now Roloff in 1981, following Bauernfeind (1980, 182), thought that vv.8-14 went back to tradition. He writes:

'The figure of Barnabas may have stood at the centre of the piece of tradition (sc. vv.8-14). He is the central figure who is regarded by the people as the father of the gods, Zeus, whereas Paul is clearly subordinate to him in v.12; cf. v.14. (The explanation that Luke finds for this is completely artificial...) Presumably here we have a Barnabas legend set in Antioch. In it Barnabas is portrayed as the great missionary, who in an exemplary way withstands typical situations of the Gentile mission' (213).

The following considerations tell against such a theory. Paul is not taken to be Zeus because the role of Hermes fits him, since he is the one who speaks (cf. the examples of Hermes as *hegemon tou logou*, etc., cited by Conzelmann 1987, 110). The attribution of a 'superior' position to Barnabas is only apparent and arises out of the insertion of the results of Luke's reading (against Weiser 1985, 351; cf. also Schneider 1982, 156).

There is an analogy to the interpretation of Paul as Hermes in the designation of Moses as Hermes by Egyptian priests in Artapanus's history of Moses. According to Alexander Polyhistor in Eusebius, Artapanus says:

'This Moysos was the teacher of Orpheus. As a grown man he gave men many useful things: he invented ships, stone-lifting equipment, Egyptian weapons, machines for irrigation and war and philosophy; he also divided the state into thirty-six districts and assigned to each district the god who was to be worshipped in it, and he (taught) the priests hieroglyphics... moreover he assigned the priests the best land. He did all this to secure sole rule for Chenephres. For earlier, when the masses of the people had been unbridled, they had sometimes driven out kings and sometimes appointed them, mostly the same ones, but now and then also others. So for these things Moysos became beloved among the people and was thought by the priests worthy of godlike honour, and called "Hermes", (the last) because of the interpretation (*hermeneia*) of the hieroglyphs' (Fragment 3.4-6, based on the translation by Walter 1976, 129f.).

Now there is certainly a degree of difference in the interpretation of the name Hermes in the two stories. In the Moses story the derivation of the cultural achievements of Egypt from Moses is connected with the identification of Moses with Hermes. In the Paul narrative the designation of Paul as Hermes is derived from the fact that Paul is the spokesman/protagonist. But the two stories belong closely together because in both cases Moses or Paul is depicted as a miracle worker.

Cf. Artapanus: 'Now when the king of the Egyptians heard of the arrival of Moysos, he summoned him and enquired of him for what purpose he had come. He said (he had come) because the Lord of the world was commanding him to release the Jews. When he heard that he had him shut up in prison. But the following night all the doors of the prison opened of their own accord and some of the guards died (for fear), while others fell fast asleep and their weapons were broken. So Moysos escaped and came to the royal palace. There he found the doors standing open and went in (unhindered) because there too the guards were drunk with sleep, and woke the king. Terrified by what had happened, he commanded Moysos to tell him the name of the God who had sent him, by which he mocked him. Then he bent down to his ear and mentioned it (in a whisper); when the king heard him he collapsed without a sound, but with the support of Moysos he regained consciousness' (Fragment 3.22b-25: Walter 1976, 133f.).

The healing of the lame man by Paul in Acts 14 corresponds to Moses' miracles. Cf. also the connection with the miraculous release in Acts 16.25ff. For literature, in addition to the commentaries see O'Neill 1970, 145.

The conclusion to be drawn from this is that in his account of Paul/Hermes and Barnabas/Zeus in Lycaonia in Acts 14, Luke was especially stimulated by literary models, on the basis of which he composed this stirring story. It should be noted that the story narrated by Ovid took place in Phrygia, which is adjacent to Lycaonia. It is therefore no coincidence that at this particular point in Acts Luke made use of the knowledge he had gained from reading (the working-in of local colouring as in 17.16-34; 19.23-40). Meeks 1983, 15, by contrast, thinks the scene historical.

[14-17] For *diarrhexantes ta himatia* in v.14 cf. 22.23; for v.15 cf. 3.12. The stress that the apostles are human, to be found in v.16, also appears in 10.26. For the whole section cf also the remarks on 17.16-34.

[18] *molis* and *ochloi* (plural) are Lukan in language. The verse takes up the situation presupposed, that the priests want to offer sacrifices to Barnabas and Paul (v.13). The speech barely deterred them from this purpose.

[19-20a] The section is redactional in that again (after 14.2) Jews address the crowd (*peithein*, cf.14.5). But it goes beyond 14.2 in that together they even stone Paul; here the plan from 14.5 is in fact carried out. Thus

162

from 14.2 via 14.5 a redactional arch spans over to 14.19-20a. It is no objection that the people's change of view could not clearly be made comprehensible. For both the worship of Barnabas and Paul and the motive of persecution (instigated by the Jews) are Lukan. Nevertheless the account of the stoning of Paul may derive from tradition (for the reason see III below).

[20b-28] The phrase 'on the next day' in v.20b is redactional (cf. Schneider 1982, 67 n.68). Verse 21 is predominantly Lukan in language. For the terminology of the preaching cf. Conzelmann 1960, 221; in particular a comparison with 8.25,40 is instructive. However, *matheteuein* occurs only here in Luke-Acts (elsewhere in the NT only in Matt.13.52; 27.57; 28.19), but in connection with the Lukan *hikanoi* and *hypostrephein*. *episterizein* in v.22 appears only there and in 15.32, each time in an ecclesiological context. The whole verse is focussed on Luke's church and deals with Christian life.

'This does not mean that Christian existence as such is thought of as *thlipsis*, but only certain aspects of it (*pollai thlipseis*). It is possible that this is a current expression, perhaps corresponding to the *polla pathein* of Mark 8.31. The whole context (NB *emmenein te pistei*) shows that it has no eschatological meaning for Luke. The same is shown in Acts 20.33, where the word is used to describe the sufferings of Paul the confessor' (Conzelmann 1960, 99, cf. ibid., 155f., 234).

Verse 23 depicts the appointment of presbyters. Luke imagines that the church constitution of his time already existed in the time of Paul. Verses 24-26 are travel notes composed in Lukan language (favourite Lucan words are *dielthein, elthein, lalein ton logon, katabainein*). However, that does not necessarily rule out the possibility that these notes are tradition. Verse 26 links back to 13.1-3. Barnabas and Paul return to Antioch, 'from where they had been handed over to the grace of God for the work that they had fulfilled' (v.26b). Verse 27 sums up the fruits of the journey ('God has opened the way to faith for the Gentiles') which will be further debated in Jerusalem in the next chapter. Verse 28 'creates one of the Lukan pauses' (Conzelmann 1987, 113).

III Traditions

It is very probable that tradition underlies vv.19-20a. The reason for this is:

1. The verses can be easily detached from the action. 2. The transition from v.18 to v.19 and from v.20a to v.20b is extremely harsh. Moreover there is no reason for the appearance of 'disciples' in v.20, since previously

there had been no mention of the foundation of a community in Lystra (cf. Roloff 1981, 214); 3. Paul alone stands at the centre (Barnabas is forgotten). 4. The passage has a parallel in II Tim.3.11 (which has the same sequence of stations as Acts 13-14).

Luke has already used the above tradition in vv.5f., where Paul and Barnabas escaped from Iconium to Lystra because of the threat of stoning, and previously at 13.50 (where they are driven out of Antioch). As II Tim.3.11 shows, it is attached to Paul, and reports his suffering in three cities (Antioch, Iconium, Lystra) and – we may add – a stoning in Lystra which almost cost him his life. Within the framework of the analysis of the tradition it is impossible to make any clear statement about the instigators of the stoning (see below under IV). (The figure of Barnabas in 13.50; 14.5 is evidently a redactional addition.)

If the suffering of Paul at the three places mentioned is shown to be part of the tradition, so too are the travel stations of Antioch, Iconium and Lystra. In addition, Derbe may be regarded as a travel stage in the tradition, since it is closely connected with Lystra (14.6; cf. 14.20).

The question now arises whether the rest of the travel stations in Acts 14 may be part of the tradition: in v.6 Paul and Barnabas travel from Iconium to Lystra and Derbe and the surrounding area, then in v.21 back to Lystra, Iconium and Antioch; in vv.24ff. through Pisidia and Pamphylia to Perga and Attalia. From there they sail together back to Antioch on the Orontes.

Now we should note – as was already indicated in the previous section II – that the return to Antioch gives a link back to 13.1f. and shows the hand of the redactor Luke. That journey therefore must be excluded as an element of the tradition. On the other hand, at first glance there seems to be no redactional interest in the statement that Paul and Barnabas twice went through Antioch (13.14/14.21), Iconium (13.51/14.21) and Lystra (14.6/14.21) (see Derbe [14.6/14.20). But it should be noted that on the return journey presbyters are appointed here (v.23) and other admonitions given. This chronological distancing of the two actions which relate to Luke's present gives them more emphasis (they arise out of a special visit, an extra action, by the missionaries). For these reasons, in this chapter we cannot assume any further places to which Paul (and Barnabas) travelled in the tradition other than the stations mentioned at the beginning (Antioch, Iconium, Lystra and Derbe).

Therefore analysis of the tradition in Acts 14 does not favour the theory of a consecutive source in Acts 13-14.

IV Historical

The missionary journey with the stations of Derbe, Lystra, Iconium and Antioch is a historical fact (for the chronology see Lüdemann 1984, 262f.). For further justification see the analysis of 13.13-52.

The historical value of the above tradition in vv.19-20a is to be rated highly. Paul himself reports a stoning in II Cor.11.25 – but without giving the place. The tradition in Acts 14.19-20a helps us to know the historical location of this dangerous punishment. Paul suffered it in Lystra – in the middle of the 30s, when he was carrying on a mission in various cities of southern Galatia (Derbe, Lystra, Iconium and Antioch) in connection with his activity in Syria and Cilicia (Gal.1.21). Now above under III the question whether Jews or Gentiles carried out the punishment of stoning on Paul was left open. That Jews instigated the punishment is supported by the fact that they above all had the penalty of stoning as part of an orderly legal process (cf. above, 90f.). Therefore the majority of scholars have not discussed this question further and have presupposed – often tacitly – the Jewish punishment of stoning in Acts 14.19f., where they have accepted the historicity of the scene at all (cf. Stählin 1980, 195; Marshall 1980, 239). However, there are important objections to this proposal: 1. the Jewish stoning is carried out outside the city (cf. Acts 7.58 – however, against this one could refer to II Chron. 24.21 [the stoning of Zechariah in the forecourt of the temple, cf. II Chron.10.18]). 2. The Jewish stoning was a death penalty. No one (but Paul) survived it. 3. Stoning was a widespread form of lynch law in pagan antiquity (cf. Apuleius, *Met* I,10,1; II,27,4; X,6,3). 4. The resistance of the Jews to Paul in this text is Luke's creation. So we have some justification for advancing the hypothesis that in Lystra Paul was 'stoned' in a riot by Gentile inhabitants of the city. Such an action could have brought about the death of the victim, but this need only have been an attempted stoning, or Paul may just have had stones thrown at him, and was able to escape. At all events, the proposal made here has the advantage of fitting meaningfully with II Cor.11.25 and at the same time lending historical colour to Paul's own remarks made there.

If we anticipate the results of the analysis of Acts 16.1-5 here, it should be added that in Lystra Timothy was probably converted by Paul and won over as a fellow-worker, and that Paul (with Timothy) went on into Galatia from southern Galatia northwards, through Phrygia (cf. Acts 16.6, a passage which certainly has a genetic connection with ch.14). Because of II Cor.1.19 (cf. I Thess 1.1; 2.1ff.) this stoning could have taken place on the first journey to southern Galatia (for further justification see 175f. below).

As I have already mentioned above, the return to Antioch, including the travel notes in 14.24f., is redactional. (Perhaps this verse reflects the historical fact that Barnabas returned to Antioch alone.)

Acts 15

I Division

15.1-3: Sending of Paul and Barnabas from Antioch to Jerusalem because Christians in Judaea demand circumcision. Their journey through Phoenicia and Samaria
4-29: Jerusalem conference
    4: Reception in Jerusalem and (first) report on the success of the mission to the Gentiles
    5: The objection of Pharisaic Christians: the need for circumcision
    6: The assembly of apostles and presbyters
    7-11: Peter's speech
    12: Summary note about the report by Paul and Barnabas
    13-21: James's speech
    22-29: Sending of Paul and Barnabas together with Judas Barsabbas and Silas to Antioch with a letter
        22: Decision by the community
        23-29: Wording of the letter
30-35: Paul and Barnabas return from Jerusalem to Antioch with Silas and Judas
    30: Letter handed over in Antioch
    31: The joy of those who read the letter
    32-33: Activity of Judas and Silas in Antioch; they are sent back to Jerusalem (v.34 is not part of the original text)
    35: Activity of Paul and Barnabas in Antioch
36-41: Barnabas and Paul part over John Mark
    36: Proposal by Barnabas to visit the communities founded earlier
    37: Barnabas wants to take John Mark along
    38: Paul refuses, because Mark had left them in Pamphylia
    39a: Clash between Barnabas and Paul
    39b-41: Barnabas takes John Mark along to Cyprus, Paul takes Silas to Syria and Cilicia

II Redaction

[1-3] The section has the stamp of Lukan language: v.1, *katelthontes, adelphous, ethei*; v.2, *ouk oligos* (cf. Radl 1975, 433), *zetematos*; v.3, *men oun, dierchonto, ekdiegoumenoi, charan*. In addition it is striking that individual phrases in vv.1-3 match others in the immediate context,

either previously or susequently: v.1, 'Unless you are circumcised according to the law of Moses' corresponds to v.5, 'It is necessary to circumcise them and to charge them to keep the law of Moses' (cf. v.24); v.2, 'When dissension and dispute (*zetesis*) arose' corresponds to v.7, 'And when there was a great dispute (*zeteseos*)'; the phrase 'to the apostles and presbyters to Jerusalem because of this disputed question' (*zetematos*) corresponds to v.6: 'the apostles and presbyters (were gathered together) to consider this matter (*logou*)'. In terms of content vv.1-3 are an exposition of the problem to be 'resolved' in what follows.

[4-29] *paragenomenoi, paredechthesan* and *ekklesias* are redactional in language. The dovetailing with the context makes the Lukan derivation of v.4 certain. Cf. 'by the church and by the apostles and by the presbyters' (v.4) with v.22, 'the apostles and presbyters with the whole church'; 'and they told what God had done with them' (v.4) picks up 14.27 ('they told what God had done with them') and appears similarly in 15.12. *haireseos* and *pepisteukotes* in v.5 are Lukan language. The verse repeats the demand for circumcision which was the occasion for sending Barnabas and Paul from Antioch to Jerusalem. Now it is made once again in Jerusalem by Pharisaic Christians. *autous* (v.5b) seems left hanging; if we are to identify any point of reference it is to Paul's companions in v.2 (cf. Zuntz 1972, 242). But this expedient is forced (v.2 is quite a long way away). Rather, Luke wants once again (after v.1) to give a general description of the problem with which the subsequent passage is concerned (cf. also Wellhausen 1914, 26f., for the character of v.5 as an insertion); v.6, the gathering of apostles and presbyters, provides the framework for the following speech and the account by Paul and Barnabas. Note that, as often in Acts, Luke's view of the constitution of the Jerusalem church comes through. (Strangely, Roloff regards Luke's account of the composition of the earliest Jerusalem community as 'solid historical information' ([1981, 224].)

On Luke's level, we should not see v.6 as the description of a more intimate gathering, since v.12, which presupposes the same audience as v.6, already speaks again of *plethos*. Verse 7a is a Lukan introduction to Peter's speech, which follows (vv.7b-11). Verses 7b-9 sum up what has been set out in the narrative in Acts 10f. Verse 7b gives the impression that the Cornelius episode happened a long time beforehand (*aph'hemeron archaion*). Verse 8 reminds the readers how the Spirit was bestowed on the Gentiles in the person of Cornelius. Verse 9 evaluates the vision in 10.9-16. Verses 10-11 draw the consequences of the Cornelius story, of which there is yet another reminder in connection with the disputed question which is now under discussion. In v.11 ('by the grace of the Lord Jesus we believe that we shall be saved') Luke is being Pauline, as he already was in 13.38f. Because of the reference to the context (14.27), v.12 is redactional. The tension between the word *plethos* (which is Lukan language) and 'apostles, presbyters' (v.6) probably does not go back to tradition, but is a careless piece of narration on Luke's part (Dibelius 1956, 95 n.6), though of course a basis in tradition cannot be ruled out. Verse 13 is the introduction to James's speech (*sigesai* picks up *esigesen* in v.12). Verse 14 is deliberately archaic ('Symeon' for 'Peter'). By referring back to the speech which Peter has just made, James refers indirectly to the Cornelius story. *ex ethnon laon* (cf J.Dupont, *NTS* 31, 1985, 321-35) similarly refers back to it, but also forward to vv.16-17 where it is first given its content (see what follows). Verse 15 is an introduction to vv.16-18: the verses are a quotation from the LXX (the MT is anti-universalistic). It does not wholly fit the context of the question whether Gentile Christians are to observe the law of Moses, but it must have been extremely welcome to Luke, as it accords with his ecclesiology. The new *laos* consists of Jews (v.16) and Gentiles (v.17). Through v.17a the restoration of Israel and the Gentile mission are brought into a causal connection (*hopos an*).

'The one is therefore meant to produce the other; the restoration is aimed at bringing in the Gentiles. So we should probably explain Luke's meaning like this: the true Israel will only be achieved when the Gentiles are brought into the community of the people of God. But that means that there is only one *laos*; this is at the same time the *laos* which was gathered together from the Jews after Pentecost and the *laos* from the Gentiles to be added in the subsequent period' (Lohfink 1975b, 59f.).

Verse 19 first of all seems to end up in a general approval of the acceptance of Gentiles, but v.20 then limits this by the 'conditions' of the Apostolic Decree (for this see III below) and v.21 justifies this as follows: 'For from early generations Moses has had in every city those who preach him, for he is read every sabbath in the synagogues.' That probably means that the Apostolic Decree is 'necessary because all over the world there are Mosaic Jews and the disputed issue which has just been discussed' (Schille 1983, 322). Verses 22-29 are Lukan throughout: v.22, for *edoxe* + dative cf. Luke 1.3 and v.25. The content of the letter in vv.23-29 takes up the content of the decree in v.20 and in syntax recalls the prologue Luke 1.1-4 (for this cf. Harnack 1906, 153-6; see ibid. on the Lukan language of the letter). Cf. further 23.26-30 as an analogy for the incorporation of a 'letter' in the account.

[30-35] The language of the section has a Lukan stamp: cf. v.30, *men oun, apolythentes, katelthon, synagagontes, plethos*; v.31, *echaresan, paraklesei*; v.32, *epesterixan, kai autoi*; v.33, *apelythesan, aposteilantes, chronon*; v.35, *dietribon, euaggelizomenoi, logon tou kyriou*. The information that Judas and Silas are prophets (v.32) recalls 13.1, as does the note that Paul and Barnabas had worked in Antioch (v.35).

[36-41] The section reports the parting of Paul from Barnabas. This parting is necessary at this point because from now on there is no longer any room in the Pauline mission for a representative of the Antiochene community. The story is told in a plausible way, and there was good reason for the separation (which was already prepared for by the previous chapter). The dispute arose over John Mark, who had turned his back on Paul and Barnabas in the middle of the missionary journey in Pamphylia (13.13). The theory that this section is redactional is supported by observations on Lukan language: v.36, *eipen pros, kateggeilamen, kata polin, logon tou kyriou*; v.37, *kaloumenon*; v.39, *apochoristhenai*; v.40, *paradotheis te chariti tou theou* (14.26), *adelphon*; v.41, *diercheto, episterizon*. Also in support of redaction is the observation that Paul – not Barnabas – parted company with the brothers in Antioch (v.40). The note about Silas (v.40) causes difficulties if this is the same person as the companion of Judas Barsabbas (vv.22,27,32f.). For he returned to Jerusalem and therefore cannot function as Paul's companion, which is what v.40 wants. There is an explanation of the difficulty if Silas is seen as redactional in vv.22,27,32f. and as part of the tradition in v.40 (cf. Weiser 1984, 153). Another possibility is that Luke has been careless here (cf. Harnack 1908, 159-98).

The function of Acts 15 in the framework of Acts

The redaction-critical analysis of Acts 10f. produced the following result. Through the revelation of God to Peter the will of God was made known that from now on the Gentiles are a legitimate part of the people of God, without any qualification. This will of God is presupposed as valid in Acts 15 – with one small qualification: the Gentiles are to observe the demands of the Apostolic Decree. Acts 15 is the junction at which the transition from the mission undertaken under the auspices of Antioch to Paul's independent mission takes place. It is legitimated by the Jerusalem church before it has really begun – for reasons of salvation history.

III Traditions

Because of the thorough Lukan revision indicated above, it seems hopeless to extract any consecutive source in ch.15. On the other hand there should be no dispute that Luke composed Acts 15 on the basis of traditions (oral or written). That is true both of the quotations in vv.16-18, which Luke will already have found in this collection, because they are in tension with the context (see above, 168 and Weiser 1985, 373 [bibliography]), and also of the conference.

However, Dibelius differs. He thinks that the account of the conference does *not* derive from tradition: Luke only knew 'of a conflict about the circumcision of the Gentile Christians in Antioch, which was arbitrated in Jerusalem' (1956, 98). He composed Acts 15 on this basis and put the decree at the end of the 'council', but that too goes back to tradition which has nothing to do with the conference: 'In doing so, he was following the custom of the ancient historians of incorporating into their work the text of documents, either ancient or fictitious' (1956, 99). But such a view is too one-sided, for even apart from vv.1-3, the basis of which in tradition Dibelius does not question, traditions about the conference may be worked over in Acts 15. In favour of the correctness of this assumption is, first of all, the course of events that can be reconstructed from Gal.2. For if Luke was not an eye-witness and there are some parallels between Acts 15 and Paul's conference report (see the participants, the agreement, the question of circumcision, etc.), on what else but tradition could these parallels rest? Also in favour of a basis in tradition is the specific character of some accounts: the personal names (Paul, Barnabas, Peter, James, Judas, Silas), the description of the problem and finally also the 'solution' opened up by the decree.

If these observations show the probability of a basis of Acts 15 in tradition and at the same time give two criteria for reconstructing the tradition in this text (concreteness and − more important − agreement with the course of the conference as it can be reconstructed from Gal.2), it must be stressed once again that only elements of tradition can be extracted. In my view the following can be seen:

1. Barnabas and Paul go together to Jerusalem (the link with Antioch is part of the Lukan framework).

2. In Jerusalem there are negotiations between the Jewish Christians there and Barnabas and Paul over the mission to the Gentiles.

3. The gathering takes place both at the level of the community (v.12) and in the group of apostles (v.6). Luke mixes the two together but still indicates the negotiations of different bodies.

4. A party in Jerusalem (v.5) and in Antioch (v.1) calls for the circumcision of the Gentile Christians.

5. The mission to the Gentiles is basically approved (vv.10f.,19).

6. The Gentile Christians who are at home in Syria and Cilicia are enjoined to observe the demands of the Apostolic Decree. (The version of Codex D is secondary.) The specific form of address should be noted in this context.

7. Probably Judas Barsabbas was a member of a delegation to Antioch.

His link with Silas derives from Luke (see above on 15.40). For the question whether Barnabas belonged to this delegation see IV below.

[36-41] Elements of tradition are the separation of Paul from Barnabas (v.39), Paul's journey with Silas to Syria and Cilicia (v.41, cf. Gal.1.21) and the activity of Barnabas and Mark on Cyprus (v.39, cf. 13.4,13).

IV Historical

The collection of Old Testament quotations under the heading of 'mission to the Gentiles' (v.16-18) comes from a Greek-speaking community in the environs of Luke's church. There they served the purpose of confirming an existing practice. Further information about chronology and geography is impossible to get.

Because of their many parallels with the account in Gal.2.1-10, the elements of tradition connected with the conference suggest that they and Paul's account relate to one and the same event, the Jerusalem conference. For there are the following agreements between Gal.2.1-10 and the elements of tradition mentioned:

1. Barnabas and Paul go together to Jerusalem (Acts 15.2/Gal.2.1).

2. They take part in a conference about the mission to the Gentiles (Acts 15.12/Gal.2.1,9).

3. The conference is held both at community level (Gal.2.2a/Acts 15.12) and in a smaller group (Gal.2.2b,7/Acts 15.6). In connection with the gathering in the smaller group Paul speaks of those of note (Gal.2.9), the tradition in Acts 15.6 of the apostles.

4. One party calls for the circumcision of the Gentile Christians (Gal.2.4f.: 'the false brethren'/Acts 15.5, 'Christian Pharisees').

5. The occasion for the conference was a set of similar demands to those made at the conference (cf. Lüdemann 1984, 64-75).

6. According to both accounts the Gentile mission was fully recognized at the conference (Acts 15.10f.,19; Gal.2.9).

7. We learn nothing of the Apostolic Decree in Paul's account. Nevertheless Paul's account might allude to the Apostolic Decree or a regulation similar to it in the statement: 'Those of note laid nothing *additional* upon me' (Gal.2.6d). The decree (or a form similar to it) may have been imposed on the largely mixed community of Antioch on whose behalf Barnabas was at the conference, whereas Paul's predominantly Gentile-Christian communities did not have anything imposed on them (cf. Lüdemann 1984, 64-71 for the question touched on here). If it is certain that following the conference Barnabas again travelled to Antioch, perhaps along with Judas he took the rule for mixed communities to the community there.

171

So all in all there is a high degree of historical reliability in the elements of tradition underlying Acts 15.1-35.

Since Acts 15 is quite frequently regarded as a reliable account of the Jerusalem conference at the narrative level, I shall now stress the differences between Luke's account and what really happened (as far as it is possible to reconstruct this on the basis of Gal.2 and the traditions contained in Acts 15):

1. Contrary to his own account in Gal.2, Paul is sent to Jerusalem from Antioch as a delegate, and at the conference, like Barnabas, only has the role of a spectator.

2. Luke brings the conference forward in order to legitimate the Pauline mission before its real beginning (Acts 13-14 is a model journey). (That is not to claim that Luke knew of the real point in time when the conference was held. But it would have been impossible for him to give an account of the 'council' at the time of Acts 18.22, in the middle of the Pauline mission.)

3. In the interest of the unity of the church, Luke suppressed reproofs to the point where they are virtually unrecognizable. So here (as elsewhere in Acts) he suppresses the person of the Gentile Christian Titus, about whose circumcision there was a dispute at the conference. Furthermore, he distances the agreement to make a collection from the account of the conference (and later from the story of Paul's last journey to Jerusalem, Acts 21), because as Paul had regarded it as a symbol of unity (cf. Rom.15.27), it would have made clear the danger of a split in the church. Instead of this he advances the collection to 11.27ff.

4. Luke gives the impression that the dispute ended with the Jerusalem conference. But the letters of Paul tell another tale (cf. Lüdemann 1983, 103-65).

'Acts smoothes down the waves with sacred oil: Paul indicates that events were all too human. To him the earliest period does not appear in the haze of sacred history, but he allows himself quite an ironical tone about men like James and Peter. It should finally be noted that the dispute is not, as it seemed to be in Acts, settled and ended with the apostolic decision, but still went on for a long time' (Wellhausen 1914, 29f.).

[36-41] The elements of tradition probably reflect the historical separation of Paul from the Antioch community, although it cannot be demonstrated that this tradition has any connection with the incident at Antioch (Gal.2.11ff.). Moreover at the redactional level a conflict over principle which we can no longer recognize is shifted into the personal sphere, and the opponents at the Antioch interlude are James's people and not Barnabas. Verses 40f. probably derive from Paul's departure for Syria and Cilicia after the Cephas visit (cf. Lüdemann 1984, 153). It is attractive to regard the statement in the tradition that Silvanus was Paul's companion

as accurate (cf. I Thess.1.1). (For the identity of Silas and Silvanus see Bauer 1979, 750.) In that case Paul probably got to know Silvanus on the Cephas visit. For the information about Barnabas and Mark see 170f. above.

Acts 16.1-5

I Division

16.1a: Journey from Derbe to Lystra
1b-3: Timothy is circumcised and taken along (from Lystra)
4: The Apostolic Decree is handed over to the communities there
5: Short summary: strengthening and growth of the communities

II Redaction

[1a] Paul's journey to Derbe and Lystra is a Lukan duplication of Acts 14.6f., 20f. (cf. Schwartz 1963, 134f., and following him Wellhausen 1914, 31). After the conference Luke narrates further journeys by Paul to these cities, since only at the beginning of Paul's independent mission does he want to report that Timothy was his companion (probably there is some indication here of knowledge of the significance of Timothy for the independent Pauline mission).

[1b-3] The section has Lukan linguistic colouring (a selection is: v.1b, *kai idou, onomati*; v.2, relative connection, *emartyreito* (cf. 6.3 [of the seven Hellenists]; 22.3 [of Ananias]). Luke's reason for the circumcision of Timothy is given explicitly in v.3: Paul circumcises Timothy because of the Jews in those places; they knew that his father was Greek. So Timothy is circumcised, because Paul wants to go on a mission with him among Jews and because the Jews had learned that Timothy's father was Gentile. Luke evidently presupposes that Timothy is a Gentile because he had a Gentile father. Now as Luke's Paul can have only Jewish colleagues for the mission among the Jews (cf. Conzelmann 1987, 125; similarly already Wendt 1913, 241, who regards Luke's view as that of Paul), he has to make his colleague a Jew by circumcision.

To this explanation Schmithals 1982 objects that in Acts Timothy never goes into a synagogue with Paul (145). But that does not in any way change Luke's scheme of going to the Jews first. Moreover none of Paul's companions (apart from Barnabas) ever appears with Paul in the synagogue. Because of Acts 21.21, the question of cirumcision indirectly provides material for conflict (against Schmithals, ibid.). But Schmithals is right that the statement about the circumcision of Timothy is based on tradition and is historical (see IV below). I do not fully understand the protest of Schille 1983, 333, against the above explanation (cf. his opinion: 'Or has Luke's scheme of first going to the Jews proved his undoing? In that case this verse would be evidence that Luke had not reflected on the matter!' [ibid.]), and his own theory ('Luke thinks that Paul is supplying what Timothy lacks in order to give him full worth in the eyes of the Jews' [ibid.]) is probably just a variant of the view he rejects.

Thus Luke limits the remark made in Acts 15 (by Peter and James) about the freedom of Gentile Christians from circumcision - at least at this point, which is about the Pauline mission among the Jews. This *a priori* rejects attacks on Paul (cf. Acts 21.21). (However, this qualification is purely theoretical, since Luke's church is no longer carrying on a mission to the Jews [see below, 264].)

[4] This verse is a reference back to the account of the Jerusalem conference. It indicates that the decisions made there in the interest of the continuity of the church were also implemented. It should be noted that the verse says only that the Apostolic Decree was passed on to the communities founded before the conference. Derbe and Lystra are mentioned explicitly in v.1. As the author understands things, one could also add Pisidian Antioch and Iconium (cf. also 15.23; the Christians of Antioch and Syria/Cilicia as those to whom the decree is addressed), which would then have been included in the *poleis* to which Paul travelled. Luke does not report later that the communities founded after the conference received the apostolic decree. It has a function only in salvation history - no present significance for Luke's community.

[5] After 6.7: 9.31 the verse is a short summary and refers to the passages there.

III Traditions

[1a] The stations Derbe and Lystra on the journey seem to be part of the tradition, though with the qualification that they have a genetic connection with those mentioned in Acts 14. In other words, Luke has duplicated them (see below under II).

[1b-3] Tradition may also underlie the narrative about Timothy (the person of Silas is forgotten, but Silas appears later [16.19], and not

174

Timothy, until Timothy suddenly returns in 17.14f.). The following elements are probably part of the tradition: Timothy's arrival from Lystra (v.2), his descent from a mixed marriage (Jewish mother, Gentile father) and Paul's acquaintance with the Christian Timothy. (II Tim.1.5 and 3.15 attest the fact that personal traditions about Timothy were in circulation.)

Probably the report about the circumcision of Timothy by Paul is also part of the tradition. The reason for it might have been that Timothy was the son of a Jewish woman. Rabbinic law usually defines the status of a child by the father, but in mixed marriages by the mother: cf. MKidd 3.12 (see the commentary by Schiffman 1981, 117ff., and Cohen 1986, 264f.).

Cf. also MBik 1.4: 'These may bring (sc. the first-fruits) but they may not make the avowal: the proselyte may bring them but he may not make the avowal since he cannot say, "Which the Lord sware unto our Fathers for to give us". But if his mother was an Israelite he may bring them and make the avowal. And when he prays in private he should say, "O God of the fathers of Israel"; and when he is in the synagogue he should say, "O God of our fathers"' (H.Danby, *The Mishnah*, Oxford 1933, 94).

The rabbinic legal view given above was not just formed in the second century CE (Cohen 1986, 265-7 differs) but was probably already part of a *halachah* (for details see Schiffmann 1981, 121, who points out that the narrative parts of the books of Ezra/Nehemiah [Ezra 9.2; 10.2,10; cf. Neh.13.23] are concerned only negatively with the instances of the marriage of a Jew with a non-Jewish woman [the legal texts Ezra 10.11; Neh.10.31; cf. Neh.13.23 prohibit intermarriage regardless of which partner is Jewish]). If it underlies the tradition in Acts 16.3, a circumcision of Timothy was in accordance with the law.

According to Haenchen, Luke took the story of the circumcision of Timothy from a tradition which is genetically connected with Gal.5.11. The passage mentioned seems to reflect rumours that even as a Christian Paul taught circumcision: 'Here then Luke has not... tendentiously replaced the truth known to him by a patchwork of his own; rather was he the victim of an unreliable tradition' (Haenchen 1977, 482; Schille 1983, 333 n.15 does not even consider this a possibility).

IV Historical

Paul's journey through Derbe and Lystra (and Iconium and Antioch) is certainly historical, since the places are on the land route from Syria/Cilicia to Ephesus.

Paul's association with Timothy is also historical. But it should be stressed *against* the tradition (or Luke) that Paul himself converted Timothy: cf. I

Cor.4.7, 'Therefore I have sent to you Timothy, who is my beloved child...
in the Lord...' In the context Paul calls the Corinthians (like Timothy) his
beloved children (v.14). He has given birth to them through the gospel.
Therefore it is natural also to assume this for Timothy. Paul converted
him, like the Corinthians, to faith in Christ. This conversion took place
on the way to Greece, where Timothy, along with Silvanus and Paul, was
among the preachers in the mission on which the community in Corinth
was founded (II Cor.1.19; cf. also I Thess.1.1 in conjunction with I
Thess.2.1ff.). If the chronology suggested on 10-16 above is correct, the
time of Timothy's conversion (against Acts) was *before* the conference,
i.e. during Paul's first stay in Lystra (Acts 14.6 – see 165 above; cf.
similarly Roloff 1981, 240, with a different chronology and a reference
to I Cor.4.17).

In earlier times or more recently the historicity of the circumcision of
Timothy was rejected with reference to relevant passages in Galatians.
Here is an illustration from recent years:

'That Paul circumcised Timothy after he had become a Christian "because of the Jews
in the region" (16.3) must be doubted. In that case Paul, who not long beforehand
had argued so passionately at the apostolic conference for the recognition of the
uncircumcised Gentile Christian Titus with full rights and had stood out against his
circumcision (Gal.2.3; cf.also 5.11) would now have acted quite differently' (Ollrog
1979, 21). 'We must certainly reflect that Titus was a Gentile Christian and Timothy
a Jew by Jewish law. But the question of circumcision was not an adiaphoron to which
I Cor.9.20 could be applied (Gal.5.2f.; Rom.2.25-29). For him it was a matter of
salvation. Circumcision, says Paul, is of no use before God (I Cor.7.18f.; Gal.5.6;
6.15), but faith alone (Rom.3.20). By contrast anyone who is circumcised is subject
to the law (Gal.5.2)' (Ollrog 1979, 21 n.72).

But these assumptions are mistaken because the polemical statements
of Galatians are not timeless dogmatic statements, and Paul's concept of
freedom allowed him 'to become a Jew to the Jews' (I Cor.9.19). In other
words, for utilitarian reasons, because it furthered the preaching of the
gospel, Paul could very well have circumcised a colleague who came from
a mixed marriage, all the more since his mother was Jewish and thus
Timothy was a Jew by rabbinic law. To circumcise Timothy would not
have amounted to 'a contempt for baptism' (thus Weiser 1985, 402),
because according to Paul 'everyone is to remain in the state in which he
has been called' (I Cor.7.20). In the case of Timothy this was the Jewish
state. Paul's intrinsic attitude to the act of circumcising a Jewish Christian
is expressed in I Cor.7.19: 'Circumcision is nothing and the foreskin is
nothing'. Later he takes part in a Jewish ceremony in Jerusalem with a
similar attitude (Acts 21).

So (with Schmithals 1982, 146; Schneider 182, 200f. is more cautious)
we must accept the historicity of Timothy's circumcision (against Lüde-

mann 1984, 153; Weiser 1985, 402 [with bibliography]) though – and this should be stressed – Luke's reason (Paul circumcises Timothy because of the Jews who knew that he had a Gentile father) does not reflect the matter correctly and also (against Acts) circumcision was not performed on Timothy as a Christian at a significantly later date but when he was newly converted (before baptism?).

It is quite possible that the case of Timothy's circumcision was exploited by Paul's opponents in Galatia. As Gal.5.11 shows, Paul was accused of occasionally having himself preached circumcision (cf. Wikenhauser 1921, 291f.). Perhaps too the conference called for the circumcision of Titus by referring to Timothy.

Acts 16.6-10

I Division

15.6-8; Zig-zag journey from Phrygia to Troas
9-10: Paul's vision of the Macedonian and the decision to travel to Macedonia

II Redaction

The whole section is stamped with Lukan language (e.g. v.6, *lalesai ton logon*; v.7, *poreuthenai*, etc). The accumulation of participles is Lukan, as is the direct speech in v.10b with the finite verb at the beginning (cf. 8.14). Is 'we' in v.10 (*ezetesamen*) attached externally to *hemin* (v.9 end)?

As to content: the mention of the Holy Spirit (v.6) or the Spirit of Jesus (v.8) is Lukan. It demonstrates that the salvation history is guided by the Spirit. The dream vision (v.9) may also be Luke's work (cf. the parallels in Acts noted in Nestle/Aland[26] in the margin at 9.10 and the excursus 'Paul's Dreams and Visions' in Weiser 1985, 406-15). With it Luke marks the special character of the transition from Asia to Europe. Generally speaking, the zig-zag journey is meant to make a contrast to the straight-line mission into Europe which is the will of God.

III Traditions

[6-8] The stations 'Phrygia and the land of Galatia' appear in 18.23 in reverse order (see there). The fact that the journey is zig-zag and the many (redactional) warnings by the Holy Spirit suggest that here Luke has suppressed material and only reported bits and pieces. What is left is the fragment of an itinerary (cf. Dibelius 1956, 12, 129f., 176, 197f.) with the stages 'Phrygia, Galatia, Mysia, Troas'.

[9-10] Apparently the tradition already contained a note about the significance of the move over to Europe. (This seems mainly to emerge from the historical considerations which follow.) It was then expressed by Luke through the artistic scene in vv.9f.

IV Historical

The stages in the tradition (Phrygia, land of Galatia) may be historical, even if Luke has put them at the wrong point chronologically. In terms of tradition and history they belong to the journey which Paul made before the Jerusalem conference through Syria, Cilicia and southern Galatia (Derbe, Lystra, Iconium) to north Galatia and from there by Troas to Macedonia (for the itineraries in v.8 and Troas as a favourable place from which to travel on to Macedonia see W.P.Bowers, *JTS* 30, 1979, 507-22). However, Paul only seems to have carried on a mission in Troas later (II Cor.2.12/Acts 20.6).

It was said above that historical reasons led to the assumption that there is a tradition behind vv.9f. which knew of the significance of the move to Europe for Paul. The reason for this is that it emerges from Phil.4.15 that Paul regarded the transition to Europe as a new beginning of his proclamation of the gospel (on Weiser 1985: 'in Paul himself there is no such stress on the move to Europe' [410]; against this see Lüdemann 1984, 103-7). That passage gives the impression that there was no real Pauline mission before the mission to Greece. Thus despite all the redaction, vv.9f. show how significant Paul and his colleagues felt the move to Europe to be. (Anyone who cannot follow these considerations would have to assume that Luke rightly reproduced Paul's estimation of the mission to Greece by chance. And anyone who wants to replace 'chance' by 'knowledge' in this statement is in fact putting forward a version of the hypothesis about tradition advanced above.)

178

Acts 16.11-40

I Division

16.11-12a; Travel account: From Troas to Philippi
12b: Explanation
12c: Arrival and lengthy stay in Philippi
13-15: Conversion of Lydia
16-18: Healing of the girl with the spirit of divination
19-24: Imprisonment of Paul and Silas
25-34: Miraculous release of the two of them and conversion of the warder
35-39: (Official) release
40: Farewell to Lydia and the brethren

II Redaction

[11-12a] For *anachthentes* cf. Luke 8.22; Acts 13.13; 18.21; 20,3,13; 27.2, etc. *euthydromein* appears in the NT elsewhere only in Acts 21.1.

[12b] The text of this part of the verse is uncertain (cf. the variants and Wikgren 1981). The Egyptian text hardly makes sense: 'Macedonia was not a *meris*, "district", rather the *province* of Macedonia was divided into four "districts"... *prote*, "first", designates a city as the capital... But Philippi, as a colony, was neither a provincial capital nor a district capital' (Conzelmann 1987, 99). With Nestle/Aland²⁶ (the proposal in fact goes back to Johannes Clericus) we should probably read *protes meridos* for *prote tes meridos* (dittography of *te*). That produces the correct statement that Philippi is a colony and a state in the first district of Macedonia (cf. Wikenhauser 1921, 334f.). The relative pronoun *hetis* reflects Lukan terminology (cf. Radl 1975, 420). The explanation of the special political status of the city of Philippi is unique in Luke's writings (but cf. similar explanations in 8.26; 13.8; 17.21). Does this indicate special local knowledge on Luke's part or does the explanation go back to his original material?

[12c] *diatribontes* and *hemeras hikanas* are Lukan in language.

[13-15] The following derive from Lukan language: v.13, *elaloumen*; v.14, *tis... onomati*; v.15, *oikos*. As to content: going to the place of prayer (v.13) is based on the Lukan scheme of approaching the Jews first, although the designation *proseuche* is striking, as it is singular in Acts (see below III). Women play a special role in Luke's writings (but by way of qualification here see Jervell 1984, 146-57).

[16-18] A break is evident at the beginning of v.16. The following narrative is introduced with the Lukan transitional phrase in the genitive absolute ('now it happened that as we were going to the *proseuche*...) and has only an external link with the preceding story through the keyword *proseuche*. It takes us back before the Lydia story, in that the incident described is said to have taken place on the way to the place of prayer. The information 'she did that for many days' (v.18a) also completely breaks through the chronological framework to which v.18b is a link backwards. Paul drives out the evil spirit. Verse 18a is in tension with v.16a and certainly is Lukan. 'Paul must have been carrying on missionary activities for some time' (Conzelmann 1987, 131). The Lukan significance of vv.16-18 is to dissociate Paul's action from magic. However, almost against his will (*diaponetheis*, v.18) Paul has to make use of magical means to drive out the evil spirit. (For the redactional shaping of vv.16-18 cf. also Schmithals 1982, 150.)

[19-24] *exelthen* in v.19 picks up *exelthein* and *exelthen* (v.18b,c). The content of v.19 ('now when her owners saw that their hope of gain had "departed", they seized Paul and Silas...') confirms the above characterization of the Lukan significance of vv.16-18 (= the way in which it distinguishes Paul's action from magic). But in that case v.19 and the subsequent accusation may be redactional, the latter because it has nothing to do with the previous story. The charges mentioned in vv.20f. ('These men are causing unrest in our city. They are Jews and preach customs which we as Romans may neither accept nor observe') have nothing to do with Paul's exorcism, and Luke presents them in such a way that they can be rejected.

Haenchen 1977; Elliger 1978, 56f. etc., differ. But here in most cases commentators historicize all too quickly; cf. simply Haenchen, *Die Apostelgeschichte*, KEK 3, Göttingen ⁷1975, 483 (the English translation, from the earlier 1965 edition, does not contain this statement): 'Paul here did act against the laws which in fact applied in a Roman *colonia*: Jews – although otherwise by and large tolerated – might not make propaganda for their cult among the Romans' (483); 1971, 496 is slightly different: 'A travel narrative seems to underlie verse 20f., since Luke would not produce any such accusation on his own.' But see the subsequent explanation in the text on v.37!

paraggeilantes and *asphalos* in v.23 are Lucan language, as is the introductory relative pronoun *hos* in v.24 (cf. Radl 1975, 420).

[25-34] Verses 30-34 may come from Luke; the dialogue (vv.30-32) corresponds to the Lukan way of shaping scenes. The question of the

prison warder ('Sirs, what shall I do to be saved?') echoes the address
'Sirs' in v.19 (the owners of the girl with the spirit of divination), cf.2.37;
Luke 3.10,12,14. On the other hand the scene focuses on the question of
conversion/salvation which is important to Luke. Peter's answer 'You and
your house will be saved' (v.31) appears here redactionally as it does in
the Cornelius story (11.14). The word *oikos* refers back to v.15. The
description of the sermon (v.32) and the way in which the preachers are
taken into the warder's house (v.33) are motivated redactionally. The
terminology *elalesan... ton logon tou kyriou* (v.32) and in v.33 *paralabon*
and *parachrema* are certainly Lukan, as is *pepisteukos* in v.34.

[35-39] These verses resume the main action without taking note of the
miraculous release. Verse 37 finally gives Luke's understanding of v.20.
Silas and Paul are Romans: in so far as being a Jew is associated with
magic — a traditional association (cf. Hengel 1974, 240f.), which is also
instanced in Acts (cf.13.6; 19.13-16) — Silas and Paul are not Jews. The
real culprits who practise magic are the accusers of Paul and Silas, the
kyrioi of vv.16 and 19. The order for them to be released from prison and
the way in which they are escorted out of the city (vv.35-39) vindicate
Silas and Paul in the eyes of their Roman readers.

Cf. already Schille 1983: 'The true Romans of the story are the missionaries who were
initially calumniated as Jews. They not only take heed of Roman law but see that it is
observed' (370).

[40] Paul and Silas enter Lydia's house. Here there is a redactional link
back to v.15, and the Philippi story is rounded off. Note the Lukan word-
play in v.40: *exelthontes... eiselthon... exelthan* (cf. the word-play with
exelthein in vv.18f.).

From the perspective of redaction criticism, the close link between the
story of the release in this chapter with the releases described in Acts 5
and Acts 12 should be noted. In all the passages God frees the Christian
missionaries; here the story in Acts 16 is elaborated in the most miraculous
way, and in addition contains a conversion story which has been composed
by Luke. The miraculous action of God through the apostles is thus clearly
in the service of their mission.

III Traditions

Schenk 1984 has recently put forward the theory that 'what Acts 16.11f. writes about
Paul in Philippi might — apart from the use of secondary material filled in with formal

181

models customary elsewhere in Luke – be completely dependent on the information in Paul's letters' (339). In my view Schenk's argument is *quite impossible*, so I shall not take further note of it here and shall continue to assume that Luke did not use the letters of Paul. This rejection of Schenk's somewhat casual but typical theory is not meant to malign the merits of his commentary.

[11-12a] The chronicle-like style suggests that we should assume tradition.

[13-15] The remarkable phrase in v.13, 'where we *thought* that there was a "proseuche"', perhaps reflects an eyewitness report (cf. Cadbury 1955, 776, who refers to the remarkable phrase, but thinks that perhaps it has a basis which is inexplicable to us). Because it is singular in Acts, the term *proseuche* suggests tradition, as does the name of Lydia, the specific details of her origin (against Schille 1983, 341f., who questions the connection between Lydia and Philippi) and her baptism. Because it corresponds with v.31, the *oikos* formula at this point seems to derive from Luke, although conventionally it is taken to be tradition (cf. Klauck 1981,51-6) and at other points certainly does reflect reliable tradition (see 201f. on Acts 18.8). For *sebomene* cf. the summary remarks at 155 on 13.43.

[16-18] The healing story goes back to tradition. Stylistically it ends with the statement: 'And at the same hour the spirit departed from her.' It is no longer possible to identify its exact beginning, as the construction in the genitive absolute is Lukan. But at this point the structure indicates that it might have been a complete story of an exorcism.

Schille 1983 differs: 'It is impossible to imagine an independent account of an exorcism without the demonstration of the miracle and the concluding chorus' (346).

[19-24] The note about Paul's physical chastisements by the Romans (vv.22f.) may go back to tradition, above all for historical reasons (see IV below).

[25-34] The tradition underlying vv.25-29 (the beginning is uncertain) can be termed a miraculous release. It has numerous pagan parallels (Euripides, Nonnus, Philostratus - cf. also the story from Artapanus cited on 162 above [for a summary comment on this see Weinreich 1968, 167]). It is impossible to decide whether Paul and Silas were already a pre-Lucan ingredient of the legend about the release (in that case vv.25-29 would derive from an independent legend – thus Dibelius 1956, 23f.). I tend to attribute the insertion of the two missionaries to Luke, since they could be replaced by other figures without damaging the sense. In that case the miraculous release could be regarded as prompted by Luke's reading (cf.

the narratives in chs.5 and 12, which show that Luke knew ancient stories of miraculous releases).

[37] Paul's Roman citizenship is not part of the traditions which can be recognized in this section, but may have belonged to the tradition at Luke's disposal and have been used by him at this point (cf. Weiser 1985, 430). It is discussed in summary form at 240f. on Acts 22.24-29.

IV Historical

[11-12a] The stages in the journey are certainly historical. In Phil.4.15f. Paul himself speaks of the beginnings of the mission in Philippi. The stages which he mentions most emphatically, 'Troas, Samothrace and Neapolis', are the natural stopping places on the way to Philippi.

[13-15] Lydia and her connection with Philippi are historical. That is supported not only by the name but by the specific remark that she is a dealer in purple. (Schille's assumption that she came from Lydia [1983, 343] is in my view improbable.) In that case, Lydia's baptism and her hospitality to the missionaries are also historical facts. *proseuche* denotes either a synagogue building ('*proseuche* is the main official designation for the synagogue building down to the early imperial period in the Greek-speaking Diaspora' [Hengel 1971, 171]) or a place of prayer. Certainly it is not in keeping with the synagogue building 'that only women were there' (Conzelmann 1987, 130), but that may be redactional (see above, 180). The river may be the Gangitis, which comes within about a mile of the city to the west (cf. Elliger 1978, 48f.; see ibid. on the geographical and archaeological details; but cf. also the healthy scepticism of Meeks 1983, 211 n.237, about attempting to locate the *proseuche* too exactly). The river provided the water needed for the ritual washings. Probably the best explanation of the pieces of information from tradition in v.13 (synagogue/place of prayer, river) is that these are historical facts which are to be connected genetically with Paul's first mission in Philippi. (Another point in time is ruled out because of vv.14f.)

[16-18] The historicity of the traditions in this section is probably an open question. On the one hand it must be stressed that Rom.15.18f. and II Cor.12.12 *clearly* attest that Paul did miracles. On the other hand the genetic connection of the tradition here with a Pauline miracle is uncertain. In addition, the tradition of a Pauline miracle in Philippi may also have arisen on the basis of a miracle at another place.

[22f.] The maltreatment of Paul and Silas by the Romans agrees with what Paul himself says about his own and Silas's suffering in Philippi (I Thess.2.2). Although it is regrettable that I Thess.2.2 does not give any more information about the circumstances of this maltreatment, there certainly seems to be a genetic connetion (cf. Walter 1978).

'In II Cor.11.25 Paul himself reports that he was beaten three times by the Romans, and in I Thess.2.2 we learn from him that he arrived in Thessalonica after having suffered maltreatment earlier in Philippi. So we find ourselves on historical ground' (Schmithals 1982, 151).

[25-29] The release reported in vv.25-29 is certainly quite unhistorical (cf. Zeller 1854, 253: 'anyone who has not sold his soul to the crassest belief in miracles will inevitably take offence at the miracle in this story'). However, on the basis of the tradition in vv.22f. it is possible to say that Paul and Silas were also arrested in connection with the maltreatment. In that case there would be a historical nucleus to vv.25-29, and the verses would contain a correct account of the release of Paul and Silas, albeit decked out with miraculous features. As I Thess. 2.2 shows, Paul and Silas in fact escaped the maltreatment.

Acts 17.1-15

I Division

17.1: Journey by Amphipolis and Apollonia to Thessalonica
2-3: Sermon in the synagogue
4: Partial success of the sermon among the Jews and great success among the godfearers and wives of the well-to-do
5-9: The unsuccessful attack of the Jews of Thessalonica (on Paul and Silas); accusations against Jason and other brethren
10: Flight of Paul and Silas to Beroea
11-12: The success of the preaching among the Jews and among the well-to-do women and men in Beroea
13: Agitation against Paul by the Thessalonian Jews in Beroea
14-15: Paul escapes to Athens accompanied by brethren from Beroea. Instructions to Silas and Timothy, who have remained behind in Beroea, to come to Paul as soon as possible

II Redaction

Although some of the passages in this section are based on tradition, vv.1-15, which report the mission of Paul and Silas in Thessalonica and Beroea, have been shaped by Luke. Thus the accounts of the mission in Thessalonica (vv.2-9) and in Beroea (vv.10b-12) have similar structures (the mission begins in the synagogue; the sermon is based on scripture; conversion especially of the well-to-do women; persecution). Moreover both narratives are dovetailed: v.11 refers back by comparison to v.15, and v.13 introduces the Jews from Thessalonica. Finally, the present section is bound up with the context: v.1a continues 16.40 and v.15 is a transition to the next place, Athens.

[1] Verse 1a is a travel note; v.1b prepares for v.2a.

[2-3] The verses can be said to be completely redactional; thus the sermon to the Jews is based on Luke's scheme of approaching the Jews first (v.2, see especially the phrase 'according to his custom' which echoes Luke 4.16); similarly the content of the sermon that the Christ had to suffer in accordance with the scriptures and rose again on the third day (v.2f. – cf. Luke 24.25-27,44-46; Acts 2.22-36; 3.18; 8.32-35; 13.27,29). The note that Paul preached to the Jews on *three* sabbaths (v.2) can be explained by the observation that 'three' is a favourite number of Luke's (Lüdemann 1984, 177-9). Verse 3b, like Acts 1.3, is a transition from the third person to direct speech in the first person (for its redactional character see on the passage concerned).

[4] The note about some conversions of Jews is schematic. For the redactional function of the statement about the conversion of a crowd of Gentiles see below III, 186. The news of the conversion of the wives of the well-to-do seems to be redactionally suspect because of the parallels in 17.12 (see below); 13.50.

[5-9] The rebellion of the Jews of Thessalonica against Paul (v.5) corresponds to the Lukan pattern. The accusation of causing political unrest (vv.6b-7; cf. 16.20; 24.5) is put in such a way that the readers can see through it and reject it (cf. Conzelmann 1960, 141-9). For the duplication of the charges against Paul see the accusation by the Jews against Jesus before Pilate (Luke 23.2-4 [Mark differs]). For the redactional description of the tumult (*demos* [v.5] = *ochlos* [v.8]) cf. 19.32f. (see below 217).

[10] *paragenomenos* is redactional in language; Luke requires an immediate entrance into the synagogue.

185

[11-12 (for v.13 see v.5; for 14-15 see below, 188)] The relative clause introduced by *hoitines* outwardly echoes *hoitines* in v.10. The phrases 'accept the word' (cf. Luke 8.13; Acts 8.14; 11.1 - but cf. also I Thess 1.6; 2.13), 'act in this way' (cf. 7.1; 24.9), *men oun* and the litotes *ouk oligoi* (cf. v.4) indicate the redactor. The relationship of the Christian message to scripture is a Lukan theme. Both verses are variants of v.4 (cf. the introductory remarks on the section vv.1-15) where as a narrative contrast there is a stress on the positive attitude of the Jews in Beroea in comparison to the negative attitude of those in Thessalonica. The whole passage is a piece of Luke's narrative skill. For the way in which the conversion of the wives of the well-to-do is conditioned by the redaction see v.4.

Elliger 1978 wants to regard the conversion of the wives of the well-to-do in Beroea as historically probable. He thinks that there are indications on inscriptions 'that women played a greater role in Beroea than elsewhere' (116). But the historical accuracy of 17.12 in no way follows from that.

III Traditions

[1a] This part of the verse contains tradition about Paul's itinerary.

[4] The note about the success of Paul's preaching among the Gentiles derives from tradition, though the formulation could also be understood in terms of redaction (the remark about the conversion of a crowd [*plethos* – note the Lucan language] of godfearing Gentiles brings out the contrast with the conversion of only a few Jews). Ultimately historical considerations (see below, IV) suggest that v.4 reproduces tradition.

[5-9] A piece of tradition underlies this. This assumption is supported by narrative tensions in the text: in literary terms the verses are only loosely connected with what has gone before. The figures of Paul and Silas are nowhere mentioned explicitly. They appear only behind *autous* (v.5 – cf. v.7a), whereas *autous* (v.9) is no longer Paul and Silas but Jason and the rest (of the brethren). That is, Paul and Silas are associated only externally with the scene by Luke (for a parallel see the scene 19.32-40 – see there). Furthermore, elements in the content support the assumption of tradition in vv.5-9: 1. The verb *ochlopoein* is singular. 2. The name of Jason is introduced abruptly (cf. similarly the introduction of Sosthenes in 18.17 and Alexander in 19.33). At first glance it is not even clear whether Jason is a Christian, as he is merely giving lodging to Christians (brethren). But we may presuppose that he was a member of the community. Moreover he may be identical with the Jason of Rom.16.21. 3. The phrase 'present before the public assembly' (*proagagein eis ton demon*) is a juristic term

186

(Conzelmann 1987, 135, cf.25.26). 4. It is not clear who instigates the uproar against the Christians. Grammatically speaking it is the Jews (but even in v.9 the Jews are apparently still the subject), but from the context it is the mob. (However, it should be clear that the Jews have been introduced by Luke, see II above.) The politarchs indicate tradition:

'The most important task of these officials was their jurisdiction. In addition, they had to summon the city council, over which they presided, and the popular assembly, to which they presented plans worked out in the council for voting on. The special status of the office also emerges from the fact that the year was named after a politarch, the *archon eponymos* (the "name-giving" official) and the politarchs also enjoyed great respect after the end of their period in office' (Elliger 1978, 93).

6. The phrase 'receive a caution' (*lambanein to hikanon*) is too specific not to go back to tradition. (However, it is also a novellistic motive.)

Even if we add together the six individual elements mentioned, we do not yet arrive a coherent story, but rather at the outlines of a tradition (of the Thessalonian community [?]; cf. similarly most recently Schille 1983, 352f.). It had the following content: the Thessalonian Christian Jason and other fellow Christians were harassed by their fellow countrymen, were to have been brought before the popular assembly, and were set free by one of the politarchs after a caution.

The following questions remain open: 1. Was a gathering in the house of Jason part of the tradition? 2. What role was played by the mob in the uproar? 3. On what charges were proceedings brought against Jason and the brethren? (Both charges mentioned in vv.6b-7 make good Lukan sense, see above 185 [on Schille 1983, 351f. who regards the second accusation in v.7 as authentic].)

For the mission in Beroea and the itineraries of Silas and Timothy see IV below.

IV Historical

Paul's itinerary (v.1a) which took him from Amphipolis and Apollonia to Thessalonica is certainly historical, even if Luke puts it in the wrong historical context (see 14 above). On the mission on which Paul founded communities in Greece he travelled on the via Egnatia from Philippi via Amphipolis and Apollonia to Thessalonica. The next stage was Beroea.

Paul's stay in Thessalonica was much longer than the report presupposes (cf. Lüdemann 1984, 177). The reason is that Paul worked in Thessalonica so as not to be a burden on anyone (I Thess.2.9). There he often received support from Philippi (Phil.4.16). However, only the redactor Luke presupposes that Paul was merely three to four weeks in the city.

The report about the winning over of many Gentiles is shown to be historical by what is said in I Thessalonians. The same may be true of the uproar over Jason. I Thessalonians presupposes that the Gentile-Christian Thessalonians were put in difficulties by their fellow-countrymen (I Thess.2.14). The one note of caution suggests the reliability of the tradition. As a result of state intervention Jason was brought with other Christians (from his house, in the middle of a gathering of the community?) before the court on a charge the precise nature of which remains unclear. The charge was dismissed with a caution. The above considerations could therefore be a more specific version of the information in I Thessalonians. (However, the event may also have taken place at a later point in time.)

Verse 10 reflects the existence of a Christian community in Beroea; there is no reason to doubt its historicity, although Paul himself does not mention it. According to the tradition in 20.4 one of Paul's companions, Sopater (cf. Rom.16.21, Sosipatros), came from Beroea. The community there will probably have been one of the churches in Macedonia which took part in the collection (cf. II Cor.8.1).

The itineraries of Timothy (and Silas) in vv.14f. (18.5) do not correspond with what Paul says. According to I Thess.3.2 Paul sent Timothy from Athens to Thessalonica (and he met Paul again in Corinth). Consequently he had travelled with Paul to Athens. According to Acts (17.14) Paul left Timothy and Silas behind in Beroea and met them again in Corinth (18.5). We will prefer Paul's remarks to those in Acts and might add that probably Paul also sent Silas back from Athens to Thessalonica. In that case the mission of Timothy and Silas consisted in strengthening the Macedonian communities. On the other hand they may also have brought a gift of money for Paul from Philippi (II Cor.11.9: see Lüdemann 1984, 97).

How did the itineraries of Timothy and Silas come to be changed in Acts? Conzelmann 1987, 136, attributes this to a tendency to simplify (as does Roloff 1982, 253). However, that, does not yet convey the redactor's meaning. Probably Luke changed the itineraries of Paul's companions because he wanted to reserve Paul for the section on Athens (cf. similarly Schille 1983, 352). For this reason he deals with the itineraries of the two companions before Paul comes to Athens (vv.14-15), and that involved the changing of details as described above.

Acts 17.16-34

I Division

17.16-20: Paul's arrival in Athens and encounter with the philosophers
  16a: Travel note
  16b: Paul's anger at the idols in the city
  17-18: Paul in the synagogue and in the market place. Reaction of the Stoics and Epicureans
  19-20: Paul on/before the Areopagus. Content of his teaching
21: Explanation about the Athenians for the readers
22-31: Paul's speech on/before the Areopagus
  22-23: Introduction
  24-25: I. God the Creator needs no temple
  26-27: II. The seasons and limits given by God and the determination of human beings
  28-29: III. The affinity of human beings to God
  30-31: The possibility of repentance and the future judgment
32-34: Reaction of the audience: some reject Paul and some join the movement

II Redaction

[16-20] These verses are shaped by Luke throughout. Verse 16, which speaks of Paul's anger about the idols in Athens, prepares for v.23. It is a Lukan transitional verse. For the phrase 'his spirit grew angry within him' cf.15.39.

It is 'oriental Greek to the third power. But that is precisely the way Luke writes. He writes Acts 20.10: *he psyche autou en auto*, and he distinguishes wherever possible between the human *pneuma* (the psyche) and human beings themselves'; cf. Luke 1.46f.; 23.46; Acts 7.59; 19.21; Luke 8.55 (Harnack 1913a, 13f.).

Verse 17 contains the Lukan scheme of going to the Jews first, but it is striking that in contrast to other passages we are told that Paul preached both to the Jews in the synagogue and the Gentiles in the market place (or more precisely to passers-by there) *at the same time. dielegeto*, like the preaching in the market place, recalls Socrates (cf. Schille 1983, 354). Verse 17 outlines a scene with local colouring (cf. 19.23-40). It is to be regarded as a literary creation. Here the contrast between the two schools merely serves to create a milieu (cf. Conzelmann 1987, 139). Again Luke seems to produce a notional parallel to Socrates. Like Paul now, Socrates argued with the representatives of philosophical schools, who accused him of introducing new gods (cf. Plümacher 1972, 19).

'Paul speaks in the market place to everyman – like Socrates. They think he is

189

introducing new gods – like Socrates. And Socrates came before the court on that account and was sentenced to death' (Haenchen 1971, 527; for the whole question of 'Socrates and Christianity' see E.Fascher, *ZNW* 45, 1954, 1-41 [with bibliography]).

As later in v.32, in v.18 Luke contrasts two groups in the audience, both of which have reservations about Paul's preaching (cf. similarly 2.12). 'Jesus and the anastasis' as the object of proclamation probably reflects the misunderstanding of Christian preaching by the Gentiles in terms of a divine pair, which is what Luke intended (cf. Haenchen 1971, 518 n.1). In vv.19-20 Luke mentions 'the best known place of judgment in Athens... for narrative effect in order to produce a worthy scene for Paul's speech' (Overbeck 1870, 277). 'Areopagus' (on which see Elliger 1978, 173-9) can mean two things: 1. the hill of Ares, but this would be far too small for the scene; 2. the legal authorities. The latter is suggested by *en meso* (17.22; cf. 7.33), *epilabomenoi* (a word which Luke likes using) and *ho Areopagites* (17.34). Paul is taken along to give an account of the new teaching. But the subsequent 'sermon' is not a speech in his defence, and v.21 then makes it quite clear that there is no accusation. Moreover in v.20 the author again proves to be at work when, taking up motives mentioned earlier (v.18), he recalls the accusation against Socrates: Paul is accused of introducing strange things (*xenizonta tina*) – which picks up v.18: *xenon daimonion dokei kataggeleus einai*. This seems to allude to the accusation against Socrates that he was introducing *kaina daimonia* (Plato, *Apol* 24b; Xenophon, *Mem* I 1,1) (but against this Hommel 1955, 150f.). However, the charge of leading the youth astray is absent.

[21] This verse is directly addressed to the readers (cf. 8.26; 16.12; 23.8). The curiosity of the Athenians was proverbial; cf. the instance in Conzelmann 1987, 140, and the reference to Chariton I, 11, 6-7 (ibid., 139). By picking up the theme of the curiosity of the Athenians the verse gives the whole scene further local coluring. Cf. also the redactional Atticisms (*spermologos* [v.18], *kainoteron* [v.21], *legein... e akouein* [v.21] – on this see Norden 1913, 333-6 and the qualifications made by Plümacher 1974, 243).

[22-31] As the theological explanation of the note about *preaching* in v.18, these verses are the only discourse addressed to Gentiles in Acts (cf.14.15ff.). Its starting point in v.22 is a commonplace often expressed in praise of Athens, namely its claim through its many cultic images and festivals to be the most pious city in Greece (cf. the instances in Weiser 1985, 464). The reference to the inscription on the altar in v.23 may also derive from Luke. It takes up a type of inscription known to have existed in Athens, though as yet there is no archaeological evidence for it (but in

190

contrast to 17.23 this is a reference to inscriptions which are dedicated to unknown *gods* [in the plural]) and alters it for his purpose (monotheism) by replacing the plural (*theois*) with the singular (*theo*: cf. Conzelmann 1987, 140 with examples). At the redactional level the speech shows its concern to pick up previous knowledge of the Christian God by means of the theme of affinity with God and the works of creation (cf. also the quotation from Aratus in v.28). Luke hardly imagined that the discourse he makes Paul give was the model for sermons to Gentiles (against Dibelius 1956, 81 n.1), since the Areopagus speech is not a sermon. However, the question remains, as with all the discourses in Acts, as to how this discourse is related to types of sermon in Luke's time (though it is not the subject of this work – see the commentaries); but cf. the questions asked in terms of motive history under III.

It is sometimes argued that the Areopagus speech derives from a secondary revision of Acts (Norden 1913, 37-55, 311-32 – Norden's work is basic for the analysis of Acts 17). But the parallels in content noted by Harnack 1913a between the speech and Luke-Acts tell against this. I shall go on to list them, following Harnack, along with the singular features of the speech, in order to bring out the redactional elements of the Areopagus speech:

1. God the Creator (v.24) – cf. Acts 4.24; 14.15: LXX.

2. God the Lord (v.24) – cf. Acts 10.36, 'He is Lord of all': LXX.

3. God does not dwell in temples (v.24) – cf. Acts 7.48: LXX.

4. God is not served by human worship because he does not need anything (v.2) – there is no parallel in this form in Luke-Acts (Stoic and LXX).

5. God the giver of being and of all gifts (v.25) – cf. similarly Acts 14.17 (Stoic background and LXX).

6. Descent of all human beings from the one (v.26) – cf. how Luke makes Jesus descend from Adam in Luke 3.23-28.

7. God, who guides the history of the nations (v.26) – cf. similarly Acts 14.16.

8. The task imposed on human beings of finding God (v.27) – cf. Acts 14.17.

9. God is near to every human being (v.27) – cf. Acts 10.35.

10. Pantheism (v.8) – there is no parallel in Luke-Acts. The pantheism is Stoic; but cf. also LXX.

11. Divine *genos* of humankind (vv.28f.) – Greek poets, no parallel in Luke-Acts, but cf. LXX.

12. Idols are not permitted (because they are nonsensical) (v.29) – no parallel in Luke-Acts, but cf. also LXX.

13. The previous ignorance of human beings, from whom God has looked away in disapproval (v.30) – cf. Acts 3.17; 13.27; 14.16.

191

14. A new revelation of God has been given in the present to all people (v.30) – cf. Luke 2.10 (the whole people).

15. The new preaching begins with repentance (v.30) – cf. Acts 2.38; 3.19; 13.14; 20.21; 26.20.

16. The coming judgment (v.31) – cf. Acts 24.25.

17. The *aner horismenos* (v.31) – cf. Acts 10.42.

18. The resurrection of Christ (v.31) – often in Acts.

Of these eighteen points, fourteen are attested in Luke-Acts. Only four (nos. 4, 10, 11, 12) are not there, but they are the characteristic feature of this speech, 'namely what Luke had to say to the Gentiles in this solemn didactic discourse, and they fit in harmoniously with his known ideas' (Harnack 1913a, 25; Harnack goes on to list the stylistic similarities between the Areopagus speech and Luke-Acts).

[32-34] For v.32 cf. the comments above on v.18: both groups in the audience have reservations about Paul's preaching (see 2.12). For v.33 see Luke 4.30; v.34 has Lukan linguistic colouring, cf. esp. *kollethentes, onomati, heteroi syn autois* (Luke 24.33; 8.3).

III Traditions

[16-20] The arrival of Paul in Athens from Thessalonica reflects tradition (see IV below). It is no longer possible to recognize a basis in tradition for vv.16b-20.

[22-31] Nauck 1956 discovered three different groups of motives in the Areopagus speech: creation (vv.24-26a, 27-28), preservation (v.26b) and redemption (v.31), and succeeded in demonstrating the same scheme of motives in the missionary literature of Hellenistic Judaism (Sibylline Oracles, fragments I and III [Nauck 1956, 26-8 (analysis of the text), 32-4 (comparison with the Areopagus speech), 51f. (text in a German translation)]). In addition, he indicates the occurrence of the same scheme in early Jewish and early Christian writings: cf. the additional texts in Nauck 1956, 46-52 (I Clem.19.2-21.1; 33.2-6; *ApConst* VII 34; VIII 12; *EpAp* (beginning); Eighteen Benedictions; Prayer of Manasseh). His conclusion is that 'the structural pattern which is frequent in tradition (makes it) advisable not to take the combination of the three themes in the Areopagus speech as Luke's theological conception. For it is probable that the basis of the mission speech is not Luke's creation, but that it was known to him from mission praxis' (300). We must accept this verdict and add that we are led to assume tradition not by stylistic criticism but

by a history-of-religions comparison or an analysis of motives (cf. the sub-title of Nauck's work).

Haenchen 1971 criticizes Nauck: 'We should not speak of a scheme *creatio-conservatio-salvatio*... it is "nowhere carried out as a strictly ordered schema" (Conzelmann, 29), not even in the Areopagus speech whose wide arches span from Creation to Judgment' (524 n.5). But this objection misses Nauck's thesis. A strict pattern cannot be expected either in the Areopagus speech, which according to Nauck too is only based on the schema mentioned, or in the texts cited, as they too only reflect more or less exactly the scheme of motives mentioned, and all are of different genres. We need to take into account slight deviations and a degree of flexibility. Note further that Nauck goes on to differentiate the schema he discovers into a more conciliatory type (Aristobulus, Areopagus speech) and a sharply accusing type (Sibyllines, Paul [cf. below]). The former excuses the ignorance of the Gentiles, the latter does not. This differentiation will not be noted in what follows.

[32-34] The name of Dionysius the Areopagite probably comes from tradition. This is the best explanation of the redactional information that Paul appears before the Areopagus. Cf. Baur 1866: 'but if he (sc. Dionysius) was converted as an Areopagite, it must also be presupposed that the Apostle appeared before the assembled court of judgment' (194).

Similarly the name Damaris may be part of the tradition. This assumption is supported by the consideration that Damaris – not elsewhere instanced as a woman's name (cf. Bauer 1979, 170) – does not fit in the context of the speech on/before the Areopagus. 'A pious Jewish woman or a woman in the community would not of course appear in Athens in public with men' (Jervell 1984, 188 n.30). Schille 1983 derives the information in v.34 from information about the founding of a community, 'from which it does not follow either that Paul founded the community or that it was founded on this journey' (360).

IV Historical

Paul's journey from Thessalonica to Athens (during the mission on which the community was founded) is historical (see I Thess.3.1f.).

It should be stressed that Paul, too, presupposes in various remarks the scheme of motives in the Areopagus speech which is rooted in tradition, as in the kerygmatic formulation of I Thess.1.9f. (cf. Wilckens 1974, 81-91 – Holtz 1978, 461-3, etc. differs) and in Rom.1.18-2.10 (cf. creation [1.20,25], knowledge of God [1.19f.], worship of God [1.23,25], repentance [2.4], judgment [2.5f.,8] and salvation [2.7,10]). By way of qualification it should first be said that the theme of preservation does not appear explicitly either in I Thess.1.9f. or in Rom.1.18-2.10. But it is presupposed as an extension of remarks about creation. Then there are considerable

193

differences between Paul's remarks and the tradition of the Areopagus speech. The latter has two proofs for the knowledge of God by natural man: 1. from the works of creation; 2. from affinity to God. The latter is inconceivable in Paul because of his view of the alienation of human beings from God (see Rom.1.21, etc.); the former also appears in Paul (see Rom.1.20a), but only as a lost possibility (cf. Rom.1.20b and the summary in Rom.1-3). Therefore we shall have to delete these two features of the speech as unhistorical. But at the same time, because of the tradition worked on in Paul and in Acts 17 it is possible that the latter is in a genetic relationship to a speech given by Paul in Athens, if it may be presupposed that Paul also carried on a mission in Athens among the Gentiles. Certainly it did not begin with an unknown god – there never was such an inscription (see above, 190f.); moreover the altar helps to provide a link which was not made by the historical Paul, one which was demonstrated above to be redactional – nor did Paul give a speech on the Areopagus. Nevertheless it can be assumed that in his attempts at mission in Athens Paul gave one speech (or more – see the explanation below) to the Gentiles, the basis of which has perhaps been preserved in the tradition of Acts 17 (cf. Nauck 1956, 45). On the other hand, in my view the stronger possibility is that Luke and Paul know a similar type of sermon to the Gentiles (for the distinction see above, 192f.) independently of one another. In that case we would not have the genealogy indicated above.

There are various possible places for such a sermon: the synagogue, the market place, Paul's workshop (on which cf. Hock 1980, 37-42). The remarks made above cannot be understood to indicate that Paul only gave one sermon in founding the community. We should think, rather, of several, each of which contained the motives indicated above. (For Paul the missionary cf. Meeks 1983, 26-8.)

The persons of Damaris and Dionysius the Areopagite are probably historical. But they should not be connected with the mission on which Paul founded the community, since the house of Stephanas (from Corinth), with whom Paul had not yet come into contact during his stay in Athens, was the first-fruits of Achaea (I Cor.16.15). Moreover we may make the well-founded historical assumption that Paul did not have much missionary success in Athens, for an Athenian community has no recognizable role in his plans for his mission, journeys and collection. Moreover it is only around 170 CE that we hear of a Christian community in Athens (Eusebius, *Church History* IV, 23, 2f.: the letter of Dionysius from Corinth to the community of Athens [the assertion by Dionysius in it that Dionysius the Areopagite had been the first bishop of Athens belongs in the realm of legend]).

So generally speaking, the historical results from the basis of the tradition contained in Acts 17.16-34 are relatively thin. It should not be objected to this that in Acts Athens is the only place in which Paul preached without prompting a persecution. Therefore the whole episode can be regarded as good historical tradition (thus Lake/Cadbury, *Beg.* IV, 208). For the lack of a theme of persecution is explained by the fact that in this chapter Paul turns almost exclusively to the Gentiles, and the Jews appear only on the periphery. (The educated Gentiles of Athens dispute but do not turn violent [an apologetic motive!]). But E.Meyer's theory must also be rejected: 'The reliability of Luke's account of events in Athens cannot be confirmed better than by this letter (sc. I Thess.)' (III, 108). For in I Thessalonians Paul is not talking about events in Athens and gives us no indication in this connection.

Acts 18.1-17

I Division

18.1: Journey from Athens to Corinth
2-3: Paul as tentmaker/leather-worker with Aquila and Priscilla
4: Paul preaches every sabbath in the synagogue
5-8: Intensified mission work by Paul
9-10: Vision of Christ
11: Note of time (eighteen months)
12-17: Paul before Gallio

II Redaction

[1] For *meta tauta* cf. the Lukan parallels 7.7 (quotation); 13.20; 15.16 (quotation); Luke 5.27 (Mark differs); 10.1; 12.4 (Matthew differs); 17.8; 18.4.

[2-3] These verses show Lukan colouring in language and syntax: cf. *onomati, to genei* (cf.4.36; 18.24), accusative with infinitive introduced by *dia* (twice); *chorizesthai* picks up *choristheis* (v.1). The style with an accumulation of participles is similarly redactional. But the sentence introduced with *kai heuron* has become a monstrosity (for the explanation cf. III below). 'All the Jews' is a Lukan generalization (cf. Luke 2.1; Acts 11.28; 21.30, etc. and Lüdemann 1984, 11, 35 n.38). This passage fits in well with the Lukan tendency to dovetail world history and salvation

history. It should be noted that here the Roman emperor Claudius is connected with salvation history for the second time, after 11.28. However, a redactional tone does not necessary mean that the information related to Claudius is not tradition, namely that Priscilla and Aquila arrived in Corinth in the year in which Claudius issued his edict on the Jews and that they met Paul there.

Hyldahl 1986 has pointed out, in my view rightly, that *prosphatos* (v.2) focusses on the arrival of Paul in Corinth. 'Aquila and Priscilla had come from Rome... shortly before he arrived there' (124). He continues: 'From the perspective of the author of Acts, who wrote later, this is not the slightest suggestion that Paul, too, had already come to Corinth at that time' (ibid.). In my view the last statement is vulnerable. But even if it were right, the theory that Hyldahl puts forward on the basis of Acts 18 would be improbable. He thinks that Priscilla and Aquila came to Corinth in 41 CE (= the year in which Claudius issued his edict on the Jews, see below 200f.) and that Paul arrived there only in 49 CE (ibid.). For there is a connection between the edict of Claudius, Aquila and Priscilla, and Paul at the level of tradition. By *prosphatos Luke* is making clear the chronological relationship between the arrival of Aquila and Priscilla and that of Paul. – Moreover Hyldahl 1986, 122-4, is probably wrong in disputing that traditions of more than one stay in Corinth have found their way into Acts 18 (on this see 10-12 above).

[4] This verse corresponds to Luke's scheme of going to the Jews first. It is also redactional in that in anticipation of the next unit, vv.5-8, it describes the two groups to which Paul's preaching is addressed: Jews and Gentiles. The verse is also to be described as a transition to v.5, which in Lukan language (Lüdemann 1984, 157 n.49) describes Paul's intensified activity in mission. Verse 4 provides the intrinsic presupposition for this missionary activity, in describing how Paul preaches every sabbath in the synagogue, a lesser missionary activity practised once a week.

[5-8] Verse 5b forms as it were the further exposition and explanation of the persuading of the Jews in the first part of the transitional v.4. When this fails, with a symbolic action (cf. Acts 13.51; Neh.5.13), Paul turns away from the Jews and to the Gentiles (v.6: 'Your blood be on your head! I am innocent; from now on I will go to the Gentiles'). This is a further explanation of the second half of the transition in v.4 to the persuading of the Greeks. The following elements in vv.5f. are Lukan:

Verse 5: *diamartyromenos* (for the content of the testimony, namely that Jesus is the Christ, see the [redactional] passages 9.22; 17.3; 18.28; 28.31). Verse 6: the construction in the genitive absolute, *eipen pros, apo tou nyn, poreusomai. antitassomai* occurs only here in Luke, though the Jewish attitude of repudiation and their blasphemy (*blasphemeo*) are typical of him. *onomati* (in conjunction with *tis*, v.7) is redactional (cf.v.2). According to Weiser 1985, *syn holo to oiko autou* (v.8) and the *oikos* formula in 16.15, 32, 34 are part of the 'Lukan elements of the composition which heighten the effect' (424). But tradition may also underlie them (see below III, 198).

[9-10] For *horama* as a Lukan means of description cf. the comments on 16.10. The vision of Christ intensifies the drama of the scene. It makes good redactional sense, since first it explains the long duration of Paul's stay in Corinth (v.11, eighteen months), and secondly it illustrates the significance of the Christian community in Corinth in Luke's time (cf. I Clement). Thirdly, it above all serves to provide a transition to the Gallio episode which follows, by announcing in anticipation that Paul will not undergo any suffering.

[11] See III below.

[12-17] The report of the 'trial' before Gallio also contains redactional features. Paul must not say a word, so that the accusation by the Jews can be repudiated. Even before he can speak, Gallio rejects the Jewish charge and thus shows himself to be a model statesman, who does not want to intervene in the dispute between Christians and Jews (cf.23.29; 25.18). The following detailed traces of Lukan redactional activity can be found: v.12, *homothymadon, egagon...epi*, the Jewish action against Paul (cf.13.45, 50; 14.2, etc.). The content of the charge that Paul teaches worship of God which is contrary to the law (*para ton nomon*, v.13) corresponds with that of the charges against him in 16.20f.; 17.6f.; 21.28; 24.5f. (cf. Conzelmann 1960, 159-61). *sebesthai ton theon* echoes *sebomenon ton theon* (v.7). *mellontos anoigein to stoma, eipen pros* in v.14 are Lukan in language. For *onomata* (persons) in v.15 cf. 1.15. Verse 16 does not reflect any redactional activity (*apelauno* appears only here in the New Testament). *pantes* in v.17 is part of Luke's generalizing (cf. v.2).

Elliger 1978 infers the following historical information from this section: 'that the accused gets no opportunity to speak can... only (sic!) be understood on the assumption that Gallio *a priori* wants to dissociate himself from the Jews and their quarrels. Therefore he possibly interprets the Jewish charge in quite a different sense from that which was probably intended. The *nomos* against which Paul is supposed to be offending is probably, as elsewhere, the Roman law and not the Jewish law. However, Gallio understands it to be the latter, since otherwise he could not *a priori* dismiss the dispute as a matter concerned only with Jews. But in that case he can let the matter drop with a good conscience. For it does not lie within his sphere of competence, as it does not pose any danger to public security. That means that Gallio is perhaps acting blamelessly as a statesman, but the rejection of the accusation is in no way any comment on Paul. He is driven away from the *bema* with the other Jews (v.16) and is left to the hostility of his fellow countrymen. Nothing can allay our suspicion that Gallio himself was familiar with the antisemitic impulses of the crowd of bystanders, to whom Gallio's decision had given free rein – Sosthenes the president of the synagogue is beaten. In Rome Gallio had witnessed the Jewish unrest under Claudius, and his brother Seneca had spoken of the *gens sceleratissima*. Even for Gallio Paul was just a Jew' (236f.).

These remarks of the learned author shows us the dilemmas facing historicizing exegesis. It rejects *without any reason* the redaction-critical perspective and gets entangled in historical difficulties. For it is inconceivable that Paul could not have said anything. Moreover v.16 leaves it open whether Paul was also driven off. Finally, it is clear from the tension between verses 17 and 16 (see III below) that the text must first be read at the redactional level. (It is historically inconceivable that Gallio should drive away the Jews and that subsequently a Jew should nevertheless be beaten.)

III Tradition

[1] Paul's journey to Corinth is tradition.

[2-3] Paul's manual work as a tentmaker or leather-worker (for the translation of *skenopoios*, cf. below, 202) with Aquila and Priscilla, including the connection between their arrival from Rome and Claudius's edict against the Jews, also seems to be tradition. At the same time this presupposes that Paul's arrival in Corinth is also to be put in immediate proximity to the edict of Claudius at the level of tradition (see above 196 on Hyldahl's theory, which is rather different). Now above, under II, I mentioned the possibility that the note about Claudius was redactional, and was one of those passages in Luke-Acts which dovetail world history with salvation history. However, although we can see what this means for Luke, the following reasons suggest that vv.2-3 come from tradition. 1. The compactness of the clauses in vv.2 and 3 is best explained on the hypothesis that various traditions have been forced together in them. 2. That Paul finds a welcome with Aquila and Priscilla because they practise the same craft (and not primarily because of the same faith) is a singular and quite untendentious report (against Roloff 1981, 270, this is *not* the Lukan pattern of going to the Jews first). 3. Another factor which tells in favour of tradition in vv.2f. (and 18f.) is that Luke imagines Aquila and Priscilla as Christian teachers (in v.26 they give Apollos help in the Christian 'way'), and there is no trace of that in these verses. 4. The information that Aquila comes from Pontus (cf. Acts 2.9) is also untendentious.

[5-8] The arrival of Silas and Timothy from Macedonia (v.5) might also

198

go back to tradition (cf. II Cor.11.9; Phil.4.15), as might Paul's teaching in the house of Titius Justus (v.7) and the conversion of Crispus, the president of the synagogue (v.8). In all cases these are specific pieces of information and untendentious. – The report of the conversion of the house of Crispus is in all probability likewise tradition, for historical reasons (see 204 below).

[9-10] The verses do not seem to have any basis in tradition (see 197 above).

[11] The note of time, 'eighteen months', does not derive from Luke and is therefore tradition.

[12-17] Elements of tradition in this section are the note about the 'trial' before Gallio and the name of Sosthenes, the synagogue president. It is hard to say what the tradition looked like before Luke created the (non-) trial before Gallio; but I would like to repeat my suggestion 'that Luke had a tradition in which one of Paul's visits to Corinth was connected with the person of Gallio and that Luke then developed this tradition – in accord with his theology – into the episode of a nontrial of Paul before Gallio. Luke possibly received from the same tradition the person of Sosthenes, who gets beaten by the Corinthians after the nontrial. This is likely in light of the observation that the figure of Sosthenes, seen in terms of literary criticism, does not fit very well into the Lukan scene of the Jews' accusation and Gallio's response. The scene seems to have reached its conclusion when the Jews are driven away from the tribunal (v.16). The following report about the beating of Sosthenes in v.17 comes a little too late and stands in tension with v.16; it presupposes that the ruler of the synagogue evidently was not driven away – otherwise the people would not have been able to beat him before the tribunal. For this reason, it is most probable that Luke found the persons of Gallio and Sosthenes together in the same tradition about one of Paul's visits to Corinth. It is likely that Luke developed this tradition into a "nontrial", where the Jews spoke against Paul before Gallio, and that he exemplified the punishment of the Jews by having the ruler of the synagogue, Sosthenes, beaten' (Lüdemann 1984, 160f.).

Weiser 1985 has argued against this proposal as follows:
'It does not follow from the fact that this is an "account of a nontrial with a purpose" (Lüdemann) that Paul was not involved in the event but that in accord with Luke's consistent purpose in shaping the narrative Paul himself was only to speak in the account of his trial in chs.22-26' (487). The high proportion of redactional work by Luke must not 'lead us to dispute a basic accusation by the governor against Paul any more than, for example, in the Philippi scene in 16.19-24' (ibid.). Therefore it may be

assumed that: 'Paul was accused by Jews before Gallio. The charge was dismissed as insufficient. Thereupon the mob, hostile to the Jews, beat the Jewish spokesman Sosthenes' (ibid.).

Against this: Weiser is *not* in a position to establish the historical course of events which he has just depicted on the elements of tradition which underlie the passage (especially the accusation of the Jews, the redactional character of which he rightly stresses, 488). Moreover, a historical dilemma remains: why did the mob which was hostile to the Jews beat the Jewish spokesman (sic! – here Weiser tacitly changes the text of Acts, which still spoke of a synagogue president) Sosthenes and not the *Jew* Paul? Finally, concerning the Philippi scene in 16.19-24 more information than in this specific case is at our disposal, all the more so since Paul speaks about events there in I Thess.2.2.

What is the relationship between the two elements of tradition that we have discovered above? In my view they can be divided into two blocks, vv.1-11 and vv.12-17. This assumption is supported by (*a*) literary, (*b*) factual, and (*c*) chronological reasons.

(*a*) 1. The note about eighteen months (v.11) evidently refers to the period reported in vv.2-8 (10). 2. The sentence 'Now when Gallio was proconsul in Achaea ...' begins as abruptly as if there had been no previous indication that Paul was staying in Corinth. The question also remains open who had previously been proconsul (during the eighteen months [v.11]). 3. Verses 12-17 are quite comprehensible on their own and in form-critical terms are clearly marked off from vv.1-11 as a 'dramatic episode'.

(*b*) In v.8 the synagogue president is called Crispus, but in v.17 he is called Sosthenes. Now in the Jewish communities there was always only one synagogue president (cf. Lüdemann 1984, 159). It is therefore more probable that the names of the two synagogue presidents reflect different points in time.

Against such a conclusion it may be argued that in Corinth a new synagogue president replaced the old one when the latter, like Crispus, adopted the new faith. But it is possible to say that only if Luke was an eyewitness or has taken the basic material throughout the chapter from the diary of a companion of Paul. As such assumptions must be ruled out, we have to rely on literary analyses and accuse the objection above with being historicization on the wrong object (cf. Lüdemann 1984, 159 and n.53).

(*c*) The expulsion of Jews from Rome probably took place in the first year of Claudius, 41 CE (cf. Lüdemann 1984, 164-71). The most recent commentaries either ignore this finding (Schneider, Schille), or take note of it and then regard 49 CE as more probable than 41 CE because it fits better with the rest of Paul's chronology (Weiser 1985, 489 – he surreptitiously gives the self-contradictory statements of Orosius the same weight as those of Dio Cassius, a procedure on which I do not need to comment), or give an objectively false account of the evidence (cf. Roloff

1981, 270, according to whom Suetonius *dates* the expulsion in 49 CE).
The authors cited in Lüdemann 1984, 192 n.99 and 292, rightly argue
against this; cf. now also Hyldahl 1986, 124 and n.26. The 'rehabilitation'
of the information in Orosius by T.Holtz (*Der erste Brief an die Thessalon-
icher*, EKK XIII, 1986, 18 n.48) is inadequate in both method and content
(for 'policy hostile to the Jews' read in ibid., 'policy friendly to the Jews').
I have not found the recent defence of 49 CE as the date of the edict of
Claudius by P.Lampe (*Die stadrömischen Christen in den ersten beiden
Jahrhunderten*, WUNT II, 18, Tübingen 1987, 7f.) any more convincing.
2. Gallio was proconsul in Achaea in 51-52 CE (cf. Lüdemann 1984,
163f.).

IV Historical

The traditions in vv.1-11

Paul's journey from Athens to Corinth for purposes of his mission is in
accord with the letters of Paul (cf. I Thess.3.1f.,6).

The tradition about the arrival of Priscilla and Aquila in Corinth is
confirmed by the evidence in Paul. First, the letters of Paul make it probable
that the date of Claudius's edict against the Jews (= 41 CE) corresponds
to the time when Paul preached and founded the community in Corinth
(Lüdemann 1984, 173-5). Secondly, the couple Priscilla and Aquila appear
in I Cor.16.19 and Rom.16.3; in I Cor.16.19 they send greetings to the
Corinthians and this presupposes that they know them (however, this is
disputed by Schille 1983, 363). The most probable explanation of the
presence of Aquila and Priscilla among Paul's followers in Ephesus is that
they had come to know him on the visit on which he founded the
community in Corinth.

Were Aquila and Priscilla already Christians when they came to Corinth,
or did Paul convert them? Luke seems to accept and tacitly presuppose
the former (cf. 18.26). However, the tradition (vv.2f.) does not presuppose
that the couple belong to the Christian church, but explains Paul's
association with them by referring to their shared craft. There is therefore
something to be said for the historical conclusion that the couple only
became Christians as a result of their meeting with Paul (Weiser 1985,
490, differs). (Aquila and Priscilla were not the first to be converted in
Corinth, since Paul calls the members of the house of Stephanas the
aparche tes Achaias [I Cor.16.15].)

The expression *te kat'oikon auton ekklesia* (I Cor.16.19) denotes the
house community which gathers around Aquila and Priscilla. (For the
house community in the letters of Paul see Klauck 1981, 21-47. For the

ground plan of a Corinthian house from the time of Paul cf. Murphy-O'Connor 1983, 153-5: the dining room [*triclinium*] had an area of forty-one square metres.) It gives a first indication of the couple's prosperity. (That is also suggested by their journeys; the stages Rome – Corinth – Ephesus – Rome can be reconstructed from Paul's letters.) This will have allowed them to employ other people, one of whom will have happened to be Paul. Paul's own remarks make it clear that he did manual work in Corinth (I Cor.4.12 etc.). The further information in Acts that like Aquila and Priscilla he was a tentmaker or leather-worker (*skenopoios*, for the discussion cf. Hock 1980, 20-5; Weiss 1959, 185f.; Bauer 1979, 755; Lampe, *BZ*, NF 31, 1987, 256-61) cannot be demonstrated from the letters. However, because of the historical reliability of the other information in vv.2-3 we should not doubt this report.

Paul greets the couple in Rom.16.3. Since the assumption that Rom.16 is based on a letter to the Ephesians creates more new difficulties rather than solving old ones, we must begin on the presupposition that ch.16 is part of Romans and assume that at the time of the composition of the letter the couple were in the world capital. There is a plausible explanation of their presence in Rome if we assume that having been expelled in 41 they had returned to Rome towards the end of the reign of Claudius. (According to Rom.16.5 a house community again gathered around them.)

Paul's emphasis on the couple in Rom.16.4 because they had risked their lives for him suggests that this action took place in connection with dangers to which Paul had been exposed in or around Ephesus (cf. I Cor.15.32; II Cor.1.8f.). As this help and the mention of the couple in I Cor.16.19 presuppose their presence in Ephesus until shortly before the third visit to Corinth, Aquila and Priscilla will have returned to Rome fairly recently. Their return to their old abode was of considerable significance for Paul's mission plans. Evidently – along with others mentioned in the list of greetings, Christians known to Paul – they were to prepare the base for Paul's future missionary work in Spain, namely the community in Rome, for Paul's coming or ensure that he had a warm welcome there (the above follows Lüdemann 1984, 174f.).

The tradition about the coming of Silas and Timothy from Macedonia to Corinth is historically credible; the presence of Timothy and Silas at the time of the visit on which Paul founded the community in Corinth is confirmed by the note in II Cor.1.19 which refers to his first sermon. Moreover the presence of Paul's two companions in Corinth is attested by the prescript of I Thessalonians (1.1), which was written in Corinth. It follows from I Thess.3.6, where Paul is in Corinth and Timothy is expected to arrive from Thessalonica, that Timothy and Paul did not arrive in Corinth at the same time. To this degree not only may the order in Acts 18 (first work with Priscilla and Aquila, then the arrival of Timothy) in the first part be correct, but the chapter will also contain accurate information about the presence of Timothy and Silas at the foundation of the community.

Now it follows from Paul's letters that he had also been given gifts of money from Philippi when he first founded the community (cf. Lüdemann 1984, 103f.). It is therefore quite probable that Timothy was the member of a delegation which brought gifts to Corinth for Paul. Paul's remark that he sent Timothy back from Athens to Thessalonica (I Thess.3.1f.) does not contradict that; Timothy's visit to Thessalonica may also have been made with a view to making a detour to Philippi. The report in Acts 18.5, in Lukan language, that after the coming of Timothy and Silas from Macedonia Paul was 'wholly taken up with preaching', may be the redaction of a tradition firmly bound up with the coming of Timothy and Silas, which reported a gift of money to a Philippian community. Now if we combine the letters and Acts, new light is shed on the circumstances and the aim of the gift of money from Philippi. Timothy evidently had to play an active role in bringing the gift, and the purpose of the gift was probably to release Paul from the need to work daily so as to further the preaching of the gospel. In that case the remark 'he was wholly taken up with preaching' (Acts 18.5) may have preserved a correct historical nucleus.

The tradition that Paul preached in the house of Titius Justus cannot be either confirmed or challenged by the letters of Paul. It seems to me to be historically credible, since Paul needed a place to preach in when he was in Corinth, and there is no plausible reason why the name Titius Justus should have been invented. In other words, Paul lived with Aquila and Priscilla but preached in the house of Titius Justus. (Another possibility, which I think to be improbable, is that we see a change of abode reflected in v.7 [thus Theissen 1979, 251; cf. also Codex D].)

The tradition of the conversion of Crispus by Paul is confirmed by the letters if – and it is hardly possible to doubt this – Crispus in 18.8 is the Crispus of I Cor.1.14. In I Cor.1.14 Paul goes on to mention the baptism of Crispus, while at best it is mentioned indirectly in Acts 18.8 (v.8b). Acts 18.8 reports the conversion of the house of Crispus, and Paul does not say anything about this. Still, the latter may be regarded as historical. If the head of a house was converted, so too were its members. Cf. also I Cor.1.16 as evidence that remarks about the baptism of households are very old (for the problem cf. Klauck 1981, 51-6). The designation of Crispus as synagogue president does not appear in the letters of Paul, but it may be historically credible. For the high reputation of a synagogue president (on this see Theissen 1979, 235f.) would well explain why in this case Paul departed from his usual custom of not baptizing new converts (I Cor.1.14). But if Crispus was the synagogue president and became a Christian (baptized by Paul), then his conversion might have acted as a signal in Corinth. Therefore v.8b ('and many Corinthians who heard [of it] believed and were baptized') is a historically reliable statement.

The conversion of Crispus took place during the visit on which Paul founded the community, since Paul did not visit the community between the first mission in Corinth and I Corinthians.

2. The traditions in vv.12-17

That Paul was in Corinth during the proconsulate of Gallio is confirmed by Pauline chronology (Lüdemann 1984, 171-3). But the analysis of the tradition given above does not allow us to talk of a trial of Paul before Gallio for the reasons indicated.

The person of Sosthenes is hardly identical with the co-author of I Corinthians. (Moreover it is not even indicated that Sosthenes became a Christian.) Rather, Sosthenes is the name of the man who was synagogue president of the Jewish community in Corinth for about ten years, after the former president Crispus had joined the Pauline community. This evidence allows the conclusion that a Jewish community continued alongside Paul's community in Corinth in the time of Gallio.

Acts 18.18-23

I Division

18.18-19a: Journey from Corinth to Ephesus
19b-21a: Paul preaches in the synagogue of Ephesus
21b-23: Journey by Paul through Palestine to Antioch, strengthening the brethren in Phrygia and Galatia

II Redaction

[**18-19a**] The language of all v.18a has Lukan colouring (*prosmeinas, hemeras hikanas, tois adelphois*). The expression 'Syria' (cf. 20.3; 21.3) is a redactional glance forward either to the journey to Palestine or to the subsequent journey to Antioch which is its destination and the starting point of the next journey. A break is visible in v.18b, which indicates Lukan work on existing material. Syntactically, it seems natural to relate *keiramenos* to Aquila. In that case Aquila would have had his hair shorn in Cenchreae, one of the two ports of Corinth, because he had made a vow (cf. Wellhausen 1907, 143). But the remark is quite isolated in the context and is not in an authentic setting (cf. Wellhausen, ibid.). Instead of regarding v.18b as the remnant of a source which reported an oath by Aquila and otherwise does not become visible anywhere (!), we should ask whether the present text does not have redactional significance, if – as is possible - *keiramenos* is related to Paul. 'A (Nazarite) vow counted as a meritorious work; one could be released from it only at the Temple' (Conzelmann 1987, 155). As Luke makes the vow happen on the way to Jerusalem (cf. the remarks above about 'Syria' in v.17), the information that Paul had his hair cut because of a vow makes good (Lukan) sense: on the way to Jerusalem (= to the Temple) Paul shows himself to be faithful in fulfilling the Jewish law (cf. 21.23f.). The stylistically harsh position of *keiramenos* (if it refers to Paul) is then to be explained by the observation that had *keiramenos* been put immediately after *Syrian*, 'and with him was Priscilla and Aquila' would have been a very harsh addition. The statement just quoted may possibly be Luke's, as 18.24-28 presuppose the presence of the couple in Ephesus (v.19). But it may reflect tradition (this even seems to be more probable for historical considerations, see below, 208f.).

[19b-21a] The whole section has a clear redactional stamp. This conclusion follows on grounds of content and form (literary-critical grounds). The statement 'he left them behind (in Ephesus) but he himself went into a synagogue' (v.19) gives the impression that the synagogue is not in Ephesus. That this was not intended is shown by v.21b, the note about the departure from Ephesus, and v.21a, the glance forward to a return by Paul to Ephesus 'if God wills' (which takes place in 19.1ff.). After 'if God wills', the travel account of vv.18-19a is continued with Paul's departure from Ephesus. This recognition of the redactional origin of vv.19b-21a gained by literary-critical means can be further supported by observations on the content: v.19b contains the well-known Lukan pattern of going to the Jews first; Paul preaches first in the synagogue. Verse 21 foresees a possible return by Paul. But 19.1, in which this takes place, speaks only of an 'arrival' of Paul in Ephesus, as though he were there for the first time. So there is tension between the redaction (in v.19b-21a) and existing material (in vv.18,19a, 21b ff.)(see below, III).

We can discover the occasion for the composition of Acts 18.19b-21a from the following text (vv.24ff.), which demonstrates that there were already Christians in Ephesus before Paul's arrival: in that case, by this scene Luke wants to make Paul 'the first Christian preacher in the city' (Conzelmann 1987, 155).

[21b-23] *kathexes* in v.23b is redactional, as is *mathetas* (v.23c), as this expression is a favourite term for the disciples in Luke. The accumulation of participles is a characteristic of Lukan style.

III Traditions

The section vv.21b-23 poses great problems for interpreters because it is so brief.

'The verses... give an... impression of being an epitome... The details are understandable only to the author of the epitome' (Conzelmann 1987, 156). The other possibility (which Conzelmann considered) that Luke himself 'took scattered reports and from them fashioned a journey' (ibid.) is improbable because the redactional significance of such a journey is not clear. Paul's so-called second journey to Jerusalem (11.27-30; 12.25) – which is a creation of Luke's – is different from Acts 18.22 in its redactional intent. Moreover unlike 18.22 it does not have the character of an epitome. It is equally impossible 'to speak of a topographical redaction which is meant to sound probable precisely because of detours in the route mentioned' (Schille 1983, 368). For in what does the redaction consist? Rather, it seems likely that here Luke has used a list of stations from the tradition which included the journey to Jerusalem (cf. Lüdemann 1984, 156). So he is writing here in connection with tradition which embraces vv.18-19a and vv.21b-23 (for the stations cf. also 225 below).

IV Historical

The list of stations in the tradition is historical in that Paul did in fact undertake a journey from Greece to Palestine/Syria, after which he took part in the Jerusalem conference. (Given this, a journey to Antioch between the conference visit and the last journey to Jerusalem is as improbable as one to Jerusalem – on Weiser 1985, 502; cf. also the remarks on 14 above.) On the presupposition that such a hypothesis is correct, there are two possible routes: (*a*) Paul went from Caesarea direct to Jerusalem (Acts 18.22b); in that case Titus already accompanied him on his journey from Greece. As according to Gal.2.1 Paul went with Barnabas to Jerusalem, he met him somewhere that we can no longer discover (we are to rule out the possibility that Barnabas went with Paul from Greece or Ephesus to Palestine). This proposal has the advantage of bringing the individual

206

stations mentioned in 18.21-23 into line with the places that we can discover from the letters of Paul (cf. Lüdemann 1984, 152-7). The weak point is the position of Barnabas. – (*b*) Paul travelled with Titus from Greece to Caesarea, and then to Antioch, from where he went with Barnabas to Jerusalem (for the conference), taking Titus along with them. This suggestion has the following advantages. 1. It does justice to the character of the travel account in 18.21-23, which depicts a journey to Antioch. 2. Barnabas can meaningfully be given a place in Paul's journeys because presumably he will have been in Antioch shortly before the conference (Acts 15.1ff.; Gal.2.13) and will have gone with Paul (in this case) from Antioch to Jerusalem. 3. The episode at Antioch would be plausibly connected with the conference as its occasion (see Lüdemann 1984, 75f.). The weak point of this theory is that Acts 18.23 does not report any journey from Antioch to Jerusalem, and 18.22b (*aspasamenos ten ekklesian*) would have to be regarded as a redactional note [a redactional anticipation of the later journey from Antioch to Jerusalem – which is not described]). However, these two difficulties may not be insuperable if we recall how Luke's account tends to move *in a straight line*. (He does not report Paul's journey to Arabia [Gal.1.17] either, but has him remaining in Damascus [Acts 9.19ff.], nor does he narrate the intermediate visit to Corinth [cf. Lüdemann 1980, 94 and 132 n.171].)

Acts 18.24-28

I Division

8.24-26: The preaching activity of Apollos in Ephesus and his instruction by Aquila and Priscilla
27-28: Apollos's journey to Achaea and his preaching among the Jews

II Redaction

[24-26] The language of the section is Lukan: cf. just the introductory phrase v.24, 'Now a Jew by the name of Apollos'; v.25, *akribos*; v.26, *parrhesiazesthai*. In v.25 Apollos is deliberately introduced as a 'semi-Christian', though he was instructed in the way of the Lord and taught correctly about Jesus (*ta peri tou Iesou* – cf. Luke 24.19); he knows only the baptism of John (cf. the redactional parallel 19.3). Priscilla and Aquila

explain the way of the Lord more precisely to him (v.26), i.e. they introduce him to full Christianity. 'Luke did not feel how nonsensical it was to say that Apollos knew the teaching of Jesus precisely and yet only came to learn it now' (Meyer III, 113).

The above account is Luke's redactional work which seeks to rescue Apollos for Pauline Christianity as Luke understands it, but on the other hand it has great difficulty in suppressing pre-Pauline tradition attached to Ephesus.

[27-28] *paragenomenos* in v.27 is Lukan in language. The preaching of Apollos to the Jews in v.28 is based on the redactional scheme of going to the Jews first. The content of the preaching (the christological proof from scripture) is redactional (cf. above on 18.5).

III Tradition

The character of the person of the Jew *Apollos* in the tradition emerges from the tension between the redactional work and the material which it uses. Apparently the person of the *Christian* pneumatic Apollos (cf. v.25: 'ardent (*zeon*) in the Spirit' – cf. Rom.12.11) was rooted in Ephesus. The pre-Pauline Christian community ('the brethren', v.27), which commended Apollos to Achaea (Corinth) (for the place see on 19.1), is also part of this tradition.

The assumption which is sometimes made that the tradition spoke of a *non-Christian* Jew who gave enthusiastic teaching in the synagogue and was converted by Aquila and Priscilla, is improbable. The fact of the existence of pre-Pauline Christianity in Ephesus also tells against that. (Moreover, as became clear under II, Apollos's preaching in the synagogue in v.26 is based on Luke's scheme of going to the Jews first.) The thesis that (only) Priscilla taught Apollos (thus Schüssler-Fiorenza 1983, 179) is hardly correct.

Schille 1983 disputes that the verse cited above belongs to the tradition: 'Anyone who detects pre-Pauline traces here is burdening... redactional associations with historical weight' (375). That is hardly right. Schille (similarly Meeks 1983, 41) overlooks the fact that with 18.19f. Luke – glimpsing pre-Pauline Christianity in Ephesus – at least indirectly claims that Paul was the first to preach in Ephesus (Paul in fact speaks only in the synagogue). – For the question of the historical Apollos cf. the survey in Weiser 1985, 505f.

For historical reasons Aquila and Priscilla may also have been part of a tradition attached to Ephesus (cf. I Cor.16.19). But it is not clear whether Luke connected Apollos with the couple in a narrative or whether that was already in the tradition. Weiser 1985, 508, makes the latter assumption; he argues that the couple gave lodgings to Apollos but did not instruct him further.

IV Historical

It emerges from the Pauline letters that *Apollos* was active alongside Paul in Ephesus (I Cor.16.12) and was also known in Corinth, where he went after Paul's departure. In I Cor.3.6 Paul can say that he himself had planted and Apollos watered. A party in Corinth called itself after Apollos (I Cor.1.12). From Corinth Apollos had travelled to Ephesus and here showed himself to be uncertain whether he should come straight to Corinth, as the Corinthian community (or some members of the Corinthian community) wanted (I Cor.16.12).

The tradition which spoke of Apollos as 'ardent in the Spirit' may be historically reliable, since it is confirmed by the evidence of I Corinthians, and by the close association between the Corinthian enthusiasts and Apollos that can be inferred from that. So Apollos was an early Christian pneumatic. In type he corresponded to Stephen, Philip, the pneumatics at Corinth and the itinerant missionaries of the tradition about the sending out of the disciples (for this cf. Lüdemann 1983, 111, 136f.).

Perhaps the figure of Apollos (*Alexandreus to genei*) demonstrates the existence of a Christian community in Alexandria in the forties (Schille 1983, 374, differs).

The above tradition, according to which the church in Ephesus was not founded by Paul, is indirectly confirmed by the letters: 1. I Cor.16.8 gives the impression that Paul is on alien ground; 2. In contrast to the churches of Galatia, Achaea and Macedonia founded by *Paul*, the community of Ephesus did not take part in the collection. Appeal should not be made to Acts 20.4 against the latter theory, since in that list there are no names from communities which which we know for sure to have taken part in the collection and to have sent escorts (Corinth, Philippi). Cf. also the reasons which Ollrog 1979 gives for the absence of delegates from Corinth accompanying the collection (56f.). However, Paul's companion Trophimus, mentioned in 20.4, may have come from Ephesus (cf.21.29).

Acts 19.1-7

I Division

19.1: (While Apollos is in Corinth) Paul encounters disciples of John in Ephesus
2-4: Conversation about the Holy Spirit and baptism
5-6: Baptism of the disciples of John by Paul; the Spirit is bestowed on them and they speak with tongues
7: Information about numbers

II Redaction

[1] This verse links the story in vv.1-7 with 18.24-28. Apollos, who is instructed by Aquila and Priscilla in Ephesus as described, is moved to Corinth, while Paul comes to Ephesus. (Note that an encounter between the two of them is avoided.) Here v.1 picks up the itinerary broken off in 18.23. Paul is in Galatia and Phrygia, 'up country' (*ta anoterika mere*), in the area lying in the interior of Asia Minor, and from here he comes to Ephesus, as he had planned in 18.21.

[2-4] Paul's question whether the disciples of John have received the Spirit is a construct and presupposes that baptism and Spirit belong together, which of course the disciples of John cannot know because of their present status. 'The peculiar expression "baptized into John's baptism" results from Luke's concern to avoid speaking about a baptism in John's *name*' (Conzelmann 1987, 159). The hand of the redactor is evident in v.4 in the fact that in contrast to Luke 3.16 (parr. Mark 1.7ff./Matt.3.11f.) John the Baptist is said to have called for faith in *Jesus* (Acts 13.24f. then again runs on synoptic lines).

[5-6] The baptism of the disciples of John in the name of Jesus has been prepared for by v.4. The speaking in tongues in v.6 connects back to the Pentecost account (Acts 2).

[7] The number twelve probably comes from Lukan redaction (cf. the number seven in Acts 19.14); the expression 'about' (*hosei*) is certainly Lukan.

The section 19.1-7 has parallels to 18.24-28 which are to be explained in terms of redaction: in both cases those involved know only the baptism of John. In each instance it has to be surpassed, either by Apollos being

210

more accurately informed about the Christian way or by the disciples of John in Ephesus being baptized and only then receiving the Holy Spirit. By telling the stories in parallel Luke is saying indirectly that Apollos, too, only received the Holy Spirit by being instructed. In this way Luke endorses the view described in the previous pericope that non-Pauline forms of Christianity first need to be sanctioned by Jerusalem-Paul (cf. already 8.14ff.).

III Traditions

The narrative about the existence of disciples of John might be part of a tradition. Perhaps their contact with disciples of Jesus in the period after Easter might also be an element of this tradition. However, in my view it cannot be demonstrated that the tradition reported the *conversion* of disciples of John or that it was attached to Ephesus. Rather, Luke needed the tradition for Ephesus in order to make the disciples parallel to Apollos and in this way to be able to express Apollos's inferiority. Otherwise Luke has no independent interest in the disciples or John.

The content of the preaching of John the Baptist (19.4) is part of the tradition, apart from the redactional change (that John called on people to believe in Jesus). It was already in Q and was not part of the tradition about the disciples of John.

IV Historical

Either the historical nucleus of the tradition is a group of disciples of John who had come into contact with Christian groups (cf. John 1.35-42) or, if Luke was the first to construct the contact between disciples of John and a Christian group, the tradition consisted simply in the remark about the existence of a group of disciples of John. If the first-mentioned possibility is right, we have an analogy for this in the disciples of John attacked by the Johannine community (cf. John 1.20; 3.28) and in a later account in the Pseudo-Clementine Recognitions I, 54; 60 (however, that may also be a redactional construction – cf. Lüdemann 1983, 239f.). It is almost superfluous to observe that the existence of disciples of John in Ephesus cannot be inferred on the basis of Acts 19. (W.Baldensperger, *Der Prolog des vierten Evangeliums. Sein polemisch-apologetischer Zweck*, 1898, 93-9, which regards Apollos as a disciple of John, is still worth considering.)

211

Acts 19.8-22

I Division

19.8: Paul preaches in the synagogue for three months
9-10: Paul leaves the synagogue and preaches for two years in the school of Tyrannus
11-12: Summary: Paul's miracles and their consequences
13-16: The failure of the Jewish magicians and especially the seven sons of the high priest Sceva
17-20: The effect of the failure on the local magicians: acknowledgment of guilt and burning of the magical books. Redactional concluding formula (v.20)
21-22: Paul's travelling plans

II Redaction

[8] This verse is based on Luke's scheme of going to the Jews first. (This is renewed preaching to the Jews after 18.19, and will lead to separation from them.) In addition the information about the time during which Paul preached to the Jews is redactional, because 'three' is a favourite Lukan number. The phrase *peithein peri tes basileias* is also Lukan, because in the New Testament only Luke connects *basileia* with remarks about preaching (cf. 8.12). Cf. also 28.23,31 as striking parallels to v.8.

[9-10] Paul's turning away form the Jews in v.9 as a consequence of their guilt is a redactional stereotype. For *hodos* cf. below on v.23. The remark 'all the inhabitants of Asia heard the word of God' is a Lukan pleonasm. The 'Jews and Gentiles' (vv.10; 17, etc.) as those to whom the preaching is addressed also appears in a redactional context in 18.4.

[11-12] The verses 'provide (on the basis of hearsay about handkerchiefs and aprons) a succinct picture of Paul the miracle worker, a picture from a later time (cf.5.12-16). This note serves as the preparation for an episode: the miracle worker is contrasted to those who have no real power' (Conzelmann 1987, 163).

[13-16 (for the redactional position of the pericope and its significance in the context see below on vv.17-20)] Verse 13 is a redactional introduction to the story which follows (for it cf. the synoptic parallel Mark 9.38-40/ Luke 9.49f.). The terminology is Lukan; cf. just *epecheiresan* (in the NT only in Luke [Luke 1.1; Acts 9.29]). In content 'the mention of Paul in the usurped formula of invocation' (Klein 69, 274) might be Lukan, since it is the necessary presupposition of the answer by the demon in v.15, and 'thus makes possible the lack of exposition in the individual episode' (Klein, ibid.). The number 'seven' in v.14 is perhaps redactional (see below III). *pneuma poneron* in v.15 appears only in Luke apart from Matt.12.45 (Q): Luke 7.21; 8.2; 11.26 (= Matt.12.45); Acts 19.13,16. Similarly v.16 has features of Lukan language: *traumatizein*, like *trauma* (Luke 10.34), is attested elsewhere in the New Testament only in Luke (cf. also Luke 20.12); *amphoteroi* occurs more often in Luke (8 times) than elsewhere in the NT (6 times).

[17-20] These verses look suspiciously like redaction throughout (for the details cf. Weiser 1985, 525f.). They sum up the consequences of the previous narrative. Verse 17a refers back explicitly to vv.13-16. (Perhaps it is even a kind of choral conclusion, in which case it should be attached to vv.13-16; cf. Pereira 1983, 182-7.) Verse 17b ('and fear fell on all of them and the name of the Lord Jesus was praised') corresponds to 2.43; cf.v.20 ('so the word of the Lord grew and increased in power'), which has a parallel in 2.47. Luke gives a religious significance to the preceding story, which was not without its comic elements. The Christian power — and only that – is superior to the demons, as is demonstrated in vv.18f.

[21-22] The verses have Lukan features (cf. esp. Radl 1975, 103ff.). The journey of Paul envisaged here corresponds to the beginning of Jesus' journey (Luke 9.51). The vocabulary is Lukan (*eplerothe, etheto, en to pneumati*), as is the theological content (cf. the divine *dei*) and the sending out in pairs (cf. below, 215).

III Traditions

[9-10] Tradition probably underlies the information that Paul taught for two years in the school (*schole*) of Tyrannus. *schole* 'could be the name of a synagogue, a place where members of pagan cult associations met, or an auditorium' (Schille 1983, 378).

[13-16] The verses are to be regarded as a legend (from the tradition) with a burlesque basis, or as a joke. Certainly Luke has worked over the language and content of the passage, as became clear under II. But he did not invent this episode. Rather, he might have worked it in as the result of his reading in pagan literature. There it may have only spoken of two exorcists (see *amphoteroi* [v.16]; however, in Acts 23.8 this expression denotes more than two – though in other passages of Luke-Acts, as usual

it denotes only two). Were that the case, the number seven would derive from Luke. Dibelius aptly explains on vv.13-16 that the underlying tradition was for entertainment and had no religious or personal interest.

'The evil spirit will not be driven out by unauthorized exorcists, who have simply borrowed a formula which they have heard used by genuine exorcists – this is the sense of the story, told in a strain which is not without its comic element. It is not clear whether the misused formula was ever a Christian one, for the anecdote is embedded in a summary passage (19.11-13, 17-19), so that we no longer have the beginning of it. We have no description of the details of the incident and it is only at the end, and rather surprisingly, that we hear anything of the house in which the story takes place. Even if the incantation had been Christian in the first place, the story was certainly not fashioned by Christian interests' (Dibelius 1956, 19). In his criticism of Dibelius, Klein 1969, 175f., fails to recognize that he derives Acts 19.13-16 from tradition (and not from redaction, as Klein, ibid., thinks).

It should be stressed here that criteria of content rather than language lead to the assumption of a tradition as the basis of vv.13-16.

[21-22] Because of their detail, the travel plans derive from tradition (Luke, the redactor, formulates them as having occurred to Paul himself) as do the names Timothy and Erastus. For the latter cf. Rom.16.23; II Tim.4.20; the (partial) identity of the three companions of Paul called Erastus is possible, but not certain. For a summary account of Erastus see Ollrog 1979, 5f., 53, 58. For the question of the identification of Erastus with the Erastus known from a Latin inscription from Corinth cf. Klauck 1981, 33 n.42.

IV Historical

The note in v.9 that Paul worked for two years in Ephesus is historically credible (Lüdemann 1984, 178f.). As the indication of place is linked with that of time and the latter is reliable, one might also be inclined to regard the information about the place as historically correct. *schole* might denote the hall of the orator Tyrannus, i.e. the private auditorium in which the orator was accustomed to teach and which Paul had hired for his missionary activity. This information enriches our information about the way in which Paul worked. (The community in Ephesus is not considered.)

The reading of the Western text in v.9 is a curiosity: Paul taught between the fifth and the tenth hour (= 11 a.m. to 4 p.m.), i.e. during the midday rest.

For form-critical reasons alone the joke told in vv.13-16 is unhistorical. The travelling plans in vv.21-22 are historical in that according to I

214

Cor.16.5 Paul in fact wanted to go through Macedonia to Achaea (Corinth). He had only contemplated the journey to Jerusalem mentioned in v.21 in I Cor.16.4, and we hear of a journey to Rome only some years later (Rom.1.13), when Paul had also firmly resolved on the journey to Jerusalem (Rom.15.25). Thus at this point Luke has so compressed a travel note which comes from tradition and is in itself historically correct that it is no longer completely accurate. Paul in fact sent Timothy to Macedonia. From there he was to go on to Corinth (I Cor.16.10; 4.17). It is unclear whether Erastus accompanied him. Although in antiquity people did not usually travel alone, Lukan interest in sending people out in pairs (Luke 7.18 [Matt differs]; Acts 9.38; 10.7, 20 – cf. also Jeremias 1966) and Paul's silence probably tell against this.

Acts 19.23-40

I Division

19.23: Introduction: The stir (*tarachos*) over the 'way'
24-29: The revolt against Paul kindled by Demetrius the silversmith
   24-25a: Demetrius gathers the craftsmen
   25b-27: Speech by Demetrius
   28-29: Reaction of the gathering with acclamation of Artemis; the unrest extends to the whole city and two of Paul's companions, Gaius and Aristarchus, are seized
30-31: Paul is prevented from entering the gathering: (*a*) by disciples; (*b*) by the friendly Asiarchs
32-34: General confusion in the gathering
   32: General ignorance about the reason for the gathering
   33: Attempt at a defence speech by the Jew Alexander
   34: The anger of the crowd against the Jew Alexander with (renewed) acclamation of Artemis
35-40: The town clerk gives a soothing speech and calms down the uproar
   35: That the city is the temple-keeper is the reason for the
   36: Appeal to keep the peace
   37: An indication that the men arraigned are neither temple robbers nor blasphemers
   38: Demetrius and the craftsmen can go to the courts
   39: The regular assembly of the people is open to the Ephesians
   40: Danger of a charge of rioting, because of the (possible) offence of groundless commotion. The assembly breaks up

[23] *egeneto de* is a Lukan introductory formula (cf. 4.5; 8.1; 9.32; 14.1; 16.16; 19.1) which is followed by a redactional note of time (*kata ton kairon ekeinon*). The Lukan litotes *ouk oligos* (cf. 17.4,12) is taken up again in v.24. *hodos* as a term which Christianity uses to describe itself also appears in the absolute in 9.2; 19.9; 22.4; 24.14,22 and may be redactional (Burchard 1970, 43 n.10 [bibliography] differs). As there was already mention of the way (+ genitive) in 16.16 (*hodos soterias*), 18.25 (*hodos tou kyriou*) and 18.26 (*hodos tou theou*), the absolute *hodos* (19.23), may be picking that up. At the same time v.23 is a Lukan sentence introducing the following episode, which is meant to describe a conflict over the Christian way.

[24-29, 30-31] The introduction of the protagonist Demetrius follows, with the Lukan *tis onomati*. The theme of *ergasia* already appears in 16.16. There the profit came from a girl with a spirit of divination; here from making silver temples of Artemis. *epistasthe* is Lukan language, as is *hikanon* (v.26). The assertion put in the mouth of Demetrius that Paul has convinced many people throughout almost all Asia (v.26a) is a Lukan pleonasm. The indication of the content of Paul's sermon refers back to 17.29, where there was already polemic against the gods made with hands. Verse 27 heightens the danger posed by Paul by pointing to the possibility that he will destroy the sanctuary of Artemis, although all Asia (note the contrast to v.26 [almost all Asia has been convinced by Paul]) and the whole world worship Artemis. Verses 28-29 describe the vigorous reaction of the craftsmen, which ends in an acclamation of Artemis. The way in which the unrest among the craftsmen seizes the whole city (v.29a) is part of Luke's dramatic techique. The language is redactional (cf. *eplesthe, hormesan, homothymadon*). At the climax of the riot indicated in this way Paul's companions Gaius and Aristarchus are seized and dragged into the theatre (v.29), but they play no further role in the course of the narrative (though cf. v.37). One gets the impression that by *artificially* introducing them, Luke wanted to describe the conflict in accordance with the 'heading' in v.23 as a conflict over the Christian proclamation. This impression is strengthened in vv.30-31: finally the hero appears on the scene and of course wants to go to the gathering. But he is prevented by the disciples (*mathetai* – a Lukan word), and some of the Asiarchs friendly to Paul even tell him not to go. Paul (and his companions) plays no further role in the narrative after that. He has evidently heeded the request of the brethren and the Asiarchs. The action in v.32 picks up v.29, with the two episodes of the seizure of Paul's companions and the advice to Paul in between. (The keyword *theatron* [v.29], to which the insertion had been attached, is picked up again at the end of v.31, i.e. at the end of the insertion.) This confirms the conclusion drawn in v.29 that Luke has introduced not only Paul's companions but also Paul himself into the action in order to describe the conflict, in accordance with the 'heading' in v.23, as a controversy over Christian preaching.

Regardless of the overall significance of the whole pericope, the action of the Asiarchs conceals a subsidiary aim of the narrator: the Asiarchs (for whom see L.R.Taylor, *Beg.* V, 256-62) were drawn from the leading families of the Roman province of Asia. They held office for a year as representatives and high priests of the confederation of Asian cities, and their task (which was half religious and half political) was to ensure that Asia was loyal to the Roman state and law. This confederation was responsible for the popularity of the cult of the reigning emperor and the goddess Roma; to this end it established and maintained temples for the confederation. In the light of this function of the Asiarchs and their intervention on Paul's behalf Luke could stress through vv.30-31, with *apologetic* intent, that important representatives of political life were on Paul's side and protected him from harm, because they were convinced of his innocence.

The reason for the intervention of the Asiarchs is not in fact mentioned, but Luke mentions in passing that the Asiarchs had been friendly with Paul (v.31). For this reason the apologetic explanation must be expanded to the effect that in stressing the friendliness of the Asiarchs Luke is indicating that Christianity is to be found all over the world (on this see Lüdemann 1984, 18f.). If the apostle Paul was even friendly with some of them (the remark in vv.30f. is unique in this respect – but cf. also 27.3) it must be said *a priori* that the apostle Paul, a leading representative of Christianity, is on the same level as leading representatives of the Roman state.

[32-34] The description of the riot in v.32 is the product of Luke's narrative art, cf. similarly 21.34, which sometimes matches it word for word. The designation of the gathering as *ekklesia* may be attributed to redactional variation. The same term is also used in vv.39f., whereas we have *demos* in vv.30, 33, and *ochlos* in vv.33-35. (Luke similarly varies the terms he uses to describe the riot: *tarachos* [v.23], *sygchysis* [v.29], *stasis* [v.40] and *systrophe* [v.40]). Verse 33 is difficult to understand: 'Some of the crowd prompted Alexander, when the Jews put him forward; but Alexander motioned with his hand and wanted to make a defence to the people.' The meaning is probably that because of the riot over Paul(!) the Jews felt threatened and therefore put Alexander forward with the intent of dissociating the Jews from Paul (Christianity). The recognition that Alexander is a Jew (v.34) leads to an acclamation of Artemis which refers back to v.28. The note about the period of two hours further intensifies the drama of the scene. The uproar caused by Paul is taken out on a Jew (this is a remote recollection of the Gallio episode [18.12-17], in which the anger of the people similarly falls on a Jew after Paul has been removed from the scene by the narrator). Is the underlying concern here to differentiate Jews from Christians, as in Acts 16.20f.?

[35-40] The speech by the town clerk has been fashioned by Luke; in v.35 the speaker makes a reference to the city as temple-keeper and in so doing gives reasons for the demand for peace and prudence made in v.36. Verse 37 refers back to v.29, the action against Paul's two companions. By stressing that the Christians are neither temple robbers not blasphemers, the speaker protects them from such an accusation. (As the Jew Alexander is not so protected, the justification of the action against him – for whatever reasons – remains.) Verses 38-40 refer back to the speech of Demetrius (vv.24-29). In this way the speaker refers to circumstances of which he can no know nothing, given the way that events are described, since Demetrius made his speech to a closed gathering. Demetrius himself does not appear again, and the crowd does not know why it has gathered. Nevertheless the speaker is well informed. Verse 39 refers back to v.32 (*en te ennomo ekklesia* picks up *he ekklesia sygkechymene*). Just as a speech – by Demetrius – caused the riot, so it is calmed down by another speech – that by the town clerk, which discusses one by one the points in the conflict which has broken out: as far as the Christians are concerned it does not make any claims as to the innocence of those who have been dragged before the gathering (their innocence is briefly and conclusively presupposed in v.37). Demetrius and his craftsmen are reminded that the courts are available to them and the Ephesians are reminded of the regular assemblies of the people. The real aim of the speech is to dispute the justification for the riot. It therefore ends with a warning against the threat of an accusation of *stasis* (v.40).

III Traditions

The analysis of the redaction has shown that Luke has artificially inserted the figure of Paul and his two companions (he has both names from tradition, see IV below) into the story of the riot in Ephesus, in order to give it a Christian flavour. He had to do that if the episode was to depict a conflict over the 'way' (v.23). Therefore it should be stressed at the beginning of this stage of the work that the story is based on a secular tradition. That *a priori* rules out some analyses of the tradition behind the present story: e.g. Schille's theory (1983, 382f., 390, etc.) that 19.24-40 goes back to a tradition connected with the founding of the community. That is improbable because it does not take account of the secular character of this passage. The same objection must be made to Roloff's suggestion. He comments on this passage:

'The basic element is probably a local Ephesus tradition which retained the memory of a critical situation from the early period of the community and fixed the decisive experience gained in it at a particular point: in their struggle against polytheism the

218

Christians did not go beyond the bounds of the law; they therefore cannot be attacked in law (v.37)' (1981, 291).

Similarly, Weiser's suggestion that Aristarchus (v.29) was part of the pre-Lukan tradition (1985, 543) is hardly convincing, since the verse in question is an artificial insertion. The demonstration by Weiser in this connection that in Philemon 24 Aristarchus 'had close contact with Paul imprisoned in Ephesus' (ibid.) and his theory that there is a genetic connetion between the Demetrius episode and the imprisonment of Paul in Ephesus stand and fall with the correctness of the (disputed) theory that Paul was imprisoned in Ephesus. Moreover in Philemon 24 Aristarchus is explicitly *not* called a fellow-prisoner (like Epaphras) but a fellow-worker (along with Mark, Demas and Luke). (But according to Weiser the tradition was specifically about Aristarchus [for him and Gaius see further under IV below].)

The narrative (like the account in Acts 17.16.16-34 earlier) shows a good deal of local colouring. This includes 1. the figure of Demetrius, who earns his living by making souvenirs for the temple of Artemis; 2. the cult of Artemis in Ephesus (cf. Elliger 1983, 113-36) – it was world famous, and the temple of Artemis was regarded as one of the seven wonders of the world (on these see W.Ekschmitt, *Die Sieben Weltwunder*, Mainz 1984); 3. the theatre of Ephesus (on this see Elliger 1985, 140f.); 4. the figure of the town clerk; 5. the role of the city as temple-keeper; and 6. the fact that there was hostility to Jews in Ephesus (cf. Josephus, *Antt* XIV, 225-30, 234, 237-40, 262-4: Josephus reproduces official documents which contain the privileges of the Jews and exemption from military service, sabbath observance, etc. We may be allowed to conclude that the Jews were vigorously denied all this, cf. Elliger 1985, 154f.).

So although the story contains many individual elements of tradition, it is hard to get a whole narrative from Acts 19 (when the clearly Lukan additions have been detached). Wellhausen's 'solution' (1907, 17) merely shifts the problem. He had thought that in Acts 19 Luke made use of the account of an antisemitic riot which he had read somewhere (Alexander, who appears abruptly, was one of the most important indications of this). But as long as no literary analogy to such a riot can be produced (say from a local history which reported an incident between Jews and supporters of Artemis), Wellhausen's suggestion remains no more than a possibility, even though he takes the secular character of the material seriously. Somewhat more probable is the assumption that in Acts 19 Luke himself is testing his narrative skill on the basis of his general knowledge of Ephesus and presenting his own theological ideas about the political harmlessness of the Christians and the missionary power of the Christian faith (see II above).

Against this, however, see Conzelmann 1987: 'Nevertheless, while Luke does compose scenes, he does not invent stories such as this. The intermezzo with Alexander remains unexplained' (165). Against this: the intermezzo with Alexander is not a story but perhaps part (at one time a decisive part?) of such a story. We also find an Alexander as an opponent of Paul in I Tim.1.20; II Tim.4.14. Does he have any connection with the Alexander in this story? (For the problem of the traditions in Acts 19.23-40 cf. also Elliger 1985, 138-40.)

Fortunately the fact that the origin of the traditions in Acts 19 is an open question has no bearing on the historical question.

IV Historical

Paul himself talks three times about dangers which threatened him in Ephesus. Once he fought against 'animals' (I Cor.15.32 – probably to be understood metaphorically [but Hyldahl 1976, 24f.n.8 differs]); the other time he already expected to die (II Cor.1.8). Finally, the report in Rom.16.4 that Priscilla and Aquila risked their necks for Paul may focus on an event in or near Ephesus in which Paul's life was in danger. (Perhaps it is identical with the incident mentioned in II Cor.1.8.) But there is no way from the three (or two) events to Luke's version of Acts 19.23-40, far less to the version in the tradition, if there was one. (Cf. also the above objections [218f.] to the theories of Schille, Roloff and Weiser.)

The names of Paul's companions Gaius and Aristarchus (both from Macedonia, v.29) certainly denote historical figures. (It can be demonstrated from 20.4 that Gaius derives from tradition since there is mention there of a Gaius from Derbe. Had Luke introduced Gaius 'into the narrative in 19.29 from 20.4, then it could not have escaped him that there was mention there of a Gaius *from Derbe*' ([Ollrog 1979, 47 n.216].) However, it does not follow from this that the information came from a tradition attached to Ephesus (on Ollrog 1979, 46f. n.216; cf. also 219 above on Weiser). Aristarchus also appears in 20.4; 27.2 (cf. Ollrog 1979, 46f.).

The conclusion to be drawn from this is that unfortunately Acts and its traditions do not give us much help in adding historical substance to Paul's activity in Ephesus. The historical problem of Luke's account of Paul's activity in Ephesus therefore amounts to this: 'Luke gives the longest time to this period of Paul's activity and has the least ancient material for it' (Schille 1983, 392).

Acts 20.1-16

I Division

20.1-3: Journey by Paul from Ephesus through Macedonia to Greece (Achaea) and resolve to return to Macedonia because of harrassment by the Jews
4-5: List of Paul's companions and their journey to Troas
6: Journey by Paul and his companions, described as 'we', from Philippi to Troas
7-12: The story of the young man Eutychus
13-16: Travel notes: from Troas to Miletus

II Redaction

[1-3] The section displays Lukan linguistic characteristics (e.g. *meta-pempsamenos, mathetas, poreuesthai, treis, hypostrephein*; cf. also the participial style). Verses 1f. refer back to 19.21. Paul covers his further itinerary as he planned in 19.21: he goes to Macedonia and then to Greece. Verse 3, the report of the revolt of Jews against Paul, fits Luke's scheme.

[4-5] *hemas* (v.5) already anticipates the journey. It relates to Troas, whereas the persons designated 'we' are only in Philippi. Of course *houtoi* (v.5) includes all the seven companions of Paul mentioned earlier. Expedients like supposing that the *houtoi* denotes only Paul's companions from Asia (Tychicus and Trophimus) are over-hasty historicizing (against Schneider 1982, 282 and often).

[6] The information that the group departed after the days of unleavened bread is probably Lukan. Luke loves to incorporate Jewish feasts in his work for the purpose of dating (cf. v.16).

[7-12] Verse 7 derives from the redactor: a seam is evident in the verse, since *autois* appears quite abruptly. (Luke probably means the Christians in Troas.) The verse also contains a glance forward to future events: the breaking of the bread, the departure next morning and the sermon till midnight. It is therefore redactional, and introduces a tradition which begins in v.8, which follows (see II below). In v.7 *dielegeto* is Lukan language; cf. also the genitive absolute. *hikanai* and *tis... onomati* in v.8 stand out as being Lukan, as do 'we', which clashes with 'they' in v.12 (*egagon*), and the number of (Lukan) participles in vv.9f. Verse 11 really does not fit into the narrative at this point, as it interrupts Paul's consoling remark about Eutychus and the reaction of the audience which is closely

connected with it; in redactional terms it connects it with the theme of the 'eucharist' addressed in v.7. It should not be objected to this that:

'In reality, in the original legend the narrative point lay in the unswerving certainty with which Paul continues the worship immediately after the raising from the dead, for it is precisely here that his sovereignty is demonstrated. In comparison with this the noting of the miracle (v.12) remains quite peripheral' (Roloff 1981, 297).

Against this it must be said that great stress is placed on v.12, and the eucharistic theme (see IV for the basis for it) already appears in the redactional v.7. The story may have been inserted here because on the one hand Luke had no traditions for Troas at this point and on the other he still had not given any account of that city (cf. 16.8). Moreover with this story Luke again draws a parallel between Paul and Peter, of whom he had already reported a raising from the dead (9.36-42: the raising of Tabitha). It cannot be objected against this that the character of this story is different (more profane). For that is a result of the distinctive character of the tradition (see below 223f.), which Luke may have taken over without changing it much apart from speeding it up with his participial style and inserting Paul and his companions (similarly to 19.23-40).

[13-16] Only the reason for the haste of the journey (v.16: Paul wants to be in Jerusalem by Passover at the latest and sails past Ephesus so as to waste no time) looks like redaction (see also on v.6). No further note is taken of this wish in the account of Paul's arrival in Jerusalem (21.17). Moreover the theme of haste (v.1) is in tension with Paul's next action. From Miletus he sends for the presbyters of Ephesus so that he can speak with them in Miletus (v.17). But that took far more time than if he had spoken with them in person in Ephesus. 'It would have taken at least five days for the Ephesians to reach Miletus (the distance from Miletus to Ephesus is about thirty miles as the crow flies; the distance by land was considerably greater). Samos would have been a more convenient meeting place' (Conzelmann 1987, 171). However, both haste and delay are to be seen as redactional themes.

'The significance of the combination of haste (as a basic motive) and elements of delay is to depict the course of the martyr to the executioner as voluntary and yet compelled (cf. the Gethsemane episode in the passion tradition)' (Schille 1983, 401).

III Traditions

[1-3] Despite the redactional influence in the arrangement of the travel information, this ultimately goes back to tradition (cf. the analysis of 19.21). The information which goes beyond 19.21, that Paul did not

222

travel from Achaea to Syria by sea but chose the way round via Macedonia, probably goes back to tradition, because it is accurate and unbiased, and belongs with the detailed travel description in vv.13-16.

[4-5] The list of Paul's companions is certainly tradition, and their journey to Troas is also likely to be, because that too is a precise and unbiassed piece of information.

[6] The same goes for the journey of Paul and his companions, described as 'we', from Philippi to Troas.

[7-12] The following episode has a number of peculiarities. Dibelius sums them up as follows:

'The mood of the story is as secular as possible; this is seen particularly in the rationalized description of the miracle. We should expect Eutychus to be dead after his fall from the window, then everything that follows would be a great miracle. But the storyteller leaves open the question as to whether it is a miracle: "he was taken up as dead". Paul throws himself on him and embraces him. It is not made clear whether this happens in order to conjure the soul or to examine the unconscious boy; we are left equally uncertain as to whether Paul is seen as a worker of miracles or a doctor: "his life is still in him"... the sceptical reader is intended to be interested by the very fact that the matter remains unexplained: "they brought the boy alive"... The secular manner of telling the story, to which, in some sense, even the lamps in the room belong, is in accordance with the secular conclusion; only the occasion of the accident and the height of the fall are described; there is no edifying motif, neither is there any mention of prayer before the boy is restored to life, nor of praise to God afterwards. The whole account concludes: "they were not a little comforted." Dismay now gives way to peace of mind' (1956, 17f.).

Dibelius concludes from this that the story is not Luke's.

'Thus we are dealing with what was originally a secular anecdote, probably containing a humorous undertone. Although the room was brightly lit, the boy fell asleep: the length of the speech was the reason! But the speaker made good the harm he had caused. How he did it we do not know. It is improbable that Christians with a literary education would have told of one of Paul's deeds in this style. I should prefer to assume that a current anecdote has come to be applied to Paul, that Luke found it in this form and introduced it into his narrative' (1956, 18f.).

We can follow Dibelius's characterization of the Eutychus anecdote even if, *pace* his suggestion, Luke himself may have transferred the story to Paul (see below).

What is the character of the tradition inserted by Luke at this point? Is it an anecdote already transferred to Paul before Luke (so Dibelius), a legend about Paul which circulated in isolation (Roloff 1981, 297), a miracle story (Conzelmann 1987, 170), or a kind of mission story (Schille

223

1983, 399). In my view all proposals of this kind (with the possible exception of Dibelius's theory) are improbable, as they do not take enough account of the *secular* character of the narrative. Moreover they are over-hasty in presupposing that *Paul* was an element of the story in the tradition. The difficulties are best removed by the hypothesis that the tradition is another consequence of Luke's (secular) reading which he has Christ-ianized in the way indicated above. (For an imitation of the story of the disciple Eutychus in the Acts of Paul [Martyrdom of the Holy Apostle Paul] see Hennecke-Schneemelcher-Wilson, *New Testament Apocrypha* II, London and Philadelphia 1965, 383f.)

[13-16] These travel notes are probably part of the tradition because they are so matter-of-fact and simple.

'It is inconceivable that Luke should have included insignificant and unimportant stations in his account of the journey if he had not had a description of the route at his disposal. In support of this we may quote the mention of Attalia in 14.25 (where, characteristically, the "Western" text completes the information by noting an evangelizing venture), of Samothrace and Neapolis (16.11), Amphipolis and Apollonia (17.1), Caesarea and, probably, Jerusalem (18.22). The sentence in 20.13,14 which is completely unimportant for both the story of the mission and for the biography of Paul belongs here also: "But we went on in advance in the ship, to Assos, intending there to take in Paul... He had arranged this as he himself wanted to go on foot. When he met with us in Assos, however, we took him on board and went on to Mitylene"' (Dibelius 1956, 197).

Conzelmann (1987, 171) challenges such an assumption: this is just a list of stages. Here, too, that does not point to the reproduction of a source but to a construction by the author; only then can we understand why the route first went through Miletus. Against Conzelmann, such an insignificant statement as v.14 does *not* thus become understandable (for Conzelmann's theory see also Georgi 1965, 88 n.338). It is therefore better to keep to Dibelius's hypothesis.

IV Historical

[1-3] Paul's journey from Ephesus through Macedonia to Corinth is historical (see the remarks on 19.21). However, there are doubts about the tradition that Paul chose to go round via Macedonia and Asia Minor on his last visit to Jerualem. For Rom.15.25 shows that Paul has the collection from Macedonia and Achaea with him in Corinth and – granted all the gaps in our knowledge – probably sailed directly from Corinth to Palestine-Syria. If this assumption is right, we may conjecture that the itinerary of the tradition in vv.1-3 gives the stages covered by Paul when

he went to Palestine/Syria and took part in the Jerusalem conference (see above 206f. on 18.22). Of course it is also possible that his detour through Macedonia and Asia Minor was necessitated by external circumstances. In that case v.1-3 would correctly denote stations on the last journey to Jerusalem.

[4-5, 6] There is a widespread view that the list in v.4 is that of the delegates from the communities which brought the collection. This assumption can appeal to I Cor.16.3; II Cor.8.19. It emerges from these passages that the communities of Macedonia and Achaea which are involved (will) provide members from their midst to bring the collection. The historical difficulties in identifying these names with the brethren involved in bringing the collection are as follows: in Acts 20.4 names are missing from those very communities which we certainly know to have participated in the collection: Corinth and Philippi. I therefore think it illegitimate to combine the list with the collection (Ollrog 1979, 52-58 differs: he thinks that 20.4 is part of the 'we' report; the 'we' is the voice of the representatives of the communities from Corinth and Philippi, and so they are not mentioned in 20.4 [56f.]). Generally speaking, historically the list goes back to companions of Paul who supported him in his missionary activity in the region of Troas (cf. II Cor.2.13). To say more would be to convey less (historically).

[7-12] No further reason need be given as to why the Eutychus episode is unhistorical (cf. what is said above about its secular basis). However, the information 'on the first day of the week' (v.7) is historically valuable, as it is the first evidence of the Christian celebration of Sunday (in Luke's time; cf. Rev.1.10; Did.14.1; – I Cor.16.2 is not clear, especially as saving money for the collection is not connected with worship). It follows conclusively from this that Luke relates *klasai arton* to the eucharist.

[13-16] The tradition gives the course of the journey of Paul (and his companions) from Troas to Miletus (or Ephesus), whence Paul goes on to Palestine/Syria (cf. above 224f. on vv.1-3 and the historical possibility of such a journey).

Acts 20.17-38

I Division

(by criteria of content, cf. Schneider 1982, 293)

20.17-18a: External framework: Paul sends for the presbyters of Ephesus from Miletus
18b-35: Speech in Miletus
  18b-27: Paul and his conduct
    18b-21: Retrospect on his own activity in Asia
    22-24: Prospect on his own fate (introduced with *kai nyn idou*)
    25-27: Declaration of innocence (introduced with *kai nyn idou*)
  28-35: Direct paraenesis
    28-31: Instructions to the elders (testament)
    32: The communities are committed to God (introduced with *kai ta nyn*)
    33-35: Reference to his own example and to the words of Jesus
36-38: Farewell scene

II Redaction

The Miletus speech is the only address given by Paul to Christians in Acts. It is also singular in that it describes the situation which arose after Paul's farewell/death. To this extent the speech is addressed to Luke's church.

'What is put on the lips of Paul in 20.18-35 is carefully balanced... here every sentence is the sum and conclusion of all that Luke wants to say about the church in Luke-Acts. Therefore it is of the greatest importance that now for the first and last time in Acts the term *ekklesia tou theou* is used' (Lohfink 1975b, 89).

With this description of the Miletus speech I have already anticipated and described the address as redactional (cf. Prast 1979, 28-38). In genre it is to be described as a farewell discourse or testament. From the milieu of the Old Testament and Judaism see Josh.23; I Sam.12; I Macc.2.49-68. Cf. also Berger 1984, 75-80, for the form-critical question, with the introduction of pagan analogies.

The following elements certainly derive from Luke (this is just a selection; for further Lucan linguistic pecularities in this section cf. Lambrecht 1979, 325; Prast 1979, 39-56; Aejmelaeus 1987, 89-195. Aejmelaeus thinks that Paul's letters [especially I Thessalonians] are used in the Miletus speech):

[17-18a] The existence of presbyters reflects the constitution of Luke's

226

church (cf. 14.23; 15.2,4,6,22f.; 21.18); *paregenonto* is Lukan in language.

[18b-35] *peirasmon* in v.19 refers the readers back to the *peirasmoi* of Jesus (Luke 22.28). The harrassments of the Jews fit Luke's scheme. Verse 20 has a close parallel in v.27 (for the construction cf.10.47). In v.21 the pair 'Jews-Gentiles' (cf. on 18.4) and the theme of witnesses (cf. in the context vv.23, 24,26) is redactional. *kai nyn* in v.22, like *kai nyn* in v.25 and *kai ta nyn* in v.32, is a sign of a Lukan division. Verses 22f. contain the theme of the Spirit and refer back to 19.21. *dromos* in v.24 corresponds with Luke's view of Paul's activity as a journey (cf. Lüdemann 1984, 13f.). For *kerysson ten basileian* in v.25 cf. Luke 8.1; Acts 8.12; 19.8; 28.23,31 (Conzelmann 1960, 113-19). The declaration of innocence in v.26 has a striking parallel in 18.6. For v.27 cf. v.20.

Verse 28 contains the Lukan theme of the Spirit. Verse 31 adds the two years and three months of 19.8,10. *to logo tes charitos autou* corresponds word for word with 14.3; for 32b cf. Acts 26.18. For v.33 cf. 3.6 (parallel between Peter and Paul). Verse 35b is a reference back to the Gospel of Luke (cf. the remarks on 228 in connection with Horn 1983).

[36-38] The motive of prayer and the gesture of prayer in v.36 are Lukan (cf. 21.5 and Radl 1975, 159-62), as is the theme of the solemn escort (cf. 21.5). Verse 38 points back to v.25.

The Miletus speech is a testament by the Paul of Acts to the Lukan church. Luke has deliberately put it at a turning point in events (cf. Dibelius 1956, 158), since Paul is going to his arrest and imprisonment. It stresses the integrity of the founder of the church: he did not fall short in any way in preaching the gospel (that is said twice, vv.20, 27). The foil to such an assertion is provided by the church situation which arose in the period after Paul's death, in which Gnostic teachers put the Lukan norms in question. Against them appeal is made to Paul himself. He already knew, and indeed prophesied, the future situation, and thus safeguarded the Lukan norms. In all probability the teachers attacked in v.29 advanced their own interpretation of Paul. It may be supposed that they had a Pauline secret teaching accessible only to the perfect (vv.20,27 attack that) and emerged in and/or around Ephesus (that is why the presbyters of Ephesus are addressed – Maddox 1982, 69, disputes the reference to Ephesus; cf. the indications in II Tim.1.15 [see I Tim.1.3]). To this degree the speech serves to consolidate the Lukan understanding of Paul.

Luke adds a paraenetic focus to the speech, which really ends at v.32: Paul has given the communities an example of how not to be a financial burden on others *and* how one should accept the weak. (Evidently this reflects the contradiction that if one does not work one cannot support even the weak.) 'In the speech Paul's manual work serves to give an example of how the elders should help the poor and sick members of their church' (Lambrecht 1979, 321). The support of the weak is based on a saying of Jesus (on which see under III): 'It is more blessed to give than to receive'. Here Luke refers the readers back to 2.45; 4.34 and especially to the Gospel, which contains paraenesis about doing good that is worth following. Luke's Paul thus impresses on his community that they must take the ethics of the gospel to heart (cf. Horn 1983, 50-3).

III Tradition

Two questions must be distinguished at this stage of the work: 1. the basis of the speech in tradition; 2. the basis in tradition of a meeting between the presbyters from Ephesus and Paul in Miletus and its relationship to the stages of Paul's journey.

1. The basis of the speech in tradition

ekklesia tou theou (v.28) appears elsewhere in the NT only in the Pauline corpus. The second half of the verse poses difficult problems. Who is the subject? How is *idiou* to be understood (as an adjective or as a noun)? It is clear that the blood of Jesus has no significance in Luke's soteriology, and that therefore, as already in the first half-verse, Luke is deliberately being Pauline. The obscurities mentioned above may simply arise because Luke is putting one formula after another (cf. Conzelmann 1987, 174ff.), a further argument that here we have the use of individual traditions from the sphere of the Pauline mission and not of letters of Paul.

Verses 29-31 perhaps presuppose Mark 13.21-23 (cf. Lambrecht 1979, 327f.).

The remark in v.34 that Paul fed himself by the work of his hands may derive either from Luke's knowledge of the letters of Paul (cf. I Thess.2.9; I Cor.4.12, etc.) or – more likely – from oral tradition about Paul (cf.Acts 18.3). The latter suggestion is supported by the consideration that Paul's manual work must have been generally known in the Christian churches (cf. Lambrecht 1979, 321).

The saying of Jesus, 'It is more blessed to give than to receive' (v.35), does not appear in this form either in the canonical Gospels or in early Christian literature. It has a certain affinity to a Persian maxim which can be reconstructed from Thucydides II, 97, 4, *didonai mallon e lambanein*, and which has an interesting parallel in I Clem.2.1: *hedion didontes e lambanontes* (the author is praising the positive characteristics of the Corinthian community). Probably the saying of Jesus is a Christianization of an originally secular saying (a proverb?) by Luke or his community (for an analogy cf.26.14), in which the Christian *makarion* has replaced an original *hedion*. For the comparative see 5.29 (for the discussion of v.35 see especially Haenchen 1971, 594 n.5 [with bibliography]).

Schmithals 1982 has offered a completely different analysis of the tradition, which must be discussed here because of its novelty. In his view the basis of the farewell speech in Miletus derives from a traditional speech which is contained in 20.18b, 19a, 25a, 26-32 (187f.) and is part of a Paul-source which underlies Acts 13-28 (15). The speech in the tradition presupposes 'the same situation as we encounter in the post-Pauline Pastoral Epistles' (190). The common opponent is a dualistic Gnosis (I Tim.6.20; Titus 1.16) which knows mythological speculations (I Tim.1.4; 4.7; Titus 1.13f.; 3.9), appeals to the Old Testament law (I Tim.1.7), is hostile to the body (II Tim.2.18) and ascetic (Titus 1.13ff.), and knows salvation only for pneumatics (I Tim.2.4; 4.10). 'In its original version the present speech by Paul is the only one in the Paul-source used by Luke, and its central passage. So this source pursues the same aim as the Pastorals, namely to fight against the Gnostic false teachers who had found their way into the Pauline communities, and it might derive from the same author' (191). Schmithals thinks that Luke made the speech delivered against Gnostics into one delivered against hyper-Paulinists, who were threatening the Lukan communities (190).

By way of criticism: 1. The same reasons can be advanced against the reconstruction of the Paul source with the sole help of the Lukan context as against the reconstruction of the itinerary on the sole basis of Acts (cf. Lüdemann 1984, 25-9). 2. Schmithals' theory about the original Miletus speech is a third-degree hypothesis and is therefore extremely improbable. 3. Schmithals' theory about Gnosticism, which is one of the main pillars of his reconstruction, has proved to be extremely improbable (cf. Lüdemann 1975, 24-6; 1984, 206-10; 1983, 103-61). But it should be stressed that the thematic relationship between the Pastorals and Acts which Schmithals has made a theme deserves more attention. (There is a different assessment of Schmithals' position in Plümacher 1984, 126-7.)

2. The basis in tradition of a meeting between Paul and the presbyters of Ephesus in Miletus

The most probable assumption might be that the tradition reported a stay by Paul in Miletus (on his way through?). Roloff 1981 differs. He thinks it possible 'that the account of the journey in the tradition contained the report of a meeting between Paul and delegates from the community in Ephesus' (301). Conzelmann 1987 thinks that Luke seems to have an account of a meeting in Miletus (173).

IV Historical

For the reasons given, the speech cannot make any claim to historicity. Similarly, considerable doubt about a meeting between Paul and delegates from Ephesus is legitimate, as there is no basis in the tradition for this. Nevertheless Miletus may be historical as a stage on Paul's travels. However, we do not have any way of giving it a precise historical context. Either Miletus really was a stage on Paul's last journey to Jerusalem (thus the Lukan context), or Paul interrupted his journey to Palestine/Syria there (18.22) before going on to take part in the Jerusalem conference.

Acts 21.1-36

I Division

21.1-16: Journey from Miletus via Rhodes and Patara to Jerusalem
  1-3a: From Miletus to Tyre
    3b-6: Stay with the disciples in Tyre, their warnings not to go to Jerusalem. Farewell scene
  7a: From Tyre to Ptolemais
    7b: One-day stay with the brethren in Ptolemais
  8a: From Ptolemais to Caesarea
    8b-9: The stay in Caesarea with Philip, the father of four virgin daughters endowed with the gift of prophecy
  10-14: Prophecy of Agabus and reaction of Paul and his companions ('we')
  15: From Caesarea to Jerusalem
    16: Lodging in the house of Mnason
17-36: Paul in Jerusalem until his arrest
  17-19: Paul and his companions received by the brethren. The next day Paul reports to James and the elders the success of the Gentile mission
  20-21: The Christian zealots and the rumours about Paul that have come to them
  22-26: The advice given to Paul about the Nazirate and about paying for four Nazirites so that they can fulfil their vows. The readers are reminded of the Apostolic Decree (v.25)
  27-36: Riot in the temple at the instigation of Jews from Asia. Paul is arrested

II Redaction

[1-16] The section alternates between travel notes and short reports on lodging with Christian brethren (see the division). That gives the

230

impression of redactional shaping (although it does not conclusively rule out the possibility that all the accounts of lodging belong to the tradition – see III below). The scheme is probably meant to express the participation of the churches of Palestine in Paul's journey.

We find some typical Lukan expressions scattered through the section. Here is a selection: v.2, *anechthemen*; v.4, *mathetas*; v.5, *eporeuometha, propemponton*; v.6, *hypestrepsan*; v.7, *aspasamenoi*; v.10, introductory participial construction and the phrase *tis... onomati* (cf. on v.10 also Radl 1975, 137f.).

Redactional shaping of the content can be seen in the following passages: v.4, the warnings by the Spirit not to go to Jerusalem; similarly 21.12 (see the analysis of the redaction on vv.10-14); v.5, the gripping portrayal of the farewell scene for the purpose of heightening the drama; the theme of prayer (cf. 20.36). The note in v.8 that Philip was one of the Seven is a reference back to Acts 6, to remind the reader. There is a narrative explanation in 21.33 of the second part of the remark in v.11, that in Jerusalem Paul will be bound by the Jews and handed over to the Gentiles. In v.12 Paul is warned by his companions and the Christians in Caesarea not to go to Jerusalem. The warnings repeatedly given to Paul (cf. already v.4b) are Lukan redaction. They are closely connected with the theme of the Spirit. On the one hand they are attributed to the Holy Spirit, yet on the other the Spirit actually ordains that the apostle shall go to Jerusalem (cf.20.22; 19.21). In v.13, Paul is ready – like Jesus – to die in Jerusalem (cf. Haenchen 1971, 602). Dying for the name of the Lord Jesus recalls 20.23, which talks of Paul having to suffer. The motive of lodging (vv.15-16) appears often in Luke (cf. Cadbury 1926).

[17-36] Verse 17 contains Lukan vocabulary (cf. *apedexanto, adelphoi*). At the same time a seam (which is redactional) is visible in this verse. Although Paul is already in Jerusalem with his companions (v.16 describes them lodging with Mnason in the holy city – but see the alteration of the geography by D; for the problem see Weiser 1985, 596), with the help of a participial construction in the genitive absolute, which often occurs in Acts, Paul and his companions are once again despatched there. Here v.17 clashes with v.22: in v.17 the (whole) community (= the brethren) greet the apostle, whereas according to v.22 (the) members of the community will hear that Paul is in the city (Suhl 1975, 290, following Haenchen 1971, 609 n.3 [with bibliography], thinks that precisely because of v.22, v.17 [*hoi adelphoi*] cannot denote the whole community. But *hoi adelphoi* tells against that; moreover Suhl historicizes too quickly, instead of asking what elements of tradition may be present). If v.22 derives from tradition (cf. III below), then v.17 can best be understood as redaction. In v.18 the

same leading body of the Jerusalem community appears as in Acts 15, namely the presbyters. Verse 19 clearly refers back to 15.4, 12.

With vv.17-19, which he has shaped himself, Luke shows that the Jerusalem community maintains a good relationship with Paul to the end. Under the theological pressure of such a view he fails to note the clumsiness of bringing the apostle to Jerusalem twice (vv.6,17), and he has all the brethren greeting Paul, although many of the 'brethren' will only hear of his arrival in the city later.

Lukan intervention can be recognized in a number of passages in vv.20-21, 22-26. The first part of v.20 contains the reaction to the report by Paul (v.19, which is redactional), cf. 11.18. *myriades* (v.20b) derives from Luke's tendency to increase numbers (cf. 1.15; 2.41; 4.4). The remarks about Paul's participation in a Jewish ceremony in vv.23-24b, 26 are contradictory. If we take the story as it stands, then it first reports that Paul has made a Nazirite vow (vv.24a, 26) and secondly that he pays the expenses of four others so that they may fulfil their Nazirite vows (v.24b; cf.v.27). But a Nazirate lasts at least thirty days, and not seven, as Luke seems to assume (v.27). It therefore seems likely that the remarks about Paul's Nazirate are wholly attributable to Luke, whereas v.24b reflects tradition (see III below). (In 21.24 is Luke possibly thinking of the vow in 18.18? In that case Paul would have had his hair cut for the last time in Cenchreae and after that would have kept his vow throughout his journey[s].) Verse 25 is a reminder to the reader of 15.20 (and is redactional).

If we read the text as Luke intends, we get the following development:

The presence of numerous Christian zealots and the existence of rumours that Paul is teaching the Jews in the Diaspora to apostatize from the law cause James and the presbyters to ask Paul to demonstrate his own fidelity to the law. He is to sanctify himself along with four Nazirites and meet the cost of cutting their hair, so that all may recognize that he is faithfully fulfilling the law. Paul follows this advice, which was clear to the leaders of the Jerusalem community from the beginning. For they had never doubted his loyal observance of the law.

The redactional significance of the section is clear: to the last Paul moves within Judaism. He is never guilty of any transgression of the law. On the contrary, he circumcised Timothy (16.3), himself made a vow (18.18) and also observed the law during his last visit to Jerusalem.

The phrase 'lay hands on someone' (v.27) also appears in 4.3; 5.18; 12.1. Verse 28 is Lukan in that Paul's preaching, like that of Stephen before him (6.1), is wrongly seen by the Jews as directed against the law and the temple. Verses 30-34 contain Luke's description of a riot (cf. similarly 19.27, 32-34). In it vv.31f. depict the state intervention in the dispute between Jews and Christians in accordance with a well-known pattern.

The redactional significance of the whole section is that it fulfils a prophecy: Paul is handed over by the Jews to the Gentiles (21.11). This creates the presupposition for the following apologetic discourse delivered by Paul, which foists the blame for the controversy between Christians and Jews on the latter and on occasion commends Christianity to the Romans.

III Traditions

[1-16] The report is based on a source which contained a journey of Paul from Miletus to Jerusalem. (For the question whether this was the conference journey or the collection journey see 235 below.) However, it is the painstakingly precise character of the report rather than the 'we style' which supports this view.

Schille differs: 'The stages are not copied from an itinerary but are simply the result of a wise description of the route' (1983, 407).

I shall go on to clarify the questions whether and to what extent the reports over and above the itinerary itself go back to tradition and whether, if they do, they were part of the source mentioned, which reported a journey of Paul from Miletus to Jerusalem.

The details of the stay with Philip in vv.8b-9 may have been part of the source. Luke does not invent stories, but reports them on the basis of tradition. The account of the four prophetic virgin daughters of Philip is in all probability part of the tradition, since it fits the traditions of the Hellenists, which report their spirit-filled activity (see above, 105) and is an interesting and unbiased detail. (In Luke's time virginity was probably not yet a general church ideal [on this see Harnack 1904, 267 n.1].) But it is not clear whether it was part of the source.

Polycrates of Ephesus (in Eusebius, *Church History* III, 31,3) reports on Philip and his three (sic!) virgin daughters in Hierapolis (or Ephesus). Although he includes Philip among the twelve apostles, the mention of the prophetic daughters might be evidence that the tradition here originally meant the evangelist Philip (cf. perhaps in this sense the Montanist Proclus in Eusebius, *Church History* III, 31,4). See also the narrative of Papias (in Eusebius, *Church History* III, 39,9), about the stay of Philip with his daughters in Hierapolis. However, he confuses the evangelist with the apostle Philip in the same way as Polycrates does (cf. Körtner 1983, 144-6).

The story of Agabus in vv.10-14 might have been part of the tradition which Luke used. Certainly redactional features were unmistakable (see above). But the name Agabus and his prophetic activity certainly come

233

from a tradition. However, it is not certain whether Agabus is in the right chronological context at this point in Acts. For he also appears in 11.27f. in connection with a journey by Paul to Jerusalem, though this is to be seen as a model journey – created by Luke by using individual traditions connected with journeys by Paul to Jerusalem. Therefore the Agabus story may have been part of the source I have mentioned.

The report about the lodging in the house of Mnason (v.16b) derives from tradition. This is suggested by: 1. the redactional character of vv.17ff. (see above, 231f.); 2. the name Mnason; 3. the interesting information that Christians from Caesarea had given Paul lodging in Jerusalem. At the same time this makes it probable that v.16b was part of the source material.

[17-36]The report that at the time of Paul's collection visit James was head of the Jerusalem community (vv.17-19) might be tradition.

The following elements of tradition can be seen in vv.20-26: 1. Many Jews who are zealots for the law belong to the Jerusalem community (cf. the tension between v.17 [which is redactional] and v.22 noted at 231 above). 2. Rumours go the rounds that Paul is teaching the Jews to apostatize from the law of Moses and dissuading them from circumcising their children (v.21). After the previous (Jewish) portrait of the apostle these rumours would *not* be expected in Acts and may therefore derive from a tradition. 3. Paul takes part in a Jewish ceremony and pays the expenses of four Nazirites so that they may fulfil their vows. Such an act was regarded as a pious work (cf. Josephus, *Antt* XIX, 294) and has nothing to do with making a Nazirite vow. Finally, the information 'seven days' may derive from tradition. It seems that we should follow Haenchen in connecting this information at the level of the tradition with Paul's visit to the temple: Paul had to make an agreement with the priest involved to pay the expenses, and at the same time regain his purity as someone coming from abroad.

'Paul accordingly... went with the four Nazirites to the Temple and there reported first his own purification... and secondly the *ekplerosis ton hemeron tou hagnismou* (of the Nazirate of the four). The date could then be fixed on which the appropriate sacrifices – for which Paul paid – were to be presented: it was the seventh day, on which he himself was to be cleared from guilt' (Haenchen 1971, 612).

For 'seven' as an element of the tradition (v.27), see what has been said above.

The name of Paul's Gentile companion Trophimus in v.29 is equally part of the tradition in this section (cf. the list in Acts 20.4). Jews hostile to Paul said that Paul took Trophimus into the temple (this charge is

234

probably part of the tradition – Luke declares it and the charge against Stephen [6.13f.] to be false witness [see above, 83f., 89]).

One can also ask whether v.35 does not also reflect tradition:

'When Paul comes to the steps, he is carried by the soldiers to keep him safe from the violence of the pressing mob. But if one carries an unpopular person on one's shoulders, one does not withdraw him from the assault of the mob: he is now completely exposed to every stone that is thrown. In reality a pressing crowd can be effectively blocked in other ways. Paul had to be carried because after the lynching attempt by the mob he was no longer able to climb the steps himself. But Luke could not report that – according to him indeed Paul will immediately deliver a speech from those very steps!' (Haenchen 1971, 618).

This results in the following outline for the source: Paul travels with companions from Miletus via Caesarea to Jerusalem. He is offered hospitality in Caesarea by the Hellenist Philip and in Jerusalem by the Hellenist Mnason. In the Jerusalem community, which is faithful to the law and is presided over by James, his person is controversial, since rumours are going the rounds that his attitude is antinomian and that he is against the circumcision of Jewish boys. Paul counters this by paying the expense of four Nazirites who are fulfilling their vows. The source probably ended with Paul's presence in the temple, to which he had gone for his own purification. Its content (cf. especially the position of James) suggests that it fits only the third and last visit by Paul to Jerusalem.

In a way which is no longer clear, Paul's companion Trophimus and the charges against the apostle which were prompted by his person ('Paul has brought Gentiles into the temple' [v.28]) belong to that source (cf. below, 249f.), as perhaps does also the description of details of Paul's arrest (see above on v.35), but this must remain quite uncertain.

The development I have just described is the best argument for the assumption of a *continuous* source. For the report follows a straight line and has no tensions or breaks.

IV Historical

Our answer to the question of the historical reliability of the above source must be a positive one. The individual elements are confirmed or shown to be probable by other information independent of Acts 21:

The report about the abode of the Hellenist Philip (Caesarea) is credible, as is that about the activity of his daughters as prophets. It fits the pneumatic-eschatological character of the preaching of the Hellenists well (cf. also *TestJob* 48-50 [description of the prophetic activity of the three daughters of Job]).

It is quite possible that Paul found lodging with a Hellenist (Mnason), because earlier he had a close connection with the Hellenist circles. (Mnason, like Barnabas, comes from Cyprus, 21.16.)

James's position as leader is confirmed by other sources (for a comprehensive account of this see Hengel 1985), as is the nomistic character of the Jerusalem community in the 50s (cf. Lüdemann 1983, 92 n.99). Paul's participation in a cultic act is to be deemed probable because of his understanding of freedom (cf. I Cor.9.19ff.).

Finally, the charge against Paul expressed in v.21 may be historical, and accurately convey the reservations of the Jerusalem Christians about him.

The evidence of Acts about this 'must be rated all the higher, as it is to be regarded as having been forced on him (sc. Luke) even against his will by the power of historical truth. Accordingly, the fact remains that according to the personal testimony of the author of Acts himself, the Jewish Christians in Jerusalem saw Paul as an apostate from the law and a preacher of the same apostasy among Jews and Gentiles. If they had this view of him, no one could be blamed for the conclusion that in instances which, like those that immediately follow, are the undeniable result of the same view and disposition, they cannot have been as indifferent and impartial as is usually assumed' (Baur 1866, 230).

At all events, the accusation in v.21 has a point of contact in what was happening in at least some of the Pauline communities. Certainly we do not find anywhere in the letters of Paul which have come down to us anything that corresponds to the charge in Acts 21.21. But the circumstances described in v.21 were a possible consequence for Jews who lived in the Pauline communities. If the Torah was at best provisional in comparison with the new creation in Christ (I Cor.7.19: Gal.6.15), those who were born Jews were inevitably alienated fom the law as a result of such a praxis and no longer circumcised their children (cf., rightly, Hengel 1985, 97). Verse 21 therefore gives reliable historical information about the possible consequences of Pauline preaching and praxis among Jews and about the reservations of the Jerusalem community over Paul.

Now of course we know from Paul's own testimony that the aim of the last journey to Jerusalem was to bring the collection from the Pauline communities there. The question is why there is nothing about that in the source worked over in Acts 21. According to the remarks made above on the historical reliability of Acts 21, it seems impossible that the source contained no reference to the collection. This raises the question: why does Luke *delete* any reference to the collection in that chapter? The question is made all the more urgent if Acts 24.17 contains a note about the significance of Paul's last journey to Jerusalem. The only possible answer to the last question is that in Acts 21 Luke deliberately avoided the theme of the collection, because the source which he used reported a failure to deliver it, or reported that it was rejected (cf. now similarly Pesch II, 222). Because of his view of the church, Luke cannot bring himself in this chapter to report that Paul's work of unity was a failure (for details see Lüdemann 1983, 96-8). Unfortunately, in his learned article Hengel 1985 – who thinks that Luke was an eyewitness on Paul's last visit to Jerusalem – does not say anything about the collection and regards Luke's portrait of James in Acts 21 as historically reliable (95f.). But that leaves the great riddle why the 'eyewitness' Luke does not report any help from James after Paul was arrested.

Acts 21.37-22.29

I Division

21.37-40: Conversation between Paul and the chiliarch; Paul is given permission to speak to the people
22.1-21: Paul's speech to the Jews in Jerusalem
    1-2: Address. Paul speaks in Aramaic
    3-5: Paul's life up to the Damascus event
    6-16: Description of the Damascus event
    17-21: The vision in the Jerusalem temple
    22-23: The furious reaction of the Jews
    24-29: Paul in the Roman barracks. Attempt at flogging. Appeal to his Roman citizenship

II Redaction

[21.37-40] The section is redactional throughout. It provides a first contact with the Roman officer and from the start stresses that Paul has nothing to do with the charge of *stasis* with which he is burdened in Jerusalem. The apostle is not, as is wrongly assumed, that Egyptian who had organized a revolt (v.38, the reference to the Egyptian, may not be used directly for chronological calculations [cf. the anachronism in 5.36f.]: on Jewett 1982, 102). Cf. the redactional litotes *ouk asemou* in v.39; v.40 prepares for the speech which follows. For the rhetorical gesture cf. 12.17; 13.16; 26.1.

[22.1-21] The beginning of v.1 corresponds to the introduction to Stephen's speech (7.2); in it Luke's Paul specifies the purpose of the address at this point: it is 'a defence before you'. Verse 2 refers back to 21.40b: Paul speaks to the people in Aramaic (he had still been speaking Greek to the officer). In v.3, Paul (the Lukan Paul) uses a threefold scheme (cf. 7.20-22 [of Moses]) to describe his upbringing: he was born (*gegennemenos*) in Tarsus, brought up (*anatethrammenos*) in this city (viz. Jerusalem), educated (*pepaideumenos*) at the feet of Gamaliel. The threefold scheme was customary in Hellenistic literature to describe an upbringing (cf. Lüdemann 1984, 39 n.72 [bibliography]). So Luke's Paul (and with him the author of Acts) belongs to the educated world. Like 7.58f.; 8.1-2; 9.1-2 earlier, vv.4-5 depict Paul's activity as a persecutor. The section vv.6-16 is a variant on the account of Paul's conversion which also underlies Acts 9 (for details see there). In the synoptic comparison of the three accounts of the conversion made above, we saw that 22.15 differs from 9.15 in stressing that Paul will be a witness to all people of what he has seen and heard. Thus Luke regards the conversion as a call, and this is made quite clear by the next section. The temple vision in vv.17-21 interprets the conversion as a call (cf. especially v.21b, 'Go, for I shall send you to the Gentiles'). Lukan language in vv.17-21 includes: v.17, *hypostrepsanti, ekstasei*; v.18, *speuson, en tachei*; v.19, *epistantai*; v.21, *exapostelo*. Verse 20 is a redactional reference back to 7.58; it is in tension with the context, which in v.19 already depicts Paul's activity as a persecutor outside Jerusalem *after* his activity in Jerusalem, and therefore sounds lame. The best explanation of this is that Luke worked over existing material (cf. under III).

[22-23] The phrase 'raise the voice' occurs outside this passage (v.22) in the New Testament only in Luke-Acts (Luke 11.27; Acts 14.11). The furious reaction of the Jews is a stylistic ingredient of the scene. The demand for Paul to be removed from the face of the earth (v.22) refers to the same attitude of the Jews as 21.30 (25.24 will then refer back to the present scene). So Paul's speech was a failure. Significantly the Jews interrupt Paul when he talks about his mission to the Gentiles.

[24-29] These verses depict Paul's appeal to his Roman citizenship. The information that he is a Roman citizen fits well with the apologetic bias of Luke-Acts (cf. Lüdemann 1984, 18f. [and bibliography]). However, redaction and tradition need not always contradict one another (see below, III). The parallel relationship beween this scene and 16.19-40 is instructive. In both passages the appeal to Roman citizenship is delayed (cf.22.25 with 16.37), and accordingly Paul is first open to acts of violence by the Roman authorities (cf. 22.24 with 16.22f.). On each occasion the cruelty of the Roman authorities (see the passages mentioned above) is

contrasted with their fear when they discover that Paul is a Roman citizen (cf. 22.29 with 16.38). The narrative intent of all this is probably to stress Paul's Roman citizenship and to make 'the apostle appear all the more clearly to be under the protection of the Roman state against Jewish acts of violence' (Overbeck 1870, 395; cf. also ibid., 394f., on the relationship of this narrative to 16.19-40).

III Traditions

[21.39] For the tradition of Paul's origins in Tarsus and his citizenship of that city see 241 below.

[3-5, 6-16] For the tradition of Paul's activity as a persecutor and the Damascus event see above on Acts 9.

The question whether the indication that Paul grew up and was educated in Jerusalem derives from tradition, despite the redactional tendency of the remark in v.3, can be answered only after historical considerations can be decided on (see IV below).

[17-21] Despite Lukan linguistic elements, the basic structure of this section, without v.20, is tradition. 'Luke could hardly have himself invented such a massive appearance of Jesus as portrayed in vv.17f.' (Burchard 1970, 163), although 9.17 refers to an appearance of Jesus (*ophthe*) to Paul. The tradition (against 9.28; 26.20) probably does not presuppose any Pauline preaching in Jerusalem (cf.v.18, 'They [sc. in Jerusalem] will not accept your testimony about me'). The tradition is unique in that it locates Paul's call to be a missionary to the Gentiles not in Damascus, but apparently in the Jerusalem temple. Furthermore, in contrast to Paul's own testimonies the move to the Gentiles is justified by unwillingness of the Jerusalem Jews, which is established *a priori*, to accept his testimony.

[24-29] As has been shown above, the pericope with the statement that Paul is a Roman citizen fits the Lukan tendency well. But in all probability the individual report (not the whole scene, vv.24-29) goes back to tradition, since Paul's Roman citizenship seems to be historical (cf. IV below).

By way of addition, it should be noted that Stolle 1973 – without giving any reason – regards vv.23-29 as part of a pre-Lukan 'prison report' (265f.).

IV Historical

For the historical questions related to Paul as a persecutor and the Damascus event cf. above 114f. on Acts 9.

Since so far there is no evidence of the training of Pharisees outside Jerusalem, the remark in v.3 that Paul was brought up as a Pharisee in Jerusalem may be part of the tradition and therefore historical. That need not exclude his attending a school in Tarsus (cf.21.39). It is impossible to make any probable statement about the duration of Paul's stay in Jerusalem.

Paul's vision in the temple is certainly unhistorical in that it suggests that Paul received his calling as apostle to the Gentiles in the Jerusalem temple. For according to Gal.1.15 Paul was called to be apostle to the Gentiles near Damascus. It is an open question where, when and why such a tradition was formed, unless one were to connect Paul's own report in II Cor.12.1-5 with this; it likewise speaks (*a*) of an ecstatic experience; (*b*) of a vision (*idein*, Acts 22.18 – *optasia*, II Cor.12.1); and (*c*) of an audition (*auton legonta*, Acts 22.18 [,21] – *arrheta rhemata*, II Cor.12.4).

Excursus: On Paul's Roman citizenship

In this excursus I shall give positive reasons for assuming that Paul had Roman citizenship. First of all, however some inadequate arguments against such a view must be discussed critically.

1. At no point does Paul mention his Roman citizenship: against that, there was nowhere any occasion – even in the catalogue of his vicissitudes in II Cor.11.23ff. (on Wengst 1987, 74, 203, who thinks that the fact that Paul does not mention his citizenship in II Cor.11.25 at least means that he did not attach any importance to it).

2. Paul was flogged three times (II Cor.11.25): against that, the Lex Julia (for details see Sherwin-White 1963, 57-60; Mommsen 1901, 89) indeed does not allow the flogging to be inflicted on Roman citizens as a punishment. But there were often offences against this law (cf. H.Windisch, *Der zweite Korintherbrief*, 1924, 356), and it is not certain whether Paul would have appealed to his Roman citizenship over a flogging matter. In addition, there was always the problem how he could have proved his citizenship. 3. The contradiction between Paul's manual labour (which is evidence that he came from the lower middle class) and his Roman citizenship (which would indicate that he belonged to the upper class) tells against the latter, as the former is indisputable (Stegemann 1985, 483-5): against that, (in the early Empire) citizenship was in no way bestowed only on prominent citizens (cf. below for freedmen). Moreover Paul's manual work was probably motivated by his rabbinic training and therefore cannot be used as conclusive evidence for defining his social status (Hock 1980, 22-5 [bibliography] differs, followed by Stegemann 1985, 483, making the correct observation that the rabbinic texts about study of the Torah and manual labour only come from the middle of the second century [but does that exclude an earlier provenance?]).

Positive proof that Paul was a Roman citizen. The apostle bears a Roman name, Paul. Paulus is a *cognomen* or *praenomen* (see the examples in Cadbury 1955, 69f.). The name is rare in the East and indicates high birth (Mommsen 1901, 82 n.3). Its use can be explained in two ways: (*a*) the Latin name Paul is the result of assimilation, in order to make social contacts or even dealings with the Roman authorities easier (see Juster 1914 [vol.II], 226 etc. for the assumption of Latin and Greek names by Jews). Here 'Paul' may be a phonetic equivalent of 'Saul' (but according to Dessau 1910, 352, the name Paul is not a phonetic rendering of the Hebrew *Sha'ul* into Greek or Latin [against Sherwin-White 1963, 153f.]; according to G.Mussies, in S.Safrai and M.Stern [eds.], *The Jewish People in the First Century* II, 1976, 1052, the Greek name which corresponded with Sha'ul was *Aithetos*); cf. the survey in Leon 1960, 120, of phonetic equivalents between Semitic and Roman names among the Jews of Rome. Perhaps Luke even wants to indicate (despite Acts 13.9, a passage which presupposes that the apostle already bore the name Paul) that Paul only gave himself this name after his meeting with the proconsul Sergius Paulus. (*b*) The name Paul goes back to the fact that the apostle was a Roman citizen. Roman citizens had the right and duty to bear a Roman name (see Juster 1914 [Vol.II], 221). If Jews became or were Roman citizens, they therefore took a Roman name. Here it seems worth taking into consideration the fact that Paul had citizenship as the descendant of a freedman (cf. Cadbury 1955, 74-6, and the qualifications in Sherwin-White 1963, 151f.), for 'the legal freeing of a slave by a Roman citizen (secured) him citizenship without more ado..., without the need for any state consent' (Meyer 1961, 186). However, the freedman (and his children) did not get unlimited citizenship immediately, so that in fact he (they) could be regarded only as (*a*) second-class citizen(s) (cf. Meyer 1961, 186f.). – Finally, the following two reasons suggest that Paul's Roman citizenship is a historical fact: 1. If the apostle's imprisonment in Jerusalem is a fact, his transportation to Rome can best be explained by an appeal to the Roman emperor by the Roman citizen Paul (see below, 254). 2. Paul travelled amazingly often through colonized territory (Philippi, Corinth, Pisidian Antioch), and one explanation of his wish to go to Spain (Rom.15.28) could be that he could be sure of finding Roman colonies there. For along with Gaul, Spain was at the centre of the deliberate policy of Romanization (see Meyer 1961, 319f.).

To conclude: in all probability Paul was a Roman citizen. Whether at the same time he was also a citizen of Tarsus (Acts 21.39) is not so easy to decide. At all events, being a citizen of Tarsus did not rule out being a Roman citizen, for the rule that Roman citizenship was incompatible with citizenship of another city had already been relaxed at the end of the Republic and in the early Principate (Sherwin-White 1963, 182).

For the question of Paul's Roman citizenship see now the comprehensive study by W. Stegemann, 'War der Apostel Paulus ein römischer Bürger?', *ZNW* 87, 1987, 200-29: he argues that the author of Acts concluded from Paul's transportation to Rome that he was a Roman citizen.

Acts 22.30-23.35

I Division

22.30: The Sanhedrin is summoned by the chiliarch
23.1-9: Paul before the Sanhedrin and the reaction of the Pharisees and Sadducees
    1: Declaration of innocence
    2-5: The exchange between the high priest Ananias and Paul
    6: Paul's stratagem
    7: Dispute between Sadducees and Pharisees
    8: Explanation about the two parties
    9: The Pharisees support Paul
10: Paul escorted to the barracks
11: Paul hears the Lord by night: he will also bear witness in Rome
12-35: Paul taken to Caesarea; how this came about
    12-15: Jewish plot against Paul
    16-22: Plot reported to Felix by Paul's nephew
    23-35: Paul taken to Caesarea with a letter from the chiliarch Claudius Lysias to Felix

II Redaction

[22.30] This verse is a redactional preparation for Paul's speech before the Sanhedrin. (In anticipation of the historical analysis it can be said that the summoning of the Sanhedrin *by a Roman officer* is probably unhistorical [cf.Matt.2.4], as is his participation in the session [23.10]; against Schürer 1979, 223; cf. rightly Stählin 1980, 288.)

[**23.1-9**] The scene has some peculiar features which so far have not been noted in the secondary literature because of over-hasty historicizing; cf. e.g. Meyer III, 66; Haenchen 1971, 639; Radl 1975, 184. The presence of the chiliarch is not presupposed as it is in 22.30; 23.10. Paul seems to be handed over (without protection) to the jurisdiction of the high priest (v.2). The very muddled character of the section is also worth noting. Thus Paul stands up several times without giving a real speech. Moreover the dialogue structure in vv.2-5 with three speakers is unusual for Luke. Paul's insult to the high priest and his apology in v.5 is also a remarkable feature: here Luke shows the apostle to be sorry for transgressing the law (even though he only broke the law out of ignorance). The peculiarities of this scene suggest that particularly in the first part Luke formulated it in connection with tradition, even though he has given the whole the stamp of his theology, as the following survey will show.

242

Verse 1 produces a further declaration of innocence ('Brethren, I have lived before God in all good conscience up to this day'). Contrary to the accusations against him (cf. 21.21, 27-29), Paul has lived as a faithful Jew. Verses 4f. demonstrate his fidelity to the Law; he would not have addressed Ananias as he did had he known him to be high priest. In vv.6-9 Paul takes the initiative, plays the Jewish parties of the Sadducees and Pharisees off against each other, and thus paralyses his judges. The statement that he is a Pharisee and is being judged on account of the resurrection of the dead (v.6) is a wise move which immediately results in a split between the parties present, as intended. The phrase 'while he was still speaking' (v.7a) uses the literary technique of interruption. Although everything has really already been said, it seems that the speech is forcibly broken off (cf. 10.44). The remark by some Pharisees, 'We find nothing wrong in this man. What if a spirit or an angel spoke to him?' (v.9) recalls Gamaliel's advice in 5.38f. (which is redactional). Until the opposite is proved, Paul is an 'orthodox' Jew.

The whole episode vv.7-9 seems to be a construct and does not show any signs of tradition. It is a 'scene arranged by the author of Acts' (Baur 1866, 236). Moreover the sympathy of some Pharisees for Paul clashes remarkably with the accusation that the apostle had taken Gentiles into the temple. For this would inevitably have shown the Pharisees how dangerous Paul was. In my view the clash is satisfactorily explained by the hypothesis that 23.7-9 are redactional, while the actual accusation stems from tradition (see above).

The hypothesis mentioned can stand independently of any estimation about the theology of the Pharisees before 70 CE (cf. the argument between Rivkin 1978 and Neusner 1971), since it is about the desecration of the temple by a Gentile. In the view of the Pharisees, that too carried the death penalty; cf. the warning inscription on Herod's temple in Jerusalem: 'Let no foreigner (*allogenes*) enter within the screen and enclosure surrounding the sanctuary. Whoever is taken so doing will be the cause that death overtakes him' (translation from Deissmann 1927, 80; there is also a photograph of the inscription there; cf. also Strobel 1980, 22-24, with further examples).

[10] The verse takes up 22.30. It is a transition to the next scene (vv.12-35). Between v.10 and vv.12-35 Luke inserts:

[11] Paul will bear witness in Rome as well as in Jerusalem. This is an anticipation of his stay in Rome and indicates the wider context. Paul's activity accords with his commission (22.15). His way is dominated by the divine *dei*.

[12-35] The language and content of the section has been shaped by Luke at the following points: v.12, genitive absolute; v.14, relative connection

with *hoitines, heos hou*; v.16, *nyn oun, akribesteron* (the comparative occurs only here in the New Testament and is attested in 23.20 in connection with this passage together with 18.26 and 24.22; it has the function of showing the pseudo-hearing to be a continuation of the one begun in ch.23); *ta peri, tou* + infinitive; v.16 *paragenomenos* (cf.Jeremias 1980, 152); v.18, *men oun*; v.19, *epilabomenos*. The report about Paul's nephew in vv.20-21 takes up the narrative of vv.12-15 (as an analogy cf. the repetition of 10.30-32 in 11.4-17). Also Lukan are *men oun* (v.22) and the transition into direct speech, as in 1.4, 17.3, etc. The numbers involved in the escort (200 foot soldiers, 70 cavalry and 200 spearmen) conflict with its task of conducting a *secret* mission. Here, as elsewhere, Luke exaggerates, and thus gets entangled in contradictions (cf.11.27-30). Verse 24 contains a Lukan transition from direct to indirect speech. The letter from Claudius Lysias to Felix (26-30) is redactional throughout: the form of v.26, the prescript of the letter, matches the prescript of the letter in 15.23ff. (which is Luke's; cf. II Macc.11.16,22,27,34). Verse 27 contains the Lukan *syllambanein* (in the sense of 'arrest', as in Luke 22.54; Acts 1.16; 12.3 [cf. Schneider 1982, 339 n.36]). The statement in the letter about Paul's arrest does not fully agree with the account in 21.30-38; 22.22-29. According to the present letter the chiliarch has saved a Roman citizen from the Jews; according to 21.33, 38 he arrests him as a rebel, and only later discovers that the apostle is a Roman citizen. According to the letter the chiliarch had asked Paul's accuser to apply to the governor in Caesarea. However, we heard nothing of this in the previous narrative. These tensions should not be exploited in favour of the assumption of tradition. For here Luke is once again making use of the freedom to present the same narratives with only approximately identical content (cf. similarly the relationship betwen 11.14 and 10.5,32 and between 11.15 and 10.44); he makes the chiliarch argue from his 'present' knowledge and generously forget his wrong behaviour in 22.24. The phrase *zetemata tou nomou* in v.29 likewise occurs in 18.15. The invitation in v.30 to the Jewish accusers to bring their charge before Felix is conceivable only after Paul has successfully been moved away.

On the letter in vv.26-30 Conzelmann aptly remarks:

'...it serves to illumine the situation from the Roman standpoint (as Luke understands it). Legal innocence is acknowledged by the first Roman functionary who dealt with the matter. The view is the same as in the Gallio scene: the Roman does not state that Christianity is identical with Judaism, but rather that the whole matter is of no concern to Rome' (1987, 195).

Verse 31 reports the execution of the order described in v.23, *dia nyktos* takes up *apo trites horas tes nyktos* (v.23). Here Luke presupposes that it is possible to arrive at Antipatris the same time (cf. rightly Weiser 1983,

623). Hengel 1983b differs: 'In a march which also extends through the night the troops reach Antipatris, about forty-five miles from Jerusalem' (119). But such a view is possible only if one presupposes that Luke is being imprecise at this point and at the same time has a generally correct view of the geography of Palestine. *hypostrephein* (v.32) is a favourite Lukan word; v.33 reports the delivery of the letter reproduced in vv.26-30 and accordingly the command of v.24 to hand over Paul to Felix. The participial style in v.34 is Lukan; v.35 prepares for the next scene.

III Traditions

[23.1-9] Reasons have been given above for the suggestion that in vv.1-5 Luke is formulating the passage under the influence of tradition. We can now be more specific, to the effect that Luke knew of Paul's insult to the high priest (cf. Schwartz 1963, 166f.). He reproduced this correctly (v.3), but changed v.5 to match his own theology. The tradition may also have reported that Paul was handed over to the high priest's penal jurisdiction.

[23.12-35] The account stands out from vv.1-9 by its relative breadth and specific detail: the planning of an attempt on Paul's life, its discovery by his nephew, the transportation of Paul from Jerusalem to Caesarea, the name Claudius Lysias, Felix – these are details which might go back to tradition. The best answer to Zeller's question 'how the author could have known all these details so precisely' (1854, 287) is the hypothesis that at this point the author used a tradition which contained the details listed.

Schmithals 1982 takes a quite different view: 'There is no trace of a source even in the present section. This is an original narrative by the author Luke which may contain no historical information and which is to be understood wholly in terms of Luke's tendencies as an author' (209).

Evidently the tradition does not presuppose a previous trial. (However, the redactional v.15 [see above, II, for *akribesteron*] makes it seem a continuation of the pseudo-hearing begun in v.1.) We may conjecture that the conspiracy and its discovery were already connected in the tradition.

Hengel 1983, 119-21, has pointed out that Acts 23 presupposes exact geographical knowledge (the citadel Antonia, Antipatris, Caesarea) and that the action is plausible in the light of the history of the time. He thinks that Josephus could hardly have described the action by Claudius Lysias more accurately. Therefore the report must 'ultimately' derive from an eye-witness (= Luke) (120). But it is impossible to accept such a judgment. Luke gets the distance between Jerusalem and Antipatris wrong (he presupposes that a distance of forty-five miles can be covered in a night, see above), and more importantly: a generally convincing piece of local colouring does not

245

conclusively demonstrate the historicity of a scene (cf. Acts 19.23-40 and also 11 above on the 'Karl May rule').

Hengel's view that the report ultimately goes back to Luke as eye-witness is precisely what the author wanted to achieve: the account leaves almost no room for an eye-witness since everything that happens (the conspiracy, its betrayal and the moving of Paul) takes place in secret, but by the motive of secrecy indicated above, Luke suggests to the reader why the episode had so far remained unknown and was only now being brought into public view by him.

IV Historical

Hypothetically the following historical facts can be assumed to be the basis of the tradition in this chapter.

1. Paul had been handed over to the high priest's penal jurisdiction and had insulted him. Since in my view no clear reason can be given for developing such a tradition, it is likely to be historical.

2. The moving of Paul from Jerusalem to Caesarea to the governor Felix on the instigation of Claudius Lysias. (The details of the move must remain uncertain and are highly novellistic.)

3. The move was for technical reasons connected with the trial (Caesarea was the seat of the governor, the supreme judge of the province) and there was also a motive for it in the threat posed to Paul by his Jewish enemies. This detail (from the tradition) is confirmed by the overall situation of the apostle's last stay in Jerusalem: Paul was arrested (or taken into protective custody) in connection with a Jewish riot against him. It is worth following E.Schwartz in seeing the charge that Paul had brought Gentiles into the temple (21.28; 24.6) as the occasion for his arrest:

'The non-Jew who entered the inner area of the temple was an outlaw. If the Jews put up with it, the Romans authorities did not of course intervene; but if a born Jew caused a Gentile to transgress the commandment (which is what Paul was accused of) and if this incited the Jews to a rebellion, he could be prosecuted for *seditio* and condemned to death' (1963, 165f.).

In all probability the Jewish charge had no basis in what had really happened in Jerusalem. Paul respected Jewish customs so far as they did not threaten the existence of Gentile Christianity, and deliberately avoided making Jewish Christians into Gentile Christians. But the charge mentioned can well be understood as anti-Pauline polemic by Jewish Christians (cf. the exegesis of 21.21).

4. The question whether the tradition has accurately depicted the details of the plot and its discovery by Paul's nephew can probably never be answered. (The involvement of the Sanhedrin in the plot may of course come from Luke, since it fits in with the redaction.) The relevant scenes

246

are elaborated in a novellistic way, and it is improbable that the nephew would have found an immediate hearing with the chiliarch. However, the existence of a sister and nephew of Paul in Jerusalem is a historical fact (vigorously disputed by Schille 1983, 428f.); they were perhaps of use to Paul on his last stay in Jerusalem.

Acts 24

I Division

24.1: Arrival of the Jerusalem delegation in Caesarea – consisting of the high priest Ananias, some presbyters and Tertullus the advocate-at-law
2-6a,8b: Prosecution speech by Tertullus (vv.6b-8a are secondary on textual grounds)
9: Endorsement of the charges by the Jews
10-21: Defence speech by Paul
22-23: Postponement of decision by Felix
24-26: Felix and Paul
27: (After two years have elapsed) Replacement of Felix by Festus

II Redaction

The scene has probably been shaped by Luke throughout.

[1] The verse takes up the narrative from 23.30. On the instructions of the chiliarch Claudius Lysias the Jews send prosecutors against Paul to Felix in Caesarea.

[2-6a,8b] The prosecution speech by the orator Tertullus begins with a *captatio benevolentiae* (v.2-4) which will be matched in Paul's defence speech (vv.10-21: v.10). The two charges against Paul are already known from previous episodes: 1. Paul is causing rebellions among all the Jews throughout the world (v.5); 2. Paul has attempted to desecrate the temple (v.6). The first charge already appears in 17.6 as a Jewish accusation against Paul, and the second refers back to 21.28.

[9] The endorsement of the accusations by the Jews heightens the drama: *houtos echein* is a Lukan phrase (cf.7.1; 17.11).

[10-21] Paul's defence speech is closely related to the charge. Verse 10, the *captatio benevolentiae*, matches vv.2-4. *pollon* takes up *polles* (v.2). This produces the incorrect information that Felix had already been 'for many years... judge over this people', i.e. procurator in Judaea. (At most Felix had held this office only for a short period, see under IV below and Lake/Cadbury, *Beg.* IV, 300 for a parallel instance.) *dynamenou sou epignonai* (v.11) takes up *dynese... epignonai* (v.8). The information that Paul had come to Jerusalem twelve days earlier is arrived at by adding the seven days in 21.27 to the five days in 24.1. Verse 12 refers to the charges, first to the latter (the accusation of desecrating the temple), then to the charge of inciting rebellion. Verses 14-15 describe Paul's Christianity positively, in Lukan fashion: it consists in belief in the scriptures (v.14) and hope in God, the content of which consists in the expectation of the resurrection of just and unjust (v.15). Verse 16 contains yet another Lukan declaration of innocence on Paul's part:

'So I always take pains to have a clear conscience towards God and towards men' (cf. 23.1; 13.46; 18.6; 20.26).

Verse 17 is surprising in that Paul's goal on his last visit to Jerusalem consists in bringing 'alms and offerings for my people' (see under III). Verses 18-19 repeat 21.27, again rejecting the charge that Paul caused unrest (*ochlou* in v.18 refers back to *ochlou* in v.12). Verses 20-22 stress Paul's innocence yet again: neither the Asiatic Jews (of ch.21) nor the Jews present can demonstrate that Paul had done wrong. Verse 21 refers back to the (first) negotiation before the Sanhedrin. At that time (23.6) Paul had already said that he was being accused over the resurrection.

[22-23] The section leads to the next episode (vv.24-26). Felix's knowledge of the Christian way (v.22 [for *hodos* cf. v.14 and on 18.25]) is developed in the narrative in v.24b. The postponement of a decision by Felix until the arrival of the chiliarch Claudius Lysias serves to give time for the encounters between Paul and Felix and Paul and Festus which are described next. The way in which Paul's imprisonment is relaxed at Felix's request is a Lukan theme (cf. 27.3).

[24-26] Notable instance of Lukan language are: v.24, *paragenomenos, metepempsato, tes eis Christon... pisteos*; v.25, *dialegomenou, metalabon, metakalesomai*; v.26, *metapempomenos, homilei*.

In content the verses reflect Lukan apologetic, in that Paul finds Felix and Drusilla to be an interested audience (v.24). 'The interest in Christianity shown by those in high places is a Lukan theme' (Conzelmann 1987, 201). Moreover v.25 (Paul speaks about justice, self-control and the coming judgment) contains a characterization of Lukan Christianity developed in terms of the situation (Felix's dissipation was notorious). It is evidence that Luke 'has little connection any more with authentic earliest Christianity' (Weiss 1897, 60). Verse 26 matches the characterization of Felix in the tradition (from Josephus and Tacitus – cf. Meyer III, 46-54; Schürer 1972, 460-4). At this point it is in some tension with vv.22f., which paint a positive picture of Felix. But the information (v.26) that Felix hopes for a bribe to set Paul free – which of course is quite out of the question as a possibility for Paul after his sermon in v.25 – explains at this point why despite Paul's proven innocence he is not set free. In addition, yet again (after 16.16-24 and 19.23-27; cf. earlier 3.6; 5.1-11; 8.18-20) Luke establishes the conflict between money and the gospel (cf. Horn 1983, 55).

[27] According to Luke, the information 'two years' relates to the duration of Paul's imprisonment. *pleroun* is a favourite Lukan word (as is *charis*). The comment in v.27b that Felix did not release Paul because he wanted to show a favour to the Jews is reminiscent of 12.3 and gives a further reason why Paul was not released, which is in tension with v.26. The aim of v.22 is forgotten, namely to decide the case when the chiliarch Claudius Lysias comes.

III Traditions

Elements of tradition are evident at various places:

In v.1 Tertullus the attorney-at-law and Ananias the high priest. (For the possibility that v.1b [the laying of the charge] is part of the tradition cf. below on vv.22f.)

In v.17 Luke has allowed the tradition about the collection, which he knew from another source but suppressed in ch.21 for redactional reasons, to slip in here incidentally.

However, we cannot completely rule out the other possibility, that Luke knows the Jewish custom of pilgrims bringing alms to Jerusalem on their journey. That would also make good Lukan sense. In that case the note could not conclusively be related to the collection (cf. Pereira 1983, 225-7).

While vv.22-23 make sense in the present context (they prepare for the next scene in vv.24-26), the following observation by E.Schwartz suggests that they are based on tradition:

In *anebaleto autous ho Phelix* and *diagnosomai ta kath'hymas* 'the pronouns cannot cover the two parties but only denote those who want something from Felix, the *petitores*; and they were the Jews' (1963, 161 n.2). However, in the Lukan context they have to refer both to the Jews *and* to Paul (Paul had been the speaker since v.10).

Accordingly, the tradition contained the report of the laying of charges by the Jewish authorities (Ananias and Tertullus) against Paul before Felix (in reality Festus, see below 254f.) in Caesarea (cf. v.1b). As the substance of the charge we can substitute the accusation of desecrating the temple which was shown to be part of the tradition above on Acts 21.28 and in the general comments on 246f.

For the characterization of Felix (vv.24-26) as part of the tradition cf. under II.

Luke knows the replacement of Felix in office by Festus (v.27) from a tradition. It reported that Paul was a prisoner in Caesarea when the change took place (cf. the tradition about Paul's stay in Corinth in the time of Claudius). The indication of time, 'two years', also goes back to tradition (cf. Haenchen 1971, 68).

On Schmithals 1982: 'The two-year period also appears at 28.30 (cf.19.10) with a Lukan bias... (cf. the stress that Christianity is politically innocuous)' (215). Against Schmithals: why should the two years here denote political harmlessness?

So for historical reasons the 'two years' might refer to the duration of Felix's term of office; cf. below.

IV Historical

All the elements of tradition that have been reconstructed might have a high claim to historical probability.

The name of the high priest Ananias (who was high priest from about 47 to 59 CE [cf.Schürer 1979, 231]) and the attorney-at-law Tertullus (not known from other sources)(v.1).

The report about the collection, as it is confirmed by the letters of Paul (but cf. the qualifications under III) (v.17).

The laying of the charges by the Jews before Felix is plausible after Paul has been moved to Caesarea (vv.22-24). But in reality this will only have happened during the term of office of Felix's successor Festus (see 253f. below).

The information that Felix was procurator for two years (v.27) corresponds with the combination of statements by Tacitus (*Ann* XIII, 14: at the end of 55 Nero deposes Felix's brother Pallas from being head of the financial administration of the empire [*libertus a rationibus*] and strips him of any influence) and Josephus (*Antt* XX, 182: after Felix is replaced by Festus, the leaders of the Jews of Caesarea accuse Felix before the emperor Nero. It is only because of the intervention of Pallas, whom Nero prized highly *at that time* [*malista de tote dia times agon ekeinon* - note the *tote*], that the charge was evidently rejected). The report given by

Josephus is probably not exclusively gossip (thus Conzelmann 1987, 195, following E.Schwartz) but is accurate in that Pallas intervened on behalf of his brother at a time when Nero held him in high esteem (see the particle *tote*). That was no longer the case after his deposition. (Jewett 1982, 40-44 [bibliography] puts forward another view of the Pallas problem; it needs a thorough new investigation.)

The following historical sequence emerges from the elements of tradition which have been recognized as reliable. Paul was in a Roman prison in Caesarea. The Jewish authorities, led by the high priest Ananias, travelled to Caesarea for a trial of Paul under Felix, and brought with them Tertullus, an attorney experienced in Roman and Jewish law. No trial took place during Felix's two-year procuratorship, but the Jewish authorities did appear before Felix. A trial probably did not take place because Paul only came to Caesarea towards the end of Felix's term of office (in the year 55 – for the dates see Lüdemann 1984, 192f. n.102), or for unknown reasons Felix dragged out the trial.

Schwartz regards a conversation between Felix, accompanied by Drusilla, and Paul as historically probable. Paul brought a gift of money to Jerusalem and Felix could have assumed from his knowlege of this that Paul was not without means and could be supported by the Christian brethren (1963, 160-2). But this view comes to grief on the fact that the section vv.24-26 is redactional throughout.

Acts 25

I Division

25.1-5: Festus and the leaders of the Jews in Jerusalem
  1: Festus comes from Caesarea to Jerusalem
  2-3: Accusation by the high priest and first men of the Jews against Paul and their wish to have Paul brought to Jerusalem (to ambush him on the way)
  4-5: Rejection of this wish by Festus and invitation to the Jews to lay the charge in Caesarea, where Paul will be
6-12: Trial before Festus in Caesarea
  6: Journey by Festus from Jerusalem to Caesarea to open the trial
  7: Accusation by the Jews
  8: Defence of Paul
  9: Pseudo-question by Festus about the possible conveyance of Paul to Jerusalem
  10-11: Paul appeals to Caesar
  12: Festus accepts Paul's appeal
13-22: Festus tells Agrippa about Paul. Agrippa's wish to hear Paul

23-27: (The next day:) Solemn entry by Agrippa and Berenice. Festus presents Paul. Festus wants Agrippa to compose a covering letter (for the emperor) which gives the reason for Paul's arrest

II Redaction

[1-5] Lukan language is visible at the following points (a selection): v.1, *treis*; v.3, *metapempsetai*; v.4, *men oun*. In content vv.2f. are a variant on the ideas known from 23.15: the Jews want to lure Paul into an ambush. So here they ask Festus to send Paul to Jerusalem. Festus's refusal to meet the Jews' wishes is in tension with v.9. But the expected answer to the pseudo-question in v.9 results in the same answer as vv.4f. So the tension can be understood in terms of the redaction and should not be used for source-critical operations.

The section looks like a doublet to ch.24. In both instances the (leaders of) the Jews appear before the procurator (once in Caesarea and then in Jerusalem) to lay a charge against Paul. It is almost certain that Luke was aware that the two scenes were parallel. For the redactional significance and the evaluation of this observation see below, 253f.

[6-12] The following words stand out as Lukan language (a selection): v.6, *diatripsas*; v.7, *paragenomenou, katapherontes, apodeixai*; v.7, genitive absolute; v.9, *katathesthai*; v.10, *eipen*; v.11, *axion thanatou pepracha* (cf. Luke 23.15; Acts 25.25; 2.31), *men oun*; v.12, *syllalesas*.

This section is even more clearly than vv.1-5 a doublet to ch.24. Verse 7 is a repetition of 24.2ff. But (in contrast to the earlier passage) we learn nothing about the content of the Jewish charges (the readers know about them). There is a similar parallel between v.8 and 24.10ff., which depict Paul's defence. Even in v.8 there is only a summary report of Paul's defence, though in contrast to the charges made by the Jews (v.7), v.8 is a succinct summary of the apostle's defence:

'I have not offended either against the law of the Jews or against the temple or against the emperor' (for the Lukan significance see Conzelmann 1960, 142f.)

Verse 9 varies the thought of 24.27 that the procurator wanted to do the Jews a favour. To this end Luke makes Festus ask the pseudo-question whether he should take Paul to Jerusalem and have him judged there. The notion is redactional. (For the 'contradiction' between v.9 and v.4 see above on v.4.) The answer expected is needed for vv.10-11 and v.12, where Paul's coming to Rome, announced long beforehand to the readers and to Paul himself (19.21; 23.11), can be stated on the narrative level. Verse 10 is a Lukan glance forward to the appeal to the emperor which is narrated later: 'Paul's words *epi tou bematos Kaisaros hestos eimi, hou me dei krinesthai* can only express what is later said more simply: *Kaisara epikaloumai*' (Mommsen 1901, 84 n.6).

However, Wellhausen thought that he could demonstrate a tension between v.10 and vv.11f. Verse 10 referred to the judgment of the procurator and only vv.11f. to that of the emperor. He writes: 'But in that case how can he (sc. Paul)... at the end appeal fron the procurator to the emperor, and in the same breath, as if the one did not contradict the other, but followed from it' (1914, 52). But the difficulties are resolved if we understand v.10 as a Lukan glance forward.

In v.11 Paul appeals to the Emperor, and Festus accepts this appeal in v.12: 'You have appealed to Caesar, and to Caesar you shall go.'

[13-22] Festus's report about Paul to Agrippa repeats what we already know (see a similar narrative technique in Acts 10f.) and prepares for the next scene.

[23-27] For an analysis of the language cf. Radl 1975, 200. Paul's meeting with Agrippa and Berenice (cf. v.13) fulfils Agrippa's wish to make Paul's acquaintance, expressed in v.22. In vv.24-27 Paul is presented yet again (by Festus), and v.25 repeats that Paul has done nothing worthy of death. The scene before Agrippa and Berenice is a doublet to that before Felix and Drusilla (24.24-26). It serves redactionally to stress the status of Luke's Paul in world history. Moreover 9.15 is fulfilled with Paul's appcarance before king Agrippa.

III Traditions

That chs.24 and 25 are doublets, as demonstrated above, might be evaluated as follows – incorporating the results of the analysis of ch.24. For ch.25 Luke has the account of a trial before Festus which for redactional reasons he already used as the basis of ch.24 and decked out with speeches by both parties. The tradition used in ch.25 probably excludes the possibility that there had already been a public hearing of Paul, 'whether before the Sanhedrin in Jerusalem or before the Roman procurator in Caesarea in the presence of members of the Sanhedrin' (Wellhausen 1914, 51).

The tradition may have contained a remark about the appeal to the emperor. Since as a rule this appeal was possible only for Roman citizens, the tradition might have depicted Paul's appeal to the emperor with reference to his Roman citizenship. By comparison, Luke evidently does not limit the possibility of an appeal to the emperor to Roman citizens

253

(cf. 25.10f.; 28.18f.). At this point he has disrupted an original connection, as in ch.16, where he gave a false explanation of the need to circumcise Timothy which goes against the tradition (see above, 176f.).

We would very much like to know whether the scene in vv.23-27 goes back to tradition. That is perhaps suggested by the fact that 24.24-26 is an imitation of it. But there is no possibility of defining the contours of the tradition (perhaps a meeting between Paul and the brother-and-sister couple – but to what end?).

IV Historical

In all probability there was a trial of Paul before Festus in Caesarea in which the Jewish leaders of Jerusalem were involved; in the wake of this, Paul appealed to the emperor, referring to his Roman citizenship (for the legal questions cf. Mommsen 1901; Cadbury, *Beg.* V, 297-338; Stolle 1973, 266 n.97; Haenchen 1971, 667 n.2; J.Bleicken, *Senatsgericht und Kaisergericht*, AAWGH.PH 53, Göttingen 1962). The immediate reason for this is not clear. (Had the apostle been condemned to death because of incitement to riot, or did he fear such a sentence?) At least it can be said that in this way he was sure of carrying out his plan to travel to the capital of the Roman empire after completing the collection.

Acts 26

I Division

26.1: Introduction
2-23: Paul's speech
  2-3: *Captatio benevolentiae*
  4-8: Summary retrospect on Paul's life and the charges against him
  9-23: Paul's life from his active persecution of the community to his own persecution
    by Jews
24-29: Conversation of Paul with Festus and Agrippa
30-32: Paul declared innocent by Agrippa and Festus

II Redaction

The whole chapter is a redactional construction with the aim of providing variations on what we already know and in addition demonstrating once again the claim of Christiantity to public status. Paul's great speech in his defence (vv.2-23) no longer makes sense in the course of the action since his appeal to the emperor and its acceptance by Festus means that he is already certain to go to Rome.

[2-23] After the *captatio benevolentiae* in vv.2-3 (cf.24.20), vv.4-8 give a summary retrospect on Paul's life and on the charge against him. In it v.8, like 24.15 previously, stresses Paul's good Jewish faith: God raises the dead (cf. v.23). Paul is judged because of the hope of Israel (vv.6f.; cf. 28.20; 23.6; on this see Haacker 1985 [with bibliography]: Haacker thinks that in his confession of the hope of Israel the Lukan Paul and thus Luke himself are showing solidarity with Israel and therefore also with the Jews living in Luke's present: but cf. Acts 28.28 [see below 264]).

Verses 9-23 are a variant on the conversion stories of chs.9; 22 (for detailed analysis see on Acts 9). Some deviations from the parallels bring out Luke's intention: v.15 contains the statement, 'Saul, Saul, why are you persecuting me? It is hard for you to kick against the goad.' The second half of the verse is either a Greek proverb (cf. 20.35c as a saying of the Lord) or comes from Euripides (*Bacch* 794f.) (see the commentaries). Here Luke shows his education (yet again) and gives theological expression to the fact that it is vain to struggle against God. There is a parallel in content in the (redactional) saying of Gamaliel in Acts 5.38f. Verse 16b speaks of an appearance of Jesus to Paul (*ophthen soi*) – this is a recollection of the christophany to the historical Paul (cf. I Cor.15.8 and already Acts 9.17 [not as an ingredient of the narrative of Paul's conversion but as part of Ananias's speech]). Verses 16-18 are explicitly a description of a mission of Paul to the Gentiles grounded in the christophany. Verse 20 is an address to the readers, to repent and turn to God (cf. Conzelmann 1960, 99-101). With the participle *syllabomenoi*, v. 21 refers back to 23.27. Verses 22f. develop the christological kerygma in formal language. Paul has only proclaimed 'what the prophets and Moses said would come to pass: that the Christ must suffer, and that, by being the first to rise from the dead, he would proclaim light both to the people and to the Gentiles' (vv.22f. – cf. vv.6f.).

[24-29] In v.24 the Gentile Festus interrupts Paul's speech at the theme of resurrection – not by chance (cf. 17.31f.). Verse 25 associates Paul's preaching with *sophrosyne* (a completely un-Pauline term). The Paul who is accused by Festus of *mania* is contrasted with the Greek virtue of

sophrosyne, which Paul has. 'He speaks "words of truth and prudence", which therefore express the objective truth' (Haenchen 1971, 688). Verse 26 stresses the claim of Lukan Christianity to be a public matter: 'This was not done in a corner' (cf. Wengst 1987, 89-104). Verse 27 depicts Agrippa as a loyal Jew who according to v.28 is brought to the verge of conversion.

[30-32] This section makes Agrippa and Festus state that Paul is innocent. *Here the apologetic has reached its narrative climax.*

Section III (and accordingly IV) must be omitted here, since like 25.13-27, Acts 26 (apart from the elements of the conversion/call story which come from tradition [see above, 115f.]) is a redactional composition by Luke. (However, reference should be made to Schille 1983, who identifies 26.16-18 as an 'ordination formula' [450f.].) Cf. Wellhausen 1914: 'The result of 25.13-26.32 is nil: things remain as they were. Weizsäcker rightly regards the whole section as a mere excrescence' (53).

Acts 27

I Division

27.1-5: Journey from Caesarea to Myra
6-44: The shipwreck on the voyage from Myra to Malta
   6-8: Difficult voyage from Myra to Fair Havens
   9-12: Voyage continued despite Paul's warning
   13-20: Shipwreck
   21-26: Those on board encouraged by Paul
   27-32: Sighting of land; the attempt of the crew to flee is prevented by Paul
   33-38: The meal at sea and the unloading of the ship
   39-44: The ship is beached and all are saved

II Redaction

[1-5] 'Italy' in v.1, as in 18.2; 27.6, stands for Rome; *tou* + infinitive and *onomati* are Lukan language, as are *epibantes, anechthemen* in v.2 and *katechthemen* in v.3. The remark that the centurion Julius allowed Paul to be cared for by his friends recalls 24.23. In this way the Romans show

256

respect to Paul. The notion of their friendly disposition similarly appears in 28.2 (cf. also 19.31). The prepositional construction (here *dia*) with the accusative + infinitive is frequent in Luke. *katelthomen* in v.5 is Lukan language.

[6-44] The analysis of the redaction has to begin from the following observation: large parts of the text make use of technical nautical expressions and lead us to forget that this is an account of the voyage of Paul and his companions. Moreover, in connection with this, it is striking that the text mentions Paul only in four passages, and that these can be detached from the action without difficulty.

Now it is often said: 'That in Acts 27 Paul plays a special role only in the insertions fits the situation precisely: Paul was going to Rome as a defendant facing a life-and-death charge on board a prison transport... And the particular stress on nautical features in Acts 27 can be explained from the fact that the other journeys took place at favourable times of the year and therefore did not call for any unusual nautical measures' (Kratz 1979, 336f.).

However, these consideration are an over-hasty historicization. The first concern must be the literary form of the text.

The four passages which stand out (see above) involve the following verses: 9-11; 21-26; 31,33-36; 43.

[9-11,21-16] The passages indicated depict Paul as a prophet of disaster whose advice is not taken (vv.9-11) and as a prophet of eventual rescue (vv.21-26) which takes place because according to the divine plan (*dei*) Paul has to appear before the emperor in Rome (cf.25.11f.,21,25-27; 26.32), and God has given him all his fellow-voyagers (v.24; cf.v.44b). The apostle explicitly refers in vv.21,26 to the advice that he had given before the disaster (v.21b: 'You should have listened to me, and should not have set sail from Crete and incurred this injury [*hybris* – cf. v.10] and loss [*zemia* – cf. v.10].' Cf. also the way in which *parainein* [v.9] is picked up in v.22 and *psyche* [v.10] in v.22b.). At the same time v.26 points forward to 28.1.

[31,33-36] After thwarting the plan of the crew to flee (v.31), Paul invites all those on board to take food (vv.33-36). The link forward (vv.37ff.) is uneven; in v.37, in between the eating and being satisfied, the number of those on board is given as 276. This figure is evidently a remnant of the old report, which had nothing to do with Paul. Luke perhaps found the occasion for the insertion of vv.31,33-36 with a meal in the middle, in the food reported in v.38. As an analogy cf.v.12, the discussion which was possibly the external occasion for inserting Paul's advice in vv.9-11.

257

[43] The soldiers want to kill the prisoners because of the shipwreck, so that no one escapes (v.42). But the centurion plans to save Paul (cf. the signs of his friendliness to Paul as early as v.3) and first orders all those who can swim to jump overboard, after which the non-swimmers get to land on the wreckage. As we are not explicitly told what happened to Paul, for whose sake the centurion gave the above orders, we are to conclude:

'The story of the centurion's apt decision thus, obviously, has nothing to do with Paul; it belongs to the description of the voyage, and, by the introduction of four words, has been made into an account concerning Paul' (Dibelius 1956, 205).

With the four insertions Luke is expressing this:

1. Although he is a prisoner, Paul is the one who has control and is the only one to keep calm. While his first speech (v.10) was rejected (v.11) and there was no reaction to his second speech (vv.21-26), the third (vv.31,33-34) gets a positive reaction (vv.32,36). Paul has beome a model to all, and the scene of the meal with thanksgiving to God (v.35) becomes the climax (cf. Reicke 1948, 410; Kratz 1979, 331f.).

2. The shipwreck is a narrative means by which Luke can show that the journey to Rome is in accord with God's plan. The buffeting of nature cannot hold up the divine plan.

3. The rescue of Paul (and all those sailing with him) from shipwreck once again proves the apostle innocent in the eyes of the reader (cf. D.Ladouceur, *HTR* 73, 1980, 435-49 [bibliography and sources for this *popular* view, which probably would not have found any echo before a Roman court]).

4. On the presupposition that the following definition of the original material is correct, in Acts 27 Luke shows once again that he has ventured into Hellenistic literature. By taking over this material he caters to the taste of his Hellenistic readers (see Plümacher 1972, 14).

III Traditions

[1-5] The name of Julius the centurion of the Augustan cohort (v.1) might reflect tradition, like the name of the Thessalonian Christian Aristarchus (v.2). His appearance at the beginning of this journey is all the more remarkable, as he was also already Paul's travelling companion on the last journey to Jerusalem (19.29; 20.4).

The journey from Caesarea via Sidon and Cyprus to Myra (according to the Acts of Paul, the apostle was active here as a missionary miracle-worker [see Hennecke-Schneemelcher-Wilson, *New Testament Apocry-*

pha II, London and Philadelphia 1965, 333f., 363f.]) could go back to tradition. For in comparison with the subsequent episode it is told both briefly and pertinently (v.5: this distinction must be stressed, *inter alia* against Weiser's theory that vv.1-5 were an ingredient of the subsequent travel account [1985, 659-61]). But it may equally well derive from Luke, who in that case would have used it to prepare for the journey which follows.

[6-44] The report of the ensuing shipwreck is a coherent one, once the redactional additions have been excluded. Verse 8 ('...we came to a place called Fair Havens, near which was the city of Lasea') is picked up by v.12 ('and because the harbour was not suitable to winter, the majority advised to put to sea from there...'). Indeed it might almost be said that the removal of vv.9-11 is needed to make the original connection understandable again.

Verse 20 ('And when neither sun nor stars appeared for many a day, and no small tempest lay on us, all hope of our being saved was at last abandoned') is picked up by v.27 ('When the fourteenth night had come... about midnight the sailors suspected that they were nearing land').

For v.43 see 258 above.

Only vv.31, 33-36 cannot be clearly demarcated by literary means, but only in an approximate way. It should be noted that escape (v.30) is a theme of romances. However, the course of the action (in the tradition) is clear: the ship nears land, so the 276 people travelling in it throw the grain (or their own provisions? – cf. vv.18f.) into the sea to lighten it.

Because of its detailed knowledge of navigation, the tradition thus discovered is striking and differs from the accounts of voyages in Acts 20.1-21.16 by its detail and the nautical technical terms (only in two passages in Acts 20.1-21.16 are there nautical techical terms: 21.1, *euthydromein* and 21.3, *anaphainein; apophortizesthai*). The narrative resembles the many parallels of accounts of voyages in ancient literature (cf. Plümacher 1972, 14f.n.43; Robbins 1978), which like them have a narrative in the first person plural and partly go over into the third person plural (cf.27.17). (In many cases these were prompted by the voyages of Odysseus [*Od* IXf.].) The account probably has no genetic connection with the journey from Caesarea to Myra, nor is it by an eye-witness (in terms of genre the 'we' goes with accounts of voyages), but is a literary entity, the result of his reading to which Luke has added the person of Paul at the passages mentioned. Given the wealth of instances which Weiser 1985, 660, has produced (cf. also B.E.Perry, *The Ancient Romances*, Berkeley 1967, 326f.) there should no longer be any dispute here. Lucian, *De mercede*, 1f., is particularly interesting for a *Sitz im*

Leben of this narrative type: he says that some people invent stories of their rescue from a shipwreck in order to be regarded as friends of the gods and to receive support. The only open question is whether Luke took over a complete account or possibly formulated it himself on the basis of Hellenistic models (thus Schille 1983, 469). However, in the last instance there is no answer to the question how the figure of Paul can be excised so cleanly.

IV Historical

[1-5] If the stages in the journey underlying 1-5 go back to tradition, they might provide some historically reliable information about Paul's last journey and perhaps derive from Aristarchus's report. But for the reasons mentioned under III, a last doubt remains. If the stages on the journey do not derive from tradition, there is no guarantee that the elements of tradition (Aristarchus, Julius of the Augustan cohort) have been given their correct historical setting by Luke at this point.

[6-44] These verses (without redactional additions) are the result of Luke's readings and probably have no point of reference in history. The assumption by Dibelius 1956, 'that, whether through Luke's being an eye-witness, or whether by means of someone else's tradition in his possession, the recollection of Paul's stormy journey to Italy' (7f.) was the occasion for the composition of this voyage is therefore unnecessary, though we cannot arrive at complete certainty. In all probability Paul did not suffer any shipwreck before Malta on his last journey to Rome, but he will have sailed there, since the account in 28.11f. might reproduce reliable tradition of a journey from Malta to Rome (see below, 265).

For H.Warnecke, *Die tatsächliche Romreise des Apostels Paulus*, Stuttgart 1987 (who claims that Paul was not shipwrecked off Malta but off the western Greek island of Cephallenia) see the devastating review by J.Wehnert, *Lutherische Monatshefte* 21, 1989, 98-100.

Acts 28.1-10

I Division

28.1-2: Rescue off Malta and friendly reception
3-6: Paul survives the poisonous snake-bite
7-10: Further miracles by Paul

  7: Paul received by the chief man of the island, Poplius
  8: Healing of Poplius's father by Paul
  9: Summary: Paul's activity as a miracle-worker
  10: Honour shown by the people of Malta and provisions for the continuation of the voyage

II Redaction

[1-2] Lukan language can be found in v.1, *diasothentes* (cf.27.44); v.2, *pareichon*. Friendly welcome after a shipwreck is a theme of travel accounts (cf. Robbins 1978, 229f. [with examples]). In that case, in composing this scene Luke would have kept to a literary model. The *philanthropia* shown to Paul and his companions by the barbarians recalls the friendly treatment of Paul by the centurion Julius (27,3, *philanthropos*). – Moreover the fate of the non-Christians involved in the shipwreck is not discussed further, since it is superfluous to the further action.

[3-6] The accumulation of participles (v.3), the direct speech (v.4), *men oun* (v.5) and the genitive absolute (v.6) are clearly redactional features. By means of this secular miracle (there is no reference to Jesus), Luke wants to show the overpowering might of the divine man Paul (significantly, in contrast to 14.11-18, there is no repudiation of the view that Paul is a god). So with this story Luke shows that nothing – not even a lethal snake-bite – can prevent the protagonist from reaching the goal that has been appointed by God (cf. Luke 10.19).

[7-10] Lukan terminology can be seen at the following points: v.7, *hyperchen, choria, onomati, anadexamenos, treis, exenisen*; v.8, *egeneto de* + infinitive, *pros hon, eiselthon, proseuxamenos, epitheis tas cheiras* (cf. v.10): v.9, *hoi loipoi, proserchonto*; v.10, *hoi kai, anagomenois, ta pros*.

    Luke seems to have had Luke 4.38-41 in mind when writing vv.8-9. On this presupposition the following parallels become understandable: Luke 4.38, *synechomene pyreto megalo* (Mark differs) corresponds to *pyretois kai dysenterio synechomenon* (Acts 28.8); Luke 4.40a, *asthen-ountas* (Mark differs) corresponds to *astheneias* (Acts 28.9); Luke 4.40b, *tas cheiras epitiheis* (Mark differs) corresponds to *epitheis tas cheiras* (Acts 28.8). In the one case we have the healing of a mother (Luke), in the other that of a father (Acts). – Such a view is supported by the fact that the order is the same in each case: miracle (Luke 4.38-39/Acts 28.8)/ summary (Luke 4.40-41/Acts 28.9), which is already provided by Mark 1.29-34. Therefore Acts 28.8-9 can probably be regarded as a Lukan composition on the basis of Luke 4.38-41 (on Kirschschläger 1979, 521, who sees the working-over of a 'tradition' in Acts 28.8-9).

The redactional significance of vv.7-10 matches that of vv.3-6: Paul's power as a divine man is demonstrated. At the same time, Paul's dealings with the 'first man' of the island demonstrates once again the social dimension or the universality of Christianity (cf. Paul's dealings with people in high positions elsewhere in Acts).

III Traditions

The story of Paul's survival from a poisonous snake-bite is either the result of Luke's reading (cf. Dibelius 1956, 8 n.16) which has a basis in tradition in secular miracle stories (cf. the commentaries) or derives from a personal legend which came into being later (cf. Schille 1983, 471f. [aretalogy]).

The name Poplius (the Greek form of the Roman *praenomen* Publius) and the explanation that Poplius was the 'first of the island' (*protos tes nesou*) probably reflect tradition, since this title is also attested elsewhere for Malta (cf. Wikenhauser 1921, 343-6). Luke might have used a station which connected Paul's stay on Malta with the person of the first man of the island, Poplius (as an analogy cf. Acts 18.12-17). This verdict may be thought optimistic, and the elements of tradition mentioned can be attributed to Luke's general knowledge. But in that case it would be hardly possible to explain how Luke could have spoken accurately of the 'first of the island'.

IV Historical

The tradition of a stay by Paul on Malta might be historically reliable, as might its chronology. It took place when Paul was on his way to Rome as a prisoner. (Paul had no previous possibility of staying on Malta.) No further information is available about the person of the first man of the island, Poplius. (Curiously, Judge 1964, 24, seems to regard v.6 as a historically reliable statement.)

262

Acts 28.11-31

I Division

28.11-16: Journey from Malta via Syracuse, Rhegium and Puteoli to Rome and welcome by the Christian brethren there. Paul's privileges in his Roman captivity: private quarters watched over by a guard

17-28: Paul meets with the Jews of Rome and preaches (v.29 is secondary)

30-31: Paul preaches unhindered for two years (in his Roman abode [?])

II Redaction

[**11-16**] The following linguistic elements are Lukan: v.11, *treis* (cf. v.12), *anechthemen*; v.14, *adelphous* (cf. v.15).

A tension is visible in vv.14-16 (as a parallel instance cf.21.15-18 and the commentary by Weiser 1985, 672). Verse 14b reports the arrival of Paul and his companions in Rome (*kai houtos eis ten Romen elthamen*), while v.16a depicts yet another arrival in Rome (in accord with v.16a and in tension with v.14b, v.15a reports that the Christian community sent out representatives to meet Paul at the Forum Appii [about forty-three miles from Rome] and Tres Tabernae [about thirty-three miles from Rome]). Conzelmann (1987, 224) has explained the tension by saying that Luke has anticipated the arrival in Rome by v.14b. But the reason for this (about which Conzelmann says nothing) is not clear. (Or is v.14b to be understood as a *hysteron proteron* which anticipates the final destination of the journey and at the same time makes possible the linguistically skilful connection *kakeithen* [v.15]?) The other possibility put forward by Haenchen (1971, 719) seems more probable: v.14b is part of a travel account, while v.15 is a redactional elaboration of it in which Luke was concerned to present the reception of Paul by the Roman community as being like that of the Jerusalem church in 21.17. However, Luke does not return to this later, because the existence of that Christian community would have got in the way of the conversations with the Jews (cf. the failure to mention the Jerusalem community in Acts 22-26). Verse 16 fits the redactional view of Luke well, namely that on the whole the Romans were well disposed to Paul (cf. 27.3 as a parallel to v.16 and the Roman protection of Paul from the Jews in Acts 22-26). However, redaction and tradition need not always clash.

[**17-28**] The verses are Lukan throughout (cf. similarly Roloff 1981, 370, who also includes vv.30-31 in this judgment). The section is marked out by particularly numerous Lukan characteristics of language; cf. just for v.17: *egeneto de* + infinitive, *treis, sygkalesasthai, synelthonton, andres adelphoi, enantion, lao, ethesi, patroois*. So there is no need of further investigation of the Lukan language in this section.

The content is a last discussion by Luke of Paul's relationship with the Jews and repeats what has been said earlier. Paul has not acted either against his people or against his ancestral customs (v.17; cf. 25.8; 21.21). The Jews compelled him to appeal to the emperor when the Romans had wanted to free him (vv.18f.; cf.25.9-12). Paul is in prison for the hope of Israel (cf. 23.6; 24.15f.; 26.6). Verses 21f. contradict v.15. In contrast to vv.21f. v.15 presupposes a Christian community in Rome. It is probably not mentioned in vv.21f. because Luke needs Paul to be first to preach the gospel in Rome, so that he can make him enter into dialogue with the Jews in the city (Roloff 1981 differs: Luke is silent about the community because he knows that its relationship to Paul was not clear [372]. The view he expresses that if the above view that there were already Christians in Rome was right, Luke would similarly have had to have keep quiet, is also unconvincing, see above on v.15). The connection between *basileia* and verbs of proclamation is Lukan (cf. on 19.8 and v.31). The preaching before the Jews (v.23) once again sums up the Lukan kerygma. The reaction of the Jews is described redactionally in such a way as to give the expression that the majority of them are a hopeless case.

However, Harnack thought that the statement in v.24, 'And some of them were ocnvinced by his words but others were unbelieving', does not match the final conclusion very well: 'Know then that this salvation of God has been sent to the Gentiles: they will listen.' Therefore v.24 is the ingredient of a tradition. But v.24 shows 'an effect with which the terrible cursing of the Isaiah quotation does not fit well; it comes like a pistol shot' (1906, 93 n.3). However, 17.4; 19.9 show similar redactional reactions by the Jews to Paul's preaching. Moreover in content the stress lies on the fact that Paul's preaching produces a division among the Jews. Verse 24 can therefore well be understood as redactional preparation for what follows (cf. Roloff 1981, 374).

[26-28] The quotation yet again repeats that the gospel will now be preached only to the Gentiles (see 13.46f.; 18.6). Conzelmann (1960, 145-50) is right in saying that the Lukan church is Gentile Christian (cf. the survey by Sanders 1984 [lit.]), however much one may regret its historical consequences.

[30-31] The language of v.30 is Lukan (*enemeinen, apedecheto, eisporeuomenos*). Verse 31 gives a redactional description of Paul preaching the gospel unhindered in Rome. Behind this is some apologetic concern. The Roman state is told, 'Let it be so'.

III Traditions

The journey from Malta to Rome via Syracuse, Rhegium and Puteoli may be part of the tradition. Perhaps Aristarchus is the one who reported it. (Weiser 1985, 673, takes the travel account as part of the narrative of the voyage used in Acts 27.)

The narrative about the reception of Paul by representatives of the Roman community (v.15) was no longer part of the tradition (see 263 above on the form of the scene). However, Luke knew the existence of the Roman community and may indeed have written Luke-Acts in Rome (though of more recent commentators Roloff 1981, 5 ["Italy"] is the only one to advocate this theory).

The information about Paul's imprisonment in Rome (vv.16,30) might go back to tradition, because it is hard to see why Luke should have created the specific information of v.16 (the *koine* reading is secondary, cf. Conzelmann 1987, 224) and v.30. *enemeinen... en idio misthomati* is almost unanimously translated 'in his own hired dwelling'. But there is no evidence for this translation; it could equally well be translated 'he lived at his own expense' (cf. Bauer 1979, 523; Lake/Cadbury, *Beg.* IV, 348: and for the controversy see the literature in Schneider 1982, 420 n.95).

From the information 'two years' it is often argued that the author knew of the change which took place later (Paul's martyrdom, see 20.18-38) and kept quiet about it for apologetic reasons (cf. Haenchen 1971, 732; Conzelmann 1987, 224; cf. also Schneider 1982: 'For Luke's conception the two-year stay of Paul as a prisoner immediately precedes his death' [412]). One can only say that because of the hints in Acts 20.18-38, etc., Luke knew that Paul died a martyr death, but preferred not to report it. We cannot discover when this happened from either the elements of tradition in the text or from the redactional content.

IV Historical

The tradition that Paul was transported from Malta via Syracuse, Rhegium and Puteoli to Rome is a historical fact.

The information in the tradition about Paul's imprisonment is probably historically reliable. It was the *custodia libera et aperta et in usum hominis instituta* in which as a rule the accused was guarded by two soldiers – in Paul's case one. In this custody it was conceivable that the prisoner could go about his business. So Paul will have practised his craft (regardless of how we translate *misthoma*), and will have contributed to the cost of the soldier who guarded him (for the above see Wikenhauser 1921, 360; Sherwin-White 1963, 108-19).

We may conclude from I Clement 5.5-7 that Paul died as a martyr in Rome:

I Clement 5.5-7: 'And Paul, because of jealousy and contention, has become the very type of endurance rewarded; ⁶He was in bonds seven times, he was exiled, he was stoned. He preached in the East and in the West, winning a noble reputation for his faith. ⁷He taught righteousness to all the world; and after reaching the furthest limits of the West (*terma tes duseos*), and bearing his testimony before kings and rulers, he passed out of this world and was received into the holy places. In him we have one of the greatest of all examples of endurance.'

The text is already heavily stylized and contains elements of a 'rhetorical panegytic modelled on the classical motif of the truly wise man battling in the arena of the spirit' (Bornkamm 1971, 105). The phrase 'limits of the West' either derives from the fact that the author inferred from Rom.15.24f.,28 that Paul had carried on a mission in Spain (cf. also the probable use of II Cor.11.23-33 at the beginning of v.6), or describes Rome as the limits of the West (for the author the westernmost point and the place of Paul's martyrdom are identical [cf. Lindemann 1979, 78]). Despite the stylization mentioned and the evidence that nothing is said about the circumstances of Paul's death, that he died a violent death in Rome is not in doubt (I Clement is a letter from the Roman community), since the words 'bearing his testimony before kings and princes' (*martyresas epi ton hegoumenon*) refer to his martyr death (cf. I Tim.6.13; MPol.1.1; 19,1,21f.), an interpretation which is further confirmed by the clause 'he passed out of this world' (*kai houtos apellage tou kosmou*) which follows immediately. Cf. Bornkamm 1971, 105f.

We do not know the exact date of Paul's death. Nero's persecution of Christians in 64, which is described thoroughly by Tacitus (*Ann* XV, 44), has been suggested (cf. also Suetonius, *Nero* 16). But an earlier date is also possible if Paul was found guilty in the trial brought on by his appeal to the emperor (cf. Weizsäcker 1902, 457f.). Moreover chronological considerations generally suggest that the date of Paul's arrival in Rome is to be put before 60 CE (cf. Lüdemann 1984: arrival and arrest in Jerusalem 52 or 55 [262f.], which would give 54 or 57 for the date of Paul's arrival in Rome. There is another calculation in Jewett 1982, 44f., who gives 61 as the *terminus ad quem* for Paul's arrival in Rome [in my view this calculation is made on doubtful presuppositions]).

If Philippians was written from Rome (of the more recent commentaries on Acts only Roloff 1981, 372, decides on this theory), then at least this letter sheds some light on the obscurity of Paul's 'activity' in the capital. In that case Phil.1.15-17 would focus on the situation in Rome, and one could connect it with some enmity towards Paul which can no longer be specified (on this cf. Lüdemann 1983, 152-8; and cf. the use of Philippians [alongside Colossians and Philemon] to portray conflicts in the Roman community by Weiss 1959, 382-92, and Meyer III, 490-500). However, unfortunately it is not certain that Philippians (and Philemon and Colossians) was written in Rome.

Bibliography

Preliminary note. In order to save space, from the start I have abbreviated the works I have cited, by giving just the name of the author and the publication date of the edition I have used. On the whole bibliographical references to the passage in question are given in full, and are not included in the index. Similarly, I have not included dictionary articles from *RAC*, *TRE*, *TDNT* and *EWNT* in this bibliography. For the extent of the literature used see 23 above.

Aejmelaeus, Lars, *Wachen vor dem Ende*, Schriften der Finnischen Exegetischen Gesellschaft 44, Helsinki *1985*

– , *Die Rezeption der Paulusbriefe in der Miletrede (Apg 20:18-35)*, Annales Academiae Scientiarum Fennicae B.232, Helsinki *1987*

Aune, David E., *Prophecy in Early Christianity and the Ancient Mediterranean World*, Grand Rapids *1983*

Barrett, Charles Kingsley, *Luke the Historian in Recent Study*, London *1961*

– , 'Light on the Holy Scripture from Simon Magus (Acts 8,4-25)', in J.Kremer (ed.), *Les Actes des Apôtres*, BETL, Gembloux and Leuven *1979*, 281-95

Bauer, Walter (, F.W.Arndt and W.F.Gingrich), *A Greek-English Lexicon of the New Testament and Other Early Christian Literature*, Chicago ²*1979*

Bauernfeind, Otto, *Die Apostelgeschichte*, THK 5, Leipzig *1939*; reprinted in id., *Kommentar und Studien zur Apostelgeschichte*, ed. V.Metelmann, WUNT 22, Tübingen *1980*

Baur, Ferdinand Christian, *Paulus, der Apostel Jesu Christi*, Stuttgart *1845*, second edition ed. E.Zeller, I,II, Leipzig *1866*, *1867*

The Beginnings of Christianity I-V, ed. F.J.Foakes Jackson and Kirsopp Lake, London *1920*-*1933* (abbreviated *Beg.* I-V)

Benz, Ernst, *Die Vision*, Stuttgart *1969*

Berger, Klaus, *Formgeschichte des Neuen Testaments*, Heidelberg *1984*

Bernheim, Ernst, *Lehrbuch der historischen Methode und der Geschichtsphilosophie* I, II, Leipzig ⁵⁺⁶*1908*, reprinted New York 1960

Beyschlag, Karlmann, *Simon Magus und die christliche Gnosis*, WUNT 16, Tübingen *1974*

Bihler, Johannes, *Die Stephanusgeschichte im Zusammenhang der Apostelgeschichte*, MTS.H 16, Munich *1963*

Bornkamm, Günther, *Paul*, London and New York 1971, reissued *1985*

Bovon, François, 'Tradition et rédaction en Actes 10,1-11,18', *ThZ* 26, *1970*, 22-45

– , *Luc le théologien*, Neuchâtel and Paris *1978*

– , *Lukas in neuer Sicht*, Biblisch-Theologische Studien 8, Neukirchen-Vluyn *1985*

Brinkman, John A., 'The Literary Background of the "Catalogue of the Nations" (Acts 2,9-11)', *CBQ* 25, *1963*, 418-27

Bruce, Frederick Fyvie, *The Acts of the Apostles*, London ²*1952*

Bultmann, Rudolf, *Exegetica*, ed.E.Dinkler, Tübingen *1967*

– , *The Gospel according to John*, Oxford *1971*

– , *The History of the Synoptic Tradition*, Oxford ²*1968*

– , *The Theology of the New Testament*, New York and London *1952, 1955*

Burchard, Christoph, *Der dreizehnte Zeuge*, FRLANT 106, Göttingen *1970*

– , 'A Note on RHEMA in JosAs 17:1f; Luke 2:15,17; Acts 10:37', *NT* 27, *1985*, 281-95

Buss, Matthäus F.-J., *Die Missionspredigt des Apostels Paulus im Pisidischen Antiochen*, Stuttgart *1980*

Busse, Ulrich, *Die Wunder des Propheten Jesus*, Stuttgart ²*1979*

Cadbury, Henry Joel, 'Lexical Notes on Luke-Acts I', *JBL* 44, *1925*, 214-27

– , 'Lexical Notes on Luke-Acts III', *JBL* 45, *1926*, 305-22

– , *The Making of Luke-Acts*, New York *1927*, reissued London 1968

– , *The Book of Acts in History*, London *1955*

– , 'Four Features of Lucan Style', in L.E.Keck and J.L.Martyn (eds.), *Studies in Luke-Acts* (FS P.Schubert), Nashville and New York *1966*, reprinted Philadelphia 1980, 87-102

Campenhausen, Hans von, 'Das Bekenntnis im Urchristentum', *ZNW* 63, *1972*, 210-53

Cohen, Shaye J.D., 'The Temple and the Synagogue', in T.G.Madsen (ed.), *The Temple in Antiquity*, Religious Studies Monograph Series 9, Provo, Utah *1984*, 151-74

– , 'Was Timothy Jewish (Acts 16.1-3)? Patristic Exegesis, Rabbinic Law, and Matrilineal Descent', *JBL* 105, *1986*, 251-68

Conzelmann, Hans, *The Acts of the Apostles*, Hermeneia, Philadelphia *1987*

– , *Theologie als Schriftauslegung*, BEvTh 65, Munich *1974*

– , *The Theology of St Luke*, London *1960*, reissued 1982

– , *A History of Primitive Christianity*, London *1973*

Dauer, Anton, *Johannes und Lukas*, Würzburg *1984*

Deissmann, Adolf, *Light from the Ancient East*, London ²*1927*

Dessau, Hermann, 'Der Name des Apostels Paulus', *Hermes* 45, *1910*, 347-68

Dibelius, Martin, 'Herodes und Pilatus', ZNW 16, *1915*, 113-26 = in id., *Botschaft und Geschichte* I, Tübingen 1953, 278-92

– , review of E.Meyer, *Ursprung und Anfänge des Christentums*, in *DLZ* 45, *1924*, cols.1635-43

– , *Studies in the Acts of the Apostles*, London and New York *1956*

– , *From Tradition to Gospel*, London 1934 reissued Cambridge *1971*

Dietrich, Wolfgang, *Das Petrusbild der lukanischen Schriften*, BWANT 94, Stuttgart, etc. *1972*

Dietzfelbinger, Christian, *Die Berufung des Paulus als Ursprung seiner Theologie*, WMANT 58, Neukirchen-Vluyn *1985*

Dinkler, Erich, 'Philippus und der ANER AITHIOPS (Apg 8, 26-40)', in E.E.Ellis and E.Grässer (eds.), *Jesus und Paulus* (FS W.G.Kümmel), Göttingen *1975*, 85-95

Droysen, Johann Gustav, *Historik: Vorlesungen über Enzyklopädie und Methodologie der Geschichte*, ed. R.Hübner, Munich = Darmstadt ³*1958*

Dunn, James D.G., *Jesus and the Spirit*, London and Philadelphia *1975*

Dupont, Jacques, *Les Sources du Livre des Actes*, Bruges *1960*

– , *Etudes sur les Actes des Apôtres*, Lectio Divina 45, Paris *1967*

– , *Nouvelles Etudes sur les Actes des Apôtres*, Paris *1984*

270

Easton, Burton Scott, *The Pastoral Epistles*, New York *1947*

Elliger, Winfried, *Paulus in Griechenland*, SBS 92/93, Stuttgart *1978*

– , *Ephesos: Geschichte einer antiken Weltstadt*, UB 375, Stuttgart, etc. *1985*

Ellis, Edward Earle, *Prophecy and Hermeneutic in Early Christianity*, WUNT 18, Tübingen = Grand Rapids *1978*

Emmelius, Johann-Christoph, *Tendenzkritik und Formengeschichte: Der Beitrag Franz Overbecks zur Auslegung der Apostelgeschichte im 19.Jahrhundert*, FKDG 27, Göttingen *1975*

Friedrich, Gerhard, 'Lukas 9, 51 und die Entrückungschristologie des Lukas', in P.Hoffmann, N.Brox and W.Pesch (eds.), *Orientierung an Jesus* (FS J.Schmid), Freiburg, Basel and Vienna *1973*, 48-77 = *Auf das Wort kommt es an*, ed. J.Friedrich, Göttingen *1978*, 26-55

– , *Die Verkündigung des Todes Jesu im Neuen Testament*, Biblisch-Theologische Studien 6, Neukirchen-Vluyn *1982* (²*1985*)

Gasque, W.Ward, *A History of the Criticism of the Acts of the Apostles*, BGBE 17, Tübingen *1975*

Georgi, Dieter, *Die Geschichte der Kollekte des Paulus für Jerusalem*, ThF 38, Hamburg *1965*

Goldstein, Jonathan A., *I Maccabees*, Anchor Bible 41, Garden City, New York *1976*

Goltz, Eduard von der, *Das Gebet in der ältesten Christenheit*, Leipzig *1901*

Grässer, Erich, *Das Problem der Parusieverzögerung in den synoptischen Evangelien und in der Apostelgeschichte*, BZNW 22, Berlin and New York ³*1977*

– , 'Die Parusieerwartung in der Apostelgeschichte', in J.Kremer (ed.), *Les Actes des Apôtres*, BETL 48, Gembloux and Leuven *1979*, 99-127

Haacker, Klaus, 'Das Pfingstwunder als exegetisches Problem', in O.Böcher and K.Haacker (eds.), *Verborum Veritas* (FS G.Stählin), Wuppertal *1970*, 125-31

– , 'Dibelius und Cornelius: Ein Beispiel formgeschichtlicher Überlieferungskritik', *BZ* NF 24, *1980*, 234-51

– , 'Das Bekenntnis des Paulus zur Hoffnung Israels nach der Apostelgeschichte des Lukas', *NTS* 31, *1985*, 437-51

Haenchen, Ernst, *The Acts of the Apostles*, Oxford and Philadelphia *1971*

Hahn, Ferdinand, 'Die Himmelfahrt Jesu: Ein Gespräch mit Gerhard Lohfink', *Bib* 55, *1974*, 418-46

– , 'Das Problem alter christologischer Überlieferungen in der Apostelgeschichte unter besonderer Berücksichtigung von Act 3, 19-21', in J.Kremer (ed.), *Les Actes des Apôtres*, BETL 48, Gembloux and Leuven *1979*, 129-54

Harnack, Adolf (von), *Geschichte der altchristlichen Literatur bis Eusebius* I.1,2; II.1,2, Leipzig 1893, 1893; *1897*, 1904

– , *Beiträge zur Einleitung in das Neue Testament* I: *Lukas der Arzt*, Leipzig *1906*

– , *Beiträge zur Einleitung in das Neue Testament* III: *Die Apostelgeschichte*, Leipzig *1908*

– , *Beiträge zur Einleitung in das Neue Testament* IV: *Neue Untersuchungen zur Apostelgeschichte und zur Abfassungszeit der synoptischen Evangelien*, Leipzig *1911*

– , 'Ist die Rede des Paulus in Athen ein ursprünglicher Bestandteil der Apostelgeschichte?', *TU* 39.1, Leipzig *1913a*, 1-46

– , 'Judentum und Judenchristentum in Justins Dialog mit Trypho', in *TU* 39.1, Leipzig *1913b*, 47-92

271

– , *The Expansion of Christianity in the First Three Centuries*, London 1904 (two vols.) reissued New York 1962

Hedrick, Charles W., 'Paul's Conversion/Call: A Comparative Analysis of the Three Reports in Acts', *JBL* 100, 1981, 415-32

Hengel, Martin, 'Maria Magdalena und die Frauen als Zeugen', in O.Betz, M.Hengel and P.Schmidt (eds.), *Abraham unser Vater* (FS O.Michel), AGJU 5, Leiden and Cologne 1963, 243-56

– , 'Proseuche und Synagoge: Jüdische Gemeinde, Gotteshaus und Gottesdienst in der Diaspora und in Palästina', in G.Jeremias et al. (ed.), *Tradition und Glaube* (FS K.G.Kuhn), Göttingen 1971, 157-84

– , *Judaism and Hellenism*, London and Philadelphia 1974

– , 'Between Jesus and Paul', in *Between Jesus and Paul*, London and Philadelphia 1983a, 1-29

– , 'Luke the Historian and the Geography of Palestine in the Acts of the Apostles', ibid., 97-127 (1983b)

– , *Die Zeloten*, AGJU 1, Leiden and Cologne ²1976

– , *Acts and the History of Earliest Christianity*, London and Philadelphia 1979

– , 'Jakobus der Herrenbruder – der erste "Papst"?', in E.Grässer and O.Merk (eds.), *Glaube und Eschatologie* (FS W.G.Kümmel), Tübingen 1985, 71-104

Hock, Ronald F., *The Social Context of Paul's Ministry*, Philadelphia 1980

Holtz, Traugott, ' "Euer Glaube an Gott": Zu Form und Inhalt von I Thess 1.9f.', in R.Schnackenburg et al. (eds.), *Die Kirche des Anfangs (FS H.Schürmann)*, ETS 38, Leipzig, Freiburg, Basel and Vienna 1978, 459-88

Holtzmann, Heinrich Julius, *Die Apostelgeschichte*, HC 1.2, Tübingen and Leipzig ²1892 (³1901)

– , 'Harnacks Untersuchungen zur Apostelgeschichte', *DLZ* 29, 1908, cols.1093-9

Hommel, Hildebrecht, 'Neue Forschungen zur Areopagrede Acta 17', *ZNW* 46, 1955, 145-78 = id., *Sebasmata* II, WUNT 32, Tübingen 1984, 83-113

Horn, Friedrich Wilhelm, *Glaube und Handeln in der Theologie des Lukas*, GTA 26, Göttingen 1983

Hyldahl, Nils, *Die paulinische Chronologie*, AThD 19, Leiden 1986

Irmscher, Johannes (ed.), *Lexikon der Antike*, Leipzig = Bayreuth ⁶1985

Jacquier, Eugène, *Les Actes des Apôtres*, EtB 17, Paris 1926

Jeremias, Joachim, 'Paarweise Sendung im Neuen Testament', in id., *Abba*, Göttingen 1966, 132-9

– , *Jerusalem in the Time of Jesus*, London and Philadelphia 1969

– , *New Testament Theology*, Vol.1. *The Proclamation of Jesus*, London and Philadelphia 1971

– , *Die Sprache des Lukasevangeliums*, KEK Sonderband, Göttingen 1980

Jervell, Jacob, *The Unknown Paul*, Minneapolis 1984

Jewett, Robert, *Dating Paul's Life*, Philadelphia and London 1982

Judge, Edwin A, *Christliche Gruppen in nichtchristlicher Gesellschaft*, Neue Studienreihe 4, Wuppertal 1964

Juster, Jean, *Les Juifs dans l'Empire romain* I-II, Paris 1914

Kirchschläger, Walter, 'Fieberheilung in Apg 28 und Lk 4', in J.Kremer (ed.), *Les Actes des Apôtres*, BETL 48, Gembloux and Leuven 1979, 509-21

Klauck, Hans Josef, *Hausgemeinde und Hauskirche im frühen Christentum*, SBS 103, Stuttgart 1981

272

– , 'Gütergemeinschaft in der klassiken Antike, Qumran und im NT', *RdQ* 11, *1982*, 47-79

Klein, Günter, *Die zwölf Apostel*, FRLANT 77, Göttingen *1961*

– , *Rekonstruktion und Interpretation*, BEvTh 50, Munich *1969*

Knox, John, ' "Fourteen Years Later": A Note on the Pauline Chronology', *JR* 16, *1936*, 341-9

– , 'The Pauline Chronology', *JBL* 58, *1939*, 15-29

– , *Chapters in a Life of Paul*, New York and Nashville *1950*, London *1954*, second edition Macon, Ga and London *1988*

– , 'Acts and the Pauline Letter Corpus', in L.E.Keck and J.L.Martyn (eds.), *Studies in Luke-Acts* (FS P.Schubert), Nashville and New York *1966*, reissued Philadelphia *1980*, 279-89

Koch, Dietrich-Alex, 'Geistbesitz und Wundermacht: Erwägungen zur Tradition und zur lukanischen Redaktion in Act 8, 5-25', *ZNW* 77, *1986*, 64-82

Körtner, Ulrich H.J., *Papias von Hierapolis*, FRLANT 133, Göttingen *1983*

Kraabel, A.Thomas, 'The Disappearance of the "God-Fearers"', *Numen* 28, *1981*, 113-26

Kränkl, Emmeram, *Jesus, der Knecht Gottes*, BU 8, Regensburg *1972*

Kratz, Reinhard, *Rettungswunder*, EHS.T 123, Frankfurt *1979*

Krauss, Samuel, *Talmudische Archäologie* III, Leipzig *1912* reprinted Hildesheim *1966*

Kremer, Jacob, *Pfingstbericht und Pfingstgeschehen*, SBS 63/64, Stuttgart *1973*

Kümmel, Werner Georg, *Römer 7 und die Bekehrung des Paulus*, UNT 17, Leipzig *1929*, reprinted Munich *1974*

– , *Introduction to the New Testament*, Nashville, New York and London ^{2}*1975*

Kürzinger, Josef, *Papias von Hierapolis und die Evangelien des Neuen Testaments*, Eichstätter Materialien Abt. Philosophie und Theologie 4, Regensburg *1983*

Lambrecht, Jan, 'Paul's Farewell-Address at Miletus (Acts 20,17-38)', in J.Kremer (ed), *Les Actes des Apôtres*, BETL 48, Gembloux and Leuven *1979*, 307-37

Leon, Harry J., *The Jews of Ancient Rome*, Philadelphia *1960*

Lesky, Albin, *Geschichte der griechischen Literatur*, Bern and Munich ^{2}*1963*

Lindars, Barnabas, *New Testament Apologetic*, London ^{2}*1973*

Lindemann, Andreas, *Paulus im ältesten Christentum*, BHTh 68, Tübingen *1979*

Linton, Olof, 'The Third Aspect', *StTh* 3, *1951*, 79-95

Löning, Karl, *Die Saulustradition in der Apostelgeschichte*, NTA NF 9, Münster *1973*

Lohfink, Gerhard, 'Eine alttestamentliche Darstellungsform für Gotteserscheinungen in den Damaskusberichten (Apg 9: 22; 26)', *BZ* NF 9, *1965*, 246-57

– , *Paulus vor Damaskus*, SBS 4, Stuttgart ^{3}*1967*

– , *Die Himmelfahrt Jesu*, SANT 26, Munich *1971*

– , 'Der Losvorgang in Apg 1, 26', *BZ* NF 19, *1975a*, 247-9

– , *Die Sammlung Israels*, SANT 39, Munich *1975b*

Loisy, Alfred, *Les Actes des Apôtres*, Paris *1920* reprinted Frankfurt *1973*

Lüdemann, Gerd, *Untersuchungen zur simonianischen Gnosis*, GTA 1, Göttingen *1975*

– , *Paul, Apostle to the Gentiles: Studies in Chronology*, Philadelphia and London *1984*

– , *Paulus, der Heidenapostel* II, *Antipaulinismus im frühen Christentum*, FRLANT 130, Göttingen *1983*

Luz, Ulrich, and Rudolf Smend, *Gesetz*, Biblische Konfrontationen 15, Stuttgart, etc. *1981*

Maddox, Robert, *The Purpose of Luke-Acts*, FRLANT 126, Göttingen *1982*

Marshall, Ian Howard, *The Acts of the Apostles*, TNTC 5, Leicester and Grand Rapids *1980*

Mattill, Andrew Jacob, *Luke as a Historian in Criticism since 1840*, PhD Vanderbilt *1959*

Meeks, Wayne A., *The First Urban Christians. The Social World of the Apostle Paul*, New Haven and London *1983*

Metzger, Bruce M., 'Ancient Astrological Geography and Acts 2.9-11', in W.W.Gasque and R.F.Martin (eds.), *Apostolic History and the Gospel* (FS F.F.Bruce), Exeter *1970*, 123-33

Meyer, Eduard, *Ursprung und Anfänge des Christentums* I-III, Stuttgart and Berlin [1-3]*1921-1923* (abbreviated Meyer I-III)

Meyer, Ernst, *Römischer Staat und Staatsgedanke*, Zürich and Darmstadt [2]*1961*

Mönning, Bernd H., *Die Darstellung des urchristlichen Kommunismus nach der Apostelgeschichte des Lukas*, Göttingen theological dissertation *1978*

Mommsen, Theodor, 'Die Rechtsverhältnisse des Apostels Paulus', *ZNW* 2, *1901*, 81-96

Muhlack, Gudrun, *Die Parallelen von Lukas-Evangelium und Apostelgeschichte*, TW 8, Frankfurt, etc. *1979*

Murphy-O'Connor, Jerome, *St Paul's Corinth*, Good News Studies 6, Wilmington, Delaware *1983*

Nauck, Wolfgang, 'Die Tradition und Komposition der Areopagrede. Eine motivgeschichtliche Untersuchung', *ZTK* 53, *1956*, 11-52

Nestle, Wilhelm, 'Legenden vom Tod der Gottesverächter', in id., *Griechische Studien*, Stuttgart 1948 reprinted Aalen *1968*, 567-96

Neudorfer, Heinz-Werner, *Der Stephanuskreis in der Forschungsgeschichte seit F.C.Baur*, Giessen and Basel *1983*

Neusner, Jacob, *The Rabbinic Traditions about the Pharisees before 70*, I-III, Leiden *1971*

Norden, Eduard, *Agnostos Theos*, Berlin and Leipzig *1913* ([2]*1923*) reprinted often

Ollrog, Wolf-Henning, *Paulus und seine Mitarbeiter*, WMANT 50, Neukirchen-Vluyn *1979*

O'Neill, John Cochrane, *The Theology of Acts in its Historical Setting*, London [2]*1970*

Overbeck. Franz, *Kurze Erklärung der Apostelgeschichte von Dr W.M.L.de Wette*, fourth edition revised and considerably extended by F.Overbeck, Leipzig [4]*1870*

– , 'Über das Verhältnis Justins des Märtyrers zur Apostelgeschichte', *ZWT* 25, *1872*, 305-49

– , *Über die Christlichkeit unserer heutigen Theologie*, Leipzig [3]*1903*, reprinted Darmstadt *1963*

Pereira, Francis, *Ephesus: Climax of Universalism in Luke-Acts*, Jesuit Theological Forum Studies 10.1, Amand, India *1983*

Pesch, Rudolf, *Die Apostelgeschichte* I, II, EKK V/1, 2, Zürich, Einsiedeln and Cologne 1986 (abbreviated as Pesch I,II)

Petersen, Norman R., *Literary Criticism for New Testament Critics*, Philadelphia *1978*

Pfleiderer, Otto, *Das Urchristentum* I,II, Berlin [2]*1902*

Plümacher, Eckhard, *Lukas als hellenistischer Schriftsteller*, SUNT 9, Göttingen *1972*

– , *Lukas als griechischer Historiker*, PRE.S 14, *1974*, cols. 235-64

– , 'Acta-Forschung 1974-1982 (Fortsetzung und Schluss)', *ThR* 49, *1984*, 105-69

Prast, Franz, *Presbyter und Evangelium in nachapostolischer Zeit*, Stuttgart *1979*

Preuschen, Erwin, *Die Apostelgeschichte*, HNT 41, Tübingen *1912*

Radl, Walter, *Paulus und Jesus im lukanischen Doppelwerk*, EHS.T 49, Berne and Frankfurt *1975*

Reicke, Bo, 'Die Mahlzeit mit Paulus auf den Wellen des Mittelmeers. Act 27, 33-38', *TZ* 4, *1948*, 401-10

– , *Glaube und Leben der Urgemeinde*, ATANT 32, Zurich *1957*

Remus, Harold, *Pagan-Christian Conflict over Miracle in the Second Century*, Patristic Monograph Series 10, Cambridge, Mass *1983*

Rengstorf, Karl-Heinrich, 'Geben ist seliger denn Nehmen', in O.Michel and U.Mann (eds.), *Die Leibhaftigkeit des Wortes* (FS A.Köberle), Hamburg *1958*, 23-33

Rese, Martin, *Alttestamentliche Motive in der Christologie des Lukas*, SNT I, Gütersloh *1969*

Riddle, Donald W., *Paul: Man of Conflict*, Nashville *1940*

Rivkin, Ellis, *A Hidden Revolution*, Nashville *1978*

Robbins, Vernon K., 'By Land and by Sea: The We-Passages and Ancient Sea Voyages', in C.H.Talbert (ed.), *Perspectives on Luke-Acts*, Special Studies Series 5, Danville and Edinburgh *1978*, 215-42

Roloff, Jürgen, *Das Kerygma und der historische Jesus. Historische Motive in den Jesus-Erzählungen der Evangelien*, Göttingen ²*1973*

– , *Die Apostelgeschichte*, NTD 5, Göttingen *1981*

Ropes, James Hardy, 'An Observation on the Style of S. Luke', *HSCP* 12, *1901*, 299-305

Rüsen, Jörn, *Historische Vernunft: Grundzüge der Historik* I, KVR 1489, Göttingen *1983*

Sanders, Ed Parish, *Paul and Palestinian Judaism*, London *1977*

– , *Jesus and Judaism*, London *1985*

Sanders, Jack T., 'The Salvation of the Jews in Luke-Acts', in C.H.Talbert (ed.), *Luke-Acts. New Perspectives from the Society of Biblical Literature Seminar*, New York *1984*, 104-28

Schaff, Adam, *Geschichte und Wahrheit*, Vienna, Frankfurt and Zürich *1970*

Schenk, Wolfgang, *Die Philipperbriefe des Paulus*, Stuttgart, etc. *1984*

Schiffman, Lawrence H., 'At the Crossroads: Tannaitic Perspectives on the Jewish-Christian Schism', in E.P.Sanders, A.I.Baumgarten and A.Mendelssohn (eds.), *Jewish and Christian Self-Definition* II, Philadelphia and London *1981*, 115-56, 338-52

Schille, Gottfried, *Die Apostelgeschichte des Lukas*, THK 5, Berlin 1983 (²*1984*)

Schläger, G., 'Die Ungeschichtlichkeit des Verräters Judas', *ZNW* 15, *1914*, 50-9

Schmidt, Paul Wilhelm, 'De Wette-Overbecks Werk zur Apostelgeschichte und dessen jüngste Bestreitung', in *FS zum 500-jährigen Bestehen der Universität Basel*, Basel *1910*, 1-53 (245-95)

Schmithals, Walter, *Die Apostelgeschichte des Lukas*, ZBK.NT 3.2, Zurich *1982*

Schneckenburger, Matthias, *Über den Zweck der Apostelgeschichte*, Bern *1841*

Schneider, Gerhard, *Das Evangelium nach Lukas I.II*, ÖTK 3, Gütersloh and Würzburg 1977 (²*1984*)

– , *Die Apostelgeschichte* I.I, HTK 5, Freiburg, Basel and Vienna *1980, 1982*

– , *Lukas, Theologe der Heilsgeschichte*, BBB 59, Königstein and Bonn *1985*

Schottroff, Luise, 'Frauen in der Nachfolge Jesu in neutestamentlicher Zeit', in W.Schottroff and W.Stegemann (eds.), *Traditionen der Befreiung* II, Munich, Gelnhausen, etc. *1980*, 91-133

Schottroff, Luise, and Wolfgang Stegemann, *Jesus von Nazareth – Hoffnung der Armen*, UB 639, Stuttgart, etc. *1978*, ²*1981*

Schürer, Emil, review of A.Harnack, *Lukas der Arzt*, TLZ 31, *1906*, cols.405-8

– , *The History of the Jewish People in the Age of Jesus Christ (175 BC – AD 135)*, I,II, III.1, 2, edd. G.Vermes, F.Millar and M.Black, Edinburgh *1973, 1979,* 1987

Schüssler-Fiorenza, Elisabeth, *In Memory of Her*, New York and London *1983*

Schwartz, Eduard, *Gesammelte Schriften* V: *Zum Neuen Testament und zum frühen Christentum*, Berlin *1963*

Schwegler, Albert, *Das nachapostolische Zeitalter in den Hauptmomenten seiner Entwicklung* II, Tübingen *1846*

Schweizer, Eduard, 'Zu Apg 1, 16-22', TZ 14, *1958*, 46

Seccombe, David, 'Was there Organized Charity in Jerusalem before the Christians?', *JTS* NS 29, *1978*, 140-3

Sherwin-White, Adrian Nicholas, *Roman Society and Roman Law*, Oxford *1963*

– , *The Roman Citizenship*, Oxford ²*1973*

Siegert, Folker, 'Gottesfürchtige und Sympathisanten', *JSJ* 4, *1973*, 109-64

Solin, Heikki, 'Juden und Syrer im westlichen Teil der römischen Welt', *ANRW* II.29.2, Berlin and New York *1983*, 587-789, 1222-49

Stählin, Gustav, *Die Apostelgeschichte*, NTD 5, Göttingen ⁷*1980*

Stegemann, Wolfgang, 'Zwei sozialgeschichtliche Anfragen an unser Paulusbild', in *EvErz* 37, *1985*, 480-90

Stolle, Volker, *Der Zeuge als Angeklagter*, BWANT 102, Stuttgart, etc. *1973*

Storch, Rainer, *Die Stephanusrede Ag 7,2-53*, Göttingen theological dissertation *1967*

Strobel, August, *Die Stunde der Wahrheit*, WUNT 21, Tübingen 1980

Suhl, Alfred, *Paulus und seine Briefe*, SNT 11, Gütersloh *1975*

Talbert, Charles H. (ed.), *Perspectives on Luke-Acts*, Danville and Edinburgh *1978*

– , *Luke-Acts. New Perspectives from the Society of Biblical Literature Seminar*, New York *1984*

Theissen, Gerd, *Miracle Stories of the Early Christian Tradition*, Philadelphia and Edinburgh *1983*

– , *Studien zur Soziologie des Urchristentums*, WUNT 19, Tübingen *1979* (²*1983*)

Trilling, Wolfgang, 'Zur Entstehung des Zwölferkreises: Eine geschichtliche Überlegung', in R.Schnackenburg et al. (eds.), *Die Kirche des Anfangs* (FS H.Schürmann), ETS 38, Leipzig = Freiburg, Basel and Vienna *1978*, 201-20

Trocmé, Étienne, *Le 'Livre des Actes' et l'histoire*, EHPR 45, *1957*

Vielhauer, Philipp, 'Zum Paulinismus der Apostelgeschichte', *EvTh* 10, 1950, 1-15 = id., *Aufsätze zum Neuen Testament* I, ThB 31, Munich *1965*, 9-27

Vogler, Werner, *Judas Iskarioth*, TA 42, Berlin *1983*

Vogt, Joseph, 'Tacitus und die Unparteilichkeit des Historikers', in H.Hommel et al. (eds.), *Studien zu Tacitus* (FS C.Hosius), Stuttgart *1936*, 1-20

Walker, William O., 'Acts and the Pauline Corpus Reconsidered', *JSNT* 24, *1985*, 3-23

Walter, Nikolaus, 'Die Philipper und das Leiden: Aus den Anfängen einer heidenchristlicher Gemeinde', in R.Schnackenburg etc. (eds.), *Die Kirche des Anfangs* *(FS H.Schürmann)*, ETS 38, Leipzig, Freiburg, Basel and Vienna *1978*, 417-34

– , *Fragmente jüdisch-hellenistischer Historiker*, JSHRZ 1.2, Gütersloh *1976* (²1980)

– , 'Apostelgeschichte 6.1 und die Anfänge der Urgemeinde in Jerusalem', *NTS* 29, *1983*, 370-93

Weinreich, Otto, *Religionsgeschichtliche Studien*, Darmstadt *1968*

Weinstock, Stefan, 'The Geographical Catalogue in Acts 2, 9-11', *JRS* 38, *1948*, 43-46

Weiser, Alfons, *Die Apostelgeschichte* I,II, ÖTK 5, Gütersloh and Würzburg *1981*, *1985*

– , 'Das "Apostelkonzil" (Apg 15, 1-35): Ereignis, Überlieferung, lukanische Deutung', *BZ* NF 28, *1984*, 145-67

Weiss, Johannes, *Ueber die Absicht und den literarischen Charakter der Apostelgeschichte*, Göttingen *1897*

– , *Earliest Christianity* (two vols), 1937 reissued New York *1959*

Weizsäcker, Carl Heinrich, *Das apostolische Zeitalter der christlichen Kirche*, Tübingen and Leipzig ³*1902*

Wellhausen, Julius, *Noten zur Apostelgeschichte*, NGG.PH 1, Berlin *1907*, 1-21

– , *Einleitung in die drei ersten Evangelien*, Berlin ²*1911*

– , *Kritische Analyse der Apostelgeschichte*, AGG.PH NF 15.2, Berlin *1914*

Wendt, Hans Hinrich, *Die Apostelgeschichte*, KEK 3, Göttingen ⁵*1913*

Wengst, Klaus, *Pax Romana and the Peace of Jesus Christ*, London and Philadelphia *1987*

Wikenhauser, Alfred, *Die Apostelgeschichte und ihr Geschichtswert*, NTA 8, Münster *1921*

– , 'Doppelträume', *Bib* 29, *1945*, 100-11

Wikgren, Allen P, 'The Problem in Acts 16.12', in E.J.Epp and G.D.Tee (eds), *New Testament Textual Criticism* (FS B.M.Metzger), Oxford *1981*, 171-8

Wilckens, Ulrich, *Die Missionsreden der Apostelgeschichte*, WMANT 5, Neukirchen-Vluyn ³*1974*

Wilcox, Max, 'The "God-Fearers" in Acts – A Reconsideration', *JSNT* 13, *1981*, 102-22

Williams, C.S.C., *A Commentary on the Acts of the Apostles*, BNTC/HNTC, London and New York ²*1967*

Wrede, William, *Vorträge und Studien*, ed. A.Wrede, Tübingen *1907*

Zahn, Theodor, *Die Apostelgeschichte nach ihrem Inhalt und Ursprung kritisch untersucht*, Stuttgart *1854*

Zimmermann, Alfred F, *Die urchristlichen Lehrer*, WUNT 2.12, Tübingen *1984*

Zimmermann, Heinrich, *Neutestamentliche Methodenlehre*, ed. K.Kliesch, Stuttgart ⁷*1982*

Zingg, Paul, *Das Wachsen der Kirche*, OBO 3, Freiburg and Göttingen *1974*

Zuntz, Günther, *Opuscula Selecta*, Manchester *1972*